Palgrave Studies in European Communication Research and Education

This series provides a diverse overview of the collaborative work of ECREA members, showcasing diversity of topics and areas within the field of contemporary media and communication research. The book series has two main objectives. The first objective is the promotion of European media and communication research. Books, published in the book series, have a strong European dimension either by virtue of inclusion of regionally and ethnically diverse voices and cases, or by virtue of comparative research. The series' second aim is to promote collaborative research, especially collaboration between our members or within and between our Sections, Networks, and Temporary Working Groups. A call for book proposals is published every year. Proposals are reviewed by ECREA book series editors and their selection confirmed by ECREA Executive Board in collaboration with Palgrave Macmillan.

Anne Mollen · Fieke Jansen ·
Sigrid Kannengießer · Julia Velkova
Editors

AI Infrastructures and Sustainability

Expanding Perspectives on Automation, Communication and Media

palgrave
macmillan

Editors
Anne Mollen
Institut f. Kommunikationswissenschaft
Universität Münster
Münster, Nordrhein-Westfalen, Germany

Fieke Jansen
Critical Infrastructure Lab
University of Amsterdam
Amsterdam, The Netherlands

Sigrid Kannengießer
Institut f. Kommunikationswissenschaft
Universität Münster
Münster, Nordrhein-Westfalen, Germany

Julia Velkova
Linköping University
Norrköping, Sweden

ISSN 2948-2372 ISSN 2948-2380 (electronic)
Palgrave Studies in European Communication Research and Education
ISBN 978-3-032-09747-7 ISBN 978-3-032-09748-4 (eBook)
https://doi.org/10.1007/978-3-032-09748-4

This work was supported by European Communication Research and Education Association.

This Palgrave Macmillan imprint is published by the registered company Springer Nature Switzerland AG
The registered company address is: Gewerbestrasse 11, 6330 Cham, Switzerland

Acknowledgements

The journey of this edited book began with a series of constant but volatile encounters among the editors and contributors of this book, channelled through our shared interest in the politics of digitization, its materialities, and profound implications for digital and environmental rights as well as social justice. Throughout our careers, we have had the privilege of connecting in various locations, each time enjoying our shared engagement with the intricate relation between digital technologies and society. These connections and shared interests have been instrumental in shaping the scope and focus of this book.

From the outset, our collective interest in these themes was nurtured through the support of the European Communication Research and Education Association (ECREA). From first discussions during an ECREA summer school over a decade ago, to repeated opportunities to present and discuss our research at several ECREA conferences and meetings, the organization's commitment to fostering emerging scholars provided us with the platform and encouragement needed to explore these ideas more profoundly. In 2023, when we proposed this book, technologies of automation had just gained another round of momentum, making matters of justice all the more pressing. In this critical moment, the ECREA Open Access Book Series offered us the invaluable opportunity to collaborate and bring our collective insights to fruition.

The timing of this book is particularly pertinent. As discussions around Artificial Intelligence (AI) and its resource consumption enter mainstream discourses, there is an urgent need to engage more deeply with its materiality and sustainability. We are deeply grateful to ECREA and the Book Series Committee—Christina Holtz-Bacha, Göran Bolin, and Simone Tosoni—for providing the opportunity to realise this joint project and outcome. We are also grateful to all contributors who shared their invaluable insights into AI infrastructures. Their varied perspectives make the book both a broad inspection of AI infrastructures and sustainability while at the same time enabling a very deep and intricate engagement with actors—humans, non-humans, and more-than-humans—and their relation to AI. Relying on our respective contacts and outreach in different fields, we are very happy to have assembled an interdisciplinary and global perspective on AI infrastructures and sustainability, embedded within the European context through our connection to ECREA. This book emerges from our long-standing engagements with the topic:

Anne Mollen is grateful for her previous encounters with Fieke Jansen, Sigrid Kannengießer, and Julia Velkova in very different settings and places, and especially for their willingness and encouragement to jointly work on this volume. Thank you for an appreciative and supportive collaboration—with special recognition to Julia Velkova for making our joint work in Sigtuna possible. She also thanks colleagues at AlgorithmWatch, the Institute for Ecological Economy Research (IÖW) in Berlin and at the Distributed Artificial Intelligence Lab at TU Berlin for their early endeavours into the sustainability of AI. Other fruitful engagements with the topic occurred in many interdisciplinary settings, among them the working group on "Sustainable AI" at the German Committee Future Earth and constant discussions among colleagues at the chair for "Media Sociology and Sustainability" at the University of Münster—notably Sigrid Kannengießer, Stephan O. Görland, nate wessalowski, Monika Dzialas, Jo-Marie Dominiak, Stephan Niemand, and Heike Haussmann.

Fieke Jansen thanks the participants of the data centre workshops for sharing their thoughts, insights, and experiences with her. A huge thanks goes to her collaborators of the Green Screen Coalition, who keep her research grounded in the struggle for sustainable futures. A few need special mention: Michelle Thorne, Maya Richman, Michael Brennan, Hanan Elmasu, Lisa Gutermuth, Claire Fernandez, Jill McArdle, and Raegan MacDonald—whose work on keeping AI infrastructures within planetary boundaries has been inspiring. Last but not least, Fieke Jansen thanks colleagues at the critical infrastructure lab—Niels ten Oever, Maxigas, Dmitry Kuznetsov, Eric Zhang, and Gargi Sharma—who are her academic home.

Sigrid Kannengießer thanks Anne Mollen, Fieke Jansen, and Julia Velkova for their collaboration in editing this book—it has been an inspiring and thoroughly positive experience! She also appreciates the wonderful team at her chair for "Media Sociology and Sustainability" at the University of Münster, Germany: Anne Mollen, Anastasia Glawatzki, Heike Haussmann, Lisa Gronau, Monika Dzialas, nate wessalowski, and Stephan O. Görland, as well as Jo-Marie Dominiak and Stephan Niemand. Thank you for your commitment. Moreover, she thanks all colleagues at the Institute for Communication Science and the Sustainability Research Centre at the University of Münster for inspiring discussions and supportive collaborations. Lastly, Sigrid is grateful for her co-authors in this book: Débora Leal and Max Krüger—this has been an intense learning process and a great pleasure, looking forward to future collaborations!

Julia Velkova thanks Anne Mollen for being the intellectual and organizational motor of this book, for her dedication to keeping us organized and on time, for taking lead in the ideation and writing of this book, and for her kind invitation to be part of this project. She also thanks the entire team of co-editors—Anne Mollen, Fieke Jansen, and Sigrid Kannengießer—for the time spent together in Sigtuna and for inspiring conversations, patience with delayed drafts, and fantastic co-editorship collaboration. Julia thanks her department, TEMA-T at Linköping University, for creating a supportive environment that enabled her to complete this book; the DataLab at TEMA for inspiring conversations and regular stimulating events; her colleagues Flora Mary Bartlett, Johanna Sefyrin, Harald Rohracher, and Laura Watts for working together and thinking about the relations between data centres and energy; and Harald Rohracher and Minna Ruckenstein for close readings and always excellent and timely comments on drafts. Julia also thanks the Profutura Scientia program of Riksbankens Jubileumsfond and SCAS for their support. Velkova's work on this book is also supported by the Marianne and Marcus Wallenberg foundation through the Megabytes vs Megawatts project under grant number MMW 2022.0070; and Reimagine ADM supported by FORTE in Sweden (GD-2022/0019) and the European union's Horizon 2020 Research and Innovation Programme, Grant Agreement no 101004509.

We extend our gratitude to all who have supported and inspired this endeavour. Special recognition goes to Anastasia Glawatzki, who provided invaluable support in finalizing this book and autonomously faced organizational challenges during hectic and sometimes confusing submission phases. We are also very grateful to the team at Palgrave for their assistance and support throughout the production process.

We are excited to share our insights and invite readers to engage with the complex and multifaceted issues addressed within these pages. We hope this collection will contribute to broadening the field and offering new perspectives on sustainability and AI, informed by our engagement with its materiality and the broader socio-political landscape.

June 2025

Anne Mollen
Fieke Jansen
Sigrid Kannengießer
Julia Velkova

Contents

1 Introduction: De-Centring Artificial Intelligence and Rethinking Sustainability 1
Anne Mollen, Fieke Jansen, Sigrid Kannengießer, and Julia Velkova

Part I Elements, Materials, Resources

2 Follow the Thing: AI 31
Ana Valdivia

3 Amazonia's Place in AI: Minerals and Mining as the Cradle of Infrastructuring 51
Débora de Castro Leal, Maximilian Krüger, and Sigrid Kannengießer

4 Growing the Cloud at the "Corner of the Atlantic": Fortaleza as a Digital Infrastructure Hub Amidst AI-Renewable Energy Paradigms in Brazil 73
Iago Bojczuk

5 Aligning Energy Grids, Clouds and Public Values in Sweden 97
Julia Velkova

6 **Aquaculture, AI, and Planetary Domestication** 117
Patrick Brodie

Part II Promises, Economies, Discourses

7 **The Cruel Optimism of the Sustainable Cloud: Fantasies and Futures of Microsoft Azure** 143
Hamsini Sridharan

8 **Narratives of Indispensability and Infrastructural Solutionism of AI Companies** 165
Salla-Maaria Laaksonen and Meri Frig

9 **Alliance or Self-Reliance in New Geopolitical Technospheres—AI Infrastructures in Poland** 189
Małgorzata Winiarska-Brodowska

10 **Discursive Infrastructuring of AI in Russia: Yandex's Sustainability Reporting** 215
Olga Dovbysh

11 **Entangled Sustainabilities: News Media Partnerships and Generative AI Market Power** 235
Anne Mollen

Part III Futures, Politics, Governance

12 **Not Seeing the Data for the Trees: How Ecological Metaphors Matter in Academic Discourse on Platforms and AI** 261
Gerwin van Schie and Inte Gloerich

13 **Responsiveness and AI in Environmental Governance: Infrastructures, Power, and Institutional Capacity** 279
Jędrzej Niklas

14 **AI Infrastructures, Total Mobilisation and Decomputing** 301
Dan McQuillan

15 **More Compute for a Burning Planet? A Scarcity Approach to AI Infrastructures** 321
Fieke Jansen and Niels ten Oever

16 The Good Infrastructure: Digital Futures, Values and Friction 341
Johanna Sefyrin and Julia Velkova

Index 363

Notes on Contributors

Iago Bojczuk is a Research Associate at the Berkeley Center for New Media (BCNM) at the University of California, Berkeley. His research focuses on digital infrastructures, science and technology policy, and the governance of large-scale complex systems. His work has been published in various lead academic journals and official UN publications. Most recently, he was a visiting scholar at Koç University in Istanbul, Türkiye. Iago earned a Master of Science from the Massachusetts Institute of Technology (MIT), where he was a Lemann Fellow, and a Bachelor of Arts (Phi Beta Kappa) from the University of Oregon.

Patrick Brodie is an Assistant Professor and Ad Astra Fellow in the School of Information and Communication Studies at University College Dublin. His research focuses on the environmental politics of digital media infrastructures. His most recent writing has appeared in journals such as New Media and Society, Big Data and Society, Information, Communication and Society, Irish Studies Review, and Edge Effects.

Dr. Débora de Castro Leal is a Researcher at the Federal University of Pará (UFPA) in the Brazilian Amazon, a Brazilian Amazon activist and consultant. Her doctoral thesis explored the use of digital technologies by rural communities in the Amazon region to interact with and resist global economic systems. She currently works as a consultant on the socio-bioeconomy of Brazil, fostering research alliances between academics and rural communities, to support the integration of rural and traditional communities into global economies. She frequently collaborates with institutions such as the Inter-American Development Bank, the Ministry of the Environment, and scientific research foundations.

Olga Dovbysh is a Postdoctoral Researcher at the Aleksanteri Institute, University of Helsinki, Finland. Her research focuses on media and internet control in restricted media regimes, journalistic cultures, and environmental and climate communication. She is a co-founder of the academic initiative "Online Talks on Eurasian Media", aimed at bringing together researchers and journalists to discuss current and emerging problems in the field of media and communication across the vast territory of Eurasia. Dovbysh's recent publications have appeared in journals such as Journalism, Digital Journalism, Media & Communication, and Social Media and Society.

Meri Frig (D.Econ) is a Postdoctoral Researcher at Aalto University, School of Business. She is specialized in corporate social responsibility (CSR) communication, and business-society relations. Her research has been published in journals such as Journal of Business Ethics, Business & Society, and Journal of Consumer Culture.

Inte Gloerich received her Ph.D. from the Media and Culture Department of Utrecht University and is a media researcher at the Amsterdam University of Applied Sciences in the Netherlands. Her work is concerned with cultures and imaginaries around emerging technologies such as blockchain and AI, especially in relation to the history and politics of knowledge production.

Fieke Jansen is a postdoc researcher and the co-pi of the critical infrastructure lab at the University of Amsterdam. Her research interest is to understand how the material impact of expanding infrastructures is shaping the management, distribution, and depletion of natural resources. Previously she was a postdoc at the Data Justice Lab at Cardiff University. She is part of the 'Exploring sustainability and environmental resilience: Sustainable AI Futures' research project, led by Professor Samantha Walton, Bath Spa University. Fieke is a former Mozilla and Green Web foundation fellow where she explored ways to frame the climate crisis as a core digital rights issue.

Sigrid Kannengießer is Professor of Communication Studies with a focus on Media Sociology. Her research focuses on digitalization, AI and sustainability, sustainable consumption, media and data practices, social movement studies, and gender media studies.

Maximilian Krüger is a Postdoctoral Researcher at the Research Institute for Sustainable and Digital Collaboration (DNZ gGmbH) in Siegen, Germany as well as at the Federal University of Pará (UFPA) in the Brazilian Amazon region. He has been a research assistant at the Chair of Information Systems and New Media at the University of Siegen since 2017. In 2022, he completed his doctorate with the title "Careful Interventions: On Care and Participation in Design for Migration and Arrival". His research focuses on the role of digital technologies in practices of climate adaptation and ecological conservation.

Salla-Maaria Laaksonen (D.Soc.Sc., Docent) is a Senior Researcher at the Centre for Consumer Society Research, University of Helsinki. Her research focuses on platform-society relations from the perspectives of communication, organization, and critical technology studies. Her current projects look at organizing with AI, activism in the hybrid media system, and the sustainability of digital media. She also has solid expertise in interdisciplinary research that uses digital and computational methods and large data sets in social research.

Dan McQuillan is a Senior Lecturer in Critical AI at Goldsmiths, University of London. After a Ph.D. in Experimental Particle Physics, Dan worked with people learning disabilities & mental health issues, created websites with asylum seekers, ran social tech camps in Kyrgyzstan and Sarajevo, and worked for Amnesty International and the NHS. He is the author of "Resisting AI: An Anti-fascist Approach to Artificial Intelligence".

Anne Mollen conducts research on automation, algorithms, and "Artificial Intelligence" at the Institute of Communication Studies at the University of Münster. Her research focuses, among other things, on the sustainability of AI, automation and democracy, algorithms and social justice. She holds a Ph.D. from the University of Bremen. As an expert on AI and digitization, Anne has advised various civil society organizations and political bodies on national, European, and global level on issues of automation.

Jędrzej Niklas is a socio-legal scholar whose research explores the role of emerging digital technologies in the operations of state and public institutions and their social justice implications. He holds a Ph.D. in law (international public law) from the University of Warsaw, and previously worked as a postdoctoral researcher at the London School of Economics, University of Leeds, and Cardiff University.

Johanna Sefyrin is an ssociate Professor and docent in information systems at the division of digitalization and information systems, Linköping University, Sweden. Her research has over the years concerned gender, participation, knowledge, and power related to information systems design and use in Swedish public sector, participation related to smart grids, and digital divides in library contexts. Currently she is studying imaginaries of robotization related to the automation of administrative work in municipal contexts, and questions relating to data centers and sustainability.

Hamsini Sridharan is a Ph.D. candidate in the School of Communication at USC Annenberg, located in Los Angeles, CA. She studies historical and contemporary entanglements of digital technologies with environmental imaginaries and speculative futures, asking how such entanglements shape the critique, contestation, and governance of technology.

Niels ten Oever is an Assistant Professor of AI and European democracies and co-principal investigator with the critical infrastructure lab at the University of Amsterdam. He is a visiting professor with the Centro de Tecnologia e Sociedade at the Fundação Getúlio Vargas. Niels teaches courses in politics and technology, has implemented technology projects on five continents, and has participated in many governance and standard-setting processes, such as in the IETF, ICANN, ITU, ICANN, and 3GPP. His research focuses on how norms, values, and ideologies get inscribed, resisted, and subverted in communication infrastructures through their transnational governance.

Ana Valdivia is a Lecturer in Artificial Intelligence (AI), Government & Policy at the Oxford Internet Institute at the University of Oxford. Her interdisciplinary work, situated at the intersection of Critical Data Studies and Computer Science, has made significant contributions to tech surveillance and society, algorithmic fairness, and digital sustainability. Her current work examines the trade-off between environmental costs and social benefits of AI by investigating its supply chains, from mineral extraction to electronic waste dumps. Ana is currently an Associate Editor for Big Data & Society and a Visiting Research Fellow at the UCL Centre for Capitalism Studies.

Gerwin van Schie is an Assistant Professor at the Media and Culture Department of Utrecht University in the Netherlands, where he investigates racism in Dutch algorithmic governance. In addition, he is interested in how botanical metaphors mediate and obfuscate the racist, colonial, and capitalist foundations of various forms of digital culture.

Julia Velkova is Professor of Media and Culture at Linköping University, and a Profutura Scientia fellow at the Swedish Collegium for Advanced Studies. Her work currently explores the cultural production of obsolescence and infrastructure endings; as well as the intersections of data infrastructure, energy politics, and questions of sustainability. She is co-editor of "Media Backends: Digital Infrastructures and Sociotechnical relations", "Beyond Academic Publics: Conversations about Scholarly Collaborations with Cultural Institutions", and author of many articles on infrastructure politics published in lead academic journals.

Małgorzata Winiarska-Brodowska is an Assistant Professor at the Department of Journalism and International Communication, Institute of Journalism, Media and Social Communication, Jagiellonian University in Krakow, Poland. She is vice-president of the European Communication Research and Education Association (ECREA). She is also active in the Una Europa alliance. Her research interests lie at the intersection of media, politics, and international relations. She has published in the field of political communication, media & AI, organizational and strategic communication, as well as quality assurance in the higher education institutions.

List of Figures

Fig. 4.1	A 2017 collage in Folha de S. Paulo, one of Brazil's most widely read newspapers. The headline, part of a longer edition commissioned by the state government, refers to submarine cables enabling connectivity "From the World to Ceará and From Ceará to the World," underscoring the city's cross-continental links (Folha de S. Paulo, 2017)	79
Fig. 4.2	Illustrative poster displayed on the government's website showcasing the projected electricity consumption by the data center sector, including Ceará (Ministério de Minas e Energia, 2024c)	88
Fig. 6.1	A fully networked fish farm (Filmless, 2024)	127
Fig. 6.2	The camera and sensor device (Filmless, 2024)	128
Fig. 6.3	The climactic product shot: the camera in situ, swimming with the fishes (Filmless, 2024)	128
Fig. 6.4	The Watermoon containment tank in situ (Marøy, 2024)	131
Fig. 8.1	Volume of blog entries per company in the final filtered data (n = 497). Figure produced by authors	172
Fig. 8.2	Relative prevalence of selected keywords in the corpus over time, **a** data center, machine learning, artificial intelligence, **b** energy, carbon, water, material. Figures produced by authors	174
Fig. 10.1	Screenshot of comic 1 *Nature, Education and Health in the Cloud* (Yandex, 2023c)	225

Fig. 10.2 Screenshot of comic 6 *AI Assistant and Education* (Yandex, 2023c) 226
Fig. 10.3 Screenshot of comic 8 *Protecting Users and Data* (Yandex, 2023c) 229
Fig. 11.1 Newly reported relations between generative AI providers and news media 244
Fig. 16.1 The beginning of the cross-country ski trail Spikbodarna in Östersund in winter 2024. The trail goes partly in forest, and partly under the pylons of the electricity grid to which EDC will eventually connect. *Photo* Julia Velkova 351
Fig. 16.2 People skiing on the Spikbodarna ski-track in December 2024. *Photo* Julia Velkova 352

CHAPTER 1

Introduction: De-Centring Artificial Intelligence and Rethinking Sustainability

Anne Mollen, Fieke Jansen, Sigrid Kannengießer, and Julia Velkova

A Future where "AI Is Everywhere"

We live in a moment of extreme hype over Artificial Intelligence (AI). Data-driven decision-making and large language models (LLMs) are promoted in an expanding array of domains ranging from everyday

A. Mollen (✉) · S. Kannengießer
University of Münster, Münster, Germany
e-mail: anne.mollen@uni-muenster.de

S. Kannengießer
e-mail: sigrid.kannengiesser@uni-muenster.de

F. Jansen
University of Amsterdam, Amsterdam, Netherlands
e-mail: fieke@criticalinfralab.net

J. Velkova
Linköping University, Norrköping, Sweden
e-mail: julia.velkova@liu.se

A. Mollen et al. (eds.), *AI Infrastructures and Sustainability*, Palgrave Studies in European Communication Research and Education,
https://doi.org/10.1007/978-3-032-09748-4_1

communication to healthcare and medical practice, public administration services, education and knowledge production, agriculture, energy infrastructure management and even ice cream (Godske, 2024). Packaged and branded as "AI services", these technologies tend to be advertised through familiar tropes that emphasise their economic potential, effortless "knowledge" about the world, "creativity" in visual and textual outputs while offering digital companionship, care services and the promise to save large economies, such as those in Europe, from recession. Attributed with increasingly mythical qualities and seemingly all-encompassing powers, AI as computational data-driven practices have been, at least in Europe, promoted as the solution to most contemporary social, environmental and economic problems (European Parliament, 2025).

As a result, and with worrisome regularity, high-level events are now being held, where—as in the case of the February 2025 AI Action Summit in Paris—politicians and industries propose innovation, investment and deregulation as the way forward to carve out a place for Europe in the ongoing "AI race". Proposing a market-oriented focus that speaks to existing European and national "AI strategies", their approach calls for the allocation of unfathomable budgets for research into innovation and adoption of AI and encourages public institutions to provide access to new data sources needed to train language models (European Commission, 2025; Jansen, 2021). The message is that innovation and prosperity can only be achieved with AI, which requires infrastructural capacity. As European Commission president Ursula von der Leyen (European Commission, 2025) spelled out in Paris, it envisions a future where Europe will become "one of the leading AI continents", which "means embracing a way of life where AI is everywhere" (von der Leyen, 2025, par. 2). The European Union's response to the global AI race has thus focused on investing in expansions of computation and data centre infrastructures across the continent, exemplified by the announcement of the construction of thirteen AI gigafactories to provide the necessary infrastructure for AI-saturated futures.

This book develops a critical infrastructural perspective on these developments. It explores the inequalities, economies and societal conflicts that are emerging as industries, administrations and individuals increasingly position AI as an authority and agent of social change, while also producing the socio-material conditions for this change. Often termed as inevitable, effortless and immaterial, implementations of LLMs and data-driven decision-making depend upon the availability of human and technological infrastructures, as well as upon transnational supply chains that keep these infrastructures functioning. Hard drives to store data, processors and chips to process it, electricity to power server racks, minerals and metals, wires, expertise and people: all these entities must be sourced and arranged to form productive relations and enable AI in distinct contexts of use and imagination (Parks et al., 2023). This book investigates how AI infrastructural pervasion is embedding and extending histories of colonialism, racism, neoliberalist expansion and the exploitation of nature and people. In other words, it explores AI at the intersection of infrastructure and sustainability.

Investigating AI infrastructures and sustainability for the purpose of making AI more just is an urgent endeavour, especially with the concentrated political push to materialise an infrastructure for an AI-enhanced digital future in Europe and beyond. This concern becomes even more pressing in times when public and expert resistance to computational, data-driven approaches to the social domains are being trivialised. Societal anxieties about AI are unfolding in parallel to concerns about the significant material and infrastructural demands of these technologies and shifts in energy supply occurring in attempts to secure (presumably) clean energy sources for the massive energy needs of AI development (Bender et al., 2021; Strubell et al., 2020). Nevertheless, among policymakers, developers and marketers, the immense social and environmental justice implications of AI technologies (Crawford, 2021) are predominantly discussed as manageable based on technological progress (Sætra, 2023). As a result, attempted net-estimations of AI's environmental benefits versus its environmental risks dominate discussions in media, policy, science and industry (Kaack et al., 2022). This techno-determinist approach neglects decades of scientific knowledge on how sociotechnical transformations unfold, as well as the fact that technology is never teleology. Technologies do not roll out in an empty social space but are part of complex, friction-filled negotiations with uncertain outcomes. The manifold harms to the communities and environments along the AI supply chain, however, tend to be ignored, while the environmental and societal impacts of AI are downplayed against the potential of future benefits.

Media and communication scholars have argued that the energy and resource consumption of the digital industries cannot be separated from issues of societal and economic exclusion, demonstrating how the energy and resource demands of AI and online communication crowds out other businesses, limits local energy access and perpetuates societal inequalities and conflicts through infrastructure (Bresnihan & Brodie, 2021; Libertson et al., 2021). Taking inspiration from such investigations, the contributions of this book exemplify how potentiality-risk dichotomies and the resource fetish of sustainable AI debates conceal the complex entanglements between AI technologies and sustainability that emerge when interrogating AI infrastructures in their complexity and broadness. By adopting an infrastructural perspective and accounting for the various actors involved, this book takes the study of AI and sustainability beyond techno-solutionism, carbon accounting and net-impact calculations. It contributes to an understanding of the wide array of relations entangled with AI and its material underpinnings.

The book connects different fields within and across media and communication research, including environmental media, infrastructur approaches, critical data centre studies and human–machine communication (Edwards et al., 2024; Guzman & Lewis, 2019; Jue & Ruiz, 2021; López et al., 2024; Maxwell & Miller, 2012; Plantin & Punathambekar, 2018; Starosielski & Walker, 2016). It builds and expands upon emergent scholarship in media studies, science and technology studies (STS) and adjacent fields in the area surrounding the sustainability of digital infrastructures like data centres and their constituting elements (Brodie & Bresnihan, 2025; Diez & Bejarano, 2025; Jankovic & Keilbach, 2023; Kellog et al, 2024; Lehuedé, 2022; Pasek, 2023; Valdivia, 2024). Following Suchman's (2023) call to situate (what are being labelled as) AI technologies in their various locations and relations, the contributions to this book focus on diverse elements of AI infrastructures and the actors, relations and norms that ensue. Together, they paint a picture of how AI developments and the socio-technical relations that undergird them emerge and shape local and global conflicts, geopolitics and political economy shifts in different industrial sectors and powers.

Expanding Perspectives

This book builds and expands on contemporary media and communication approaches to technologies of automation, platforms, environmental media and infrastructural approaches. Previous research into digital media, platform infrastructures and critical data and algorithm studies has demonstrated how inquiries into the materialities undergirding digital media allow researchers to grasp the complex (geo)political, societal and economic relations through which contemporary media takes shape (Amoore, 2020; Dencik, 2022; Plantin & Punathambekar, 2018). Such studies have discussed emergent and reconfigured constellations of interests, ideologies, norms, values and power dynamics related to developing digital communication technologies. The past decades have also witnessed a boom of scholarship investigating digital interfaces, data practices and information transmission (Dencik et al., 2022; Flensburg & Lai, 2023; Milan & Velden, 2016; Ruckenstein, 2023; Parks & Starosielski, 2015). More recently, these studies have been expanded by an increasing scholarly interest in communicative AI, with a heavy focus on how research agendas for and theorisations about societal communication must be adapted as automated communication grows (Guzman & Lewis, 2019). However, infrastructural perspectives on automated technologies have been marginal and require further development. Meanwhile, other disciplines have provided insights into how AI technologies foster various forms of exploitation of natural resources and the environment, labour and working conditions and societal representations (Birhane et al., 2023; Crawford, 2021; Gray Widder et al., 2023; Miceli et al., 2022). Building on these works, there is an urgent requirement for further perspectives on the sociotechnical relations creating and surrounding AI.

This book expands perspectives in media and communication approaches to AI alongside analyses of AI as a phenomenon through its infrastructures. Specifically, it addresses two research gaps. First, it provides a missing perspective in academic discussions about the sustainability of AI. Such discussions have primarily occurred in engineering fields like machine learning (Kaack et al., 2022) or humanistic disciplines like practical philosophy (van Wynsberghe, 2021). This book brings the analysis of complex social processes in relation to AI sustainability within the range of media and communication studies, contributing new perspectives to interdisciplinary discussions on the topic. Second, it extends the work of scholars in environmental media and critical data studies, which are concerned with the materialities and environmental relations that sustain digital media (Crawford & Joler, 2018; Gabrys, 2014; Kannengießer, 2019; Parks & Wallker, 2020; Shriver Rice & Vaughan, 2020; Starosielski, 2021; Starosielski & Walker, 2016), and transfers them to the landscape of AI imaginaries, economies, materialities and governance.

Accordingly, the book orients scholarly attention towards the materialities, places, people and relations that constitute AI. It moves beyond the domain of symbolic interactions and human–machine communication while critically assessing claims that AI technologies can contribute to the efficiency and effective management of natural resources (Rolnick et al., 2022). Various questions drive its contributions. How is sustainability produced and practiced in relation to the development and maintenance of infrastructures for AI (and vice versa)? How is the relationship between AI infrastructures and sustainability constructed, by whom and to what ends? What implications does this relationship have for social, economic and environmental wellbeing? These questions are vital to ask for critically assessing how social practices are being transformed with digital technologies through four key arenas, which contributors address throughout this book.

First, current developments in the discussion of sustainability reflect an accelerated move towards techno-solutionism, in which AI technologies are increasingly positioned as actors that can produce sustainability. The potentials and risks of AI for achieving the Sustainable Development Goals (SDGs; United Nations [UN], 2015) were being discussed and criticised even before the advent of generative AI (Sætra, 2023; Vinuesa et al., 2020). However, with the intensifying societal diffusion and discussion of AI, justifications of its investment and infrastructural extension are increasingly based on claims that it will solve the climate crisis. These claims are discursively played out by key actors like OpenAI CEO Sam Altman (2024), who has made the unsubstantiated claim that AI "will fix the climate" (par. 18). There is therefore an urgent need to critically investigate how the relationship between AI infrastructures and sustainability is discursively constructed by various actors and within diverse spheres and arenas.

Along this first movement, a second tendency encompasses the increasing commodification of climate issues through AI companies that position themselves and their services as a sustainability solution for other industries. They focus on reducing sustainability to issues of efficiency, knowledge and resource optimisation, detaching AI and other industries from their polluting, extractive and oppressive realities throughout their supply chains (Dauvergne, 2022). These practices of commodifying sustainability efforts require critical interrogations into the emerging meanings of sustainability (e.g. what counts as sustainable and for whom), their implications and how they manifest within AI infrastructures.

Third, a resource-oriented escalation is ongoing, in which the current growth of AI applications results in increasing competition around resources and aggravating contestations along AI infrastructures. For example, data centre and software industries are making sustainability pledges, enrol renewable energy sources, establish carbon off-setting schemes while the optimisation of energy consumption is frequently presented as pathways to achieve NetZero emissions (Day et al., 2022). While these "green" ambitions are themselves riddled with problems, they stand in stark contrast to their industries' growing thirst for land, energy, water and critical raw materials. Emerging conflicts around these resources not only raise questions about governance and future adherence to the established values of welfare societies, but they also indicate a need for new trajectories in speaking, thinking and governing those heavily contested futures.

Fourth, current geopolitical shifts are drastically changing priorities in AI and infrastructural policies and investments. These shifts have not only shattered US–European alignments on digital policies, they have instigated a dismantling of international governance frameworks and shared norms. Consequently, ongoing geopolitical shifts have resurfaced debates on European infrastructural sovereignty (Caffarra et al., 2025), aggravating the geopolitical race for market hegemony over AI technologies and control over their constituting elements like components, datasets, models and infrastructure (while risking the side-lining of justice and sustainability concerns). These geopolitical developments not only fuel fears of missing out and being pushed to the periphery, they are the latest incarnation of a long line of colonial and imperialistic politics and practices of hegemonic powers exploiting nature and people from marginalised groups and regions.

Substantiated through these key developments, the contributions to this book exemplify how potentiality-risk dichotomies and resource-fetishism approaches that promote sustainable AI conceal the complex entanglements between nature, industry and power. Authors foreground these frictions by interrogating the sociotechnical systems that enable AI operations throughout the supply chain, from the cradle to the grave and beyond the traditional boundaries of communication studies. In this sense, the book expands perspectives in media and communication approaches to AI by focusing on infrastructure and its normative relation to sustainability alongside understandings of AI systems and discourses as phenomena that unfold across the material and social infrastructures that enable their operations. In other words, this book moves beyond the cultural imagination that AI is a progressive force and a tool with no cost. The chapters contextualise AI infrastructure expansions within local contexts and across countries, economies and cultures. These analyses expose the fact that there are no sustainable AI infrastructures *per se*. There is not one but many AI infrastructures (Mol, 2002) and ensuring sustainable and equitable AI futures requires change to current economic and political systems and values.

Infrastructural Relations

AI is not a new phenomenon. Scholars of the ideas and histories of machine intelligences have criticised the technologically-driven mythologies that depict AI and algorithms as substance-less (Elish & Boyd, 2018), powerful media (Natale, 2021) that exist beyond social and technological constraints (Amoore, 2020). Such research addresses a key concern Lucy Suchman (2023) formulated in questioning the "thingness" of AI. Responding to her call "for a keener focus on [these technologies'] locations, politics, material-semiotic specificity and effects" (Suchman, 2023, p. 4), this book positions sustainability as a central concern of inquiry for technological developments and digital services branded as AI, which are here investigated through an infrastructural lens.

Infrastructural perspectives have gained prominence in media and communications studies over the past decade. The infrastructural turn (Hesmondhalgh, 2021; Lai & Flensburg, 2023; Parks et al., 2023; Parks & Starosielski, 2015), has brought new empiric objects and sites into purview for scholars while engaging with traditional questions of media research, including how sociotechnical relations organise power, economies and knowledge. Conceptions of power within digital infrastructures research have been particularly central to such analyses, including investigations into the geopolitics, political economy and temporalities of internet infrastructures (Lai & Flensburg, 2023; Parks et al., 2023; Velkova & Plantin, 2023) and AI technologies (van der Vlist et al., 2024). The contributions to this volume are grounded in this field and expand it through a focus on sustainability. The authors investigate how infrastructural entities like platforms, undersea cables, data centres, newsrooms, mines and fish farms intersect with questions of sustainability alongside environmental and social justice.

Throughout, this book follows an approach to infrastructure proposed by Susan Leigh Star (1999) as the study of "boring things", including arrangements of people, data and code (Seaver, 2017) as much as the arrangements of matter, land, energy, markets, regulations and the humans and nonhumans involved in them (Suchman, 2023). How AI is defined affects how it is governed and which of its impacts are highlighted. For example, an emphasis on AI as an algorithmic system shaped by data practices reflects the cultural and organisational work of making social relations legible, calculable and prone to machine automation in commercial and public sector contexts and opens up issues of discrimination, humanisation and public value reconfigurations to governance and critique. Other definitions productively highlight AI "as a flow of materials (e.g., minerals and metals used to create GPUs), energy (e.g., water and electricity feeding data centres) and a set of encounters between layers of a large data infrastructure" (Cellard et al., 2025). At the same time, the point here is not to provide a single truthful definition but to highlight the political nature of definitions as knowledge devices that obscure or foreground AI's elements and aspects (Suchman, 2023).

Based on critical research on media infrastructure (Parks & Starosielski, 2015), we thus define AI infrastructures as material-discursive arrangements that enable the automated transformation of information from individual data points to agglomerated outputs through probability assessments and large-scale data processing based on respective computing means. This prompts an analysis of all the relational structures formed by materials, technologies, actors and practices through which AI emerge (Mollen & Kannengießer, 2025). This approach reflects what Brian Larkin (2013) has described as the non-positivist appearance of infrastructures and its definition as a categorial act, meaning that "any particular set of intellectual questions will have to select which of these [infrastructural] levels to examine" (p. 330). Any such categorical act will highlight certain issues and obscure others. For example, software engineering and informatics depict AI infrastructure through diagrams and charts that describe neural networks with their neurons and nodes, suggesting uniformity and distance from the actual ways these networks and industries operate in practice and their differences (Cohn, 2023). This extends a historical trajectory of technoscientific approaches to computing that emphasise its mathematical operations above any other dimension (Pasek, 2023).

When infrastructure is acknowledged as a socio-technical system it encourages inquiry into the consequences and conflicts of expansion

(Parks, 2020; Parks & Starosielski, 2015; Plantin & Punathambekar, 2018). An infrastructural perspective thus foregrounds the many relations and frictions that evolve around AI and its constituent materialities as a relevant factor within broader sustainability discussions, especially as matters of social and environmental justice. For example, contributors in this volume deconstruct how approaches focused on the supposedly sustainable extraction and management of natural resources remain intrinsically flawed by producing a narrative that neither corresponds with questions of intra-and intergenerational justice (UN World Commission on Environment and Develoment [UN WCED], 1987) nor reaches agreed-upon climate goals (Buller, 2022). Our interest thus resonates with recent calls made by scholars to expand the critical insights currently missing in computer science, industry and public policy debates concerning AI. These insights centre attention on the productions of places, transforming ecologies and lands and to recraft the stories and narratives through which we understand AI systems.

This book thus engages with the situated practices through which actors who promote and build AI solutions produce discourses and arrange materialities, cultural expectations and economies under the "AI" label across differences of definition, place, and time. Contributors discuss actors like tech companies, governments, workers, developers, end users, data centre corporations, journalists, fish, forests, activists and many more, who among other things deploy, govern, create, extract, collect, live and exist in relation to AI technologies. In this sense, infrastructures are relative (Hesmondhalgh, 2021), in so far as that they mean different things for different actors. They are also inherently relational, since "infrastructure is something that emerges for people in practice, connected to activities and structures" (Star & Ruhleder, 1996, p. 122). From a non-anthropocentric approach, this also extends to non-human and more-than-human actors.

Multiple Sustainabilities

This book embraces a broad conception of sustainability that engages justice, equality and capabilities (Sen, 2008; UN WCED, 1987), with a more-than-human and multispecies focus (Bossert & Hagendorff, 2023; Tschakert, 2022) as well as non-Western conceptions of living with and in nature (Liboiron, 2021) as central to an encompassing engagement with AI and sustainability. Contributions deconstruct the narrow discussions on the emissions and resource consumption of AI systems that have come to dominate mainstream societal, industrial and political discourses around AI and sustainability (Kaack et al., 2022; Vinuesa et al., 2020). This broad conception of sustainability is imminent when engaging with AI through an infrastructural perspective that foregrounds the many relations actors can have with different materialities (Star & Ruhleder, 1996).

Originally described by von Carlowitz in the context of forest management (Saxon Hans Carl von Carlowitz Society, 2013), the very origins of the term "sustainability" allude to an understanding of intergenerational justice, as later evoked by the UN approach to sustainability as intra-and intergenerational justice (UN WCED, 1987). Meanwhile, its historical usage to mean sustaining forestry or agriculture for future generations implies a focus on the enduring use of resources for a social entity; in other words, extraction that is constrained within limits to guarantee its continuity (Warde, 2018). Sustaining a forest for economic gains is, in other words, conceptualised as a management and knowledge problem of which trees to cut or plant, how to account for loss from diseases, and so on. Functionalist approaches to AI technologies and their potentials for SDGs (Vinuesa et al., 2020) rely on a similar understanding of sustained natural resource exploitation. They conceptualise sustainability as an issue of knowledge, efficiency and resource management and thus join a long line of techno-solutionist approaches presenting technologies in general and AI specifically as quick fixes for complex problems (Morozov, 2014; Sætra, 2023). Much of the debate on AI and sustainability is thus focused on bringing AI development and application within planetary boundaries (Raworth, 2017; Rockström et al., 2009) and using AI technologies to make industrial production more efficient and for reducing carbon emission (Kaack et al., 2022; Rolnick et al., 2022). Sustainability here offers a normative framework, focused on bringing AI technologies in line with inter-and intragenerational justice ambitions (UN WCED, 1987), in which climate change mitigation is considered a cornerstone of sustaining the planet for future generations.

With its focus on AI infrastructures as socio-technical systems, this book is a continuation of media and communication research that has discussed the connection between digital media and sustainability (Kannengießer, 2019; Maxwell & Miller, 2013; Pasek, 2023; Pasek et al., 2023) and argued that the energy and resource consumption of the digital industries cannot be separated from issues of societal and economic exclusion. Matters of resources can therefore never be separated from wider sustainability implications and, consequently, very different concepts of sustainability.

De-Centring AI and Rethinking Sustainability

With AI-saturated futures governed to become reality (Von der Leyen, 2025), it is important to address AI infrastructures as socio-technical systems constituted through networks of objects, actors, practices, norms and values, since they are shaping future societies. The study of AI infrastructures thus not only concerns how AI changes societal communication in different societal spheres (Guzman & Lewis, 2019), but how certain projections of AI-saturated futures materialise within sites, localities and relations that usually remain hidden when discussing where users and AI are interfacing. Moving beyond these commonplace understandings of the relationship between AI infrastructures and sustainability requires approaches that de-centre AI. This book takes its cue from Peña Gangadharan and Niklas (2019), who proposed de-centring as an approach to "'see through' technology, acknowledging its connection to larger systems of institutionalised oppression" (p. 882). This de-centring of AI allows a consideration of the very materiality that enables the large-scale processing of data. As chapters across this book demonstrate, these materialities must be considered in their infrastructural contexts, which are always constituted through technology, hardware, software, data sets, communities, industries, governance regimes, people, plants and many others.

De-centring AI by situating it in its local relations foregrounds inconvenient questions of how to align AI with sustainability in current governance regimes. Empirical insights from this book indicate that citizens envision better governance and alternatives to the status quo, moving toward original ideas of the welfare state, participatory approaches and de–/post-growth conceptions, inherently implying changes to current political and economic systems. By orienting our perspectives towards infrastructures and sustainability in current discussions around AI, we thus position media and communication research as relevant for interdisciplinary and policy discourses around AI and sustainability. These could possibly navigate within current regulatory and governance architectures while also engaging in contemplation about different digital futures, systemic changes and utopias with (or without) AI.

Thus, we also connect and re-position established and new directions in the field (e.g., political economy and infrastructural approaches) beyond functionalist approaches to AI and sustainability. This book demonstrates how ideas of AI and sustainability are envisioned together, how current conceptions of sustainable AI need to be deconstructed and how the shift towards AI solutionism must be problematised. Meanwhile, contributors propose rethinking sustainability according to local contexts (e.g., geopolitical, commercialisation), foregrounding how, for instance, from the Amazon to Northern Sweden, risks are outsourced to those who do not (want to) profit from AI. This book demonstrates that rethinking sustainability highlights new forms of frictions and injustice, develops new vocabulary and discourse to describe these phenomena and imagines governance for AI that accounts for both direct and indirect harms.

Rethinking sustainability thus becomes an analytical approach to question and challenge the values and worldviews underpinning AI infrastructures. In this book, for example, Seyfrin and Velkova's case study of a "good" AI infrastructure reveals that there is no single understanding of sustainability: different (and sometimes conflicting) meanings get attributed to the concept and reflect different valuations of what is "good". As such, we cannot limit questions of AI infrastructure and sustainability to its direct impact; it requires a more profound analyses of the worldviews and values that govern and organise society, including questions of what is considered valuable, what can be discarded and at what cost. This is not to say that sustainability becomes irrelevant as a concept. Indeed, the opposite must be argued when examining AI infrastructures and their social, ecological and economic impacts. Rather, we must rethink recent dominant paradigms of sustainability.

This ambition can surely be pushed further. As a book within a European media and communication-focused series, it situates the discussion within primarily European locations, industries, governance rationalities and discourses that are visible to us from our position. Contributors provide unique insights into countries and regions, such as the Netherlands and Sweden, that are struggling to govern the data centre boom. Geopolitical tensions matter fundamentally to AI relations but target specific countries very differently, as exemplified by contributions about Poland (as a Central and Eastern European example) or Yandex, a company operating within Russia's autocratic regime. Similarly, infrastructural AI components that span the world matter to how global peripheries are being re-constructed, from Ireland as a historical European periphery to Brazil, which is becoming an increasingly important network component not only due to undersea cables but its access to minerals and hydropower. Despite geographical, political and industrial shifts in relation to AI infrastructures and sustainability, colonialist logics and distributional injustices persist. Across this book, contributors exemplify how these extractive frontiers are being renegotiated in industries as diverse as agriculture, forestry, journalism or technology. However, this is by no means exhaustive; this book emerges within the context of ECREA, and as a result the chapters present only a fraction of local perspectives, mostly within Europe, and cannot account for the very relevant African or Asian perspectives, and for other regions around the world.

Contributions: From the Cradle to the Commodity

Despite their different foci on AI infrastructures and sustainability, all chapters in this book highlight that even though AI is touted as shiny new technology, underlying industrial logics in digital industries continue to shape old trajectories of power agglomeration, exploitation and distributional injustices. The book is structured into three parts, moving from the "birth" of AI resources in Amazonian mines into its manifestation within discourses and industries and towards projections of AI futures in politics and governance.

The chapters in the first part of the book, "Elements, Materials, Resources", engage with the materialities of AI infrastructures, how they are produced and understood and their implications on ideas of sustainability. Contributors engage with the politics of employing minerals, fish, sub-sea cable network systems, electricity and other materialities in the service of cloud computing, expanding objects and matters of mediation within media and communication research. The authors reveal and discuss the different socio-ecological sustainability implications caused by extraction and exploitation as well as the entangled industrial logics, matters of territoriality and politics in the context of media and communication as a discipline.

The second part of the book, "Promises, Economies, Discourses", focuses on the ways AI infrastructures and sustainability are imagined by different actors in different arenas and from different geopolitical positionings. Contributors deconstruct scientific, industry, news media and popular discourses on AI and sustainability and critically investigate the practices and representations of "sustainable AI" announced by big tech companies, science communication and journalism. Chapters explore crucial questions regarding the governance of AI-related market dynamics, digital sovereignty, responsibility and sustainability, as well as ethical questions surrounding the downstream uses of AI technologies, such as in journalism.

The third section, "Futures, Politics, Governance", analyses power asymmetries in the AI industry and their interdependence with matters of social and ecological sustainability. Authors explore options to deconstruct techno-solutionist arguments within discourses on AI infrastructures and sustainability and propose more liveable relations with AI infrastructures. They explore questions of scarcity in relation to AI, provide and develop alternative imaginaries and thereby constructively oppose techno-solutionism while simultaneously analysing the transformative potentials of AI development.

Together, these sections exemplify how AI infrastructures emerge from and within local contexts while co-producing global AI infrastructures, thus positioning their localities as crucial for understanding the planetary implications of AI and sustainability.

Elements, Materials, Resources

In her contribution, Ana Valdivia makes the point to "follow the GPU" (graphical processing units, specialised for AI applications) along the AI production chain to account for the manifold relations that must be considered in relation to AI infrastructures and sustainability. She engages with the commodity fetishism of AI, which purposefully renders its materials, infrastructures and producers invisible. Based on the method of "follow-the-thing" she traces the journey of AI chips, from mineral extractivism to e-waste, revealing the environmental costs at each stage of the AI commodity chain. She argues that such an expanded perspective is crucial to de-fetishise and nuance the cost-benefit equations within discussions of AI and sustainability.

By locating AI in the Amazon, Débora Leal, Max Krüger and Sigrid Kannengießer focus on mining as the "cradle of AI infrastructure" and exemplify how the exponential demand for computing devices results in the increasing extraction of gold, tantalum, copper, cobalt and other minerals essential for manufacturing GPUs. Within and in extension of the respective mining sites, many social and environmental justice concerns emerge in the local communities that must be accounted for when considering sustainability in relation to AI. Mining sites exemplify how pollution, health hazards, rising crime rates, sex work, and the severe endangerment of workers in illegal mining are shaping relations with AI infrastructures. The chapter argues the need to acknowledge all materials, actors and practices that are directly and indirectly involved with AI as part of an infrastructural understanding. By integrating indigenous perspectives, the chapter calls for the deconstruction of hegemonial understandings of sustainability, arguing that mining will always be exploitative and that AI infrastructures can therefore never be sustainable.

The infrastructural perspective on AI in this book thus acknowledges the highly different relations people can have with technology across the globe and even within the same country. To retain Brazil as an example, while the mining of GPU-relevant minerals in the Amazon are often made peripheral to discussions of AI and sustainability, the energy demand of AI technologies is increasingly causing the coastal region around Fortaleza to emerge as part of global AI infrastructures. Iago Bojczuk thus addresses how existing energy infrastructures that use the abundant hydropower available in coastal regions and local digital communication infrastructures, are shaping the geopolitics of AI in Fortaleza's favour as an undersea cable landing point. Bojczuk's analysis vividly exemplifies how public sector and governmental rhetorics and actions position Fortaleza as a "hub-of-hubs" that can ensure sustainable energy provision in an intensifying AI landscape that requires computing capacity and a clean energy supply. His contribution depicts Fortaleza's geopolitical position as an emerging digital infrastructure hub, where its transformation from one of Brazil's poorest regions is being pushed through state-led policies and geographic advantage that position Brazil as a competitive player in the global AI economy based on its interconnected infrastructures.

Ethical questions about public values and the common good must also be considered when analysing AI's energy demands alongside higher-level questions regarding the interrelation of AI and energy infrastructures, as Julia Velkova argues in her chapter. She analyses problems around energy access and grid capacity shortages related to data centre expansions. Investigating Sweden as a concrete case, she introduces the concept of infrastructure misalignment and demonstrates that an alliance of regional administrations, national grid operators and municipalities endanger the population's energy supply by upscaling power grids. While Sweden provides a useful example due to its growing number of data centres that are branded as sustainable, questions of the ethical distribution of resources like energy and water emerge across all regions hosting data centres. This chapter invites reflections on the embeddedness of AI infrastructures within a multitude of other infrastructures—energy infrastructures being one of them—which in turn raises question of justice, public values and the common good.

Patrick Brodie meanwhile investigates how big tech corporations frame their AI products as "solutions" to sustainability issues. Taking fish farming as his starting point, he depicts how cloud providers promise to "innovate" cultivation and extraction measures to manage limited planetary resources. Relying on theories of the metabolic rift and political ecology approaches to data, Brodie bridges regimes of datafication with the expansion of green capitalism and its reliance on infrastructures of automations as infrastructures of knowledge. Using machine learning applications to automate feeding or manage disease and parasites within fish farms, AI companies optimise extraction to (presumably) stay within planetary boundaries. As Brodie demonstrates, however, they are thus "materially shaping industrial futures" reliant on complex computing technologies and the few corporations that provide such solutions at scale, "intensifying rather than ameliorating the so-called 'externalities' of capitalist growth".

Promises, Economies, Discourses

In the second part of the book, contributors emphatically demonstrate how AI corporations are shaping narratives of sustainability as a concern solved through technology at the discursive level while also materializing corresponding infrastructures across industries. Taking "Cloud for Sustainability" tools promoted by Microsoft Azure as a starting point, Hamsini Sridharan deconstructs how the company is successfully implementing its cloud application for businesses as an infrastructure of sustainability, but doing so by actively narrowing down sustainability to a matter of data analytics. This approach, argues Sridharan, represents more than a "greenwashing" attempt: it discursively decouples sustainability from capitalism by aligning the current economic status quo with Western environmentalism. In doing so, cloud providers depoliticise sustainability, with lasting effects.

Extending this argument, Salla-Maaria Laaksonen and Meri Frig discuss the power of strategic corporate environmental communication to reinforce the infrastructural power of American big tech corporations while silencing critique. They analyse corporate blogs from the past 24 years and demonstrate how these corporations position themselves as obligatory passage points in sustainability matters. Through a nuanced discussion of the historical evolution of the messages these companies have been advancing through their environmental communication, Laaksonen and Frig demonstrate how large corporations position themselves as infrastructural providers of sustainability solutions while avoiding critique by simply eliminating it from the discourse. The authors call this approach "infrastructural solutionism" and empirically show how it strengthens the perceived legitimacy of big tech as the future providers of solutions for climate issues while simultaneously materializing these futures.

Malgorzata Winiarska-Brodowska shifts the attention of this section from corporate to public and media discourses, focusing on Poland as one of the most developed Central and Eastern European countries in terms of AI application. Poland has traditionally taken an approach of closer alignment to the US technosphere compared to some Western European states, where matters of digital sovereignty have traditionally been more prominent in the interest of promoting their own digital industries. With AI and rising geopolitical tensions undermining traditional global partnerships, questions of sustainability and AI have emerged as military and economic geopolitical concerns for Poland due to the war in Ukraine, making matters of alliance or self-reliance in AI development and application crucial.

Olga Dovbysh adds another layer to the discussion of the discursive production of relations between infrastructures for AI and sustainability by considering the case of Russia's major technology company, Yandex. Based on a visual and discursive analysis of Yandex's sustainability reporting, she reflects on the relevance of sustainability discourses around AI infrastructures in the context of an autocratic regime during its full-scale invasion of a neighbouring territory. While Yandex has considered sustainability reporting important in the past to enable cooperation with Western partners, it now frames sustainability as a matter of technological and ideological sovereignty in a country that is being globally sanctioned. This narrative around sovereignty aligns with depictions of AI as embedded in the progressive, modern lifestyles of Yandex's employees and customers. Dovbysh's analysis highlights sustainability as a matter of digital self-reliance in Russia that upholds global competitiveness and promises prosperity and progress for its citizens.

Moving towards media and publishing houses, Anne Mollen analyses partnerships between big tech and traditional news production entities and asks how these influence market concentration dynamics. Drawing on a political economy perspective, Mollen's analysis demonstrates the crucial value of news media during the deployment phase of AI systems. She shows how news media become important actors for companies developing generative AI systems as sources for training data, producing presumable authority and trustworthiness of AI-generated content and setting industry standards. News media thus become an instrument of reinforcing monopolisation over the emerging market of AI generated content. Furthermore, Mollen's analysis powerfully shows how relationships between news media and AI companies have not only economic impact, but also affect information access, the distribution and production of knowledge, the constitution of public spheres and environmental issues.

Futures, Politics, Governance

The final section examines epistemological and governance approaches to reimagine futures with computing technologies. In this context, metaphors matter for how we speak about and conceptualise AI and its infrastructures, along with how we govern and project AI-saturated futures. Gerwin van Schie and Inte Gloerich therefore unravel the biological and botanical metaphors in discourses on computation, data, platforms and AI. They argue how classical publications from platform studies effectively rely on tree-focused metaphors to exemplify the entanglements and power dynamics in platform societies. At the same time, they problematise how botanical metaphors naturalise human-made decisions about how AI and platformisation occur and manifest. While media studies have a rich tradition of discussing media ecologies, new metaphors might be needed to re-focus the naturalisation of the use of AI within platform infrastructures. The authors position the sewage system as one possible way to describe both contemporary and projected AI platformisation.

Jędrzej Niklas develops a critical discussion on the role of AI tools in the domain of environmental governance and sustainability. He argues that digital infrastructures should be considered public infrastructures regardless of their ownership because they are crucial agents in mediating collective and public interests and shaping environmental and ecological priorities. From this perspective, Niklas proposes a normative framework built around the notion of responsiveness that sees the integration of AI and data into environmental governance “as a dynamic process of political, social and technological transformation” grounded on disruptions of the status quo and communal approaches to policy changes. Illustrating this approach with a case from Poland’s forestry sector and the use of AI in managing forests, Niklas exposes the tensions catalysed by environmental governance and AI, which land between democratic participation and communal critique, as well as between institutional inertia and the need to include local knowledge and societal voices in large-scale infrastructural transformations.

Dan McQuillan positions “scale” as a key concern of current AI trajectories, which legitimises unfathomable current and future resource demands, projects ideas of unlimited growth through and with AI and advertises capabilities that (presumably) far surpass human facilities. Relying on Ernst Jünger’s notion of “total mobilization”, the chapter not only deconstructs the narrowed sustainability discussions around AI but explicates how such promissory imaginaries divert vast amounts of capital towards AI-saturated futures and the necessary infrastructures despite AI’s very harmful fallibilities, a move that is deeply entangled with far-right, eugenic and anti-democratic politics of Silicon Valley. Corresponding with de-growth approaches, he proposes applying de-computing approaches to the “de-automatisation of social relations and the disentangling of important decisions from AI’s reductive outputs”.

Further considering alternative, more sustainable computing futures, Fieke Jansen and Niels ten Oever explore the kinds of governance required to constrain infrastructure development for AI within planetary boundaries. Taking an empiric approach informed by participatory action, the authors discuss propositions forwarded by academics, civil society practitioners and policymakers during a series of workshops. Jansen and ten Oever reveal a strong desire among a plurality of European actors to reimagine the role of the state in AI infrastructure governance. An ideal state, they imagine, would promote welfare and democratic values while protecting human rights, societal and environmental justice instead of prioritising a wartime economy and market growth. In these discussions, the role of the state is reimagined as “a regulator, facilitator of different governance approaches and an investor”. Such a state, the authors argue, is a prerequisite for a more emancipatory, just computing future.

The book concludes with a discussion of questions about "the good life" in relation to AI as Johanna Sefyrin and Julia Velkova ask what a "good AI infrastructure" could look like. They use the example of a data centre located in Sweden intended to be environmentally sustainable by design. Their analysis reveals that realizing "good AI infrastructures" is not an easy feat as they identify frictions that occur among the imaginaries of different involved actors regarding the integration of this data centre into the region. While Sweden is the focus, their questions about "good" sustainable data centres could be posed regarding any data centre location. Moreover, while the design of a sustainable data centre requires specific measures and practices, the question of how all dimensions of AI infrastructures can be "good" (in the sense of "just") remains highly relevant.

Competing Interests The authors have no conflicts of interest to declare that are relevant to the contents of this chapter.

References

Altman, S. (2024, September 23). *The intelligence age*. Sam Altman. https://ia.samaltman.com/

Amoore, L. (2020). *Cloud ethics: Algorithms and the attributes of ourselves and others*. Duke University Press. https://doi.org/10.1215/9781478009276

Bender, E. M., Gebru, T., McMillan-Major, A., & Shmitchell, S. (2021). On the dangers of stochastic parrots: Can language models be too big?. In L. Irani, S. Kannan, M. Mitchell, & D. Robinson (Eds.), *FAccT '21: Proceedings of the 2021 ACM conference on fairness, accountability, and transparency* (pp. 610–623). Association for Computing Machinery. https://doi.org/10.1145/3442188.3445922

Birhane, A., Kasirzadeh, A., Leslie, D., & Wachter, S. (2023). Science in the age of large language models. *Nature Reviews Physics, 5*, 277–280. https://doi.org/10.1038/s42254-023-00581-4

Bossert, L. N., & Hagendorff, T. (2023). The ethics of sustainable AI: Why animals (should) matter for a sustainable use of AI. *Sustainable Development, 31*(5), 3459–3467. https://doi.org/10.1002/sd.2596

Bresnihan, P., & Brodie, P. (2021). New extractive frontiers in Ireland and the moebius strip of wind/data. *Environment and Planning E: Nature and Space, 4*(4), 1645–1664. https://doi.org/10.1177/2514848620970121

Brodie, P. (2023). Data infrastructure studies on an unequal planet. *Big Data & Society, 10*(1). https://doi.org/10.1177/20539517231182402

Brodie, P., & Bresnihan, P. (2025). From the bog to the cloud: Contesting eco-modernity in Ireland. In *From the Bog to the Cloud*. Bristol University Press.

Buller, A. (2022). *The value of a whale: On the illusions of green capitalism*. Manchester University Press.

Caffarra, C., Fermigier, S., Gambardella, A., Hidalgo, A., Lechelle, Y., Parsons, C., Styma, F., & Yen, A. (2025). *Deploying the EuroStack: What's needed now*. EuroStack. https://euro-stack.eu/the-white-paper/

Cellard, L., Parker, C., & Haines, F. (2025). Beyond AI as an environmental pharmakon: Principles for reopening the problem-space of machine learning's carbon footprint. *Environment and Planning E: Nature and Space*. https://doi.org/10.1177/25148486251332087

Cohn, J. (2023). EugenicTech: Three perspectives on the (b)anality of AI. In L. Parks, J. Velkova, & S. de Riddler (Eds.), *Media backends: Digital infrastructures and sociotechnical relations* (pp. 62–79). University of Illinois Press. https://doi.org/10.5622/illinois/9780252045349.003.0004

Crawford, K. (2021). *Atlas of AI: Power, politics and the planetary costs of artificial intelligence*. Yale University Press. https://doi.org/10.12987/9780300252392

Crawford, K., & Joler, V. (2018). *Anatomy of an AI system: The Amazon Echo as an anatomical map of human labor, data and planetary resources*. https://anatomyof.ai/

Dauvergne, P. (2022). Is artificial intelligence greening global supply chains? Exposing the political economy of environmental costs. *Review of International Political Economy, 29*(3), 696–718. https://doi.org/10.1080/09692290.2020.1814381

Day, T., Mooldijk, S., Smit, S., Posada, E., Hans, F., Fearnehough, H., Kachi, A., Warnecke, C., Kuramochi, T., & Höhne, N. (2022). *Corporate climate responsibility monitor 2022*. New Climate Institute. https://newclimate.org/sites/default/files/2022/02/CorporateClimateResponsibilityMonitor2022.pdf

Dencik, L. (2022). The datafied welfare state: A perspective from the UK. In A. Hepp, J. Jarke, & L. Kramp (Eds.), *New perspectives in critical data studies* (pp. 145–165). Springer. https://doi.org/10.1007/978-3-030-96180-0_7

Dencik, L., Hintz, A., Redden, J., & Treré, E. (2022). *Data justice*. SAGE Publications.

Diaz Bejarano, N., & Valdivia, A. (2025). Thirsty forests and expansive droughts: The environmental impacts of data centers in Latin America.*Environment and Planning E: Nature and Space*. https://doi.org/10.1177/25148486251409055

Edwards, D., Cooper, Z. G. T., & Hogan, M. (2024). The making of critical data center studies. *Convergence, 31*(2), 429–446. https://doi.org/10.1177/13548565231224157

Elish, M. C., & Boyd, D. (2018). Situating methods in the magic of big data and artificial intelligence. *Communication Monographs, 85*(1), 57–80. https://doi.org/10.1080/03637751.2017.1375130

European Commission. (2025, September 4). *Commission sets course for Europe's AI leadership with an ambitious AI Continent Action Plan* [Press release]. https://ec.europa.eu/commission/presscorner/detail/en/ip_25_1013

European Parliament. (2025, April 25). *Artificial intelligence: Threats and opportunities.* Topics. https://www.europarl.europa.eu/topics/en/article/20200918STO87404/artificial-intelligence-threats-and-opportunities

Flensburg, S., & Lai, S. S. (2023). Follow the data! A strategy for tracing infrastructural power. *Media and Communication, 11*(2), 319–329. https://doi.org/10.17645/mac.v11i2.6464

Gabrys, J. (2014). Powering the digital: From energy ecologies to electronic environmentalism. In R. Maxwell, J. Raundalen, & N. Lager Vestberg (Eds.), *Media and the ecological crisis* (pp. 3–18). Routledge.

Godske, B. (2024, November 27). *AI optimises ice cream for the summer.* Ingeniøren. https://ing.dk/artikel/ai-optimises-ice-cream-summer

Gray Widder, D., West, S., & Whittaker, M. (2023). Open (for business): Big tech, concentrated power, and the political economy of open AI. *SSRN Electronic Journal.* https://doi.org/10.2139/ssrn.4543807

Guzman, A. L., & Lewis, S. C. (2019). Artificial intelligence and communication: A human–machine communication research agenda. *New Media & Society, 22*(1), 70–86. https://doi.org/10.1177/1461444819858691

Hesmondhalgh, D. (2021). The infrastructural turn in media and internet research. In P. McDonald (Ed.), *The Routledge companion to media industries* (1st ed., pp. 132–142). Routledge. https://doi.org/10.4324/9780429275340-13

Jankovic, M., & Keilbach, J. (2023). Streaming against the environment: Digital infrastructures, video compression, and the environmental footprint of video streaming. In N. Verhoeff & K. Van Es (Eds.), *Situating data: Inquiries in algorithmic culture* (pp. 85–102). Amsterdam University Press.

Jansen, F. (2021). The state: A key actor in shaping data infrastructure space. In B. Herlo, D. Irrgang, G. Joost, & A. Unteidig (Eds.), *Practicing sovereignty: Digital involvement in times of crises* (pp. 20–31). Transcript Verlag.

Jue, M., & Ruiz, R. (2021). *An Elemental Politics.*Duke University Press.

Kaack, L. H., Donti, P. L., Strubell, E., Kamiya, G., Creutzig, F., & Rolnick, D. (2022). Aligning artificial intelligence with climate change mitigation. *Nature Climate Change, 12*, 518–527. https://doi.org/10.1038/s41558-022-01377-7

Kannengießer, S. (2019). Engaging with and reflecting on the materiality of digital media technologies: Repair and fair production. *New Media & Society, 22*(1), 123–139. https://doi.org/10.1177/1461444819858081

Kellogg, S., Starosielski, N., & Wiessner, M. (2024). Through the haze: Data centres' elemental aesthetics. *Journal of Environmental Media, 5*(1), 141–150. https://doi.org/10.1386/jem_00126_1

Lai, S. S., & Flensburg, S. (2023). *Gateways: Comparing digital communication systems in Nordic welfare states*. University of Gothenburg. https://doi.org/10.48335/9789188855848

Larkin, B. (2013). The politics and poetics of infrastructure. *Annual Review of Anthropology, 42*, 327–343. https://doi.org/10.1146/annurev-anthro-092412-155522

Lehuedé, S. (2022). When friction becomes the norm: Antagonism, discourse and planetary data turbulence. *New Media & Society, 26*(7), 3951–3966. https://doi.org/10.1177/14614448221108449

Libertson, F., Velkova, J., & Palm, J. (2021). Data-center infrastructure and energy gentrification: Perspectives from Sweden. *Sustainability: Science, Practice and Policy, 17*(1), 152–161. https://doi.org/10.1080/15487733.2021.1901428

Liboiron, M. (2021). *Pollution is colonialism*. Duke University Press.

López, A., Ivakhiv, A., Rust, S., Tola, M., Chang, A. Y., & Chu, K. W. (2024). *The Routledge Handbook of Ecomedia*. Studies Routledge.

Maxwell, R., & Miller, T. (Eds.). (2012). *Greening the media*. Oxford University Press.

Maxwell, R., & Miller, T. (2013). Our dirty love affair with technology. *Soundings, 54*, 115–126. https://doi.org/10.3898/136266213807299078

Miceli, M., Posada, J., & Yang, T. (2022). Studying up machine learning data: Why talk about bias when we mean power? *Proceedings of the ACM on Human-Computer Interaction, 6*(GROUP), 1–14. https://doi.org/10.1145/3492853

Milan, S., & Velden, L. V. D. (2016). The alternative epistemologies of data activism. *Digital Culture & Society, 2*(2), 57–74. https://doi.org/10.14361/dcs-2016-0205

Mol, A. (2002). *The body multiple: Ontology in medical practice*. Duke University Press. https://doi.org/10.1215/9780822384151

Mollen, A., & Kannengießer, S. (2025). Shaping AI (more) sustainably. Socio-technological perspectives on AI infrastructures. In T. Kox, A. Ullrich, & H. Zech (Eds.), *Uncertain journeys into digital futures: Inter-and transdisciplinary research for mitigating wicked societal and environmental problems* (pp. 207–218). Nomos. https://doi.org/10.5771/9783748947585

Morozov, E. (2014). *To save everything, click here: The folly of technological solutionism*. PublicAffairs.

Natale, S. (2021). *Deceitful media: Artificial intelligence and social life after the Turing test* (1st ed.). Oxford University Press. https://doi.org/10.1093/oso/9780190080365.001.0001

Parks, L. (2020). Infrastructure. In L. Ouellette & J. Gray (Eds.), *Keywords for media studies* (pp. 106–108). New York University Press. https://doi.org/10.18574/nyu/9781479817474.003.0035

Parks, L., & Starosielski, N. (Eds.). (2015). *Signal traffic: Critical studies of media infrastructures*. University of Illinois Press. https://doi.org/10.5406/illinois/9780252039362.001.0001

Parks, L., & Walker, J. (2020). Disaster media: Bending the curve of ecological disruption and moving toward social justice. *Media+ Environment, 2*(1). https://doi.org/10.1525/001c.13474

Parks, L., Velkova, J., & de Ridder, S. (Eds.). (2023). *Media backends. Digital infrastructures and sociotechnical relations*. University of Illinois Press. https://doi.org/10.5622/illinois/9780252045349.001.0001

Pasek, A. (2023). From atoms to electrons: An energy history and future of computing. In I. A. Pasek, Z. G. T. Cooper, C. K. Lin, & J. B. Kinder (Eds.), *Digital energetics* (pp. 15–42). University of Minnesota Press, meson press. https://doi.org/10.14619/0580

Pasek, A., Vaughan, H., & Starosielski, N. (2023). The world wide web of carbon: Toward a relational footprinting of information and communications technology's climate impacts. *Big Data & Society, 10*(1). https://doi.org/10.1177/20539517231158994

Peña Gangadharan, S., & Niklas, J. (2019). Decentering technology in discourse on discrimination. *Information, Communication & Society, 22*(7), 882–899. https://doi.org/10.1080/1369118X.2019.1593484

Plantin, J. C., & Punathambekar, A. (2018). Digital media infrastructures: Pipes, platforms, and politics. *Media, Culture & Society, 41*(2), 163–174. https://doi.org/10.1177/0163443718818376

Raworth, K. (2017). *Doughnut economics: Seven ways to think like a 21st-century economist*. Random House Business Books.

Rockström, J., Steffen, W., Noone, K., Persson, Å., Chapin, F. S., Lambin, E. F., Lenton, T. M., Scheffer, M., Folke, C., Schellnhuber, H. J., Nykvist, B., de Wit, C. A., Hughes, T., van der Leeuw, S., Rodhe, H., Sörlin, S., Snyder, P. K., Costanza, R., Svedin, U., et al. (2009). A safe operating space for humanity. *Nature, 461*, 472–475. https://doi.org/10.1038/461472a

Rolnick, D., Donti, P. L., Kaack, L. H., Kochanski, K., Lacoste, A., Sankaran, K., Ross, A. S., Milojevic-Dupont, N., Jaques, N., & Waldman-Brown, A. (2022). Tackling climate change with machine learning. *ACM Computing Surveys, 55*(2), 1–96. https://doi.org/10.1145/3485128

Ruckenstein, M. (2024). *The Feel of Algorithms.*University of California Press

Sætra, H. S. (Ed.). (2023). *Technology and sustainable development: The promise and pitfalls of techno-solutionism* (1st ed.). Routledge. https://doi.org/10.1201/9781003325086

Saxon Hans Carl von Carlowitz Society (Ed.). (2013). *Die erfindung der nachhaltigkeit: Leben, werk und wirkung des Hans Carl von Carlowitz*. Oekom Verlag.
Seaver, N. (2017). Algorithms as culture: Some tactics for the ethnography of algorithmic systems. *Big Data & Society, 4*(2). https://doi.org/10.1177/2053951717738104
Sen, A. (2008). *Commodities and capabilities* (13th ed.). Oxford University Press.
Shriver-Rice, M., & Vaughan, H. (2020). What is environmental media studies? *Journal of Environmental Media, 1*(1), 3–13. https://doi.org/10.1386/jem_00001_2
Star, S. L. (1999). The ethnography of infrastructure. *American Behavioral Scientist, 43*(3), 377–391. https://doi.org/10.1177/00027649921955326
Star, S. L., & Ruhleder, K. (1996). Steps toward an ecology of infrastructure: Design and access for large information spaces. *Information Systems Research, 7*(1), 111–134. https://doi.org/10.1287/isre.7.1.111
Starosielski, N. (2021). *Media hot and cold*. Duke University Press.
Starosielski, N., & Walker, J. (Eds.). (2016). *Sustainable media* (1st ed.). Routledge. https://doi.org/10.4324/9781315794877
Strubell, E., Ganesh, A., & McCallum, A. (2020). Energy and policy considerations for modern deep learning research. *Proceedings of the AAAI Conference on Artificial Intelligence, 34*(9), 13693–13696. https://doi.org/10.1609/aaai.v34i09.7123
Suchman, L. (2023). The uncontroversial 'thingness' of AI. *Big Data & Society, 10*(2). https://doi.org/10.1177/20539517231206794
Tschakert, P. (2022). More-than-human solidarity and multispecies justice in the climate crisis. *Environmental Politics, 31*(2), 277–296. https://doi.org/10.1080/09644016.2020.1853448
United Nations. (2015). *Transforming our world: The 2030 Agenda for Sustainable Development*. https://sdgs.un.org/sites/default/files/publications/21252030%20Agenda%20for%20Sustainable%20Development%20web.pdf
United Nations World Commission on Environment and Development. (1987). *Our common future*. https://sustainabledevelopment.un.org/content/documents/5987our-common-future.pdf
Valdivia, A. (2024). The supply chain capitalism of AI: A call to (re)think algorithmic harms and resistance through environmental lens. *Information, Communication & Society*, 1–17. https://doi.org/10.1080/1369118X.2024.2420021
Van der Vlist, F., Helmond, A., & Ferrari, F. (2024). Big AI: Cloud infrastructure dependence and the industrialisation of artificial intelligence. *Big Data & Society, 11*(1). https://doi.org/10.1177/20539517241232630

Van Wynsberge, A. (2021). Sustainable AI: AI *for* sustainability and the sustainability of AI. *AI and Ethics, 1*, 213–218. https://doi.org/10.1007/s43681-021-00043-6

Velkova, J., & Plantin, J. C. (2023). Data centers and the infrastructural temporalities of digital media: An introduction. *New Media & Society, 25*(2), 273–286. https://doi.org/10.1177/14614448221149945

Vinuesa, R., Azizpour, H., Leite, I., Balaam, M., Dignum, V., Domisch, S., Felländer, A., Langhans, S. D., Tegmark, M., & Fuso Nerini, F. (2020). The role of artificial intelligence in achieving the sustainable development goals. *Nature. Communications, 11*, Article 233. https://doi.org/10.1038/s41467-019-14108-y

Von der Leyen, U. (2025, February 11). *Speech by president von der Leyen at the artificial intelligence action summit*. AI Action Summit. https://ec.europa.eu/commission/presscorner/api/files/document/print/en/speech_25_471/SPEECH_25_471_EN.pdf

Warde, P. (2018). *The invention of sustainability: Nature and destiny, c. 1500–1870* (1st ed.). Cambridge University Press. https://doi.org/10.1017/9781316584767

PART I

Elements, Materials, Resources

CHAPTER 2

Follow the Thing: AI

Ana Valdivia

Take an ultimate consumable item and trace back the set of inputs that culminated in this item, including prior transformations, the raw materials, the transportation mechanisms, the labour input into each of the material processes, the food inputs into the labour. (Hopkins & Wallerstein, 2016).

The Materiality that Matters: AI, Chips, and Data Centres

On January 27th, 2025, Chinese Artificial Intelligence (AI) model-makers released DeepSeek v3, a new version of a chatbot powered by Generative Artificial Intelligence (GenAI). While this may seem like just another GenAI-powered chatbot entering the AI market, DeepSeek's model shook US stock markets. To provide some numbers about the scale of the situation, while Meta's Llama 3 cost 61.6 million USD to develop, DeepSeek claimed to have reduced costs to just 6 million USD

A. Valdivia (✉)
University of Oxford, Oxford, UK
e-mail: ana.valdivia@oii.ox.ac.uk

A. Mollen et al. (eds.), *AI Infrastructures and Sustainability*, Palgrave Studies in European Communication Research and Education,
https://doi.org/10.1007/978-3-032-09748-4_2

(The Economist, 2025). DeepSeek's breakthrough had a direct impact on the US chip designer and supplier of GPUs (graphics processing units, specialized chips for AI), NVIDIA, which saw its market value plummet by 600 billion USD on the same day. The reason is that the Chinese team demonstrated that GenAI models could supposedly achieve similar performance to competitors while using fewer chips and consuming less energy. This breakthrough challenged Sam Altman's prevailing notion that developing GenAI necessarily requires more chips, energy, and data centers (Lynn, 2024). The DeepSeek case revealed a fundamental tension: improvements in AI efficiency, and thus in sustainability, can negatively impact US stock markets and firms whose profits depend on selling more hardware resources such as chips.

This example also illustrates how technological innovation in AI efficiency exists within competing economic incentives. While there is growing interest in reducing GenAI's energy consumption to lower operational costs and environmental impact, there are simultaneously economic pressures from hardware manufacturers to maintain high resource requirements. The AI industry publicly invests in digital sustainability initiatives, yet the market's negative reaction to efficiency breakthroughs suggests complex dynamics between technological advancement, environmental concerns, and economic interests throughout the chip production supply chains, pointing out to the relevance of AI's materiality nowadays. But how we can study its materiality today?

Materiality has traditionally been understood as a relational effect, i.e., "matter that matters" (Law, 2012). As seen in DeepSeek's case, the materiality of AI—encompassing chips, data centres, and other resources essential to powering this technology—has become increasingly significant due to its political and economic influence in capital markets, reinforcing its status as "matter that matters" (Lehdonvirta, 2022; Luitse, 2024). This matter is extracted, transported and producers across the globe to make AI possible today.

Scholars from a wide range of disciplines have proposed different approaches to study the materiality of technology. For instance, STS and media scholars Kate Crawford and Vladan Joler (2018) proposed to study the anatomy of an AI system by analysing the internal structure of Amazon Echo, the device that connects users to its voice assistant, also known as Alexa. Media scholar Jussi Parikka (2021a) introduced the concept of the "Geology of Media", which explores the connections between media technologies, their materiality, hardware, energy consumption, and the geophysical environment. Parikka argues that nature both enables and bears the burden of media culture, from the extraction of metals and minerals to the accumulation of electronic waste. In fact, the making of media technologies involves manufacturing electronics and using energy to power it, which is frame in a commodity chain frame. In this vein, media scholar Sy Taffel (2021) proposed an ecological approach to examining digital media's materiality, linking media with political ecology. One important aspect of Taffel's scholarship is the stress on the relationship between media devices and environmental degradation. Taffel claims that in the current scenario of climate change it is relevant to better understand the environmental costs of the materiality media and digital technologies. Given the large and increasing number of resources needed to train GenAI products (Martin & Peskoe, 2025), scholarship has recently begun to investigate the environmental costs of GenAI by building on a traditional body of scholars analysing data infrastructure and associated environmental costs (Hogan, 2015; Velkova, 2019).

Within the recent literature on AI's environmental costs, numerous studies have examined the energy consumption associated with algorithmic training through carbon emissions. Morand et al. (2024) analysed the carbon footprint of machine learning algorithms by focusing on the energy required by graphics processing units (GPUs) for training. They found that, despite efforts to improve efficiency, AI's environmental impact has continued to rise. In a similar vein, Luccioni et al. (2023) estimated that training BLOOM, a large language model trained to be environmentally sustainable, generates a total of 50.5 tonnes of CO_2 emissions.[1]

AI also consumes vast amounts of water. During the training and development phases, water is required to cool the servers used for AI model training. Some estimations show that AI places a significant demand on water resources. For instance, Meta used 22 million litres of water to train Llama-3—an amount a Londoner would consume in just over 400 years (Valdivia, 2025). However, energy and water are also essential beyond the training phase. For example, manufacturing graphics cards requires substantial water resources (Li et al., 2023).

[1] In comparison, a flight Barcelona-London emits 0.292 CO_2 tonnes per person.

These facts illustrate the need to analyse AI's materiality and associated environmental impacts from a commodity perspective. In the context of AI, there are two types of commodities: software and hardware.[2] Data and algorithms are the software objects in the form of virtual and intangible materiality, while GPUs, memory cards, and SSD disks are hardware objects in the form of physical and tangible materiality. Within this context, part of the literature on AI's environmental costs fails to trace back the environmental impacts across both types of AI commodities (software and hardware) by connecting the various stages of the AI commodity chain, from mineral extraction to waste generation (Valdivia, 2024).

This fragmented approach prevents a comprehensive understanding of the associated environmental costs throughout the entire supply chain, including carbon emissions, water consumption, soil degradation, mass waste production, and biodiversity loss. This limitation illustrates the need to connect different stages within AI commodity chains to make visible and better estimate the balance between its environmental costs and social benefits. This chapter aims to contribute to the literature on AI and sustainability by proposing a conceptual framework that draws on critical geography and sheds light on AI commodity chains in order to defetishise its materiality (Mollen et al., 2024).

Geographies of Commodity Chains: Papayas, Mushrooms and GPUs?

Value chain, supply chain, and production network are synonymous of commodity chains, a concept that refers to a "network of labour and production processes whose end result is a finished commodity" (Hopkins & Wallerstein, 1986, p. 159). Sociologists, economists, anthropologists, historians and geographers have largely investigated commodity chains to "study patterns of development of the modem world-system" (Bair, 2014, p. 1). This method proved to be successful in advancing analytical understanding on the complexity of production networks that have become global and intrinsic within the capitalist world-economy (Tsing, 2009).

[2] I own this contribution to Dr. Valente, a colleague with whom we have had academic discussion about what does it mean to be a commodity in the digital world.

This analytical framework proposes to examine what Marx coined as "commodity fetishism" (Felluga, 2015; Marx, 1967), the idea that once commodities are purchased, the materials and human relations involved in the production of that commodity are ignored. Critical geographers such as David Harvey (1990) have drawn upon this concept asserting that "the grapes that sit upon the supermarket shelves are mute; we cannot see the fingerprints of exploitation upon them or tell immediately what part of the world they are from" (p. 423). In a similar vein, Ian Cook published in 2004 *Follow the Thing: Papaya* in which he traced the route of a papaya from a supermarket in London back to a farm in Jamaica to "unmute" commodities and explore social relations and geographies. In fact, this piece was intended as a provocation to defetishise commodity chains by connecting producers and consumers throughout different geographies, proving that it is possible to connect subjects and trace commodities across geographies. To do so, Cook proposed the *follow the thing* methodology, an approach proposed to follow the journey of commodities. This chapter builds on this scholarship to defetishise commodity chains through follow the thing analysis, focusing on the tangible commodities of AI: GPUs. First, it unveils the geographies, materialities, and social relationships involved in the production of this technology. Second, it examines and accounts for the environmental impacts, not only during the training phase of AI but across its entire commodity chain. This analysis is essential in demonstrating that the creation of AI involves not only human labour, as others have already highlighted, but also diverse geographies and significant environmental costs. Moreover, this commodity perspective challenges the prevailing "AI for sustainability" narrative and highlights persistent patterns of global distributional injustices. Examining AI through the lens of commodification does more than simply catalogue additional environmental harms along the commodity chain—it reveals how the commodification process itself actively constrains our understanding of AI technologies and their impacts. This narrowed perception obscures the full social and environmental consequences embedded in AI systems, limiting the ability to address them comprehensively.

The literature on AI commodity chains has recently emerged as a prominent field of interdisciplinary study (Brodie, 2020, 2023; Lehuedé, 2024; Parikka, 2021b; Taffel, 2023), accounting for the "organisational and geographical forces that shape the supply chains of AI" (Tubaro et al.,

2025, p. 1). This includes labour tasks related to data work in AI preparation, such as low-wage data annotators (Grohmann & Fernandes Araújo, 2021; Miceli & Posada, 2022), highlighting labour injustices and the exploitation of data labellers by "powerful forces that push such companies towards limiting the actual social impact of their business model in favour of ensuring higher profit margins" (Muldoon et al., 2023, p. 1). However, AI commodity chains also extend to miners extracting minerals for GPU manufacturing, workers in factories assembling GPUs, and e-waste dismantlers (Valdivia, 2024), exposing social relationships that are neglected under the fetishism of commodities.

The defetishisation of AI commodities involves bringing attention to its key tangible materiality: its processing units. The first marketed graphic unit for personal computing was launched by NVIDIA in 1999. It was defined as "a single-chip processor with integrated transform, lighting, triangle setup/clipping, and rendering engines that is capable of processing a minimum of 10 million polygons per second" (Gaboury, 2021, p. 254). These GPUs were developed to enhance computer graphics using parallel computation but have become key components in the development of machine and deep learning algorithms. Unlike central processing units (CPUs), which are highly flexible but process calculations sequentially, GPUs are designed for parallel processing, allowing them to run multiple iterations of the same calculation simultaneously. This capability, initially developed for rendering graphics, proved highly effective for training algorithms. GPUs could process large amounts of data at once and reduce the time needed for tasks like image recognition or text generation, but at a larger computing cost (Miller, 2022). To study the materiality of AI is to study GPUs, amongst other electronics (Rella, 2024). GPUs become part of servers located in data centres that process data and train algorithms. Data centres are in turn connected to subsea and underground cables that enable data circulation across the Internet (Munn, 2021, 2022; Starosielski, 2015). As a result, they also become key infrastructure in AI materiality. Moreover, these infrastructures, GPUs, data centres, and subsea cables, are manufactured using various materials and minerals. Their extraction, as well as their production and shipment across different geographies, entails significant environmental impacts that are unveiled when defetishising these commodities.

Following the Thing AI

Raw Materials

Minerals contribute to the materiality of AI. GPUs, for example, are classified as "semiconductors" because their electrical conductivity can be controlled—they are neither superconductors nor non-conductors. The main semiconductor material used to manufacture GPUs is silicon, which is derived from high-purity quartz. While one might assume silicon is simply sand, scholar Ingrid Burrington (2024) clarifies that "the invention of silicon chips did not rely on ordinary sand but on extraordinary crystals" (p. 14). Although silicon and quartz are not considered critical raw materials due to their abundance—silicon makes up 27.7% of the Earth's crust by mass—their extraction is concentrated in specific locations where high-purity quartz is accessible. One such location is Spruce Pine, North Carolina, which holds some of the world's largest high-purity quartz deposits. The mining company Sibelco operates in Spruce Pine, and as stated on their website, "products are exported thousands of miles from North Carolina to Asia's specialist electronics" (Sibelco, 2025, Spruce Pine section).

While GPUs are primarily made of silicon, they also contain other minerals such as aluminium, copper, tin, tantalum, gold, silver, zinc, and palladium, which are used to manufacture specific components. For instance, tantalum and palladium are used in capacitors, small components within GPUs that store and release electricity when the chip requires an energy boost. Tin, gold, silver, and zinc are essential for switches and connections within the chip. Tantalum, in particular, is sourced from various locations worldwide. According to NVIDIA's *Conflict Minerals Report*, the companies that extracts this mineral are based in Brazil, France, India, China, and Japan (NVIDIA, 2022). The chemical composition of GPUs highlights the materiality of AI and its dependence on raw materials that must be extracted for chip production. Therefore, mineral extraction has significant environmental impacts.

A recent study by Owen et al. (2023) found that at least 60% of the land used for extracting minerals essential to the green transition, many of which, such as silver, copper, tin, and zinc, are also used in electronics manufacturing, belongs to Indigenous and rural geographies. The extraction of these materials requires vast amounts of energy, contributing significantly to carbon emissions. Large quantities of water are needed to purify and process the extracted minerals, leading not only to high water consumption but also to contamination of nearby water sources. Furthermore, mineral extraction is linked to biodiversity loss, as it involves deforestation and habitat destruction, disrupting local ecosystems, including insects living underground and birds affected by noise pollution. While AI as a form of commodity is promoted as a positive development, defetishing this commodity by following a chip supply chain of a mineral constituent of AI infrastructure highlights how AI is also engaged in the historical oppressive mechanisms such as land and resource extractivism.

Chip Manufacturing

Once minerals are extracted and processed, they are shipped to factories that manufacture GPUs. Manufacturing a GPU is a complex process involving several steps. First, a company must design the chip. In the AI sector, NVIDIA has become the most prominent chip designer, particularly for GPUs. This US-based company holds 80% of the market share and has surpassed major tech firms such as Meta and Amazon in market capitalisation. The primary material used, silicon, is first purified to prepare it for chip production. It is then sliced into thin wafers, onto which intricate electrical patterns are etched to form the circuits that enable the GPU to function. These wafers are then cut into individual chips, which are rigorously tested and packaged. The entire process takes place in highly controlled clean rooms to prevent contamination, as even the tiniest particle of dust could cause defects.

The main chip manufacturers of GPUs are TSMC, Samsung, and Intel. Within this context, ASML, a Dutch company, holds the monopoly of the machinery used to manufacture the chips. Contrary to popular belief, NVIDIA does not manufacture its own chips; it is a fabless company that outsources production to these manufacturers. However, NVIDIA "is a key gatekeeper in the design of chips for AI training, and three cloud infrastructure firms—Amazon Web Services, Microsoft Azure, and Google Cloud Platform—continue to dominate the provision of networked data centre services through which many access AI services today" (Myers & Vipra, 2025, p. 39).

Among the three main chips manufacturers, TSMC is the most significant, and the geopolitical tensions between the US and China are partly driven by its factories in Taiwan. During the 1970s and 1980s, the US outsourced chip manufacturing to reduce costs, as the demand for affordable chips in laptops and other devices grew. However, due to the current geopolitical climate, the US now regrets this decision and is investing in domestic chip production, including the construction of a TSMC factory in Arizona (Jolly, 2024). As Sarah Myers and Jai Vipra posit in the latest issue of Logic(s), the political economy of TSMC, which has consolidated its dominance in chip manufacturing, relies heavily on precarious labour. The workers producing GPUs in Taiwan, many of whom are migrant labourers from Southeast Asian countries such as Indonesia, Vietnam, the Philippines, and Thailand (Tay, 2023), must endure long hours and exposure to toxic chemicals that severely impact their health: "The material conditions of chipmaking, including work that requires exposure to toxic chemicals, are obscured by influential narratives that frame chips as politically valuable resources" (Myers & Vipra, 2025, p. 42). TSMC has become so economically significant to Taiwan that in 2021, the government prioritised water supply for chip manufacturing over agriculture during one of the country's worst droughts (Zhong & Chang Chien, 2021). This decision sparked anger among local farmers, who felt unfairly blamed for high water consumption, even though chip manufacturing also requires vast amounts of water.[3] This example illustrates how the commodity chain of AI reconfigures the distribution of water, and thus of environmental justice, in ways that affect other sectors in the economy, such as agriculture and farming.

But what are other environmental impacts associated to chip manufacturing? According to Roussilhe et al. (2024), who analysed the environmental impact of 16 Taiwanese electronics manufacturers, between 2015 and 2020, these companies increased greenhouse gas emissions by 7.5% annually, final energy consumption by 8.8%, electricity use by 8.9%, and water usage by 6.1%. The research highlights a direct link between production volume and environmental impact, arguing that efficiency improvements alone are insufficient to reduce the industry's overall footprint. The study warns that the rapid expansion of the electronics sector, combined with slow adoption of renewable energy, could undermine Taiwan's carbon reduction goals and sustainability efforts.

[3] According to TSMC's (2022) *Sustainability Report*, the company used 260,000 m^3 of water per day (TSMC, 2022).

Data centres

Data centres have become a crucial infrastructure in the political economy and the ongoing race for AI innovation. This is largely due to the increasing size of GenAI models. Unlike in the past, when AI models could be trained on a laptop, today's large-scale models require significant computational power, relying on multiple GPUs housed in server rooms within data centres. These facilities not only provide the necessary processing capabilities but also store the vast amounts of data used to train and fine-tune AI models.

There are various categories of data centres, but due to the growing demand for computational power and data storage, hyperscale data centres—designed to support large-scale IT infrastructure—have seen an unprecedented surge. As a result, the materiality of the "cloud" has been increasingly exposed, revealing the immense architectural structures and vast resource consumption required to sustain it. In response to this phenomenon, scholars have highlighted that data centres have emerged as "site[s] for critical inquiry into the materialities of the Internet, the cloud, and digital technologies" (Edwards et al., 2024, p. 430). Data centres form the backbone of what is commonly referred to as "the cloud" yet studying them through commodity lens reveals their role in a global network that mobilises capital and resources (Hu, 2015, p. 4). This raises critical questions: which geographies are entangled in data center operations and what resources and commodities are being extracted and transformed to sustain them?

There is a common misconception that data centres are primarily built in cold regions. Their locations are determined by political, infrastructural, and economic factors rather than climate alone. One key reason for their widespread distribution is the necessity of proximity—being closer to a data centre ensures faster data transmission. For example, a financial broker who relies on high-speed internet cannot afford even a one-second delay, as it could mean losing millions in a transaction. This growing demand for ultra-fast communication has driven the rapid expansion of data centres across the globe. However, data centres do not just emerge anywhere; they are strategically placed in regions where political actors actively encourage their deployment. During my ethnographic research in Mexico, I found that Querétaro was an ideal location for data centres because the local government explicitly welcomed and promoted their installation (Valdivia, 2024). In addition to political support, these facilities require territories with the infrastructure to meet their immense electricity and water demands. They also tend to be established in areas with high unemployment rates, often under the promise of job creation. Yet, evidence suggests that data centres do not significantly reduce unemployment in the regions where they are built (Cummins, 2024). While they employ a large number of construction workers during the building phase—requiring expertise in industrial structures, pipelines, and digital infrastructure—once operational, they require only a minimal workforce. Typically, a data centre employs only a handful of engineers to maintain the servers and a small security team to oversee the premises. The long-term economic benefits for local communities are, therefore, often overstated. On the contrast, they create and exacerbate environmental issues, such as conflicts over water (Lehuedé, 2024; Valdivia, 2024), and electricity distribution (Brodie, 2023; Libertson et al., 2021).

A 2015 study outlining the lifecycle of UK data centres (Whitehead et al., 2015) identified the various infrastructure and components required for their operation. These include IT systems (servers, storage, and networks), electrical systems (lighting, UPS losses, switchgear), mechanical systems (free cooling fans, ventilation, chillers), and public health infrastructure (water pumps). Each of these components is built from materials such as copper, PVC, concrete, polyethylene, and steel.

As the number of data centres rapidly expands across the globe, their environmental impact has become a key focus of critique. One major concern is their significant carbon emissions. Carbon emissions depend on their energy source. If the electricity grid depends on fossil fuels, data centres emit carbon emission emerging from the energy sources. However, this depends on the location and environmental regulation. For instance, data centres in the Global North used, in general, energy from renewable sources compared to those located in the Global South. These infrastructures have also faced criticism for the vast amounts of water they consume to cool their servers. In this regard, media scholar Mél Hogan was a pioneer in analysing data centre water usage in the US as early as 2015 (Hogan, 2015).

Data centres are defetishised by uncovering cloud narratives and investigating the material commodities embedded within this infrastructure. While data centres have been investigated in the literature, pre and post the GenAI era, the follow the thing analysis developed within this chapter unveils not only its materiality, but how AI chips (Khan and Mann,

2020) are magnifying the environmental impacts of data centres. But what happens to this materiality when is no longer useful?

E-Waste

Waste is the final stage within AI commodity chains, with two primary endpoints: incineration or dumping. Extracting minerals from GPU components is prohibitively expensive, making it nearly impossible to reintroduce them into the supply chain. As a result, GPUs are typically incinerated to reduce waste volume or shipped to other countries, where local communities are left to manage the electronic waste. For instance, artist and researcher Cyrus Khalatbari (2024) discovered discarded GPUs in Accra, Ghana, home to one of the world's largest e-waste dumps. Despite its environmental and social consequences, GPU waste remains largely underexplored in academic literature, with some exceptions (Velasco González, 2016; Wang et al., 2024). Greater attention should be paid to this final phase of the commodity chain, as it has serious implications for communities and ecosystems near incineration plants and e-waste dumps.

While research on GPU waste is scarce, media scholars have extensively examined electronic waste more broadly. Jennifer Gabrys studied e-waste by "mapping the sites of its multiple transformations and by examining the residue that accumulates from these transformations" (2013, p. 24). Her analysis highlights e-waste geographies in locations such as Delhi (India) and Guangdong (China), where workers dismantle electronic components, including wires and motherboards. Indeed, e-waste geographies are often concentrated in the Global South. As Taffel (2021) posits: "wealthier nations send large volumes of toxic waste to poorer countries, where they are manually treated, with few safeguards in place to protect the health and safety of workers or local environments" (p. 178).

A recent study by Wang et al. (2024) in *Nature Computational Science* analysed how Large Language Models (LLMs) and the GPUs required to train them could exacerbate the global e-waste crisis. Given that the average lifespan of a GPU is approximately five years, these components must be regularly replaced, contributing to increasing waste generation. The researchers estimated that without proper regulation or policy intervention, LLMs could increase e-waste production by a factor of 1000 by 2030. This surge in e-waste could have severe environmental and health consequences. If GPUs are incinerated, they may release toxic particles into the air, negatively affecting the health of communities living near incineration plants. Alternatively, if discarded in landfills, the hazardous materials within GPUs could contaminate the soil and groundwater, posing long-term environmental risks.

Following the thing AI until the end, when its tangible materiality is discarded, offers a critical approach to defetishise this technology. It illustrates the material side of AI and how this technology has the potential risk to increment the amount of e-waste in the future. But by following the thing AI, that is, tracing the journey back to the beginning, to mineral extraction, illustrates how AI commodities are contributing to existing social and environmental struggles across different geographies and at different points of the commodity chain. By unveiling the materialities and supply chains behind AI, we expose multidimensional conflicts that emerge at each stage: from water rights disputes at manufacturing sites to labour exploitation in mineral extraction to waste management crises.

Conclusion

Ian Cook, in his piece *Follow the Thing: Papaya* (2004), cites David Harvey's call to "get behind the veil, the fetishism of the market" (Harvey, 1990, p. 422, as cited in Cook, 2004) urging to reveal the powerful, important, and often unsettling connections between geographies, consumers and the distant producers whose contributions to their lives remain invisible, unnoticed, and largely unappreciated when a commodity is purchased. This chapter responds to that call by challenging the fetishisation of commodities of AI that obscures its materiality, as well as geographies and bodies exposed to its environmental impacts. While AI has been promoted as a sustainable technology capable of tackling climate change, its industry is advocating for the use of more resources. Consequently, the case of DeepSeek illustrated how training algorithms with (supposedly) less resources can have a negative impact in the stock market. Getting behind the veil in the age of AI involves understanding the commodities behind this technology. To do so, this chapter contributes to *AI Infrastructures and Sustainability* edited volume by *following the thing: AI*. This methodology shows the entanglements of the materiality of AI along commodity chains, and how this materiality scales up and exacerbates environmental conflicts. GPUs, made from minerals extracted in locations such as the United States and Brazil, are assembled in Taiwan to manufacture chips before being distributed to data centres worldwide. At the end of their lifecycle, these GPUs are discarded in dumping fields in Ghana or incinerated. Several geographies around the world contribute to making this technology and its material existence possible today.

One can observe that the value generated by these commodity chains is not distributed equally. As Tsing (2015) states, "supply chains make value from translating values produced in quite varied circumstances into capitalist inventory" (p. 56). In the AI commodity chains, territories in Latin America and in the periphery within the US and Europe bear the costs of extraction operations. While regions near data centres sacrifice their water and soil, their communities do not benefit from the capital accumulated by big tech companies. Similarly, farmers in Taiwan also bear the costs of TSMC factories that extract large amounts of water to manufacture GPUs, even in drought scenarios. Within these chains, one can also identify how pollution translates into profit (Tsing, 2015, p. 56): extracting minerals from the Earth, processing these minerals to manufacture chips, manufacture these chips, assembling servers into data centres, dumping electronics in landfills. All these activities observed in AI commodity chains involve the contamination of the soil and water and human bodies (Valdivia, 2024, 2025). The environmental impacts of AI commodity chains are substantial, as this chapter highlights. By following the thing, the materiality of AI is defetishised and its costs and environmental impacts revealed.

Competing Interests The author has no conflicts of interest to declare that are relevant to the contents of this chapter.

References

Bair, J. (2014). Editor's introduction: Commodity chains in and of the world system. *Journal of World-Systems Research, 20*(10), 1–10. https://doi.org/10.5195/jwsr.2014.574

Brodie, P. (2020). Climate extraction and supply chains of data. *Media, Culture & Society, 42*(7–8), 1095–1114. https://doi.org/10.1177/0163443720904601

Brodie, P. (2023). Data infrastructure studies on an unequal planet. *Big Data & Society, 10*(1). https://doi.org/10.1177/20539517231182402

Burrington. (2024). From war crystals to ordinary sand: Excavating silicon supply chains. *IEEE Annals of the History of Computing, 46*(2), 13–23. https://doi.org/10.1109/MAHC.2024.3378121

Cook, I. (2004). Follow the thing: Papaya. *Antipode, 36*(4), 642–664.

Crawford, K., & Joler, V. (2018). *Anatomy of an AI system.* https://anatomyof.ai//span/span

Cummins, Wes. (2024, June 14). Navigating labor shortages in the data center industry. *Data Centre Dynamics.* https://www.datacenterdynamics.com/en/opinions/navigating-labor-shortages-in-the-data-center-industry/

Edwards, D., Cooper, Z. G. T., & Hogan, M. (2024). The making of critical data center studies. *Convergence, 31*(2), 429–446. https://doi.org/10.1177/13548565231224157

Felluga, D. (2015). *Critical theory: The key concepts* (1st ed.). Routledge. https://doi.org/10.4324/9781315718873

Franklin, S. (2012). Cloud control, or the network as medium. *Cultural Politics, 8*(3), 443–464. https://doi.org/10.1215/17432197-1722154

Gaboury, J. (2021). *Image object: an archaeology of computer graphics.* MIT Press. https://doi.org/10.7551/mitpress/11077.001.0001.

Gabrys, J. (2013). *Digital rubbish: A natural history of electronics.* University of Michigan Press. https://doi.org/10.2307/j.ctv65swcp

Grohmann, R., & Fernandes Araújo, W. (2021). Beyond mechanical Turk: The work of Brazilians on global AI platforms. In P. Verdegem (Ed.), *AI for everyone? Critical perspectives* (pp. 247–266). University of Westminster Press. https://www.jstor.org/stable/j.ctv26qjjhj

Harvey, D. (1990). Between space and time: Reflections on the geographical imagination. *Annals, Association of American Geographers, 80*(3), 418–434. https://www.jstor.org/stable/2563621

Hogan, M. (2015). Data flows and water woes: The Utah data center. *Big Data & Society, 2*(2). https://doi.org/10.1177/2053951715592429

Hopkins, T. K., & Wallerstein, I. (1986). Commodity chains in the world economy prior to 1800. *Review, 10*(1), 157–170. https://www.jstor.org/stable/40241052

Hopkins, T. K., & Wallerstein, I. (2016). Patterns of development of the modern world-system. *Review, 1*(4), 83–128. https://www.jstor.org/stable/40240765

Hu, T. H. (2015). *A prehistory of the cloud.* MIT Press. https://doi.org/10.7551/mitpress/9780262029513.001.0001

Jolly, J. (2024). TSMC to make state-of-the-art chips in US after multibillion subsidy pledge. *The Guardian..* https://www.theguardian.com/technology/2024/apr/08/tsmc-make-chips-in-arizona-us-multibillion-subsidy-pledge-taiwan-semiconductor

Khalatbari, C. (2024, March 13). *Faulty GPUs, gold, forks, cooking pots or iron-rods: Recycling computers in Accra, Ghana*. Medium. https://fiber.medium.com/faulty-gpus-gold-forks-cooking-pots-or-iron-rods-recycling-computers-in-accra-ghana-ec2930459778

Khan, S. M., & Mann, A. (2020). *AI chips: What they are and why they matter an AI chips reference*. Center for Security and Emerging Technologies. https://cset.georgetown.edu/publication/ai-chips-what-they-are-and-why-they-matter/

Law, J. (2012). The materials of STS. In D. Hicks & M. C. Beaudry (Eds.), *The Oxford handbook of material culture studies* (pp. 173–188). Oxford University Press. https://doi.org/10.1093/oxfordhb/9780199218714.001.0001

Lehdonvirta, V. (2022). *Cloud empires: How digital platforms are overtaking the state and how we can regain control*. MIT Press. https://doi.org/10.7551/mitpress/14219.001.0001.

Lehuedé, S. (2024). An elemental ethics for artificial intelligence: Water as resistance within AI's value chain. AI & SOCIETY, 40(3) (Mar 2025), 1761–1774. https://doi.org/10.1007/s00146-024-01922-2.

Li, P., Yang, J., Islam, M. A., & Ren, S. (2023). Making AI less "thirsty": Uncovering and addressing the secret water footprint of ai models. *arXiv*. https://arxiv.org/abs/2304.03271

Libertson, F., Velkova, J., & Palm, J. (2021). Data-center infrastructure and energy gentrification: Perspectives from Sweden. *Sustainability: Science, Practice and Policy, 17*(1), 152–161. https://doi.org/10.1080/15487733.2021.1901428

Luccioni, A. S., Viguier, S., & Ligozat, A. L. (2023). Estimating the carbon footprint of bloom, a 176b parameter language model. *Journal of Machine Learning Research, 24*(253), 1–15.

Luitse, D. (2024). Platform power in AI: The evolution of cloud infrastructures in the political economy of artificial intelligence. *Internet Policy Review, 13*(2), 1–44. https://doi.org/10.14763/2024.2.1768

Lynn, D. (2024, December 13). AI wants more data. More chips. More power. More water. More everything. *Bloomberg*. https://www.bloomberg.com/news/features/2024-12-13/ai-wants-more-data-more-chips-more-power-more-water-more-everything

Martin, E., & Peskoe, A. (2025, March 5). *Extracting profits from the public: How utility ratepayers are paying for big tech's power*. Environmental & Energy Law Program, Harvard Law School. https://eelp.law.harvard.edu/extracting-profits-from-the-public-how-utility-ratepayers-are-paying-for-big-techs-power/

Marx, K. (1967). *Capital, Volume 7*. International Publishers.

Miceli, M., & Posada, J. (2022). The data-production dispositif. *Proceedings of the ACM on Human-Computer Interaction, 6*(CSCW2), 1–37. https.www.doi.org/https://doi.org/10.1145/3555561

Miller, C. (2022). *Chip war: The fight for the world's most critical technology*. Simon and Schuster.

Mollen, A., Keilbach, J., Brodie, P., Jancovic, M., Helmond, A., Crosera, A., Velkova, J., Ochner, V., Maxigas, M., & Jansen, F. (2024). Governing digital infrastructures for a secure and sustainable future. *SSRN*. https://doi.org/10.2139/ssrn.4879449

Morand, C., Ligozat, A. L., & Névéol, A. (2024). How green can AI be? A study of trends in machine learning environmental impacts. *arXiv*. https://doi.org/10.48550/arXiv.2412.17376

Muldoon, J., Cant, C., Graham, M., & Ustek Spilda, F. (2023). The poverty of ethical AI: Impact sourcing and AI supply chains. *AI & SOCIETY, 40*, 529–543. https://doi.org/10.1007/s00146-023-01824-9

Munn, L. (2021). Chip, body, earth: Toxic temporalities of Intel processor production. In R. Barcan, F. Allon, & K. Eddison-Cogan (Eds.), *The temporalities of waste* (1st ed., pp. 47–58). Routledge.

Munn, L. (2022). Thinking through silicon: Cables and servers as epistemic infrastructures. *New Media & Society, 24*(6), 1399–1416. https://doi.org/10.1177/146144482097719

Myers, S., & Vipra, J. (2025). Complicating the US-China binary: Taiwanese semiconductor manufacturing. *Logic(s) Out of the Place, 22*, 39–48.

NVIDIA. (2022). *Conflict minerals report of NVIDIA corporation*. https://fintel.io/doc/sec-nvidia-corp-1045810-ex101-2023-april-26-19473-799.

Owen, J. R., Kemp, D., Lechner, A. M., Harris, J., Zhang, R., & Lèbre, E. (2023). Energy transition minerals and their intersection with land-connected peoples. *Nature Sustainability, 6*(2), 203–211. https://doi.org/10.1038/s41893-022-00994-6

Parikka, J. (2021a). *A Geology of Media*. University of Minnesota Press. https://www.jstor.org/stable/10.5749/j.ctt13x1mnj

Parikka, J. (2021b). *Antropocene and other essays: Media, materiality and ecology*. Mimesis.

Rella, L. (2024). Close to the metal: Towards a material political economy of the epistemology of computation. *Social Studies of Science, 54*(1), 3–29. https://doi.org/10.1177/03063127231185095

Roussilhe, G., Pirson, T., Xhonneux, M., & Bol, D. (2024). From silicon shield to carbon lock-in? The environmental footprint of electronic components manufacturing in Taiwan (2015–2020). *Journal of Industrial Ecology, 28*(5), 1212–1226. https://doi.org/10.1111/jiec.13487

Sibelco (2025). *The world's purest quartz*. https://www.sibelco.com/en/150-years/spruce-pine

Starosielski, N. (2015). *The undersea network*. Duke University Press.https://doi.org/10.1515/9780822376224.

Taffel, S. (2021). *Digital Media Ecologies: Entanglements of content, code and hardware*. Bloomsbury. https://www.bloomsbury.com/uk/digital-media-ecologies-9781501349263/

Taffel, S. (2023). Data and oil: Metaphor, materiality and metabolic rifts. *New Media & Society, 25*(5), 980–998. https://doi.org/10.1177/14614448211017887

Tay, C. (2023, October 13). Migrants crucial to microchip industry. *Taipei Times*. https://www.taipeitimes.com/News/editorials/archives/2023/10/13/2003807606

The Economist (2025, January 29). The real meaning of the DeepSeek drama. *The Economist*. https://www.economist.com/leaders/2025/01/29/the-real-meaning-of-the-deepseek-drama

Tsing, A. L. (2009). Supply chains and the human condition. *Rethinking Marxism, 21*(2), 148–176. https://doi.org/10.1080/08935690902743088

Tsing, A. L. (2015). *The mushroom at the end of the world: On the possibility of life in capitalist ruins*. Princeton University Press. https://doi.org/10.2307/j.ctvc77bcc.

TSMC. (2022). *Sustainability report*. Retrieved May 201, 2025, from https://esg.tsmc.com/download/file/2022_sustainabilityReport/english/e-all.pdf

Tubaro, P., Casilli, A. A., Cornet, M., Le Ludec, C., & Torres Cierpe, J. (2025). Where does AI come from? A global case study across Europe, Africa, and Latin America. *New Political Economy*, 1–14. https://doi.org/10.1080/13563467.2025.2462137

Valdivia, A. (2024). The supply chain capitalism of AI: A call to (re)think algorithmic harms and resistance through environmental lens. *Information, Communication & Society*, 1–17. https://doi.org/10.1080/1369118X.2024.2420021

Valdivia, A. (2025). Data Ecofeminism. In *the 2025 ACM Conference on Fairness, Accountability, and Transparency (FAccT '25), June 23–26, 2025, Athens, Greece*. ACM. https://doi.org/10.1145/3715275.373202.

Velasco González, P. (2016). Superabundant design: From waste to control in bitcoin mining. *A Peer-Reviewed Journal About Excessive Research, 5*(1), 61–69.

Velkova, J. (2019). Data centres as impermanent infrastructures. *Culture Machine, 18*. https://culturemachine.net/vol-18-the-nature-of-data-centers/data-centers-as-impermanent/

Wang, P., Zhang, L. Y., Tzachor, A., & Chen, W. Q. (2024). E-waste challenges of generative artificial intelligence. *Nature Computational Science, 4*, 818–823. https://doi.org/10.1038/s43588-024-00712-6

Whitehead, B., Andrews, D., & Shah, A. (2015). The life cycle assessment of a UK data Centre. *The International Journal of Life Cycle Assessment, 20*, 332–349. https://doi.org/10.1007/s11367-014-0838-7

Zhong, R., & Chang Chien, A. (2021, April 8). Drought in Taiwan pits chip makers against farmers. *The New York Times*. https://www.nytimes.com/2021/04/08/technology/taiwan-drought-tsmc-semiconductors.html

CHAPTER 3

Amazonia's Place in AI: Minerals and Mining as the Cradle of Infrastructuring

Débora de Castro Leal, Maximilian Krüger, and Sigrid Kannengießer

Introduction

When deconstructing the infrastructures of AI, many different components and stages become apparent. From a technological perspective, AI infrastructures include, among other things, raw minerals and technological devices, data centres, and network structures. In this chapter, we will focus on the relevance of minerals in infrastructures of generative AI,

D. de Castro Leal · M. Krüger
Universidade Federal do Pará, Belém, Brazil
e-mail: debora_leal@yahoo.com

M. Krüger
e-mail: Maximilian.Krueger@uni-siegen.de

M. Krüger
University of Siegen, Siegen, Germany

S. Kannengießer (✉)
University of Münster, Münster, Germany
e-mail: sigrid.kannengiesser@uni-muenster.de

A. Mollen et al. (eds.), *AI Infrastructures and Sustainability*, Palgrave Studies in European Communication Research and Education,
https://doi.org/10.1007/978-3-032-09748-4_3

which we see as *the cradle of AI infrastructures* because they make up the material foundation of Artificial Intelligence hardware. In doing so, we stress the relevance of raw minerals as resources integrated in infrastructures, and thereby also touch upon other related resources relevant for AI infrastructures, notably, human labour, as well as the relevance of different actors and their practices involved directly and indirectly in the processes of mineral extraction. We thereby connect to the tradition of science and technology studies that embraces a *relational socio-technological perspective on infrastructures*, arguing that AI systems are not only formed by materials and technologies, but also by actors and their practices.

Furthermore, we take a sustainability perspective in this chapter, which we define as more-than-human justice, with regard to mineral extraction for AI systems. Through this perspective, the severe impacts caused by mineral extraction in different locations–mainly, although not only, in the "Global South"—are rendered visible.

These extraction processes are embedded within a long history of colonial exploitation and dispossession. They mirror what Immanuel Wallerstein (2004) called the World System—where resources are extracted from locations which are constructed as peripheries to sustain the industrialised centres (see also Bojczuk's and Brodie's chapters in this volume). They also perpetuate colonial legacies that continue to undermine the sovereignty and self-determination of Indigenous and local communities in different regions of the "Global South". Extraction processes for raw minerals that will become integrated in AI infrastructure value chains are located at the periphery, in countries such as Brazil, Venezuela, the Democratic Republic of the Congo (DRC), and Kenya. By contrast, the development of AI applications and the creation of their financial and technological value takes place elsewhere, at the centre(s) of the world system: Europe, the USA, or China.

Focusing on the Amazon region in Brazil, which is one of the globally significant sites of mineral deposits relevant for AI systems, we foreground the severe social, ecological, and economic effects that result from their extraction. This analysis also strengthens the argument for a re-conceptualisation of what is commonly understood as sustainability, including green growth, towards a version of sustainability that focuses on more-than-human justice. As Indigenous leader Sônia Guajajara states: "For indigenous peoples, destroying indigenous forests and territories is the same as destroying ourselves. Because our territory is our body, our spirit. Indigenous peoples have known for a long time that everything in this life is interconnected. When nature is destroyed in one place, the consequences can be felt on the other side of the world" (Guajajara, 2020, para. 12). Yet mining presents a direct threat to the Amazon and its human and non-human inhabitants, as will be shown in this chapter.

The aims of this chapter are as follows: *firstly*, drawing on existing literature theorising AI infrastructures, we outline the relevance of minerals in a socio-technological conceptualisation of AI infrastructures. *Secondly*, taking a perspective of sustainability as human/more-than-human justice, we reveal the severe social, ecological, and economic effects caused by the extraction of minerals in the Brazilian Amazon region. *Thirdly*, following our broad concept of AI infrastructures, we show how these negative effects not only impact people who work directly in the mines or the ecosystems near extraction sites, but also people who are indirectly involved in the extraction processes and support the extraction, and thereby the infrastructuring of generative AI. *Finally*, we argue that there is no feasible way to extract minerals for AI infrastructures in a sustainable way, which would be ecologically, economically, and socially just, as these extraction processes are always exploitative and destructive. To *conclude*, we have adopted a normative perspective to call for more research analysing the relevance of minerals in AI infrastructures from a socio-technological perspective, as well as for political action to stop the exploitation and destruction caused by mineral extraction.

AI Infrastructures and Minerals—Taking a Socio-Technological Perspective

Although AI infrastructures have not come under intensive scrutiny as yet, they have been metaphorically described as parts of the "anatomy of AI systems" (Crawford & Joler, 2019) and theoretically conceptualised from a socio-technological perspective (Mollen & Kannengießer, 2025). The latter draws on a life cycle concept of Machine Learning that identifies raw material extraction, material manufacturing, equipment manufacturing, system development, and training, system deployment and disposal as central elements of the AI life cycle (Luccioni et al., 2022). Minerals appear at the very first stage of this life cycle, that is, the stage of raw material extraction.

Addressing the necessity of an integrative perspective that combines social and technological aspects, Mollen and Kannengießer (2025) theorise a social-technological concept of AI infrastructures that integrates their *material* aspects—for example, resources such as minerals and raw materials, hardware, and architecture, data sets of generative AI, and finally, hardware allowing usage; as well as relevant *actors*—for example, miners, workers, manufacturers, policy makers, AI developers, click workers, users (and many more); and their *practices*—for example, mineral extraction, manufacturing, developing and training or appropriation—to name only some of the relevant practices. This socio-technological perspective on AI infrastructures follows relational concepts of infrastructures that stress the relevance of *practices* (e.g. Star & Ruhleder, 1996) in bringing infrastructures into being, which the term *infrastructuring* is stressing.

What is lacking in this rather holistic conceptualisation of AI infrastructures is the acknowledgement of all the actors and their practices that *indirectly* constitute and maintain AI infrastructures. In this chapter, we focus on the moment of mineral extraction in AI infrastructures to show how indirect local relationships form part of infrastructuring. Our relational concept of infrastructures integrates and opens up to analyse the technologies, actors, and practices that are *indirectly* infrastructuring AI systems. Focusing on the stage of mineral extraction in AI infrastructures reveals the latter's complex nature, depending upon and incorporating a vast number of actors, practices, tools, and technologies. This approach compels us to acknowledge that AI infrastructures are not neutral or purely technological but are, rather, deeply entangled with histories of extraction, displacement, and resistance, and represent colonial continuities.

AI Infrastructures from a Perspective of Sustainability—Minerals in Focus

Looking at AI infrastructures from a sustainability perspective, we return to the Brundtland definition, understanding sustainability as ecological, economic, and social justice (UN WCED, 1987). In doing so, we emphasise that sustainability needs to be defined in terms of *justice* across these different dimensions. Further developing this perspective, we claim a need for justice not only for human beings worldwide, but we follow a more-than-human approach, emphasising that "more-than-human solidarity" (Tschakert, 2020) has to follow (and fulfil) the norm of "multispecies" justice (Tschakert, 2020) and "ecological justice" (Davis et al., 2019). Taking a comprehensive perspective, we define sustainability as human and more-than-human justice, applied to all humans and non-humans worldwide, today and in the future. This also reveals a contradiction inherent in the Sustainable Development Goals declared by the United Nations, which, due to its compatibility with a focus on economic growth (green or otherwise), has paradoxically rendered justice an impossible goal for our understanding of sustainability.

Looking at AI infrastructures from a sustainability perspective, research into the vast amounts of energy required for the training and use of AI applications (e.g. Dodge et al., 2022) as well as the volumes of water used to cool data centres (e.g. Li et al., 2023) has established the detrimental effects of AI infrastructure on the environment and the climate. Minerals are rarely investigated in their capacity as an existential resource for AI infrastructures. Nevertheless, there has been research on minerals in the context of digitalisation that has revealed the severe impacts caused by mineral extraction. These processes are not isolated incidents but are reflective of an ongoing colonial world order that continues to devalue Global South lives and resources to the benefit of technological advancement in the Global North.

The last 20 years have witnessed an unprecedented mineral rush and an increase in mining—both at a large scale as well as on a small, artisanal scale—mostly driven by minerals' role in digital technologies (Jacka, 2018). Mining, however, has severe effects on people and the environment. The most prominent example of the destructive effects of mining in the context of the digital economy is probably coltan in the DRC (e.g. Ojewale, 2022). While the situation in the DRC might be especially dire, it is not only there that mining has disastrous effects. These effects have been documented in many regions, from Indonesia and Papua New Guinea (PNG) to Bolivia and Peru, as well as Australia (Jacka, 2018). Even at the time of writing this chapter, a news story broke that an unknown number of illegal workers extracting gold in South Africa were trapped underground when police tried to force them out by blocking their supply of food, water and medications (Savage, 2025).

In the following section, we focus on the Brazilian Amazon region as a source of various minerals crucial for AI infrastructures, reflecting on the situation of mineral extraction in more detail. We will reveal and analyse the severe social, ecological, and economic effects that result from mineral extraction in this particular region.

Extracting Minerals in the Amazon Region in Brazil

The history of mining in Brazil is closely tied to colonialist violence and continues to reflect neo-colonial dynamics. Initially, Portuguese invaders were largely unsuccessful in locating and extracting minerals, but in the late seventeenth century, slave raiders came upon large-scale gold deposits while looking for Indigenous populations to enslave, and this unleashed an extensive gold rush period (da Costa & Rios, 2022). While for a long time mining was focused on the region of Minas Gerais (which even gained its name from the industry), the focus expanded in the twentieth century to include the Amazon rainforest region in the North of the country. Industrial mining arrived in the Amazon in the 1940s with a Manganese mine in the state of Amapá (Borges & Branford, 2020). Since then, the exploitation of minerals in the Amazon region has emerged as a crucial component of the country's strategy for development (Borges & Branford, 2020). This model prioritises economic gain over Indigenous peoples' sovereignty, environmental stewardship, and social justice, which perpetuates the colonial dispossession of land and resources in the Amazon. Alessandra Korap Munduruku, an Indigenous leader, highlights this ongoing struggle: "The government looks at our territory as a business plan. With the killing of rivers and landgrabbing, everything is covered in Indigenous blood" (Alfinito & Munduruku, 2023, Video, min 00:56).

The Amazon region is rich in a variety of minerals, ranging from Manganese, bauxite, cassiterite, tin to nickel, iron ore, gold, and rare earths such as niobium, tantalum, and coltan (Killeen, 2024a). It holds one of the biggest niobium reserves on the planet (Ribeiro, 2023). Oil has even been discovered in the region (Nogueira & Teixeira, 2024), and, in March 2025, a license for drilling was issued. All of these minerals are also crucial for the production of AI infrastructures. This richness has, of course, been recognised by policymakers in Brazil and elsewhere, and it is the source of much debate, as it creates tremendous problems for the rainforest and its human and non-human inhabitants, but also for the planet as a whole, due to the Amazon rainforest's importance for global climate. Although not everybody perceives it as such, it may present more of a curse than a blessing (Borges & Branford, 2020). In the following subsection, we will first describe the region's place in global AI infrastructures as the source of many of the minerals it requires, as well as the role of mining and related practices in the Amazon (4.1). Next, we detail the destructive effects of mining for the Amazon rainforest and its inhabitants (4.2). Finally, we describe mining's tendency to *sprawl*, and how its destructive effects are not limited to a mine's location but to practices, places, and people far removed from its geographical location (4.3).

The Place of the Amazon in AI Infrastructures

Assessing how mining in the Amazon and its disastrous consequences are entangled within AI infrastructures is not easy, as the use of illegal minerals is hard to track in technology supply chains (Farrar, 2008), even though it is known that illegal minerals do make it into highly regulated markets such as those of the EU (Wenzel, 2024). The origin is nevertheless evident and demonstrable in the case of Graphical Processing Units (GPUs) manufactured by Nvidia (see also Valdivia in this volume). GPUs are frequently used in Machine Learning due to their high calculation speed. Nvidia, one of their most important producers, is connected to mining in the Amazon in various ways (NVIDIA Corporation, 2022). In their Conflict Minerals Report, they list their suppliers, which reveals several Brazilian companies. These include companies that are based in the Amazon rainforest region or operate plants and mines there, such as Taboca Mines, Marsam Metais or Estanho de Rondonia S.A., amongst others. Marsam Metais has been involved in the processing of illegally mined gold from the Amazon (Goodman & Biller, 2022), while the mine operated by Taboca, in a town called Pitinga, is located on former Indigenous territory.

Resources for AI infrastructures in this context are not only the minerals themselves, but also the people involved in their extraction. To gain an understanding of global AI infrastructures and their mineral origins, it is necessary to broaden our perspective in order to include such extractive practices, as outlined above in this chapter.

There have been detailed investigations into mining in the Amazon, especially illegal gold mining. These studies reveal the complexity of mining practices as well as the diversity of activities and actors that develop around extraction. This complexity included, for example, a rich knowledge base about gold, developed not via formal studies of geology or engineering but by lived familiarity with the forest and mining, which matches or even rivals formal, academic knowledge about gold (Graulau, 2001). Studies also show how work in gold mining itself consists of different kinds of mining, depending on the type of deposit that is mined, and that such work is gendered. In fact, women make up between 20–37% of illegal miners in the Amazon, and have come to dominate specific kinds of mining, called *requear* and *bateiar*, which refer to different steps of extracting gold from gold-bearing gravel (Graulau, 2001). Technological advancements and innovations also play a crucial role in mining practices. Illegal miners have been characterised as technologically proficient and highly innovative (Massaro & de Theije, 2018). The uptake of new technologies by illegal miners, such as the upgrade from manual to mechanised mining, the use of an exploration drill or deploying cyanide instead of mercury to separate gold from soil, increases efficiency, which supposedly also has the potential to increase sustainability and reduce negative environmental effects (Massaro & de Theije, 2018). However, practices of innovation and increasing efficiency stay extractivist and exploitative practices and can equally lead to an increase in illegal mining activity, without actually reducing its environmentally and socially destructive nature.

Mining's Destructive Consequences

The effects of mining depend on various characteristics. To grasp these impacts, we need to distinguish between legal and illegal mining, with some threats being specific to illegal mining, which is often, but not always, small-scale and artisanal (Hentschel et al., 2002; Zvarivadza, 2018).

In general, mining in the Amazon—legal and illegal, large-and small-scale—creates a range of social, ecological and economic problems, most of which cannot be avoided (Villén-Peréz et al., 2020). The most obvious of these is deforestation. In the Brazilian Amazon, mining has caused 11,670 km^2 of deforestation between 2005 and 2015 alone (Sonter et al., 2017). Most of the mining in the Amazon takes place not in underground mines, but in open-pit or strip mines. Both of the latter, but particularly pit mines, are extraordinarily large, as they exploit minerals deposited close to the surface. To access this, a large area of forest needs to be removed. Furthermore, a "filtering" process is often applied, whereby the removed rock is treated to extract the desired minerals, meaning that pit mines cannot be refilled. A giant hole in the ground remains, and large quantities of often toxic waste material (called "tailings") are present. Furthermore, the deforested area is often much larger–by up to 12 times—than the size of the mine itself (Sonter et al., 2017). This is due to infrastructure, such as roads that are constructed to facilitate mining, as well as to the expansion of nearby settlements or cities to make space for the mining workforce (Siqueira-Gay et al., 2020). These road infrastructures become part of AI infrastructures and serve as an example here for various materials and technologies which compose AI infrastructures even though they are linked to AI indirectly. This material infrastructure leads to further deforestation projects, as roads become infrastructure for various other destructive activities such as timber exploitation or agriculture (Barber et al., 2014; Siqueira-Gay et al., 2020). Deforestation furthermore causes droughts, which exacerbate the negative impacts, causing rivers to dry up, trapping villagers in settlements that depend on rivers for transport and harming the river fauna (Staal et al., 2020; Villén-Perez et al., 2020). Here, again, the relational character of infrastructures becomes apparent, as materials and technologies, humans and non-humans become intertwined in these negative effects.

Another threat posed by mining is the accumulation of "tailings". Tailings, as noted earlier, are the waste material that occurs in industrial pit- or strip mines. The rock is removed and processed: pulverised, mixed with water and specific chemicals to filter out the desired minerals. The residue of the pulverised rock is usually highly toxic and in a liquid state (Killeen, 2024). It is often stored in repositories called tailing dams, which have been the source of some of the worst environmental catastrophes in Brazil—for example, the Fundão dam break (Pereira et al., 2024).

In addition to the problems that mining in general creates, illegal mining is especially problematic. The rate of deforestation due to illegal mining in the Brazilian Amazon increased by more than 90% from 2017 to 2020, reaching 101.7 km^2 annually in 2020 compared to 52.9 km^2 annually in 2017 (Siqueira-Gay & Sánchez, 2021). Illegal mining is also increasingly mechanised, employing large and expensive machinery (Borges & Harari, 2024). This also reveals that the border between legality and illegality in the mining sector is porous at best, as illegal mines have, for example, been found to be owned by police officers or financed by politicians' relatives; this explains how some illegal miners have been able to afford advanced machinery (Camargos et al., 2024; PODER360, 2023). Despite the smaller size of the individual mines, illegal mining occurs on such a scale that it is the source of the vast majority of gold exported from Brazil to the EU (Wenzel, 2024). Due to its unregulated and informal nature, illegal mining does not adhere to the laws and restrictions that govern other forms of mining. This means that illegal mining is a much greater threat to Indigenous communities, which face incursions into their territories by illegal mining operations, threatening protected Indigenous lands with deforestation (Mataveli et al., 2022). Whereas legal mines are required to restore mining sites, if possible (e.g. refilling pits and reforesting), illegal mines are usually simply abandoned, without any restoration (Siqueira-Gay & Sánchez, 2020). Illegal mining operations also frequently deploy highly toxic (and thus highly regulated) chemicals such as mercury or cyanide in their processes (Killeen, 2024a). These chemicals can be frequently used due to the lack of oversight and regulatory access to illegal mines (Veiga & Hinton, 2002). In particular, mercury is known to poison rivers and soils, and infiltrate all levels of the food chain as a result, becoming a threat not only to non-human but also to human life in the areas surrounding illegal mining sites (Pajolla & Rocha, 2024; Pressly, 2013; Torres, 2016). Here again, the relational character of infrastructures becomes apparent.

The consequences for the health of the affected communities are devastating, given that mercury poisoning has multiple deleterious impacts on the nervous, digestive, renal, and cardiovascular systems and is especially associated with neurological development (Vega et al., 2018). Elevated levels of mercury have been documented in women of childbearing age in several communities in the vicinity of active but also of long-abandoned mining sites (Hacon et al., 2008; Bello et al., 2023; Veiga & Hinton, 2002).

Illegal mining is also associated with an influx of people into the area surrounding the mine, with several harmful consequences for Indigenous communities. Water sources are potentially depleted by the increasing number of people who depend on them, while food sources such as plants and animals are also affected, as are cultural traditions (Villén-Peréz et al., 2020). This influx of new inhabitants is also often associated with an increase in crime and prostitution (Villén-Peréz et al., 2020), as well as clashes between miners and Indigenous inhabitants. In such clashes, illegal miners frequently kill members of Indigenous communities, as, for example, occurred in recent years in the territories of the Yanomami people (Philips, 2023). The harsh consequences for Indigenous communities of mining in the Amazon are unavoidable and hard to compensate, and pertain to both illegal and legal mining operations (Villén-Perez et al., 2020). Ultimately, the consequences of illegal mining can lead to the extinction of Indigenous peoples (Villén-Perez et al., 2020).

Mining Expands Far Beyond the Mine

Studies of mining practices in the Amazon and the people involved in them emphasise that mining—small scale or large scale—involves many different types of actors and institutions, and can hardly be understood as limited to the location of the mine (e.g. Zhouri, 2017). It is also this wide range of actors and their practices that needs to be acknowledged when taking a broad perspective on socio-technological concepts of AI infrastructures. Mining has a tendency to spread out, far beyond the borders of the actual mine. This has been demonstrated with regard to deforestation, as outlined above, but has much broader implications. Gudynas (2015) has called this tendency the "spillage effect of mining", a notion that has received widespread acceptance. Spillage effects can be observed in the geographic vicinity of the mine as well as far away. At a close proximity, mining operations lead to the development of support economies. These include businesses that specialise in the provision of tools and machinery (Hinton et al., 2003), or inputs such as charcoal, in providing loans and investments into mining ventures, as well as businesses that buy and sell gold. It also includes the provision of food or medical care, restaurants and bars, sex work, clinics and the production of traditional/natural medicine, for example, from plant roots (Graulau, 2001). Mining settlements, which in the past were usually temporary, have in recent decades gained permanence and transformed into villages or small cities (Kolen et al., 2018). All of these mining-adjacent support economies are highly gendered, as Graulau illustrates in detail, with specific roles and pressures for each gender. Tentacle-like, the effects of mining also extend much further. Mining leads to the development of large-scale infrastructure, such as roads, railroads, ports, and processing facilities such as steel plants (Sant'Ana & Alves, 2017), often in places far removed from the mine. For example, the iron ore mine Canaa das Carajas (one of the largest iron mines in the world) in the south of the Brazilian state of Pará, led to the construction of a port in the area of São Luis in the north of the state of Maranhão, 1000 km away. The effects of mining also impact the communities neighbouring the mine as well as those adjacent to its widespread infrastructure. Roads through rural or remote territories such as the Amazon rainforest can have drastic consequences for communities in their vicinity. The effects also include Indigenous communities, their evolving participation in mining, but also their attempts to prevent it, and resistance movements that form against mining and mining infrastructure, which can take a regional or national form (e.g. Sant'Ana & Alves, 2017). Illegal gold miners from Brazil also relocate to other Amazonian countries such as Suriname (de Theije & Heemskerk, 2009) and French Guyana (Le Torneau, 2021), to continue their mining operations there.

In addition, mining is deeply entangled with global businesses that buy, sell, process and invest, but also with regional as well as national policy making. This includes economic development programmes, some of which are specifically aimed at developing the mining sector, but they also include environmental legislation, as well as the protection of Indigenous peoples and their territories. For example, in order to establish the tin ore mine in Pitinga, of which Nvidia is a client, as mentioned above, the protective status of the Indigenous territory in which the tin deposits were discovered was downgraded, and the borders of the territory were altered to exclude the mine (Baines, 2008).

When AI infrastructures are conceptualised to include their constituent minerals, the people involved in mining them, and those people's practices, it becomes clear that drawing the border between what is within and what is external to AI infrastructure is difficult. The complexity of mining and its spillage effects entail that it is not a localised, but rather a spreading phenomenon, as Gudynas (2015) pointed out. Its consequences are profound, violent, and destructive to ecosystems and communities. All of these can be viewed as part of AI infrastructures, being consequent upon AI technology's need for diverse minerals from the Amazon and elsewhere.

The Impossibility of Shaping Mineral Extraction for AI Infrastructures to Be (More) Sustainable

Our chapter has traced the socio-technological relations that undergird AI systems, foregrounding its visibly negative impacts, and highlighting the deleterious effects of the fancy generative AI technologies used by so many people worldwide. These AI systems are assumed to be unattached to the people that extract the required minerals as well as to the non-human parties that are affected; in the end, however, all of these form part of AI infrastructures only situated in different moments of infrastructuring AI. The socio-technological concept of AI infrastructures we use allows us to understand these connections between all humans and non-humans in the AI life cycle. However, more research is needed to better elucidate these relationships. Moreover, we need more empirical research that investigates the nature of the extraction practices and the severe impacts presented above. Focusing on the Amazon, for example, more studies are needed that investigate, through ethnographic studies, exactly how communities are affected by mining and how they respond. While existing studies document the various devastating effects, particularly on Indigenous communities, using quantitative methods, there is very little research that probes in detail the perspectives and perceptions of the people affected and directly or indirectly involved in the mining process (Zhouri, 2017).

Applying a sustainability perspective to AI infrastructures, one last question remains: how can these processes be shaped in a more sustainable way?

While our current research provides no conclusive answer to this, it may also be the case that a definitive answer might be very difficult to find, given that we live in an "age of minerals", and mining is deeply intertwined with the global economy (Jacka, 2018; Nikiforuk, 2023). Overall, it should be stressed that the response to the challenges outlined above cannot be in terms of making mining more sustainable. We agree with the authors who point out that mining, in the Amazon and elsewhere, is always associated with environmental degradation and deforestation (see e.g. Nikiforuk, 2023; Villen-Perez, 2020). Thus, the extraction of minerals needed for AI infrastructures can never be sustainable—neither in the sense of the Brundtland definition—nor in the sense of human and more-than-human justice, because mining will always be a method of exploitation. AI technology that relies on mineral extraction cannot be sustainable, and therefore cannot be used for sustainable ends. Consequently, we must critically interrogate the foundations of AI development, as well as our understanding of sustainability, questioning in whose interests these technologies are developed and at what cost (see also the chapters by Brodie and Sridharan in this volume). A decolonial approach demands not only different practices of infrastructuring and different technological solutions but also a deconstruction of global power dynamics, prioritising Indigenous knowledge systems, land rights, and environmental stewardship over extractive economic models. Instead of attempting to make harmful practices appear more eco-friendly, we should push for systemic change that helps to repair past harms and respect the rights and independence of marginalised communities.

Recycling and the Circular Economy are two straightforward approaches that would reduce the need for new minerals. This also means investigating not only the beginning of AI infrastructures but also their ends, including when and where AI hardware is disposed of, and related practices. Wherever possible, minerals should be recycled and reused, as several companies already claim to do. Proponents of a Circular Economy assert that the goal of such an economy is only attainable by effecting a major reduction in the diversity of products and production processes, so as to facilitate their recycling. This also applies to the production of AI hardware, with a parallel requirement to reduce the number of metals and minerals processed and used in AI hardware.

While these might be fruitful and essential approaches, we do not want to give the impression that we believe them to be sufficient. In their hunger for innovation, economic growth, and technological dominance, companies and governments seem all too willing to abandon previous commitments to, for example, energy and emissions reductions as means through which to slow down climate change. Hence, a deeper and more radical change might be necessary to avoid the social and ecological destruction brought about by mining, that does not simply redesign and re-engineer AI through less data-and energy-hungry systems such as Deepseek (which also hold other problems regard social justice such as censorship within data or privacy concerns), or through better chips, but that questions the need for AI and similar technology innovations and their role in societies and economies. Some of this might be found in approaches such as post-growth or degrowth research, which argues for countries at the centre of the World System to abandon economic growth as a goal, including the abandonment of socially unnecessary and ecologically destructive forms of production (e.g. Hickel, 2023).

While this might seem radical in the current climate of an international AI race, Indigenous thinkers have long offered an even more radical critique, not only in connection with mining, but critiquing the idea of sustainable development as a whole. Ailton Krenak, an Indigenous Brazilian activist and intellectual, lost his ancestral land to 50 million cubic meters of mining tailings (Phillips, 2016). In an interview, he made the following observation about sustainability:

> How can you produce something sustainable if the extractive system is sovereign and changes the cycles of life on Earth? Sustainability is a certificate sold to fools that will last for as long as there are people buying it...

> It would be better if we called it the sustainability of the end. Everyone knows we're already over the edge.... Indigenous peoples have suffered from the invasion of their world by chaotic, predatory practices. The man outside the forest, who eats hamburgers in Europe, needs it [the Indigenous world] dead. (Guerra, 2021, question 4)

This quote represents one central challenge for AI research and politics that asks questions of sustainability: We need to think and shape AI extremely differently than asking how the production and appropriation processes can be shaped more sustainable. Instead, we need to question the economic system whose extractivist and exploitative practices materialize in AI infrastructures.

Competing Interests The authors have no conflicts of interest to declare that are relevant to the contents of this chapter.

References

Alfinito, A. C., & Munduruku, A. K. (2023). *Goldman Environmental Prize winner from Brazil*. https://www.goldmanprize.org/recipient/alessandra-korap-munduruku/

Baines, S. (2008). The reconstruction of Waimiri-Atroari territory. In A. de Oliveira (Ed.), *Decolonising indigenous rights*, (pp. 45–64). Routledge. https://doi-org.libproxy.ncl.ac.uk/10.4324/9780203449202

Barber, C. P., Cochrane, M. A., Souza, C. F., & Laurance, W. F. (2014). Roads, deforestation, and the mitigating effect of protected areas in the Amazon. *Biological Conservation, 177*, 203–209. https://doi.org/10.1016/j.biocon.2014.07.004

Bello, T. C. S., Buralli, R. J., Cunha, M. P. L., Dórea, J. G., Diaz-Quijano, F. A., Guimarães, J. R. D., & Marques, R. C. (2023). Mercury exposure in women of reproductive age in Rondônia state, Amazon region, Brazil. *International Journal of Environmental Research and Public Health, 20*(6), 5225. https://doi.org/10.3390/ijerph20065225

Borges, B., & Harari, I. (2024, June 18). *Hyundai e Caterpillar lideram ranking de máquinas usadas em garimpos ilegais [Hyundai and Caterpillar lead the ranking of backhoes used in illegal mining]*. Repórter Brasil. https://reporterbrasil.org.br/2024/06/hyundai-caterpillar-lideram-ranking-retroescavadeiras-garimpo-ilegal/

Borges, T., & Branford, S. (2020, December 21). *Historical analysis: The Amazon's mineral wealth—curse or blessing?* Mongabay Environmental News. https://news.mongabay.com/2020/12/historical-analysis-the-amazons-mineral-wealth-curse-or-blessing/

Camargos, D., Harari, I., & Junqueira, D. (2024, September 19). *PF prende milícia que controlava garimpo em terra indígena [Investigation points to police officers as owners of illegal gold mines on indigenous lands].* Repórter Brasil. https://reporterbrasil.org.br/2024/09/milicia-garimpeira-presa-extracao-ouro-terra-indigena-kayapo/

Constantinides, P., Henfridsson, O., & Parker, G. G. (2018). Introduction—Platforms and infrastructures in the digital age. *Information Systems Research, 29*(2), 381–400. https://doi.org/10.1287/isre.2018.0794

Crawford, K., & Joler, V. (2019). Anatomy of an AI system. *Virtual Creativity, 9*(1), 117–120. https://doi.org/10.1386/vcr_00008_7

da Costa, M. A., & Rios, F. J. (2022). The gold mining industry in Brazil: A historical overview. *Ore Geology Reviews, 148*, 105005. https://doi.org/10.1016/j.oregeorev.2022.105005

Davis, J., Moulton, A. A., van Sant, L., & Williams, B. (2020). Anthropocene, capitalocene, plantationocene? A manifesto for ecological justice in an age of global crises. *Geography Compass, 13*(5), e12438. https://doi.org/10.1111/gec3.12438

de Theije, M., & Heemskerk, M. (2009). Moving frontiers in the Amazon: Brazilian small-scale gold miners in Suriname. *European Review of Latin American and Caribbean Studies/Revista Europea de Estudios Latinoamericanos y del Caribe, 87*, 5–25. https://doi.org/10.18352/erlacs.9600

Dodge, J., Prewitt, T., Tachet Des Combes, R., Odmark, E., Schwartz, R., Strubell, E., Luccioni, A. S., Smith, N.A., DeCario, N., & Buchanan, W. (2022). Measuring the carbon intensity of AI in cloud instances. *ACM Conference on Fairness, Accountability, and Transparency (ACM FAccT) 2022, pages 1877–1894.* https://doi.org/10.1145/3531146.3533234

Farrar, J. (2008, March 7). The cassiterite crisis - how tech boom fuels human rights risk in Africa. *ZDNET*. https://www.zdnet.com/article/the-cassiterite-crisis-how-tech-boom-fuels-human-rights-risk-in-africa/

Feyisayo, A. (2024, March 2). How much gold is in a cell phone? *American Bullion, Inc.* https://www.americanbullion.com/how-much-gold-is-in-a-cell-phone/

Goodman, J. & Biller, D. (2022, October 6). *Brazil gold refiner Marsam linked to exploitation, stripped of seal.* The Christian Science Monitor. https://www.csmonitor.com/World/Americas/2022/1006/Brazil-gold-refiner-Marsam-linked-to-exploitation-stripped-of-seal

Graulau, J. (2001). Peasant mining production as a development strategy: The case of women in gold mining in the Brazilian Amazon. *Revista Europea de*

Estudios Latinoamericanos y del Caribe/European Review of Latin American and Caribbean Studies, 71, 71–106. https://www.jstor.org/stable/25675940

Guajajara, S. (2020, October 16). *Amazonian indigenous leader Sônia Guajajara: 'In the flames, they see money.'* Inequality.org. https://inequality.org/article/indigenous-amazon-corporate-greed/

Gudynas, E. (2015). Extractivismos en américa del sur y sus efectos derrame [Extractavism in South America and its spillover effects]. In D. Restrepo, L. Soler-Gómez Lutzelschwab, & E. Toche y Molvina Zeballos (Eds.) *Gobernanza local, pueblos indígenas e industrias extractivas transformaciones y continuidades en América Latina [Local governance, indigenous peoples, and extractive industry transformations and continuities in Latin America]. La Revista*, (Sociedad Suiza des Americanistas), *76*, 13–24. https://ssa-sag.org/bssa/pdf/LARevista_2015_No76.pdf#page=9

Guerra, G. (2021, September 23). *"The climate crisis has been foretold by native peoples from the outset," says Ailton Krenak*. Conectas. https://www.conectas.org/en/noticias/the-climate-crisis-has-been-foretold-by-native-peoples-from-the-outset-says-ailton-krenak/

Hacon, S., Barrocas, P. R. G., de Vasconcellos, A. C. S., Barcellos, C., Wasserman, J. C., Campos, R. C., Ribeiro, C., & Azevedo Carloni, F. B. (2008). An overview of mercury contamination research in the Amazon basin with an emphasis on Brazil. *Cadernos de Saúde Pública, 24*(7), 1479–1492. https://doi.org/10.1590/S0102-311X2008000700003

Hentschel, T., Hruschka, F., & Priester, M. (2002). Global report on artisanal & small-scale mining. *International Institute for Environment and Development (IIED)*. https://www.iied.org/sites/default/files/pdfs/migrate/G00723.pdf

Hickel, J. (2023, July 1). On technology and degrowth. *Monthly Review*. https://monthlyreview.org/2023/07/01/on-technology-and-degrowth/

Hinton, J. J., Veiga, M. M., & Beinhoff, C. (2003). Women and artisanal mining: Gender roles and the road ahead. In G. Hilson (Ed.) *The Socio-Economic Impacts of Artisanal and Small-Scale Mining in Developing Countries*. Swets Publishers. https://prod-edxapp.edx-cdn.org/assets/courseware/v1/6913dd84795c217cc1c8c05358d8e782/asset-v1:SDGAcademyX+NR001+2T2019+type@asset+block/Women_and_artisanal_mining_-_gender_roles_and_the_road_ahead.pdf

Instituto Socioambiental (ISA). (2002/2018). *Waimiri Atroari - indigenous peoples in Brazil*. https://pib.socioambiental.org/en/Povo:Waimiri_Atroari

Jacka, J. K. (2018). The anthropology of mining: The social and environmental impacts of resource extraction in the mineral age. *Annual Review of Anthropology, 47*, 61–77. https://doi.org/10.1146/annurev-anthro-102317-050156

Killeen, T. J. (2024a, July 12). *Industrial minerals in the Pan Amazon*. Mongabay Environmental News. https://news.mongabay.com/2024/07/more-industrial-minerals-on-brazils-borders-with-ecuador-venezuela-and-colombia/

Killeen, T. J. (2024b, March 26). *The environmental and social liabilities of the extractive sector*. Mongabay Environmental News. https://news.mongabay.com/2024/03/the-environmental-and-social-liabilities-of-the-extractive-sector/

Killeen, T. J. (2024c, September 13). *Wildcat miners: Will cyanide displace mercury?* Mongabay Environmental News. https://news.mongabay.com/2024/09/wildcat-miners-will-cyanide-displace-mercury/

Kolen, J., de Smet, E., & de Theije, M. (2018). We are all garimpeiros: Settlement and movement in communities of the Tapajós small-scale gold mining reserve. *The Journal of Latin American and Caribbean Anthropology, 23*(1), 169–188. https://doi.org/10.1111/jlca.12271

Le Tourneau, F. M. (2021). Brazilian illegal gold miners resilience in French Guiana: The garimpo as an economic and social system. *European Review of Latin American and Caribbean Studies, 112*, 1–27. https://doi.org/10.32992/erlacs.10767

Li, P., Yang, J., Islam, M. A., & Ren, S. (2023). *Making AI less thirsty: Uncovering and addressing the secret water footprint of AI models*. arXiv, 1–10. https://doi.org/10.48550/ARXIV.2304.03271

Luccioni, A. S., Viguier, S., & Ligozat, A. L. (2023). Estimating the carbon footprint of bloom, a 176b parameter language model. *Journal of Machine Learning Research, 24*(253), 1–15. arXiv preprint arXiv:2211.02001.

Massaro, L., & de Theije, M. (2018). Understanding small-scale gold mining practices: An anthropological study on technological innovation in the Vale do Rio Peixoto (Mato Grosso, Brazil). *Journal of Cleaner Production, 204*, 618–635. https://doi.org/10.1016/j.jclepro.2018.08.153

Mataveli, G., Chaves, M., Guerrero, J., Escobar-Silva, E. V., Conceição, K., & de Oliveira, G. (2022). Mining is a growing threat within indigenous lands of the Brazilian Amazon. *Remote Sensing, 14*(16), 4092. https://doi.org/10.3390/rs14164092

Mollen, A., & Kannengießer, S. (2025). Shaping AI (more) sustainably. Socio-technological perspectives on AI infrastructure. In T. Kox, A. Ullrich, & H. Zech, (Eds.), Uncertain journeys into digital futures. Inter-and transdisciplinary research for mitigating wicked societal and environmental problems (1st ed., pp. 207–218). Nomos. https://doi.org/10.5771/9783748947585-207

Moreau, F. (2024, September 16). *Gold's role in microprocessor manufacturing: Challenges and innovations.* Kitco News. https://www.kitco.com/opinion/2024-09-16/golds-role-microprocessor-manufacturing-challenges-and-innovations

Nikiforuk, A. (2023, April 7). *The rising chorus of renewable energy skeptics.* The Tyee. https://thetyee.ca/Analysis/2023/04/07/Rising-Chorus-Renewable-Energy-Skeptics/

Nogueira, M., & Teixeira, F. (2024, April 18). *Brazil's plans to drill for oil in the Amazon hit stiff indigenous resistance.* Reuters. https://www.reuters.com/world/americas/brazils-plans-drill-oil-amazon-hit-stiff-indigenous-resistance-2024-04-18/

NVIDIA Corporation. (2022). *NVIDIA corporation - conflict minerals report as required by items 1.01 and 1.02 of this form-EX-1.01-April 26, 2023.* https://fintel.io/doc/sec-nvidia-corp-1045810-ex101-2023-april-26-19473-799

Ojewale, O. (2022). Mining and illicit trading of coltan in the Democratic Republic of Congo. *Enact–Enhancing Africa's Response to Transnational Organised Crime*, 29. https://enact-africa.s3.amazonaws.com/site/uploads/2022-05-03-research-paper-29.pdf

Pajolla, M., & Rocha, A.P. (2024, June 25). How mercury gets into mining and why it needs to be banned from Brazil. *Brasil de Fato.* https://www.brasildefato.com.br/2024/06/25/how-mercury-gets-into-mining-and-why-it-needs-to-be-banned-from-brazil

Pereira, C. C., Fernandes, S., Fernandes, G. W., & Goulart, F. F. (2024). Eight years after the Fundão tailings dam collapse: Chaos on the muddy banks. *Nature Conservation, 56*, 77–82. https://doi.org/10.3897/natureconservation.56.133441

Phillips, D. (2016, October 15). Samarco dam collapse: One year on from Brazil's worst environmental disaster. *The Guardian.* https://www.theguardian.com/sustainable-business/2016/oct/15/samarco-dam-collapse-brazil-worst-environmental-disaster-bhp-billiton-vale-mining

Phillips, T. (2023, May 1). Brazil's battle to reclaim Yanomami lands from illegal miners turns deadly. *The Guardian.* https://www.theguardian.com/world/2023/may/01/yanomami-territory-illegal-miners-death-toll

PODER360. (2023). *PF identificou financiadores do garimpo ilegal em terras yanomami, Poder360 [PF identified financiers of illegal mining on Yanomami lands].* https://www.poder360.com.br/poder-justica/justica/pf-identificou-financiadores-do-garimpo-ilegal-em-terras-yanomami/

Pressly, L. (2013, September 18). *How mercury poisons gold miners and enters the food chain.* BBC News. https://www.bbc.com/news/magazine-24127661

Ribeiro, L. (2023). Amazônia: uma das maiores reservas de nióbio do planeta [Amazonia: One of the biggest reserves of niobium on the planet].

Portal Amazônia. https://portalamazonia.com/amazonia-ameaca-ou-oportunidade/amazonia-uma-das-maiores-reservas-de-niobio-do-planeta/

Sant'Ana H.A de & Alves, E de J.P. (2017). Mining-railroad-port: At the end of the line, a city in question. *Vibrant: Virtual Brazilian Anthropology*, *14*, Article e142205. https://doi.org/10.1590/1809-43412017v14n2p205

Savage, R. (2025, January 13). South Africa launches operation at illegal gold mine amid fears many dead. *The Guardian*. https://www.theguardian.com/world/2025/jan/13/south-africa-launches-operation-at-gold-mine-amid-fears-many-dead

Siqueira-Gay, J. (2021). *From intensive land use to fragmented landscapes: Perspectives on cumulative impacts of mining on forests in the Brazilian Amazon*. [Doctoral dissertation, Escola Politécnica, Universidade de São Paulo]. Biblioteca Digital de Teses e Dissertações da USP. https://doi.org/10.11606/T.3.2021.tde-07102021-150557

Siqueira-Gay, J., & Sánchez, L. E. (2020). Keep the Amazon niobium in the ground. *Environmental Science & Policy, 111*, 1–6. https://doi.org/10.1016/j.envsci.2020.05.012

Siqueira-Gay, J., & Sánchez, L. E. (2021). The outbreak of illegal gold mining in the Brazilian Amazon boosts deforestation. *Regional Environmental Change, 21*, 28. https://doi.org/10.1007/s10113-021-01761-7

Siqueira-Gay, J., Sonter, L. J., & Sánchez, L. E. (2020). Exploring potential impacts of mining on forest loss and fragmentation within a biodiverse region of Brazil's northeastern Amazon. *Resources Policy, 67*, 101662. https://doi.org/10.1016/j.resourpol.2020.101662

Smith, J. H., & Mantz, J. W. (2006). Do cellular phones dream of civil war? The mystification of production and the consequences of technology fetishism in The Congo. In M. Kirsch (Ed.), *Inclusion and exclusion in the global arena* (pp. 71–93). Routledge. https://www.taylorfrancis.com/chapters/edit/10.4324/9781315786759 5/cellular-phones-dream-civil-war-james-smith-jeffrey-mantz

Sonter, L. J., Herrera, D., Barrett, D.J., Galford, G.L., Moran, C.J., & Soares-Filho, B.S. (2017). Mining drives extensive deforestation in the Brazilian Amazon. *Nature Communications*, *8*(1), Article 1013. https://doi.org/10.1038/s41467-017-00557-w

Staal, A., Flores, B. M., Aguiar, D., Bosmans, A. P., Fetzer, J. H. C., I, & Tuinenburg, O. A. (2020). Feedback between drought and deforestation in the Amazon. *Environmental Research Letters, 15*(4), 044024. https://doi.org/10.1088/1748-9326/ab738e

Star, S. L. (2002). Infrastructure and ethnographic practice: Working on the fringes. *Scandinavian Journal of Information Systems, 14*(2), 107–122. https://dl.acm.org/doi/10.5555/782686.782695

Star, S., & Karen, R. (1996). Steps toward an ecology of infrastructure: Design and access for large information spaces. *Information Systems Research, 7*. 111–134. https://doi.org/10.1287/isre.7.1.111

Tanaka, A., Maples-Reynolds, N., & Fowler, B. A. (2022). Gallium and gallium semiconductor compounds. In G. F. Nordberg & M. Costa (Eds.), *Handbook on the toxicology of metals* (5th ed., pp. 275–288). Academic. https://doi.org/10.1016/B978-0-12-822946-0.00011-8

Torres, C. (2016, July 7). *Illegal gold mining causing mercury contamination in indigenous groups.* Mongabay Environmental News. https://news.mongabay.com/2016/07/illegal-gold-mining-causing-mercury-contamination-in-indigenous-groups/

Tschakert, P. (2020). More-than-human solidarity and multispecies justice in the climate crisis. *Environmental Politics, 31*(2), 277–296. https://doi.org/10.1080/09644016.2020.1853448

UN WCED. (1987). *Report of the World Commission on Environment and Development: Our common future.* https://sustainabledevelopment.un.org/content/documents/5987our-common-future.pdf

Vega, C. M., Orellana, J. D. Y., Oliveira, M. W., Hacon, S. S., & Basta, P. C. (2018). Human mercury exposure in Yanomami indigenous villages from the Brazilian Amazon. *International Journal of Environmental Research and Public Health, 15*(6), Article 1051. https://doi.org/10.3390/ijerph15061051

Veiga, M. M., & Hinton, J. J. (2002). Abandoned artisanal gold mines in the Brazilian Amazon: A legacy of mercury pollution. *Natural Resources Forum, 26*(1), 15–26. https://doi.org/10.1111/1477-8947.00003

Villén-Pérez, S., Moutinho, P., Nóbrega, C. C., & De Marco Jr, P. (2020). Brazilian Amazon gold: Indigenous land rights under risk. *Elementa: Science of the Anthropocene, 8*, 31. https://doi.org/10.1525/elementa.427

Wallerstein, I. M. (2004). *World-systems analysis: An introduction.* Duke University Press. https://doi.org/10.1215/9780822399018

Wenzel, F. (2024, September 2). *Nearly all Brazilian gold imported by EU is likely illegal, report says.* Mongabay Environmental News. https://news.mongabay.com/2024/09/nearly-all-brazilian-gold-imported-by-eu-is-likely-illegal-report-says/

Wheeler, A. (2018, September 29). *What raw materials are used to make hardware in computing devices?* Engineering.com. https://www.engineering.com/what-raw-materials-are-used-to-make-hardware-in-computing-devices/

Zhouri, A. (2017). Introduction–anthropology and knowledge production in a minefield. *Vibrant: Virtual Brazilian Anthropology, 14*, e142072. https://doi.org/10.1590/1809-43412017v14n2p072

Zvarivadza, T. (2018). Artisanal and small-scale mining as a challenge and possible contributor to sustainable development. *Resources Policy, 56*, 49–58. https://doi.org/10.1016/j.resourpol.2018.01.009

CHAPTER 4

Growing the Cloud at the "Corner of the Atlantic": Fortaleza as a Digital Infrastructure Hub Amidst AI-Renewable Energy Paradigms in Brazil

Iago Bojczuk

Introduction

As AI systems continue to remodel industries and daily life worldwide, the energy required to power, cool, and sustain its digital infrastructures has become a point of speculation. Estimates indicate that the data center infrastructure supporting AI is under pressure to expand, which in turn is sparking conversations about the need for more resilient and powerful data centers. In parallel, there is also a mounting debate regarding the compromises among stakeholders about the future of infrastructures' impact on pollution and the electric grid, as well as the push for "greening" AI's entire supply chain (Spencer & Singh, 2024). In Brazil, where vast renewable energy resources are seen as a competitive advantage for

I. Bojczuk (✉)
University of Cambridge, Cambridge, UK
e-mail: ib410@cam.ac.uk

A. Mollen et al. (eds.), *AI Infrastructures and Sustainability*, Palgrave Studies in European Communication Research and Education,
https://doi.org/10.1007/978-3-032-09748-4_4

energy-intensive sectors due to extensive hydropower generation, recent developments indicate rising awareness of national challenges associated with scaling energy production in juxtaposition to AI's growth. While a systematic analysis of AI's effects on the energy grid within the Brazilian context is yet to come to fruition, concerns are increasing as new data centers are constructed, strategic locations become testing grounds for expansionist industries, and novel partnerships within and beyond the digital infrastructure sector are forged. This chapter examines some of these emerging debates with a particular focus on how geography shapes discourse and facilitates the convergence of energy and digital systems, as exemplified by the Brazilian city of Fortaleza, increasingly known globally among leaders in the digital infrastructure sector.

Located in the northeastern state of Ceará, once one of Brazil's poorest states, Fortaleza has over the past decade surfaced not only as a key node in global signal traffic but also as a hub where interconnectivity potential, state-envisioned sustainability strategies, and digital aspirations driven by the private sector converge. With its strategic location connecting networks and markets across the Atlantic Ocean and serving as a significant landing point for fiber-optic submarine cable systems, the city continues to gain attention for its rapid increase in data center constructions and capital investments. At the same time, local government initiatives and financial incentives continue to promote a vision of Fortaleza as a "hub-of-hubs," where abundant renewable resources—from wind and solar to emerging green hydrogen projects—are expected to support not only Brazil's competitiveness in the digital infrastructure sector but also the growing demands of data traffic due to AI. However, beneath this future-oriented portrayal of infrastructural sovereignty and promises for a greener technological future lie significant uncertainties over how these will unfold in years to come insofar as the investments for data centers scale up and new promises for renewable energy are confluent in such rhetoric. How are Fortaleza's geographic advantages, public policies and incentives, as well as renewable energy resources converging to shape its rise as a digital infrastructure hub, and what sustainability and socio-environmental challenges does this transformation bring to the AI landscape in Brazil?

To empirically explore these points, this chapter employs a critical discourse analysis with a dialectical–relational approach (Fairclough, 2010) to examine how municipal, state, and federal discourses co-create narratives of digital and energy convergence in Fortaleza. This involved chronologically analyzing a range of key sources produced between 2015 and 2025, including news media from leading organizations, slide decks, brochures, and reports by regulatory agencies, as well as videos, maps, and policy documents issued by both the municipality of Fortaleza and the state of Ceará. Specifically, these documents and media artifacts were drawn from major national media outlets (e.g., *Folha de S. Paulo*, *O Globo*), regional newspapers (*O Povo*, *Diário do Nordeste*), and sector-specific publications, while official reports and presentations were obtained from government portals at both municipal, state, and federal levels.[1] In doing so, I approached this body of discourse through an interpretivist lens, enabling a sense-making process that brings into focus the interplay between data center and renewable energy developments. Diverse viewpoints—particularly those informed by government narratives—are brought into relief and set in contrast with wider industrial discussions around AI's role in shaping Fortaleza's infrastructural future. Through this process, I foreground diverse viewpoints—particularly those shaped by government narratives—and contrast them with broader industrial discussions about AI and its projected role in positioning Fortaleza as a growing digital infrastructure hub.

The key intervention developed through this chapter considers "growing the cloud" as fluid and dynamic processes shaped by power relations and territorial tensions that become increasingly pronounced as AI intersects with the convergence of digital and energy infrastructures. First, I analyze how Fortaleza's geographic assets, particularly submarine fiberoptic cable systems, are mobilized to attract data center investments and shape regional development. Second, focusing on Fortaleza as an energy and data center nexus, I critically assess the promises and pitfalls of AI-driven expansion against governmental strategies to position Brazil globally. I argue that Fortaleza and northeast Brazil exemplify government involvement in attracting and shaping the "cloud" via infrastructure, challenging views of digital immateriality as purely private action and contributing nuance to what Luke Munn (2023, p. 3)

[1] Materials were identified through systematic keyword searches in online Portuguese language and selected via purposive sampling to ensure the representation of diverse stakeholder perspectives. All documents were manually coded and thematically categorized to trace evolving narratives of digital infrastructure and energy convergence over the 2015–2025 period. When necessary, I also made use of the Access to Information Law to clarify whether data centers were included in particular tax schemes or other initiatives.

terms "new vectors for territorialization"—forces through which digital infrastructures reshape territories.

By examining these interconnected dimensions, this analysis contributes to interdisciplinary scholarship on digital infrastructures by providing an empirically grounded account of how technological infrastructures are embedded in—and co-produced by—social, economic, environmental, and political forces (e.g., Bresnihan & Brodie, 2021; Burrell, 2020; Johnson, 2023; Libertson et al., 2021; Velkova, 2021). Furthermore, it scrutinizes the prevailing narrative of abundant clean energy by critically evaluating how governmental discourses and regulatory maneuvers are mobilized to align infrastructural growth with sustainable development goals. Ultimately, the chapter aims to contribute to academic discussions on digital energetics (Pasek et al., 2023) through the context of a situated hub. As I demonstrate, Fortaleza's case is a powerful reminder of the critical need for interventions by researchers, as well as the public and private sectors, to collaboratively work in reimagining resilient, equitable, and environmentally integrated digital infrastructures as AI continues to drive data demands in new geographies around the globe.

A Matter of Geography? Ceará and the "Hub-of-Hubs" Imaginary

According to the Cambridge English Dictionary, the word "hub" originates from the Old English *hyb*, referring to the central part of a wheel, the rounded wooden block that holds the spokes in place much like a core from which all spokes radiate, or "the central or main part of something where there is most activity." Since the nineteenth century, this concept has been applied across diverse fields—including urban planning, industry al development, and economic and scientific spheres—while retaining consistent spelling and meaning. Around the globe, hubs of all sorts have emerged. For example, India's Bangalore and Hyderabad have served as IT centers since the 1990s and are celebrated as globally relevant "tech cities," while China's Shenzhen has transformed from a locale once obscured behind the "Bamboo Curtain" into what is now hailed as the "Silicon Valley of Hardware" (Chacko, 2007; O'Donnell, 2020). In this context, hubs, whether cities, research labs, or institutions, are spaces where new products, ideas, relationships, and modes of action are formed

(Buderi, 2022). Analytically, the concept of a "hub" explored here functions as a powerful discursive and spatial construct through which states and corporations articulate visions of progress, connectivity, and global relevance—often embedding specific political and economic logics within, through, and in relation to the infrastructures they promote.

In the fiber optic submarine cable industry, responsible for the infrastructure that transports 99% of the world's transoceanic data and connects data center facilities across geographies and jurisdictions, the concept of a geographic hub remains explicitly constant as part of the industry's expansionist strategies. This notion encapsulates the capital forces that simultaneously justify investments and reinforce narratives of connectivity. Since 2014, Brazil has experienced an exponential surge in such projects, increasing data capacities and diversifying signal routes with North American markets. Many industry experts argue that Fortaleza's emergence as a hub for international submarine cable accumulation is rooted in its unique geographic position as a stopover, its proximity to Europe and the United States via one of the shortest landing routes, and proactive policies aimed at connecting the city with other Brazilian capitals and beyond (see Figueiredo (2023) for more information on the historical context). Since the 1990s, local policies have driven Fortaleza's metropolitan expansion—marked by industrial development, coastal integration, rural urbanization, and dynamic real estate markets (Diógenes & Paiva, 2014). By the 2000s, innovative tourism and energy production, notably oil and gas, further shaped its economy, while rapid broadband growth in the 2010s secured Fortaleza's status as northeastern Brazil's city with the highest GDP per capita by the 2020s.

Throughout the 2010s and early 2020s, Fortaleza has attracted massive investments by foreign and domestic colocation data center operators, largely due to growth and access to submarine cable systems and terrestrial telecommunication infrastructure—from internet service providers (ISP) to robust fiber deployment throughout Ceará and the Northeast region. The city has gone from being largely an oil and gas manufacturing site to attracting investments across digital infrastructures from some of the largest global companies, ranging from Big Tech companies such as AWS, Google, and Microsoft, to major domestic players in the digital infrastructure sector, such as Scala and Ascenty, as well as other leaders in terrestrial fiber and edge data center sectors such as V.Tal V.tal Networks (recently renamed to Tecto Data Centers) Networks and Elea Digital.[2] This trend follows a pattern where submarine cable systems are rapidly deployed across strategic Global South locations to meet growing data processing demands (Mauldin, 2024), followed by new data center construction.[3] In Brazil, where over 80% of the population has internet access, operators find logic in profiting from the growing demand for subsea cables and data centers, often celebrated as signs of economic progress.

In 2023, Tecto Data Centers launched "Big Lobster," a 200 million reais (34.5 million USD) facility, followed by plans for "Mega Lobster," a 13,000 m^2 data center with 20 MW capacity, supported by over 550 million reais (94.9 million USD) investment, both in Fortaleza's *Praia do Futuro,* a beach area where most cables land in the city. In parallel, Ceará's renewable energy sector has also gained traction, particularly in wind generation and green hydrogen production, drawing global interest and new investment accords. At Mega Lobster's inauguration in 2024, the state's Secretary of Economic Development highlighted the state's unique advantage: "[Ceará has] abundant renewable energy resources, submarine cables that provide the best connectivity in the Americas, and the data centers are a key strategic element for creating a digital economy" (Governo do Estado do Ceará, 2024). Consequently, Fortaleza continues making headlines as *an intercontinental hub*, *a corner of the Atlantic*, and a *nodal point of global connectivity*, some of which have also been reflected in Brazilian media (Fig. 4.1).

When considering submarine cables, the newly established networks routing to and from Fortaleza promise not only to reduce latency between companies and data centers across geographies but also to expand socioeconomic opportunities where they land. Capitalizing on such a strategic location, this narrative of trans-territorial connectivity is strengthened by Ceará's robust logistics infrastructure, which includes a major airport and a maritime port with global connections, including the 19,000 ha Port of Pecém and an Exporting Processing Zone. Together, these other layers of

[2] Other key factors include the establishment of Internet Exchange Points (IXP) and the overall infrastructural capacity developed in Ceará through programs like Cinturão Digital do Ceará (Digital Belt) and Connected Ceará (Ceará Conectado), initiatives that seek to boost fiber capacity and expand internet access statewide.

[3] Locations such as Jakarta, Mumbai, Mombasa, and Djibouti City are rapidly expanding cable systems to meet rising data traffic and diversify emerging markets, attracting investments in new data center facilities.

Fig. 4.1 A 2017 collage in Folha de S. Paulo, one of Brazil's most widely read newspapers. The headline, part of a longer edition commissioned by the state government, refers to submarine cables enabling connectivity "From the World to Ceará and From Ceará to the World," underscoring the city's cross-continental links (Folha de S. Paulo, 2017)

logistic infrastructures position the state as a hub-like node—or a "trio of hubs" (*trinca de hubs,* in Portuguese), as referred to in strategic initiatives whereby flows of physical goods, industries, and data converge into the fabric of the geographical node. This development solidifies Ceará's role in global data exchange and trade and suggests an expanding cloud that is no longer dependent on other established nodes such as São Paulo, which concentrates most investments in data centers in the region (O Povo, 2019). These dynamics reveal that the "hub-of-hubs" concept fuels an imaginary framework in which data centers operate within a self-reinforcing feedback loop. In this, multiple layers of infrastructure direct investments toward a unified vision of a technologically advanced future where Fortaleza competes with other established hubs in Brazil and beyond. As of 2025, Fortaleza has 18 operational or planned submarine cable systems, with at least ten directly providing international bandwidth connecting companies and markets in other parts of the Americas, as well as Western territories of the European and African markets. Especially when promoted by government agencies at the state and municipal levels, Fortaleza is often portrayed as a key site with a business-friendly environment, policy incentives, and favorable seabed conditions that are crucial for determining the suitability for cable landing station infrastructure installation (ANATEL, 2022). In recent years, conferences and events within the digital infrastructure sector have also consistently spotlighted Fortaleza as a critical node for new cable systems in the Atlantic, showcasing it in slide decks, talks, and promotional banners. In an era where AI drives exponential data and energy demands, Fortaleza's case exemplifies how local geographies and policies are mobilized to circumvent these challenges by enabling an economic pathway forward—one in which Brazil's digital landscape is deemed competitive and sustainable, similar to other established regional hubs such as Singapore and Ireland where government has been proactive (Bojczuk et al., 2023).

Moreover, Fortaleza's example as a submarine cable hub illustrates how new systems can create cost-effective opportunities for constructing data centers that serve multiple markets simultaneously (Bragion et al., 2023). This further strengthens the rationale for investing in new facilities, especially as rising demand and electricity consumption drive the rapid growth of AI. A recent announcement by Scala Data Centers, unveiling a technologically advanced data center capable of supporting AI, further underscores this potential. During the announcement, Fortaleza's mayor, joined by media and top executives, highlighted the strategic connection between data centers and the city's airport infrastructure as part of the "hub-of-hubs" narrative put forth by the government:

> Boeing will not land on a runway meant for small planes; it will land at major airports. We already have that. What gives us a great starting advantage is the pragmatism of the operation. In Fortaleza, we are close to the cables, we have excellent connectivity and a geographic location that allows for lower latency, which is the main asset of the companies coordinating this operation. (Rodrigues, 2024)

As these new emerging patterns suggest, the expansion of submarine cables in Fortaleza paved the way for geographically diversifying Brazil's digital infrastructure market for data centers, challenging the historical concentration in other established locations of terrestrial fiber infrastructure. In becoming such, one can argue that the formation of the cloud cannot be disentangled from established and emerging nodes of connectivity; rather, it emerges through competing and fluid forces, with the government playing a central role in the Fortaleza case. After all, these assets not only drive market expansion but also enable the diversification of signal routes and bolster overall connectivity plans of the state—an infrastructure foundation that will be crucial for future AI advancements.

Local Promises and Policies: The Abundant Green Energy Narrative

Government-fueled narratives signpost Fortaleza's geographic advantage as the basis for its hub identity in digital infrastructures, aligning with the Brazilian government's portrayal of the region as a provider of abundant, sustainable energy for AI. Indeed, Brazil's renewable energy sector supplies over 89% of the country's electricity and reached 599.2 TWh in 2024 (IRENA, 2024; Ministério de Minas e Energia, 2024a), setting a global benchmark for sustainable transition.[4] Since the early 2020s, Ceará has sourced at least half its energy from renewables—with wind and solar now contributing nearly 70% of its mix compared to thermoelectric plants, and limited hydropower due to scarce surface water—while its estimated potential stands at 94 GW for onshore wind (10.7% of the country), 117 GW for offshore wind (9.5%), and 643 GW for photovoltaic generation (2.3%) (Governo do Estado do Ceará, 2021; Rolim et al., 2020). These figures are remarkable given the state's relatively small territorial footprint and are further amplified by ongoing developments in green hydrogen production in recent years. If the narrative of an expanding cloud is deeply connected to the energy to power it, that of the Fortaleza as a hub is deeply connected to the role of the state in greening that supply of electricity, and garnering perceptions of "Ceará as paradise"

[4] These developments largely stem from decades of federal policy interventions dating back to Brazil's industrialization period (1930–1980), including energy purchase guarantees, public financing, state tax exemptions, and other initiatives that diversified the country's energy matrix (Werner & Lazaro, 2023).

for renewable energy generation from those interested in investing there (Serpa, 2022).

As these numbers suggest, government initiatives—such as comprehensive tax incentives, legal certainty, streamlined environmental licensing, and enhanced energy transmission through local partnerships—have positioned Ceará as a wind power leader over the past two decades (Abreu et al., 2014), underscoring the crucial role of state policies in driving renewable energy transitions. In parallel, the state of Ceará streamlined its environmental licensing, accelerating the construction of wind and solar projects. This approach is reinforced by boosting energy transmission through partnerships with local agencies, the national grid operator, and energy research companies. These measures show that Ceará's renewable transition is driven not only by its natural resources and strategic location—with Fortaleza as its capital—but also by robust public sector involvement at both federal and state levels. This challenges the idea that market forces drive sustainability alone, highlighting state policies' critical role in renewable development and future data center projects. Continually, Ceará's government actively supports renewable industries through regulatory frameworks, fiscal incentives, and streamlined licensing. For instance, *Decree No. 32.438* of 2017 established the Industrial Development Fund and the Incentive Program for the Renewable Energy Production Chain, while later policies like *Law No. 17.553* (2021) and the *Ceará Verde State Energy Transition Plan (Decree No. 34.733)* extended preferential treatment to clean energy projects. Together, these initiatives are transforming Ceará's energy landscape by fostering renewable growth, modernizing infrastructure, and attracting targeted transmission investments.

In addition to state-wide initiatives promoting the adoption of renewable energy, Fortaleza has implemented municipal-level tax and financial incentives to foster the growth of the IT and telecommunications sector, including data processing and storage services. For instance, complementary *Law No. 340* of 2022 introduced several fiscal incentives, most notably reducing the ISSQN (Service Tax) rate to 2% for services exceeding the average prices of the previous quarter. This reduced rate specifically targets companies involved in data processing, application service provision, and internet hosting, directly benefiting data center operations.[5] What these incentives show is that a strong government presence is actively paving the way for becoming a hub for digital infrastructure designed to maximize renewable energy potential. This underscores how policy choices construct techno-optimistic visions of "greening the cloud," while potentially overlooking contentious and persistent debates surrounding equitable access to resources, economic development, and sustainability.

Between data center stakeholders and government officials, these strategic interventions often assume that large-scale wind and solar projects can seamlessly power data centers and automatically benefit local communities. However, such framing may obscure socio-environmental trade-offs, uneven benefit distribution, and corporate profits prioritized over local needs—especially as data centers are portrayed as drivers of immediate scalability. Research demonstrates that renewable energy transitions in the Global South frequently involve uneven development and social contestation. For instance, Howe and Boyer's (2019) ethnographic accounts of wind farms in Latin America reveal that green investments can inadvertently deepen inequalities, displace local communities, and restructure land rights to favor multinational interests. This necessitates, as they caution, "a more holistic reimagination of relations in which we avoid simply greening the predatory and accumulative enterprises of modern statecraft and capitalism" (p. 197). Similarly, other scholars emphasize that "even as renewable energy is pursued to fuel the cloud, the same divisions that powered industrial capitalism through fossil fuels can be reproduced" (Pasek et al., 2023, p. 106). While Fortaleza's integration of digital infrastructure and renewables positions it as a sustainable development model, it does not necessarily ensure a balanced perspective that prevents the monopolization of renewable resources at the expense of broader sustainability goals. Furthermore, there is a notable lack of data and systematic studies linking energy projects to the growing AI-driven demand in the context of data centers in Brazil, partly because regulatory bodies do not require these infrastructure owners and operators to disclose their energy usage consumption.

[5] New companies can access the reduced rate from the fourth month onwards, while those moving their fiscal domicile to Fortaleza qualify immediately. Additionally, 10% of the tax benefits shall support local economic initiatives through the Municipal Economic Development Fund.

If AI's expansion is intrinsically linked to its energy demands, Fortaleza's development as a digital hub-of-hubs hinges on a state-driven narrative that positions its energy supply as both "abundant" and "green." However, this framing reflects a technocratic approach to sustainability; that is, one that prioritizes large-scale industrial production while sidelining the social dimensions of environmental stewardship. By emphasizing energy availability for industrial and commercial use, this perspective can depoliticize energy transitions and obscure local conflicts over land use, environmental degradation, and economic inequalities. While Fortaleza's rise as a digital infrastructure hub is often attributed to its strategic geography, this explanation conceals the deeper entanglements of power, policy, and socio-environmental dynamics that shape its infrastructural development. At its core, the city's function in hosting data centers is not merely a matter of location but the result of political choices that now present renewable energy as abundant and, by extension, inherently sustainable for private sector growth. Nevertheless, this portrayal masks competing claims to resources, potentially downplaying other relevant struggles amid the pressures of an energy transition frequently framed as a corporate opportunity rather than a public good concern.

Framing energy as "abundant" risks oversimplifying sustainability, reducing it merely to powering Fortaleza's data centers rather than a broader sociopolitical process. The emphasis on attracting investments and renewable transitions lacks clarity on managing these resources sustainably beyond industrial growth. Most importantly, this weakens public sector regulation aligning cloud infrastructure with economic equity and environmental responsibility. While the abundance narrative primarily serves corporate interests, companies such as Scala, Angola Cables, and Tecto Data Centers actively promote their green portfolios and significant capital investments, reinforcing renewable-powered data centers as inherently beneficial. In many cases, public and private actors present these infrastructures as part of win-win set of relations—one that is able to address the data-intensive industry needs while boosting the expansion in sustainability efforts. Yet, if not done right or within a systematically analyzed scenario, this model risks perpetuating spatial inequalities characteristic of global technology hubs—where capital and infrastructural power are concentrated in high-profile projects, often overshadowing broader social and ecological costs by promising a future that remains unrealized. In other words, without a critical assessment of how abundance is defined, distributed, and governed, such narratives risk entrenching a technocratic model of sustainability.

Beyond the Hub: An Emerging Sustainable AI Ecosystem?

Globally, many governments lack the technical expertise or regulatory frameworks needed to effectively address the greening of data centers. Countries and jurisdictions with established data center hubs have implemented disclosure requirements to assess grid congestion; however, Brazil remains behind in this regard, particularly as hubs such as Fortaleza continue to attract investments. Nevertheless, the country is taking ambitious steps to integrate data centers, AI, and energy policies into its domestic strategies. In recent years, the Brazilian government has already framed digital infrastructure as a pillar of technological sovereignty, exemplified by the *AI for the Good of All* strategy, which envisions nearly 4 billion USD in investments between 2024 and 2028 (Conselho Nacional de Ciência e Tecnologia, 2024). Launched in mid-2024, the strategy promotes technological autonomy and global competitiveness by centering energy on Brazil's AI ambitions, diverging from Silicon Valley models with a locally driven approach. Here, the narrative that prevails is one where green energy is paramount to counteract existing extractive models of AI:

> [Brazil's vision is to build] an AI that does not exclude people…that does not increase inequalities, and that ultimately improves everyone's lives. Because there is no technology without considering people. Furthermore, a sustainable AI that leverages the diversity of our renewable energy matrix to produce technology with a smaller environmental footprint, harnessing our resources sustainably and responsibly. (CanalGov, 2024)

This commentary, exposed in a well-circulated promotional government video, outlines a vision for Brazil's AI production that leverages its strengths—especially its clean energy matrix—as a strategic asset to attract investment and establish an alternative view of "AI for All." Notably, the strategy's first pillar calls for expanding and modernizing AI infrastructure, emphasizing an enhanced data center sector where Fortaleza's strategic location and decade-long development provide a competitive edge. Central to this approach is Brazil's renewable energy installed capacity and potential, with plans for a *Sustainability and Renewable Energy Program for AI* that integrates cooling technologies and energy-efficient equipment in a way that harmonizes AI demand with surplus clean energy. What's more, the disclosed preliminary plans on developing "national data centers" in the North and Northeast regions underscore Fortaleza's potential to enhance the AI supply chain while expanding the use of the renewable energy that the government usually utilizes as a part of the public-facing campaign to emphasize that Ceará, alongside the broader northeast region, produces more clean energy that it currently demands.

Despite the ambitious plans to drive the AI sector in relation to green electricity use, the Brazilian government, at the federal level, employs only a decadal model to assess energy demands. Increasingly, such a method is challenged by the rapid construction of new data centers aimed at supporting AI growth and competitiveness. Hence, forecasting energy needs over a decade is difficult due to fluctuating demand and evolving technologies, and without specific regulatory frameworks from energy and telecommunications agencies, the hubs remain unprepared to align growth with sustainability. According to the Ministry of Energy and Mines, planning for the national electric grid must balance projected future energy consumption with the capacity of the transmission network, ensuring sufficient generation to meet demand and allow the cycle to operate smoothly (Rosa, 2024). This sentiment is echoed by the director of Brazil's National Telecommunication Agency (ANATEL), who asserts that "what they [the energy sector's regulators] can do is ensure the provision of reliable energy to support data center operations" (Mosna, 2024). Although these arguments bolster the government narrative of attracting data centers for economic gains—leveraging a surplus of cheap, reliable, and clean energy— they are yet to propose a granular and robust mechanism for developing imaginaries, standards, and policies to promote sustainable data center infrastructure.

The ongoing plans for domestic data center constructions in hubs such as Fortaleza further underscore the city's potential to strengthen the AI supply chain and boost renewable energy use, aligning with the government's campaign to brand Ceará and the broader Northeast as net clean energy producers. Though still in the planning stages, the *AI for All Strategy* positions the Northeast as a vital location for Brazil's AI and sustainable technology future. However, achieving a sustainable AI ecosystem from an energy perspective is more complex than industry or government narratives suggest, given the constraints of Brazil's current electric grid configuration and the lack of a coherent regulatory framework for data centers at a national scale. Consequently, adopting a proactive, data-driven approach is imperative to ensure accountability for sustainability practices; however, such efforts require a systematic data-driven picture of the sector's overall energy impact, including, among other things, its infrastructure and electricity consumption levels.

Between 2025 and 2037, the federal government forecasts anticipate that Ceará alone will require up to 876 MW, a demand comparable to other major data center hubs, such as those found in the states of São Paulo and Rio Grande do Sul (Fig. 4.2). Rather than controlling growth, as seen in many established data center nodes around the world, Fortaleza is embracing incentives to fuel expansion, positioning itself as a regional competitor among major data center hubs. In doing so, the city gains new significance as a location that can help shape Brazil's trajectory in greening data centers and addressing the rising energy demands of AI by utilizing renewable resources to power its infrastructure. Other estimates by the government show that electricity demand from the sector is expected to reach 9 GW country-wide by 2035 (Ministério de Minas e Energia, 2024a), driven by extensive construction projects across various states, including Ceará. Parallel to rising electricity demands, Ceará's potential for green hydrogen is under debate, driven by promises of 30 billion USD in investments as of 2024.

As these projects suggest, navigating this scenario in the context of Fortaleza as a hub will require innovative solutions to balance the technological progress of particular data center hubs with sustainability, ensuring that Brazil can meet future AI demands without compromising energy security or environmental goals.

By exposing the superficiality in this positioning of "economic gain" versus the "long-term sustainability planning" that can indeed benefit the country's hubs as they form and enhance the interface with the global supply chain of AI (through investments, constructions, equipment imports, and local training for new talent powering the sector), it becomes clear how these paths require new approaches to ensure that the development of new hubs at the digital-infrastructure-renewable-energy nexus in Brazil follows a sustainable path. Despite that, ANATEL emphasizes an economic-focused approach toward data centers at large, insisting that discussions should not become restrictive for owners and operators seeking to invest in and develop data centers to support the country's

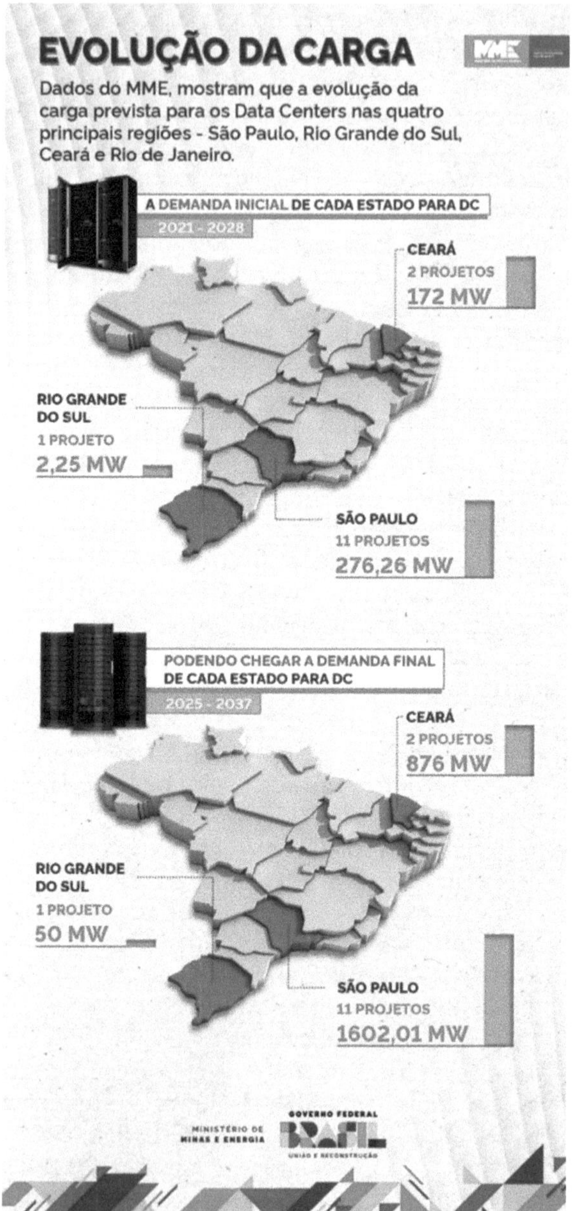

Fig. 4.2 Illustrative poster displayed on the government's website showcasing the projected electricity consumption by the data center sector, including Ceará (Ministério de Minas e Energia, 2024c)

digitalization needs and growing demands for AI development. As noted by one of the agency's officials in a recent event in the sector:

> These premises [of energy increase and AI] are based on a series of benchmarks observed in New Zealand, Australia, and the United States. In the U.S., for example, federal legislation favors state-level autonomy, leading some states to reject the installation of data centers due to high energy consumption. In other countries, there are already very restrictive policies in this regard. However, we cannot focus only on restrictive regulation. We need to envision a national strategy that promotes the development and expansion of data centers, while also considering ways to ensure this growth does not negatively impact the environment or Brazil's telecommunications infrastructure. (Freire, 2024)

This commentary signals a non-restrictive approach, functioning with a broader abundant energy framework, that is commonly articulated by many Global South countries seeking to attract technology investments with minimum policy oversight. However, as I suggest, the recognition of Ceará in the formative government strategies for AI in Brazil at large—and Fortaleza by default as an inter-regional digital infrastructure hub—gives the region the ability to shape how the discourses surrounding AI development and sustainability are envisioned in Brazil.

Indeed, there may be not a universal path to undercover all the implications revealed in the convergence of digital and energy infrastructures in support of AI's growth. A first step, however, might be to implement a more rigorous framework for collecting data and reporting on existing data center facilities—one that enhances our understanding of the true impact of the burgeoning data center sector on the electric grid amid AI-driven transformations and scrutinizes renewable energy practices. To date, regulatory best practices in this area are already underway across the broader European Union context, and increased engagement with standards and certifications could potentially further safeguard a greener pathway for development.[6] Importantly, this approach does

[6] Starting in 2026, the EU's Energy Efficiency Directive (EU/2023/1791) outline that there will be a requirement for data center operators (of ≥500 kW capacity) to report on energy performance, water footprint, and demand-side flexibility using a standard template. EU operators will be required to disclose key details—such as name, owner, location, start date, floor area, installed power, data traffic, and storage capacity—and annual metrics like energy consumption, power utilization, temperature, waste heat, water

not necessarily translate into stricter regulations but seeks an optimal path that considers sector-specific factors, existing energy configurations, current policy frameworks, and feasibility studies capable of helping holistically understand and predict externalities stemming from new renewable projects that emerge to power a growing and increasingly geographically distributed cloud.

Discussion

In light of the global surge in AI developments, the imperative is no longer merely constructing new data centers, but determining their optimal deployment locations, connections to other infrastructures, and how they intersect with other critical systems, such as the energy grid. Fortaleza's emergence as a digital infrastructure hub exemplifies this transformative shift. As argued in this chapter, this positioning relies on state-led policies and the strategic mobilization of geographic advantages—namely, submarine cables and abundant renewable resources—to establish Brazil as a competitor in the global AI economy. Yet, this techno-optimistic branding potentially conceals deep-seated socio-environmental contradictions. The case of Fortaleza as a digital infrastructure hub echoes Appel et al.'s (2018) reflection that "infrastructures are critical locations through which sociality, governance and politics, accumulation and dispossession, and institutions and aspirations are formed, reformed, and performed" (p. 3). Here, and within the framing of a digital infrastructure hub, the celebrated government discourse of "abundant energy" obscures potential land-use complexities, inequitable resource distribution, and regulatory gaps that threaten to repeat historical inequalities if left unaddressed. Unpacking these points of contention is essential not only for understanding the local dynamics of strategic locations such as Fortaleza, but also for unraveling the possible kinds of convergence that underpin infrastructural promises.

For a country of continental dimensions with enormous renewable energy potential, concerns related to sustainability occupy a paradoxical position—marginal in practice, yet central in discourse—particularly in the context of data centers and AI developments explored in this chapter. In an era marked by the rapid convergence of AI systems

usage, and renewable energy usage, all expressed as sustainability indicators (PUE, WUE, ERF, REF) per CEN/CENELEC EN 50600–4 standards.

enabled by digital and energy infrastructures, Fortaleza's rise as a strategic node in Brazil's regional and national development discourse demands more than celebratory narratives of progress and abundance. As this chapter has shown, local public stakeholders have mobilized this narrative through a form of techno-optimism to attract data center investments and promote a future-facing image of sustainability that leverages the region's renewable energy potential. Yet, beneath these discourses lie unresolved tensions—between infrastructure-led development and social equity, between energy abundance and environmental accountability, and between global competitiveness and local governance. These dynamics underscore the need for research that attends to the granular realities of nodal geographies such as Fortaleza, not only to trace how expansionist industry logics take root, but also to critically assess how they reorganize political priorities, institutional frameworks, and public understandings of what constitutes sustainable development.

Therefore, potential areas for future research could critically examine how emerging hub locations such as Fortaleza can navigate the tensions between economic incentives and digital infrastructure development in the age of AI. Rather than solely prescribing the adoption of international best practices, there is a pressing need for locally grounded, interdisciplinary studies that interrogate how digital infrastructures are shaped by—and, in turn, reshape—socio-environmental dynamics. Such assumptions are far from universally accepted, given how natural resources are distributed, how infrastructure sectors operate across jurisdictions, and the speed at which AI is advancing. In relation to this relational understanding, further scholarship could illuminate the feasibility of crafting new, context-specific governance models, accountability frameworks, and technical standards capable of harmonizing infrastructural growth with equity and ecological stewardship. Such an approach not only invites empirical work on the emerging configurations of data centers, renewable energy projects, and urban developments in places often considered peripheral, but also contributes to a broader comparative conversation about how Global South nodes can inform more inclusive and sustainable paradigms insofar as citizens and industries observe the convergence of infrastructures and narratives to sustain AI growth.

Competing Interests The author has no conflicts of interest to declare that are relevant to the contents of this chapter.

References

Abreu, M. C. S., Siebra, A. A., da Cunha, L. T., & dos Santos, S. M. (2014). Fatores determinantes para o avanço da energia eólica no estado do Ceará frente aos desafios das mudanças climáticas. *Revista Eletrônica de Administração (Porto Alegre), 20*(2). https://doi.org/10.1590/1413-2311060201238406

ANATEL. (2022). *Ata da 5a reunião ordinária do comitê de infraestrutura de telecomunicações.* https://sei.anatel.gov.br/sei/modulos/pesquisa/md_pesq_documento_consulta_externa.php?eEP-wqk1skrd8hSlk5Z3rN4EVg9uLJqrLYJw_9INcO46gZakxrC19OlgRk5hu5-BW8pSije3MPsj1iY7iRDA3h0IMm3Q4EIhbNvU5LaZYPjizbmcAL18e4QafxCZwppZ

Appel, H., Anand, N., & Gupta A. (2018). *The promise of infrastructure.* Duke University Press. https://www.dukeupress.edu/the-promise-of-infrastructure

Bojczuk, I., Silcox, N., Starosielski, N., & Vaughan, H. (2023). A new era of sustainable network hubs? The subsea cable–data center–renewable energy connection. *Submarine Telecoms Forum, 128*, 18–25. https://issuu.com/subtelforum/docs/subtel_forum_128/18

Bragion, E., Akter, H., Kumar, M., Xu, M., Abdelmoniem, A. M., & Gill, S. S. (2023). Fortaleza: The emergence of a network hub. *Internet of Things and Cyber-Physical Systems, 3*, 272–279. https://doi.org/10.1016/j.iotcps.2023.05.001

Bresnihan, P., & Brodie, P. (2021). New extractive frontiers in Ireland and the moebius strip of wind/data. *Environment and Planning E: Nature and Space, 4*(4), 1645–1664. https://doi.org/10.1177/2514848620970121

Buderi, R. (2022). *Where futures converge: Kendall square and the making of a global innovation hub.* MIT Press. https://mitpress.mit.edu/9780262046510/where-futures-converge/

Burrell, J. (2020). On half-built assemblages: Waiting for a data center in Prineville, Oregon. *Engaging Science, Technology, and Society, 6*, 283–305. https://doi.org/10.17351/ests2020.447

Canal Gov. (2024). Lula participa da abertura da 5ª conferência nacional de ciência, tecnologia e inovação. *Governo Federal do Brasil* [Video]. YouTube. https://www.youtube.com/watch?v=1IkypXIeWdE&t=523s&ab_channel=CanalGov

Chacko, E. (2007). From brain drain to brain gain: Reverse migration to Bangalore and Hyderabad, India's globalizing high tech cities. *Geo Journal, 68*(2/3), 131–140. https://www.jstor.org/stable/41148150

Conselho Nacional de Ciência e Tecnologia. (2024). *IA para o bem de todos: Proposta de plano brasileiro de inteligência artificial 2024–2028.* Governo Federal do Brasil. https://www.gov.br/mcti/pt-br/acompanhe-o-mcti/cct/legislacao/arquivos/IA_para_o_Bem_de_Todos.pdf

Diógenes, B. H. N., & Paiva, R. A. (2014). O processo histórico de metropolização de Fortaleza. *III Encontro da Associação Nacional de Pesquisa e Pós-graduação em Arquitetura e Urbanismo: Arquitetura, cidade e projeto: uma construção coletiva*, 1–15. https://www.anparq.org.br/dvd-enanparq-3/htm/Artigos/ST/ST-CDR-009-3_DIOGENES.PAIVA.pdf

Fairclough, N. (2010). A dialectical-relational approach to critical discourse analysis in social research. In N. Fairclough (Ed.), *Critical discourse analysis: The critical study of language* (pp. 230–254). Routledge. https://doi.org/10.4324/9781315834368

Figueiredo, R. C. C. (2023). Um cabo submarino na maré abolicionista: Infraestrutura comunicacional contra a escravidão no Ceará (1873–1888). *Revista de História, São Paulo, 182*, 1–32. https://doi.org/10.11606/issn.2316-9141.rh.2023.209111

Folha de S Paulo. (2017) Foco: Ceará de Oportunidades. *Estúdio Folha*. https://arquivos.sfiec.org.br/sfiec/files/files/ceara_Oportunidades_31out.pdf

Freire, A. (2024, August 13–14). *Mercado de data centers e inteligência artificial* [Conference presentation]. IV Simpósio TelComp IDP–Telecom, Tecnologia e Competição para o Futuro Digital, Brazil. https://www.youtube.com/watch?v=sGQWTNg78PI&ab_channel=Poder360

Governo do Estado do Ceará. (2021). *O hidrogênio verde*. https://www.sedet.ce.gov.br/wp-content/uploads/sites/15/2021/07/Proposta_Apresenta%C3%A7%C3%A3o-Institucional-Hidrog%C3%AAnio-Verde-Ceara.pdf

Governo do Estado do Ceará. (2024). *Ceará ganha novo data center e fortalece sua posição como polo tecnológico no Brasil*. https://www.ceara.gov.br/2024/10/17/ceara-ganha-novo-data-center-e-fortalece-sua-posicao-como-polo-tecnologico-no-brasil/

Howe, C., & Boyer, D. (2019). Joint conclusion to wind and power in the Anthropocene. In I. D. Boyer (Ed.), *Energopolitics: Wind and power in the Anthropocene* (pp. 194–198). Duke University Press. https://www.dukeupress.edu/wind-and-power-in-the-anthropocene

IRENA. (2024). *Energy profile: Brazil*. https://www.irena.org/-/media/Files/IRENA/Agency/Statistics/Statistical_Profiles/South%20America/Brazil_South%20America_RE_SP.pdf

Johnson, A. (2023). *Where cloud is ground: Placing data and making place in Iceland* (1st ed.). University of California Press. https://www.ucpress.edu/books/where-cloud-is-ground/paper

Libertson, F., Velkova, J., & Palm, J. (2021). Data-center infrastructure and energy gentrification: Perspectives from Sweden. *Sustainability: Science, Practice and Policy, 17*(1), 152–161. https://doi.org/10.1080/15487733.2021.1901428

Mauldin, A. (2024, September 24). *Escaping the matrix: AI and submarine cables.* [Conference presentation] Submarine Networks World 2024. https://www2.telegeography.com/hubfs/2024/Presentations/Submarine%20Networks%20World%202024.pdf

Ministério de Minas e Energia (2024a). Brazilian Monthly Energy Bulletin. https://eur03.safelinks.protection.outlook.com/?url=https%3A%2F%2Fwww.gov.br%2Fmme%2Fpt-br%2Fassuntos%2Fsecretarias%2Fsntep%2Fpublicacoes%2Fboletins-mensais-de-energia%2Fboletins%2F2024%2Fenglish%2F9-brazilian-monthly-energy-bulletin-september-2024%2Fview&data=05%7C02%7Cib410%40universityofcambridgecloud.onmicrosoft.com%7Ce093bcad08a64f42d68308dda4ccc0bc%7C49a50445bdfa4b79ade3547b4f3986e9%7C1%7C0%7C638847921628326613%7CUnknown%7CTWFpbGZsb3d8eyJFbXB0eU1hcGkiOnRydWUsIlYiOiIwLjAuMDAwMCIsIlAiOiJXaW4zMiIsIkFOIjoiTWFpbCIsIldUIjoyfQ%3D%3D%7C0%7C%7C%7C&sdata=caXerj21Lq0q4s4ObbVvtxHzRXrhGtPP1MvjbKGcD2w%3D&reserved=0

Ministério de Minas e Energia. (2024b). *Monthly energy bulletin Brazil.* https://www.gov.br/mme/pt-br/assuntos/secretarias/sntep/publicacoes/boletins-mensais-de-energia/boletins/2024/english/9-brazilian-monthly-energy-bulletin-september-2024/viewMinistério de Minas e Energia. (2024b). *MME identifica crescimento acelerado na demanda de energia elétrica para projetos de Data Centers.* https://www.gov.br/mme/pt-br/assuntos/noticias/mme-identifica-crescimento-acelerado-na-demanda-de-energia-eletrica-para-projetos-de-data-centers

Ministério de Minas e Energia. (2024c). *MME e EPE mapeiam soluções para atender crescente demanda dos data centers no Brasil.* https://www.gov.br/mme/pt-br/assuntos/noticias/mme-e-epe-mapeiam-solucoes-para-atender-crescente-demanda-dos-data-centers-no-brasil

Mosna, F. (2024, August 13–14). *Mercado de data centers e inteligência artificial.* [Conference presentation]. IV Simpósio TelComp IDP–Telecom, Tecnologia e Competição para o Futuro Digital, Brazil. https://www.youtube.com/watch?v=sGQWTNg78PI&ab_channel=Poder360

Munn, L. (2023). *Technical territories: Data, subjects, and spaces in infrastructural Asia.* University of Michigan Press. https://press.umich.edu/Books/T/Technical-Territories3

O Povo. (2019). *Guia de infraestrutura do Ceará, Brazil 2019–2020.* https://www.ceara.gov.br/wp-content/uploads/2019/04/infraestrutura.pdf

O'Donnell, M. A. (2020). From bamboo curtain to the Silicon Valley of hardware. *e-flux Magazine.* https://www.e-flux.com/architecture/software/337686/from-bamboo-curtain-to-the-silicon-valley-of-hardware/

Pasek, A., Lin, C., Cooper, Z., & Kinder, J.(2023). *Digital energetics.* https://doi.org/10.14619/0580

Rodrigues, L. (2024). Em meio à crise no setor, empresas de energia querem atrair investimentos em data centers no Ceará. *Diário do Nordeste*. https://diariodonordeste.verdesmares.com.br/negocios/em-meio-a-crise-no-setor-empresas-de-energia-querem-atrair-investimentos-em-data-centers-no-ceara-1.3546971

Rolim, J., Picanço, J., & Ponte, I. (2020). *Energias renováveis no ceará*. Federação das Indústrias do Estado do Ceará. https://parquetecnologico.ufc.br/wp-content/uploads/2021/01/ceara-energias-renovaveis-10nov2020-1.pdf

Rosa, G. Z. (2024). Mercado de Data Centers e Inteligência Artificial., *IV Simpósio TelComp IDP—Telecom, Tecnologia e Competição para o Futuro Digital*. Brasília, Brazil. 13-14 August.

Serpa, E. (2022). Noruegueses estão no Ceará para conhecer projeto do Hub do H2V. *Diário do Nordeste*. https://diariodonordeste.verdesmares.com.br/opiniao/colunistas/egidio-serpa/noruegueses-estao-no-ceara-para-conhecer-projeto-do-hub-do-h2v-1.3304676

Spencer, T., & Singh, S. (2024). *What the data centre and AI boom could mean for the energy sector*. International Energy Agency. https://www.iea.org/commentaries/what-the-data-centre-and-ai-boom-could-mean-for-the-energy-sector

Velkova, J. (2021). Thermopolitics of data: Cloud infrastructures and energy futures. *Cultural Studies, 35*(4–5), 663–683. https://doi.org/10.1080/09502386.2021.1895243

Werner, D., & Lazaro, L. L. B. (2023). The policy dimension of energy transition: The Brazilian case in promoting renewable energies (2000–2022). *Energy Policy, 175*, 113480. https://doi.org/10.1016/j.enpol.2023.113480

CHAPTER 5

Aligning Energy Grids, Clouds and Public Values in Sweden

Julia Velkova

Introduction

In the spring of 2023, the international military producer Nammo made the headlines in international press with the announcement that the company was unable to expand its ammunition production factory in Norway because of a TikTok data centre that had claimed all the available grid transmission capacity in the region of Hamar (Yerushalmy, 2023). Nammo's expansion was intended to help alleviate ammunition shortages that had arisen in relation to the European military support for Ukraine in its ongoing resistance of the Russian invasion. However, the TikTok data centre had highjacked all the grid capacity in the region and prevented the upscaling of ammunition production. The news was remarkable but not unique. A year earlier, housing construction in West London was halted as the local grid ran out of capacity due to a concentration of data centres in the area (Hammond & Morris, 2022). In Sweden, in 2021, Microsoft inaugurated, with great fanfare, a data centre in the Skåne province amidst

J. Velkova (✉)
Department of Culture and Society, Linköping University, Norrköping, Sweden
e-mail: julia.velkova@liu.se

A. Mollen et al. (eds.), *AI Infrastructures and Sustainability*, Palgrave Studies in European Communication Research and Education,
https://doi.org/10.1007/978-3-032-09748-4_5

the worst capacity deficit in the power grid in the history of the region; this pushed the major local industrial bakery, a plastic manufacturer, and other industries to look to establishing their production facilities elsewhere (Libertson et al., 2021). Around the same time, in the region of Mälardalen in Sweden, Amazon Web Services (AWS) established three data centres. The then CEO of the regional electricity grid warned already in 2019 that no other large electricity-intense industries would be able to connect to the grid thereafter in this region (Selin, 2018).

Contemporary debates regarding the environmental sustainability of computing and artificial intelligence (AI) systems have specified energy as a central problem. The magnitude of electricity consumed by digital infrastructure and, particularly, by data centres has been discussed at length (Cubitt, 2017; Ensmenger, 2018; Marks, 2024; Maxwell & Miller, 2012; Ortar et al., 2023). The sources of energy for computing are commonly associated today with increases in carbon emissions, leading to calls for greater environmental accountability of the digital tech sector regarding its contribution to climate change (Brevini, 2022; Dovbysh et al., 2025; Kuntsman & Rattle, 2019). Accounting for the carbon emissions of computing is in itself a contested knowledge practice (Pasek et al., 2023), which nevertheless continues to animate computer engineers' efforts to calculate, ever more precisely, the carbon emissions of AI systems, such as model training and inference (Luccioni et al., 2023).

Amidst these debates, the examples above further highlight how routine technical operations of connecting computers in data centres to power grids are not only operations that involve carbon and the environment but are also social operations that affect the distribution of access to energy infrastructure. In this chapter, I argue that whether digital infrastructures are sustainable cannot be seen as a singular expression of their link to a chemical such as carbon but is also a result of how infrastructure operations promote or compromise public values of access.[1] As new EU policies promote the development of AI factories across Europe, the question regarding equal and fair access to electricity for citizens and industries is only going to gain greater importance. In this context, it is crucial to ask: how are the compromised values of shared access to basic infrastructure, such as energy grids, imagined to be restored or addressed?

[1] I draw on van Dijck et al.'s (2018) discussion of public values as values that contribute to the common good, and the recognition that both public values and the common good are performative, historically and culturally shaped, and at stake in democratic societies.

And, what are the conditions that contribute to creating these issues to begin with? After all, software designated as "AI" has existed for decades (Suchman, 1987) and so has computing and digital infrastructure. Then, what is the problem today?

In this chapter, I propose infrastructural misalignment as a lens to engage with these questions. With this perspective, I seek to recast critique regarding the sustainability of digital infrastructure and its relationship with energy in a new direction by emphasising the importance of considering how public values are compromised or upheld across entangled infrastructure that supports the expansion of AI systems. This perspective contributes to expanding scholarly discussions on the relationship among energy, sustainability, and digital infrastructure (Bresnihan & Brodie, 2023; Pasek et al., 2023; Velkova, 2021), as well as to the understanding about the relationship between public values and algorithmic systems (Lehtiniemi, 2024; Ruckenstein & Turunen, 2019; Zakharova et al., 2024).

Misaligned Infrastructures

Following a classic anthropological definition, infrastructure can be defined as things and relationships that enable the movement of other things through forms of governance that appear detached from formal institutions (Larkin, 2013). Scholarship on infrastructure has produced a large body of research concerned with questions of citizenship, knowledge, power, and temporality in relation to distinct "forms" of infrastructure: networks of roads and railways, energy, the internet, and audio-visual and mobile media. More recently, data centres have emerged as a distinct subset of digital infrastructure that has catalysed scholarly analyses of the entanglements among data processing, digitalisation, energy, and the environment (Edwards et al., 2024).

Most scholarly discussions on infrastructure have tended to compartmentalise infrastructure and base analyses on distinct industrial segments. For example, scholars analyse space infrastructure, urban infrastructure, science infrastructure, information infrastructure, energy systems, and data centres with their distinct logics and politics, but seldom engage with their multiple interrelations and how the differences among systems are evened out and smoothened.[2] Running against this tendency, science and technology studies scholar Janet Vertesi (2014) emphasises how any infrastructure always exists as an entanglement of multiple infrastructures that messily overlap with each other. For example, power grid infrastructures co-exist and support the operations of science infrastructure, transport networks, digital computing, and many more systems. Each such infrastructure system has its own logic that supports specific rationalities, commodities, and services, often existing in misalignment with other systems. There can be numerous sources of this misalignment: different professional work practices, differing regulations and markets, varied temporalities and spatialities, drift and brokenness, as well as distinct value orientations. From such a perspective, infrastructure operations are always an ongoing accomplishment achieved through the alignment of logics, values, and other elements across profoundly heterogeneous systems.

Misalignment demands efforts by different actors to produce "fleeting moments of alignment suited to particular tasks with materials ready-to-hand" (Vertesi, 2014, p. 268) across entangled infrastructures. Using examples from the work of scientists and engineers on a robot space mission, Vertesi shows how participants of the mission align and smoothen non-aligned standards, professional identities, cultural norms, and digital technologies for communication on an everyday basis, which is achieved through mundane rituals such as phone calls, individual adjustments, or by technical means to produce coherence. Crucially, alignments are not always successful. Vertesi shows how a simple mismatch between Mac and PC infrastructural systems can leave scientists powerless, thus changing the course of expensive space mission operations. Misalignment further calls for repairs and realignments that become domains of power negotiations, as they prompt questions such as what and whose work is to be aligned, and to what end?

Digital infrastructures are no exception. They emerge in misalignment with other entangled systems. For example, certain data centre operators attempt to promote the value of data security through their infrastructures by siting computers in places that are already associated with security, such as bomb shelters and bunkers (Taylor, 2021). However, the logics that govern bomb shelters are different from those that govern data centres. Public authorities that administer the use of these spaces have to negotiate

[2] Although, of course, this topic has been addressed extensively in STS with a focus on standards, see, for example, Star and Bowker (2004).

the values of preparedness and citizen protection in case of emergencies in addition to the possibilities of commodifying such spaces, as they are available but have often been in a state of disuse for a long time (Velkova, 2023). The differing value orientations of civic defence and data centre infrastructure produces infrastructure misalignments that require public administrations to take decisions regarding what to prioritise and when as well as how to align their differing values by allowing or disallowing specific infrastructural connections.

In similar vein, multinational companies place data centres in the Nordic countries from where they can uphold the values of environmental care simply by connecting data centres to already existing infrastructure that apparently promotes these values, such as electricity grids powered by renewable electricity or district heat systems (Salling & Winthereik, 2025). In these cases, power grid providers and regional administrations have to negotiate the different spatial logics of digital and energy infrastructure, such as the emergent new geographies of intermittent renewable energy supply versus the location demands of data centres; differing temporal logics, such as the long-term planning of energy systems versus the quick pace of development of the tech sector and obsolescence of digital technologies and infrastructures (Chun, 2017; Velkova, 2019); and the different economies of energy and data.

From this perspective, data centres assume an infrastructural role for the digital economies of data and AI systems through the constant alignment of different infrastructure logics and the differing values that they seek to promote (see also Bojzcuk in this volume). But what are these values? In the next section, I suggest that infrastructural misalignments, and the resulting societal and environmental harms from them, are not an intrinsic quality of data centres but a result of a particular cultural form (Williams, 1974) of organising digital computing in the present that promotes the value of hyper-scalability, which demands the constant upscaling of entangled infrastructures to accommodate this form but fails to do so.

Hyper-Scalable Computing Meets Non-Scalable Power Grids

Contemporary AI services require computing power and, often, a substantial amount of it. This power is needed to process the data that is fed into different models, to train algorithms, and to generate estimates regarding the relevance of calculated results. Today, tech multinationals offer computing power for such operations through "cloud computing" services. Cloud computing is a contemporary form of organising computing infrastructure in which organisations aggregate computers in data centres, virtualise and group computers as logical entities, and package them as services available for rent on demand (Hu, 2015). Narayan (2022) describes how cloud computing is a form of outsourcing that enables new forms of corporate organisation of digital service provision and labour premised upon a cultural logic of "hyper-scalability" of computing and infrastructural resources. Hyper-scalable computing, as Narayan defines it, promises companies and organisations the ability to scale by providing digital services without the upfront costs of owning or managing infrastructure. Hyper-scalability makes computing appear virtually limitless and, apparently, also costless (Powell, 2024). A radical shift from earlier forms of organising computing infrastructure, cloud computing makes computational resources available "on the tap" (Narayan, 2022).

Today, AWS, Microsoft, and Google are the largest providers of such services in Europe (Narayan, 2022). These companies also promote hyper-scalable cloud infrastructure as a resource for AI development. For example, AWS offers SageModel Training, a package of algorithms, computing resources, models, and training datasets, including synthetic data modelling. Microsoft offers an entire catalogue of language and vision models as part of a package of "AI Solutions" branded under the slogan "Build and Scale Exceptional Generative AI Systems" (Microsoft, 2025, para1). On their cloud computing website, Microsoft Azure is advertised with the following promise: "Amplify human ingenuity. Dream big and create breakthroughs with the latest AI solutions. Pay as you go or try Azure free for up to 30 days. There's no upfront commitment—cancel anytime" (Microsoft, 2025, Azure AI Solutions).

These services come with a choice of locations that prospective customers can select from, where certain locations offer the attributes of "sustainability" to computing resources depending on where in the world the data centres on which these services run are located. For example, Microsoft and AWS both promote their Swedish-based data centres as offering sustainable computing and AI by associations with the energy infrastructure in Sweden, which is powered by renewable energy. Hyper-scalability promises that computing resources are available to anyone at any cost and pressurises companies to develop data centres. However, when data centres scale, energy and other societal infrastructure, such as water and energy grids, are simply unable to grow as fast, thus resulting in an infrastructure misalignment that manifests through compromising the value of equal access to basic infrastructure services.

For example, on 16 November 2021, during the COVID-19 pandemic, Microsoft announced the inauguration of a new cloud computing region that the company had produced for current and prospective users of Microsoft Azure and Microsoft 365 (Microsoft, 2021). The region consisted of three data centres that Microsoft built in three towns located far from each other—Staffanstorp, Gävle, and Sandviken—in Sweden. The centres offered initially scalable cloud services, security, local data storage (which subsequently included computers for AI-labelled services), and sustainability to prospective users.

In its compulsory inaugural press release, Microsoft emphasised that these data centres were the company's most advanced and sustainably designed ones, as they were zero waste, ran on backup power with environmentally certified diesel and 100 % renewable energy, and utilised a software that would measure the use of renewable electricity on an hourly basis. Microsoft added a commitment to use less water and produce less waste in the future in Sweden (Microsoft, 2021).

Microsoft's announcement for a new data centre and virtual cloud region came at the same time as Skåne—the Swedish region where one of these three data centres was located—experienced the worst shortage of transmission capacity in the region (Skånes effektkommission NET, 2025). In 2020, no new connections to the power grid in Skåne could be established and no existing ones could be upgraded; all the while, the electricity-intense Microsoft data centre had managed to secure connections ahead of the shortages—thus contributing to these shortages—and was preparing to open its data centre. The deficit in transmission capacity was a limitation for numerous projects in the region. Municipal plans to develop train connections in the region and citizen projects to generate solar power through their own photovoltaics (PV) installations were affected. Local companies and industries announced plans to move elsewhere (Libertson et al., 2021). The capacity deficit also resulted in queues for power grid connections that could extend to years depending on how large a connection a client would request.

Grid operators in Sweden are obliged to connect anyone who wants a connection to the grid within a two-year period or less (Swedish Energy Markets Inspectorate, 2021). When Microsoft requested a connection to the local power grid, the operator E.ON could not reject it as long as there were available capacities at the time of request, irrespective of whether granting connection would lead to capacity deficits and delays in connections for other industries. The mandate to connect anyone produces universal access to electricity as a public value, a value historically related to the development of a welfare state in Sweden. Developments such as those with the Microsoft data centre put pressure on this value not only locally but also nationally in many major towns in Sweden which, coincidentally, also host many data centres. For example, in the region of Stockholm, a data centre industrial park called "Stockholm Data Parks", established by the city of Stockholm, energy companies, and a fibre optic infrastructure provider has come to a standstill. The park is branded as "sustainable" and low carbon because it would heat the town with excess heat from data centres; however, no data centres can be built there at present because data centres in other areas of the town, together with electrifying industries and other large electricity producers, have claimed such a large volume of electricity that there are no significant capacities available in the capital. Therefore, the data centres that are part of Stockholm Data Parks are in queue until 2030, when more grid capacity is expected to become available (Stockholm City, 2025).

Deficits in grid capacity reflect a misalignment in the temporalities of scaling between data and energy infrastructure, thus compromising the public value of universal and equal access to electricity in Sweden. These issues come on top of already existing internal misalignments within the energy system—for example, between the locations where electricity is generated and where it is consumed, thus creating imbalances and the prospect of power cuts. They also put pressure on renewables that have to be produced in greater quantities to make data centres "sustainable", thus generating even further misalignments.[3]

[3] For example, the current demand for computing power for AI systems has sparked conversations regarding the production of more nuclear power and building modular nuclear reactors to be colocated with data centers (Stover, 2024), which raise societal conflicts regarding nuclear waste handling, siting, and public health.

Realignments: Upscaling Electricity Grids

The situation of the capacity deficit in Skåne triggered massive local and national efforts to produce more capacity in the power grid. The regional grid operator E.ON upgraded several transformers, entered into a new contract with a transmission line called Baltic Cable between Sweden and Germany, installed a new system to load balance transmission, and—from 2021 onwards—promoted algorithmic solutions that enticed people to shift their practices of cooking or charging cars, their use of electricity in general to free grid capacities at times when those were most needed from the perspective of the power grid (E.ON, 2025). These measures made available 1 TW of power, the equivalent of all Malmö's energy demand on a cold day. Despite its magnitude, politicians and regional grid operators deemed the new capacity insufficient in light of expected future demand by data centres, municipal electrification projects, and electrifying industries (Skånes effektkommission NET, 2025). They anticipated even higher demand and braced themselves for the need to produce even more power.

Further, the regional and municipal administrations as well as grid operator E.ON anticipated a historical increase in demand for electricity that called for what they saw as a historical upscaling of grids. Projects were launched to forecast future capacity needs (Effektprognoser, 2025). A commission on expanding the grid in Skåne was initiated in 2024; the commission reported a year later on the reinforcement projects that enabled connecting new clients that were consuming electricity equivalent to all of Malmö's energy demand. The grid operator, E.ON went to look for customers that could use all this new future capacity while being unable to handle new connections to the grid until the grid was expanded. These reactions expose, in yet another manner, the internal misalignments within the electricity system and the differing dynamics of scaling of cloud computing and energy grids. Electricity grids have to be planned long-term, years ahead, and when customers are not yet in place. Data centres mushroom wherever land is cheap and where providers can find available electricity instead of being driven by the logic of hyper-scalable cloud computing. In this misalignment, from being the source of a problem, data centres for AI re-emerge as the solution of the problem by becoming prospective customers who can justify the upscaling of the grid. A report by the Swedish national grid operator, Svenska Kraftnät, suggests that a significant proportion of these new customers will likely be data centres for AI, arguing that the grid must urgently expand to handle more demand: "The largest requests for connections of data centres amount to 500 MW of capacity from the grid, which is often difficult to realise without reinforcements of the grid" (Svenska Kraftnät, 2019, p. 13), they write, calling for more powerlines across the country.

These frenetic efforts to scale up the electricity grid expose how low carbon hyper-scalable cloud computing is created through the relationships with resources and infrastructures in concrete places with very different logics of scaling. As Anna Tsing writes, scalability efforts are always incomplete, and the inability of an infrastructure to scale exposes the failures of scaling projects (Tsing, 2012, p. 510). Electricity grids in many regions in Sweden simply fail to scale in keeping with the scales at which computing operates. In this case, infrastructural misalignment emerges as a problem of rescaling and of identifying the right scale of entangled infrastructure that would help align the compromised values of economic growth and public access to energy.

Overcoming misalignment between entangled infrastructures demands re-alignments among different values embedded in infrastructure and among different infrastructure logics. The different ways in which these realignments are executed define the premises for whom infrastructures will work, who will they prioritise and exclude, and for how long they will work. They are the core of infrastructure politics and can produce both wealth and violence (Anand et al., 2018; Rodgers & O'Neill, 2012).

In Sweden, contemporary attempts to align electricity grids to the demands of different industries envisions a major nationwide upscaling of the backbone power grid in the country for AI. The upscaling of grids is undoubtedly a lucrative business: it implies more sales for grid operators of very expensive transmission capacity that generates economic gains not just for Big Tech cloud operators but also for the energy industry. In Sweden, a major driver in the upscaling is Svenska Kraftnät, the state-owned authority tasked to plan, maintain, and operate the electricity transmission grid as well as its substations and international connections. The authority develops both the transmission grid and the electricity market in Sweden with the mandate to provide a safe, environmentally sustainable, and economically viable supply of electricity in the country and describes itself as an important actor in Sweden's climate policy (Svenska Kraftnät, 2019).

Until recently, Svenska Kraftnät focused on how to export unused energy production, thereby reinforcing transmission lines within the country to enable export. Following the crises in transmission capacities in Skåne and a few other regions, the national grid operator issued a 10-year plan for reinforcing and upscaling the grid in Sweden in general (Svenska Kraftnät, 2019). The plan involves major extensions of the grid that involve building new powerlines as well as reinforcing major existing substations and regional transmission infrastructure over the decade. The general motivation, as declared in the 10-year plan that the organisation published, is to respond to the expectations of different actors on the power grid to meet what they call the needs of "societal developments" as well as new needs, while also simultaneously helping Sweden achieve its political and environmental goals within the domain of energy (Svenska Kraftnät, 2019, p. 77). In other words, upscaling the grid is a means of aligning the grid to the appropriate transmission capacities to cover new demand.

The societal developments that the 10-year plan specifies are a combination of increased energy use by urban regions as a result of existing data centre establishments, the shutdown of local electricity production (implied to be the closure of certain nuclear power plants) that has created deficits in transmission and production capacities in many areas, and an anticipated surge in electricity demand from data centres. While there are no public numbers available, Svenska Kraftnät indicates that data centres could request capacities in the range of up to 300 MW–500 MW, which is comparable to the scale of a medium-sized Swedish town (Svenska Kraftnät, 2019, p. 13). The urban areas which face the most capacity deficit are Stockholm, Uppsala, and Malmö and Mälardalen. Except for Uppsala, the other two are places with already a high concentration of data centres or the establishment of Big Tech companies that provide computation resources following the hyper-scalability logic.

It must be noted that data centres are named as just one of four reasons to expand the grid, with the other three being to increase the ability of the grid to connect new wind power plant projects to the grid, to maintain and increase capacity to be able to sell electricity domestically and internationally, and to maintain or replace ageing elements of the power grid (Svenska Kraftnät, 2019). Of these three reasons, wind power is again indirectly related to the expansion of data centres and computation capacities. By their own accounts, a few of the major companies in the business of hyper-scalable cloud computing—Microsoft, Google, Amazon—have all proclaimed themselves as the largest buyers of newly installed renewable power energy. Specifically, in the Nordic countries, these companies have emerged as important subsidiaries of wind power plant projects, as Big Tech derisks investments in unprofitable wind power projects by committing to buy their electricity for 10–15 years; this makes the production of wind power plants lucrative for investors (Christophers, 2022). As the power grid in Sweden scales up to meet the needs of hyper-scalable computing in its multifarious forms, such as data centres and wind power generation facilities, new problems and misalignments emerge.

One such crucial misalignment is concerned with the divergent temporal horizons of cloud computing and electricity grids. The main sales pitch of hyper-scalable computing is that any computing resource, large or small, can be delivered on demand. Electricity grids can obviously not be rescaled on demand and neither can data centres. The responses to realign electricity grids to the demand of electricity driven by hyper-scalable computing are geared towards achieving greater alignment with the scalability logic of cloud computing. Energy planners do it on their own terms and time horizons. Svenska Kraftnät admits that it takes 10–12 years on average from decision to operation to expand the grid, which is apparently too long a time "when put against the expectations to be able to transition industrial manufacturing from fossil fuels to electricity, build data centres, or new housing" (Svenska Kraftnät, 2019, p. 19).

Their solution is to shorten permission times by managing different processes in parallel, particularly to begin the process of planning for new powerlines before the concession rights to operate the power lines are granted. In this manner, the time taken to install a new powerline might be reduced by 8–10 years, which is still considered too long by grid operators. However, planning for powerlines involves handling conflicts with citizens, such as farmers, indigenous people, potential archaeological sites, cultural and industrial heritage, and environments with their human and non-human inhabitants. Issues of justice and conflicts of values are bound to emerge there as well.

The Swedish Energy Markets Inspectorate (Ei) anticipates working with regions and different agencies, such as the Swedish mapping, cadastral, and land registration authority to shorten the permission processes for expanding the grid. In anticipation of conflicts, administrators in Skåne admit that in their region, this would require dialogue with communities regarding land use and siting as well as work on the aesthetic designs of substations to resolve conflicts with citizens (Skånes effektkommission NET, 2025, p. 13). The large-scale expansion of the grid in Skåne will also require agricultural land and will claim land from private owners, potentially generating disputes.

As hyper-scalable cloud computing exerts pressure on public values and generates social conflicts around already built infrastructure, upscaling and shortening temporalities of grid planning multiplies the arenas in which societal conflicts might manifest. Upscaling power grids also changes the nature of the conflicts, from disputes over access to electricity to those over land governance issues. Rather than alignments among the values of the hyper-scalability of cloud computing and universal access to electricity, the focus of responses shifts to solving issues around power grid expansion. These responses transform how power grids in Sweden are governed as well. They reduce the temporalities of power grid planning, create new arenas of contestation, and transform the administrative processes that govern these developments.

In the meantime, until power grids scale up, cloud computing infrastructure operators are adapting to longer timelines and plan with longer connections, slowing down expansions of computing infrastructures dedicated to AI systems. This temporal misalignment between the business model for on-demand AI through cloud computing, the production of data centres in anticipation of demand, and the need to search and wait for connections to power grids already generates anxiety in the data centre industries. In other words, while power grid infrastructure operators and municipalities make ten-year plans for infrastructure upscaling and are changing their work practices, the tech industry might have already moved somewhere else in search for more power, creating new misalignments and leaving infrastructure in ruins (see Brodie & Velkova, 2021; Velkova, 2025).

So, What About Sustainability?

The hyper-scalability logic around which cloud computing is currently organised enables digital companies to expand, to experiment with AI model development, and to be extremely successful (Narayan 2022). This success is premised upon pushing entangled infrastructures in misalignment in ways that affect public values. Internal misalignments as well as different spatial and temporal logics of scaling result either in shortages in computing power or in local shortages in electricity that compromise the public value of equal access to energy in Sweden. A close examination of these processes calls for more nuanced discussions on sustainability that could begin with analyses of infrastructure misalignment and attempts to realign infrastructure, thus focusing on the internal contradictions within and between digital and energy systems as well as how they promote or compromise public values of equal access to basic infrastructure.

Further, the attempts to scale up power grids as a form of alignment to hyper-scalable computing are also fragile and precarious. Power grids have slower and longer temporalities than computing infrastructure, different materialities, professional cultures, markets and regulations. In contrast, the hype around AI today calls for limitless computing here and now, organised around endless scalability. Therefore, even if grids would expand in Sweden over the next decade, as planned, companies in business with AI can easily claim these capacities too, as policymakers attempt to boost the development of computing infrastructure and prioritise it over other sectors. Thus, while cloud computing benefits from the principle of universal access to energy for everyone in Sweden, data centre operators de facto monopolise power grids, crowding out other industries and competitors, including other actors from the data centre industries.

In this context, it is unsurprising to see efforts by resourceful companies—such as Amazon, Microsoft, and Google—to invest in dedicated powerlines and even power plants, thus fending off the pressures on power grids that these very same companies are contributing to create and leading to further monopolisation and misalignments in energy production and grid management.

Importantly, the infrastructural misalignments and responses to them that I have discussed here are not exhaustive or universal by any means. They play out differently in different settings shaped by their histories, people, and industries. In certain places, they might not manifest as conflicts over energy at all but could take shape as conflicts over water infrastructure instead (Lehuedé, 2024; Valdivia, 2024). In this context, a focus on infrastructure misalignments offers a means to reimagine ways of creating aligned futures of entangled data centres and other infrastructures in ways that promote rather than compromise public values. More harmonic alignments might demand a different pace of scaling computing or different ways of organising computing altogether, following not where land is cheap and connectivity best but where there would be the least pressure on local infrastructure, communities, and industries. In other words, we need a different form of computing and varied ethical and economic models for it; such models must be considerate of the interrelations among data centre industries, which have entangled infrastructures, in ways that protect public values.

Acknowledgements I am grateful to Minna Ruckenstein, Maria Eidenskog, Harald Rohracher, Anne Mollen, Fieke Jansen and Sigrid Kannengießer for their engagement, close reading, and invaluable comments that enriched the text; as well as the REIMAGINE-ADM project team, and the seminar *AI Infrastructures and Democracy* hosted by Stefania Milan for opportunities to discuss earlier versions of this chapter.

The chapter was developed with the support of the "Megabytes vs Megawatts" research project funded by the Marianne and Marcus Wallenberg Foundation, grant no. MMW 2022.0070 and the REIMAGINE-ADM project supported by FORTE, under CHANSE ERA-NET Co-fund programme, which has received funding from the European Union's Horizon 2020 Research and Innovation Programme, under Grant Agreement no. 101004509. Julia Velkova's work is also supported by the Profutura Scientia programme of Swedish Collegium for Advanced Studies and the Riksbankens Jubileumsfond in Sweden.

References

Anand, N., Gupta, A., & Appel, H. (Eds.). (2018). *The promise of infrastructure*. Duke University Press.

Bresnihan, P., & Brodie, P. (2023). Data sinks, carbon services: Waste, storage, and energy cultures on Ireland's peat bogs. *New Media & Society, 2*(25), 361–383.

Brevini, B. (2022). *Is AI good for the planet?* Polity Press.

Brodie, P., & Velkova, J. (2021). Cloud ruins: Ericsson's Vaudreuil data centre and infrastructural abandonment. *Information, Communication & Society, 24*(6), 869–885.

Christophers, B. (2022). Taking renewables to market: Prospects for the after-subsidy energy transition. *Antipode, 54*(5), 1519–1544.

Chun, W. H. K. (2017). *Updating to remain the same: Habitual new media (1st MIT press new paperback edition)*. MIT Press.

Cubitt, S. (2017). *Finite media: Environmental implications of digital technologies*. Duke University Press.

Dovbysh, O., Laaksonen, S. M., & Pantti, M. (Eds.). (2025). *Platforms and the planet: Digital platforms and environmental responsibility*. Emerald Publishing.

Edwards, D., Cooper, Z. G. T., & Hogan, M. (2024). The making of critical data centre studies. *Convergence: The International Journal of Research into New Media Technologies*.

Effektprognoser. (2025). *Framtidens elanvändning och effektbehov på karta*. Retrieved April 11, 2025, from https://effektprognoser.se/om-projektet/
Ensmenger, N. (2018). The environmental history of computing. *Technology and Culture, 59*(4), 7–33.
E.ON. (2025). *Switch*. Retrieved April 11, 2025, from https://www.eon.se/foeretag/elnaet/switch
Hammond, G., & Morris, S. (2022, July 28). *West London faces new homes ban as electricity grid hits capacity*. Financial Times. https://www.ft.com/content/519f701f-6a05-4cf4-bc46-22cf10c7c2c0
Hu, T. H. (2015). *A prehistory of the cloud*. The MIT Press.
Kuntsman, A., & Rattle, I. (2019). Towards a paradigmatic shift in sustainability studies: A systematic review of peer-reviewed literature and future agenda-setting to consider environmental (un)sustainability of digital communication. *Environmental Communication, 13*(5), 567–581.
Larkin, B. (2013). The politics and poetics of infrastructure. *Annual Review of Anthropology, 42*(1), 327–343.
Lehtiniemi, T. (2024). Contextual social valences for artificial intelligence: Anticipation that matters in social work. *Information, Communication & Society, 27*(6), 1110–1125.
Lehuedé, S. (2024). An elemental ethics for artificial intelligence: Water as resistance within AI's value chain. *AI & Society*.
Libertson, F., Velkova, J., & Palm, J. (2021). Data-centre infrastructure and energy gentrification: Perspectives from Sweden. *Sustainability: Science, Practice and Policy, 17*(1), 153–162.
Luccioni, A. S., Jernite, Y., & Strubell, E. (2023). *Power hungry processing: Watts driving the cost of AI deployment?* ACM Conference on Fairness, Accountability, and Transparency (ACM FAccT '24), June 3–6, 2024, Rio de Janeiro. https://doi.org/10.48550/arXiv.2311.16863
Marks, L. U. (2024). Collapse informatics and the environmental impact of information and communication technologies. In A. Lopez, A. Ivakhiv, S. Rust, M. Tola, A. Y. Chang, & K. Chu (Eds.), *The Routledge handbook of ecomedia studies* (pp. 119–128). Routledge.
Maxwell, R., & Miller, T. (2012). *Greening the media*. Oxford University Press.
Microsoft. (2021). *Idag öppnar Microsofts hållbara datacenter i Sverige – skapar nya möjligheter för Sverige genom hållbar digitalisering. Microsoft Website*. https://news.microsoft.com/sv-se/2021/11/16/idag-oppnar-microsofts-hallbara-datacenter-i-sverige-skapar-nya-mojligheter-for-sverige-genom-hallbar-digitalisering/
Microsoft. (2025). *Amplify human ingenuity*. Retrieved April 11, 2025, from https://azure.microsoft.com/en-gb/

Narayan, D. (2022). Monopolisation and competition under platform capitalism: Analysing transformations in the computing industry. *New Media & Society, 25*(2), 287–306.

Ortar, N., Taylor, A. R. E., Velkova, J., Brodie, P., Johnson, A., Marquet, C., et al. (2023). Powering 'smart' futures: Data centres and the energy politics of digitalisation. In S. Abram, K. Waltorp, N. Ortar, & S. Pink (Eds.), *Energy futures: Anthropocene challenges, emerging technologies and everyday life*. De Gruyter.

Parks, L., Velkova, J., & De Ridder, S. (Eds.). (2023). *Media backends: Digital infrastructures and sociotechnical relations*. University of Illinois Press.

Pasek, A., Lin, C. K., Cooper, Z. G. T., & Kinder, J. B. (2023). *Digital energetics*. University of Minnesota Press.

Pasek, A., Vaughan, H., & Starosielski, N. (2023). The world wide web of carbon: Towards a relational footprinting of information and communications technology's climate impacts. *Big Data & Society, 10*(1), 1–12.

Powell, A. (2024). *AI is expensive*. http://eprints.lse.ac.uk/id/eprint/124175

Rodgers, D., & O'Neill, B. (2012). Infrastructural violence: Introduction to the special issue. *Ethnography, 13*(4), 401–412.

Ruckenstein, M., & Turunen, L. L. M. (2019). Re-humanizing the platform: Content moderators and the logic of care. *New Media & Society, 22*(6), 1026–1042.

Salling, C. A., & Winthereik, B. R. (2025). Inventorying data: Circumvented investment conditions by Big Tech's supply chain capitalism. *Journal of Cultural Economy, 18*(2), 266–283.

Selin, A. (2018). *Amazons etablering: Elnätet klarar inte fler stora företag*. Sveriges Radio. https://www.sverigesradio.se/artikel/amazons-etablering-elnatet-klarar-inte-fler-stora-foretag

Skånes effektkommission NET. (2025). *Skåne rustar för framtiden Så säkrar vi regionens elförsörjning tillsammans*. Utveckling Skåne. Retrieved from https://utveckling.skane.se/regional-utveckling/verksamhetsomraden/energiforsorjning/skanes-effektkommission/fokusgrupp-distribution/skanes-effektkommission-net/

Soben. (2025). *Data centre trends 2025: Power, AI, and Progress*. https://media.datacenterdynamics.com/media/documents/WP_-_Soben_Data_Centre_Trends_2025-compressed_-_Alex_Brady.pdf

Star, S. L., & Bowker, G. (2004). How to infrastructure. In L. A. Lievrouw & S. Livingstone (Eds.), *Handbook of new media: Social shaping and consequences of ICTs* (Reprint, pp. 151–162). SAGE.

Stockholm City. (2025). *Serverhallar med återvinning av överskottsvärme*. Retrieved April 11, 2025, from https://vaxer.stockholm/projekt/akalla/serverhallar-med-atervinning-av-overskottsvarme/

Suchman, L. (1987). *Plans and situated actions: The problem of human-machine communication*. Cambridge University Press.

Svenska Kraftnät. (2019). *En statusuppdatering om läget i kraftsystemet: Systemutvecklingsplan 2020–2029*. Sundbyberg. https://www.svk.se/siteassets/om-oss/rapporter/2019/systemutvecklingsplan2020-2029.pdf

Swedish Energy Markets Inspectorate. (2021). *Granskning av tidsåtgång för anslutning till elnätet* (No. PM – Ei PM2021:05). https://ei.se/download/18.508b968217d0e6c213a1550c/1638451004574/Granskning-av-tids%C3%A5tg%C3%A5ng-f%C3%B6r-anslutning-till-eln%C3%A4tet-Ei-PM2021-05.pdf

Taylor, A. R. E. (2021). Future-proof: Bunkered data centres and the selling of ultra-secure cloud storage. *Journal of the Royal Anthropological Institute, 27*(S1), 76–94.

Tsing, A. L. (2012). On non-scalability. *Common Knowledge, 18*(3), 505–524.

Valdivia, A. (2024). The supply chain capitalism of AI: A call to (re)think algorithmic harms and resistance through environmental lens. *Information, Communication & Society*, 1–17.

van Dijck, J., Poell, T., & de Waal, M. (2018). *The platform society*. Oxford University Press.

Velkova, J. (2019). Data centres as impermanent infrastructures. *Culture Machine, 18*.

Velkova, J. (2021). Thermopolitics of data: Cloud infrastructures and energy futures. *Cultural Studies, 35*(4–5), 663–683.

Velkova, J. (2025). Data infrastructures and their temporalities. In T. Venturini, A. Acker, J. Plantin, & T. Walford (Eds.), *Sage Handbook of Data and Society*. SAGE Publications.

Vertesi, J. (2014). Seamful spaces: Heterogeneous infrastructures in interaction. *Science, Technology, & Human Values, 39*(2), 264–284.

Williams, R. (1974). *Television: Technology and cultural form*. Routledge.

Yerushalmy, J. (2023, March 28). *Norwegian company says TikTok data centre is limiting energy for manufacturing Ukraine ammunition*. The Guardian. https://www.theguardian.com/technology/2023/mar/28/energy-hungry-tiktok-data-centre-ukraine-ammunition-production-nammo-norway

Zakharova, I., Jarke, J., & Kaun, A. (2024). Tensions in digital welfare states: Three perspectives on care and control. *Journal of Sociology, 60*(3), 540–559.

CHAPTER 6

Aquaculture, AI, and Planetary Domestication

Patrick Brodie

Introduction

This chapter will introduce the material implications of "cloud" and artificial intelligence (AI)-driven technologies by analysing their use and application on relatively novel (blue) terrain: aquaculture. Fish farming has seen a recent digital boom, as companies seek to innovate their cultivation and extraction measures by applying data-driven and machine-learning technologies to their operations. While AI is increasingly deployed as a silver bullet for sustainability in industries not known for their "green" credentials, from mining to industrial agriculture (Arboleda, 2020; Barney, 2022), this chapter analyses how AI systems are not only rehabilitating industrial images via digital greenwashing but materially shaping industrial futures. With calls for "green" and "blue"

P. Brodie (✉)
University College Dublin, Dublin, Ireland
e-mail: patrick.brodie@ucd.ie

A. Mollen et al. (eds.), *AI Infrastructures and Sustainability*, Palgrave Studies in European Communication Research and Education,
https://doi.org/10.1007/978-3-032-09748-4_6

new deals coalescing,[1] digital technologies are increasingly tasked with calculatively managing planetary resources for intensified forms of value extraction, mobilising "stocks" of measurable resources towards "flows" of goods and services in and through the "environment" (Barney, 2022). Managing the "blue economy" for green profit becomes an imperative inextricably entangled with the proliferation of sensing, mapping, and surveying the oceans and freshwater systems for resources. In what ways do the "cloud," and its facilitation of AI and machine-learning, operate to manage these processes within planetary limits?

Answering this question will provide preliminary research into the political ecology of data, as the geographers Jenny Goldstein and Eric Nost (2022) have referred to the growing interdisciplinary interest in how digital data operates within socio-ecological systems. In my analysis, this can be productively observed through the integration of advanced digital technologies into food production at the perceived planetary "frontiers" of green capital—and, specifically, through the processes of domestication that are made viable through scaled efficiencies in digitally-enabled tools of monitoring and intervening in fish stocks. Thinking through theories of the metabolic rift and "green extractivism" as applied in and through aquacultural (and agricultural) efficiencies, this chapter demonstrates that the regimes of calculability being innovated by and through digital technologies are intensifying rather than ameliorating the so-called "externalities" of capitalist growth.

To demonstrate this, I consider the context of AI platforms in fish farming. Beginning with a conceptual overview, the chapter then focuses on examples of these applications in action from both discursive and material standpoints. Multiple AI-driven aquatech companies have emerged over the past five years or so, using big tech cloud software and infrastructures. In many cases, these platforms are direct spinoff companies or have shareholders from big tech. To name a few, specifically related to big tech:

[1] In response to wide recognition of "green deals" of widespread infrastructural transformation for sustainability, the Sustainable Ocean Alliance in 2021 called for a "Global Blue New Deal," utilising similar arguments about the social transformation of oceanic activities.

- Tidal, the Alphabet X start-up, which spun off in 2024—Alphabet still has a significant minority stake in the company, which utilises Google cloud
- Aquabyte, which is partnered with AWS to deliver its solutions (its former tech lead jumped ship and went to Tidal once they spun off—AI fish farming appears a small ecosystem still)
- Microsoft has enabled and promoted a number of projects with start-ups and producers from South America to East Asia

Each project parrots roughly the same information, and promotes the same aims: sustainably feed the planet; optimise production of fish (largely as biomass, fixing the biomass to feed ratio); increase fish welfare; scale up production; and eventually, introduce an automated fish farm, as Aquabyte promises at the end of one AWS-sponsored webinar from 2019 (AWS Events, 2019). After analysing the politics and implications of some of these and related projects, the chapter concludes with considerations as to the planetary implications of this "teaching the cloud to fish."

Farming Fish and Farming Data at Green Frontiers

In recent years, there has been a necessary uptick in critical social scientific work addressing the datafication of environmental systems—from the "political ecology of data" (Nost & Goldstein, 2022) to the situation of the "planetary" computing apparatuses of sensing and predicting climate variations (Edwards, 2010; Gabrys, 2017), scholars have been critically approaching the nexus of "natural" measurement and calculabilities with the expansion of digital systems and their applications in wider aspects of life and economies. While there has been a wealth of research surrounding digital sensing and environmental data practices for climate action (Gabrys, 2017; Lin, 2022; Nafus, 2023; Nost, 2022; Vera et al., 2019), and the market-driven sectors of climate finance and carbon crediting have been analysed (and critiqued) in detail (Bumpus & Liverman, 2008; Lippert, 2016; Nelson & Bigger, 2022; Robertson, 2012), there has been less critical engagement with how one constitutes and makes possible the other (for exceptions, see Buck, 2022; Pasek, 2019; Whitington, 2020; Wiessner, 2024). We must confront the discursive and material economies that connect the phenomenon of datafication explicitly in lockstep with the expansion of green capitalism and its distinct calculative rationalities—which are increasingly advanced through the application of AI.

The work of the political ecology of data also makes clear that regimes of data-driven knowing and decision-making are inseparable from the infrastructures that enable their proliferation (Lally et al., 2022). These are extensions of the same capitalist epistemologies that produce "nature" for ecological value—a fact that can be productively applied to much existing work in critical data studies on the overtly extractive (and oftentimes racist, classist, sexist, and otherwise biased) algorithmic rationality and its regimes of knowledge. As Paula Ricaurte defines this era of advanced datafication,

> Data-driven rationality is supported by infrastructures of knowledge production developed by states, corporations, and research centers situated mainly in Western countries and an economic system that supports capital accumulation and economic growth. This economic model, based on epistemic dominance, is reflected in research agendas and funding. … Furthermore, entire infrastructure of the Internet supports transactions, flows, and interactions that convert any form of existence in a possible source of data. … our universe of objects and spaces has…been transformed into knowledge that fuels capital accumulation and power concentration. (2019, p. 351)

Ricaurte is speaking specifically from the analytical perspective of "data colonialism," an extension of theories that assume that the primary value of datafication is produced from its colonisation, harnessing, and extraction of value from social activity and "human life" (Couldry & Mejias, 2019). Applied to the landscape of environmental datafication, this theory runs into productive frictions. Datafication is typically embedded in mechanisms of public governance and regulation—as Adrienne Buller notes, much of the pricing of carbon, for example, is based on policies towards state penalising emissions rather than necessarily positively ascribing it value (2022). The technoscientific dimensions that this introduces across policy, science, and industry acts as a channelling mechanism for these regimes of valuation—not necessarily overtly extractive, but involved in a process of representation, quantification, and legibility, pre-empting the formation of the resource drawn from "nature" by first making it calculable (Liboiron, 2021).

As we can see, the primary assumptions surrounding the extractive dimensions of datafication already start to dissolve when dealing with the material realities of ecology and elemental circulations. The technoscientific process of "resource-making" is a process of management at multiple points in this value chain, increasingly enabled by the regimes of expanded datafication by and for AI. Geographer Gavin Bridge outlines that the concerns of "resource-making" for social scientists mean that we must "understand the political, economic and cultural processes through which particular configurations of socionature become imagined, appropriated and commodified" (2011, p. 821). That "socionature," as Bridge defines it, is part of a process of epistemological intervention and construction of material value that collapses the human/nature distinction as an overtly intentional mechanism. And this intention is being deepened—and further valorised—in the social investment in "sustainability."

In this sense, we should both salvage extractivism as a helpful heuristic for conceiving of regimes of datafication that are, at their core, about displacing and outsourcing the harms and contradictions of data-driven capitalism. At the same time, we must recognise that what often gets called the "extractive epistemologies" of datafication are more so about the management of rifting in particular ways when applied to environmental systems directly. This means that the efficient management of so-called externalities is outsourced to the "cloud" in a process of material abstraction, while simultaneously expanding necessary sites of material extraction (and its externalities) across proliferating frontiers. This extensive and intensive dynamic of extractive datafication is the result of two contradictory processes: the planetary management of resources via the productive efficiencies of digitalisation, alongside the expanding externalities of such efficiencies (Brodie, 2023). These are technoscientific processes that enable capitalist abstraction at multiple points in capitalist value chains and in different ways, to be sure, which deepens extractive epistemologies and practices into new and changing resource regimes. However, these are not just sited processes, but geographically directional mechanisms and situational applications in and through institutional orientations of technoscience-for-sustainability.

Scholars at the intersection of data and the "environment" can draw from the theory of the "metabolic rift," a foundational eco-Marxist dictum surrounding the originary disruption of ecological systems towards the capitalist production of value. As political ecologist Jason Moore notes, this theory has long—since the publication of John Bellamy Foster's Marx's Ecology in 2000—served to effectively reify "the environment" as an object of analysis for critical environmental thought.

But as Moore rescues the theory (2017), it presents a point of analysis for how the organising impulse of capitalism serves itself to instrumentalise the nature/society binary towards the production of new frontiers for valorisation. Whether conceived as "separation" or "disruption" of a primordial harmony, the nexus of this supposed binary is always available to capital because capital is foundationally a relation of production situated in and operating through so-called nature, whether in agriculture or the exploitation of industrial labour. The point being: whether reified (and naturalised) as a binary or as a somehow ecosystemic function, capital endeavours ceaselessly towards accumulation, which produces externalising effects through the production process. This is a dialectical process—value-in-motion, through so-called nature. Whatever project of correcting or stopping the "rift" needs to remove that core function of capital prior to proposing truly "sustainable" alternatives that do not rest on this relation.[2]

What is crucial to note here is that the theory of the metabolic rift concerns the moment—and knock on effects—of this disruption into the forms of management necessary to maintain production, in spite of the "exhaustion" of soil ecologies and other localised relations (see Chaudhary, 2024). For as long as the theory of the metabolic rift has been conceived, for example, it has always rested upon this exhaustion in one place towards the accumulation of capital, and this is especially prominent in the "colonies" or, today, the peripheries and semi-peripheries. The most prominent examples of the "rift" remain arguably these former colonies, peripheralised places, and semi-peripheral economies—like Ireland, Norway, Scotland, or Chile, where these experiments in industrial technoscience are being enacted to harness and harvest salmon ecologies. So even if primordial exhaustion now marches ahead towards harnessing and managing these knock-on effects of a disrupted ecology—the instrumentalisation of the human/nature binary towards a self-perpetuating schema of ecosystemic capture and profit accumulation constitutes continual process of rifting that continues to require exhaustion as its byproducts, and promotes green, digital technoscience to reduce and offset these inefficiencies of planetary ecology. It is the further production of an ecosystem—by managing and organising the necessary byproducts and externalities of intensified efficiencies, at scale.

[2] This is a crude summary of Moore (2017).

The suturing of AI into these systems of production is thus not just crass AI accelerationism, as one might cynically dismiss—it's an imaginary of a planet in which AI is not only a necessary, but an inescapable element of sustaining life dependent upon continued capitalist production and growth. And this is an image that should trouble us, when extractive logics are so entrenched as to become not only concretised through machines, but automated by machines through ecologies. As Xiaowei Wang argues in the context of the use of AI in Chinese pig farming as a mechanism of expanding the market for pork amidst health and sustainability challenges, "These technologies go on to make pork cheap, driving even more availability and demand, as people start to believe pork is a necessary part of their diet. AI is not the balm to any problem—it is just one piece of the ever-hungry quest for scale" (2020). What Moore would call "cheap nature" is produced by AI-driven efficiencies for endlessly scalable growth.

What are the core planetary values, assumptions, and temporalities encoded when corporations endeavour to "farm" solutions in the cloud? As Darin Barney and I have argued elsewhere,

> the 'farm' has become a commonplace way to describe extractive operations located in rural settings whose primary function (beyond capital accumulation) is to contribute to solving the environmental problems of cities, or 'the planet.' Data centres ('server farms'), turbine complexes ('wind farms'), photovoltaic panel arrays ('solar farms'), replanted forests ('tree farms'), aquaculture operations ('fish farms') and even land stewardship practices configured for carbon sequestration in soils ('carbon farms') together comprise the infrastructures of 'decarbonization' and 'sustainability' that make demands on the rural landscapes where they are typically located. The degrees and manner to which they return observable benefits are ambiguous, unstable and unevenly distributed. As sites of automated harvesting, computing, energy production, and carbon sequestration, these are often farms without farmers, at least in the traditional sense, a dramatic development in contexts where rurality has long been associated with farming communities. (Brodie & Barney, 2026)

Pressing on "farming" as an increasingly central metaphor in the green, digital alignments of industrialisation means also confronting the distinct technoscientific ideologies and practices being enacted. As the STS scholar Marianne Lien demonstrates, making salmon legible as a controllable "resource" is foundationally a process of domestication—central to any process of "farming" in human history (2015). While painting a perhaps too-tidy portrait of these histories, she gestures towards the distinction and genealogy of commodities from resources to domesticated things—which, while always a form of "culturing," as she denotes, also carries with it, in capitalist societies at least, a suggestion of landed expansion and scaling. In the case of fish farming, the technoscientific processes that came with domesticating salmon—fish pens further offshore, the technological monitoring of stocks, the selective breeding of species—all required capital to scale, as the process was never profitable enough for small farmers to be worthwhile. Fish farming became quite quickly an endeavour dominated by those with the infrastructural and land-based capacities to scale offshore, to the tricky (aquatic) terrain of ocean and sea. As Aquabyte founder Bryton Shang suggests, fish farmers are used to advanced technological mediation, and at the very least a necessary distance from their stocks (SiliconANGLE theCUBE, 2020)—fish arrive to shore or deck transported through tubes rather than harvested by hand or line.

Technological efficiencies and scale are necessary to domesticate this otherwise unruly species. Susanne Bauer argues, in a recent article on what she calls "salmon modelling" as a "response to policy calls for more sustainable aquaculture" that "Different from traditional bench work in the laboratory and biochemistry's 'experimental systems' and 'epistemic things' ... digital platforms in systems biology give rise to blended and distributed research configurations ... digital models may raise different questions about knowledge infrastructures, already well-known in information systems studies of cooperative practices" (2024, pp. 526–527). She continues, to "describe the chains of extraction and optimizations in and beyond the lab, such as in distributed repositories and in nutrition interventions set up as health promotion work in Norwegian primary schools" you must show "how data extracted from different experimental settings enroll both fish and humans into calculative infrastructures for *preemptive optimization*" (pp. 527–529, my emphasis). Resonating with Ricaurte's theory of the epistemic functions of data colonialism, the technoscientific decisions and practices enacted in a lab, fed by data from the field modelled in and through digital systems, are in themselves a prerequisite for scientific subjects to become commodities—for example, salmon. In short, as Bauer suggests, "digital models extract, transform, and digest—metabolize—data for specific modes of seeing and acting in the world" (2024, p. 529). Those specific modes are increasingly modes of "sustainable" commodity and value production—even if first imaginatively rendered towards sustainability offsets, they can become infrastructuralised in a way, especially if these software platforms become essential to the scalable function of the industry. What Bauer suggests is that data-driven modelling is increasingly mobilised as a part of this wider extractive ecology—rendering fish legible, alongside reducing contingencies such as health and pollution externalities, in order to become harnessed and valuable.

When a fish becomes data, it is in and of itself a resource that, put together with other fish and other data, makes the productive machinery of the fish farm run faster and more efficiently. But a fish is not data—a fish only becomes data through the sensing and computational processes that incorporate a fish's biometric and other information into and through electronic devices. Google-backed fish farming start-up Tidal's "fishal recognition" (see below) is in part the same biometric and volumetric measurement devices used for human biopolitical monitoring. But the politics of surveillance tech have at the same time a more and less extractive dimension when dealing with food: this is about rendering something legible as raw material for harvesting; while at the same time, that material is only useful for efficient harvesting and the training of AI models to optimise that harvesting into the future, rather than valuable in and of itself.

Teaching the Cloud to Fish

As my other work has focused on more explicitly, however, this focus in critical data studies and STS on the extractive dimensions and epistemologies of data-driven technologies frequently elides the material resource networks that sustain digital infrastructures (Brodie, 2024; Pasek et al., 2023). When a company joins "the cloud," which most have by this stage, they are entering into the computing apparatus of the big tech hyperscale providers, largest in market share are AWS, Google, and Microsoft. The deployment of cloud technologies and infrastructures to support industrial technoscience—especially towards extraction—is about managing and reproducing byproduct in one part of the value chain, while outsourcing "harms" and the management of contingency to the cloud. How do we square the apparently incommensurable circles of the "twin transition" of "green, digital" growth, whereby the extractive epistemologies of expanding green capitalism are facilitated and intensified by digital efficiencies driven by sensing, monitoring, processing, and acting upon ecological information?

In 2024, the Google "X" company Tidal "spun off" as an independent company. Emerging from the "Moonshot Factory" of Google's secretive R&D/start-up wing, Tidal promised to revolutionise fish farming via advanced monitoring of salmon pens—"fishal recognition," quote one tech podcast covering Tidal's technologies. Like other similar aquatech start-ups deploying AI, the company proposed solutions to the enduring problems of fish farming at scale: disease and parasites in the population; inefficiencies in feeding; the problem of effluent and other ecological "externalities" in localised environments. Sticking cameras and sensors in and around the fish pen for 24/7, real-time monitoring of fish on shore, Tidal, like other AI start-ups in the space, could promise "preemptive optimization" of fish production, to quote Bauer (2024, p. 528). In these visions, digital tech is inseparable from the imperative of sustainability: there can be no sustainable fish farming without advanced, scalable digital efficiencies.

But while such technology promises to reduce contingencies in production at the micro-scale—moving percentages of yields upwards by monitoring population health fish-by-fish—these micro-scale efficiencies are deployed towards industrialising fish farming activities at scale. This scale is essential: fish farming becomes a race to save the "planet" by producing a "sustainable" source of protein. These ideologies of efficiency, scale, and sustainability are strongly observable in the "vision film" produced for Tidal (Filmless, 2024), which begins with a spectacular overhead shot of an industrial fish farm off of a green coastline in Norway. CEO Neil Davé speaks over imagery of men in wet gear, cut before a Wall-E-like sensor:

> We started with a pretty simple concept: save the ocean, and help save the world. The challenge is that we don't know enough about the ocean to protect it in the right way for the long term. So the concept was if we can bring understanding into the ocean, we have half a chance of ensuring that it remains healthy enough to support humanity moving forward. The thing that gave us confidence to be able to tackle is the technology that you need to be able to understand the ocean at scale is now viable.

Handshakes, boats, men in wet gear and wellies, video screens, and fish swimming amongst sensors ensue, to a backdrop of dramatic, orchestral string music. During a break in the crescendo, Davé goes in for the kill, closing the deal:

> 90% of the wild fishing stocks are depleted. And we can't keep wild fishing at the rate we have. Aquaculture needs to bridge the gap between current supply and future demand – but it has to scale sustainably. And that was really the opportunity for us, was to bring technology to help overcome the challenge of sustainable scaling for the industry.

Regimes of knowing ocean ecologies are efficiently applied to problems of scaling and the "nature" of the market—supply and demand, intricately related to "collective" human intervention in planetary ecologies, proposes a kind of Malthusian ecosystem that "we" just haven't controlled well-enough (Figs. 6.1, 6.2 and 6.3).

What is important to draw from this video, which is exemplary rather than exceptional, is the focus on two aspects of AI applications for fish farming: quantification (knowing) and scale. These two factors are repeated across the industrial and promotional literature surrounding the "sustainable" production of protein for a growing planetary population. The fish farm becomes a microcosm of AI's ability to scale insights

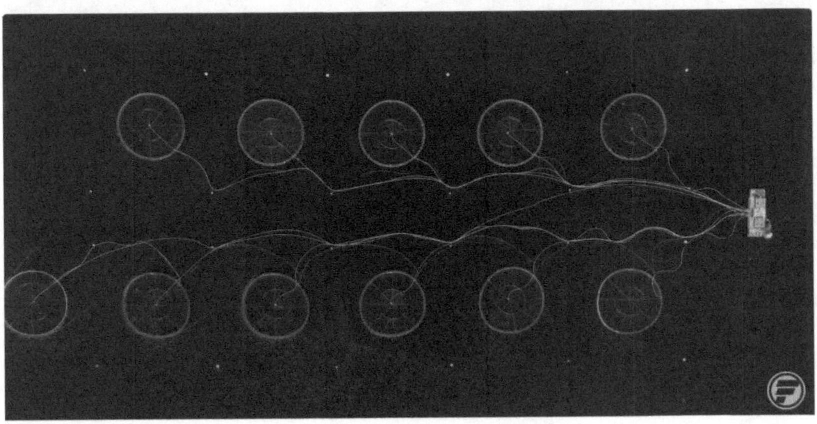

Fig. 6.1 A fully networked fish farm (Filmless, 2024)

Fig. 6.2 The camera and sensor device (Filmless, 2024)

Fig. 6.3 The climactic product shot: the camera in situ, swimming with the fishes (Filmless, 2024)

towards massively expanded production, while minimising "externalities" like pollution, disease, and mass fish death.

This is part of a wider ideology of growth and progress applied to not only fish farming, but to the ocean itself. Critical work in blue media studies has attested to the ways in which mediation of ocean environments both presents a challenge to human "observation," as well as serves to open up new frontiers for accumulation (Han, 2024; Jue, 2021). Such regimes of mediation and representation render marine environments as either: (1) potential environments to be mobilised towards human activity, for whatever purpose or at whatever scale; or (2) components to be harnessed/extracted—both via advanced (usually digital) technological means, and requiring an advance guard of imaginative orientation (e.g. rendering water a "storage medium" or seafloor geographies a "channel" for subsea cables).

This renders marine environments particularly vulnerable to the extractive calculabilities of industrial technoscience and its data-driven accounting, especially as onshore "green" frontiers recede. We can see in fish farming an example of a basic dichotomy presented: fish farming is a well-known environmental "villain," known for polluting coastal ecosystems and torturing fish by the basic function of its production at scale; but at the same time, as an ecosystemic prospect able to be domesticated and harnessed for a lower-emissions profit (it produces proportionally far less emissions than hog, sheep, and cattle farming), it represents an environment that can be calculatively controlled towards more sustainable production of protein, especially within a climate reductionist frame—where carbon and GHGs are the only concern.

The "blue revolution" promised by alignments of green/digital aquaculture inherits the promises of the "green revolution" of scaled agriculture on-land. The idea, according to Aquabyte's Shang, is that if only a fraction of the world's seas are in use for food production, why not open up this frontier? All it takes is the eventually fully-automated fish farm promised by Aquabyte—whose proportion of feed-to-protein production is nearly 1–1, and can, ostensibly, produce fully optimised fish in and from the cloud (SiliconANGLE theCUBE, 2020).

Managing Byproducts and Outsourcing Contradictions

In May 2024, news reports began to emerge about the "Elon Musk" of fish farming, Sondre Eide, and his company Eide in Norway (Eide, 2024). Already a leader in "sustainable" fish farming, the company had self-developed a new "moonshot" technology, mired in secrecy: the "Watermoon," a fully enclosed salmon pen that nonetheless remained offshore, not limiting itself to the land-locked necessities of Aquabyte's promised "fully automated fish farm in every town." 72 m below the surface, thousands of fish swim in a pen that promises "zero lice" and zero overt externalities on the surrounding ecosystem. The tantalising image of the submerged pen emerged as the banner of the article on Fish Farming Expert in May 2024 (Marøy, 2024). Reducing the externalities of fish protein production to next to zero became an exercise of intensified enclosure via cables and wires. In their *2023 sustainability report* (Eide, 2023), the company characterises Eide's approach:

> Where [prior CEO] Knut Frode took the business from the lake to the sea, Sondre is taking it further out in the world and into the cloud, with new innovations in big data, the visitor center Salmon Eye and a new brand for carbon neutral salmon. (2023, p. 6)

Innovations require simultaneous PR and machinery, and should be orientated around efficiency and sustainability—as well as expansion. As Aquabyte's founder, Shang, makes clear in his interviews and media appearances (SiliconANGLE theCUBE, 2020),[3] this is an industry that is already heavily mechanised due to the nature of its operation—usually in rough, cold seas, with difficult conditions of observation and a lot of existing estimation via monitoring. More control has always been the goal—it's just a matter of how you apply the correct technologies to truly domesticate, in ways that make scaling production commercially more feasible. At least, this is the story aquatech peddlers tell, with remotely monitored artificial ecosystems nourished by the life-cycles and ecologies

[3] This also includes an episode of the Amazon Web Services web series Let's Go Build with Werner Vogels, which highlights "innovative" technologies and companies making use of AWS infrastructures (Amazon Web Services, 2019).

they harness, with detritus and externalities managed partially on-site and partially somewhere out-of-sight (Fig. 6.4).

It is telling that Eide, a self-described and widely promoted leader in sustainability, could still only boast a 92% survival rate of its farmed salmon prior to the implementation of the Watermoon, and in spite of significant investments in "cloud" and big data technologies to monitor pens.

The Watermoon represents an intensified version of what is required to "sustainably" produce fish at scale. These experimental regimes of production within "planetary limits," aligning digital technology with green circularity, have presented a proliferation of frontiers for digital capitalism's applied efficiencies. It becomes less a matter of geographical expansion now, although that dynamic remains in place—and the location of fish farms in coastal areas is a key facet of their farming metaphor and its relationship to shifting resource regimes (e.g. usually located in places where fisheries have declined). It is also deepening relations of production in and through digital technologies—which are increasingly used towards production branded "sustainable" under industry and policy

Fig. 6.4 The Watermoon containment tank in situ (Marøy, 2024)

guidelines. This does not resolve but rather amplifies the contradictions at the heart of these dematerialised economies—like phosphorous for agriculture or feed for cattle. A process of ongoing "rifting" towards the collapse of lifeways to sustain those elsewhere—while accumulating profits for the technological managers of these processes, who take on increasingly central importance both infrastructurally and operationally.

The resource intensities of the large-scale computing required to operate AI and data-driven systems generally make them an obvious target for circularity, within which products such as fish become a material for green arithmetic. It is in this context that we see the proliferation of projects that utilise waste heat from data processing facilities for circular production (Velkova, 2016). These practices have been scaled to support the production of food in greenhouses, for example, and are frequently deployed as silver bullet "circular economy" solutions to data-driven growth at a time of decarbonisation. As Green Mountain data centres argues in a promotional video from 2023, their utilisation of waste heat for the production of food, alongside their renewable energy purchasing, means that they are not only climate neutral—they are actually "climate positive" (TBD Media Group, 2021). The production of controlled, micro-climates towards cooling servers forms a kind of thermal ecology that alignments between tech and food producers intend to utilise more widely (Frenzel & Ruder, 2023). In 2022, EcoDataCenter in Sweden announced a partnership with Wa3rm to utilise waste heat towards fish farming solutions (EcoDataCenter, 2022; also Sefyrin & Velkova, this volume). Citing successful projects like one to farm eels in Japan with data centre waste heat, a Data Centre Dynamics article announcing the partnership also acknowledges the somewhat controversial status of these technological connections (Judge, 2022). Nonetheless, promising "industrial symbiosis," Wa3rm's CORALIS initiative (co-funded by Horizon 2020) is designed to manage industrial waste ecologies towards renewed production (WA3RM, 2025)—in some ways, making byproducts into resources for further industrial growth. As the Eco-Data Centre website promises, the new facility will contribute to "a large area of food production" into the future, "Meeting the future requirements of sustainability, technology, and circularity. This is a new kind of ecosystem where we think circular from the beginning" (EcoDataCenter, n.d.).

In a 2021 article, Thomas Patrick Pringle theorises the relationships between the "tech ecosystem and the colony," a provocation which he situates in the historical development of ecosystemic thinking in a kind of manufactured colonial "holism." In his account, the environmental thinking of the technology industries promotes the discrete operations of the colony maintaining the functioning complexity of the whole. However, as he describes,

> Arguably, this expansionist use and abuse of ecological concepts and terms is in line with the rhetoric on display in a recent article by the World Economic Forum, titled "How 'agritech' could lead Africa's rising start-up scene," that refers to the African continent as the "food basket for the world" where "60% of the world's unused arable land and 54% of Africa's population [already] working in the sector [means] the continent has enormous agricultural promise." Is this tech ecosystem—Africa as smart breadbasket—designed to route the global flows of informational capital to soils already depleted by centuries of exploitation, imperial violence, and land dispossession? (Pringle, 2021)

What it seems Pringle is gesturing towards is a simultaneous intensive and extensive dynamic enabled by the "tech ecosystem" and its modes of ecological thinking: a scaling to facilitate growth, that depends on discrete, ecological micro-efficiencies. We can perhaps read a similar headline about Green Mountain Data Centres in Norway, whose waste heat will go towards lobsters, similarly. In an article titled *On the menu: Norwegian cloud lobster*, one author connects data territorialisation with the "sustainability" business: "Europe's newfound appetite for data localization and tech sovereignty is also helping a hand in pushing forward Green Mountain's sustainability business" (Pollet, 2023).

We can imagine a scenario whereby the on-land, self-contained fish farms built next to data centres are also made efficient by AI-driven applications run on the servers next door. This is the terraformed vision of Aquabyte, who promises a "fully automated fish farm in every town," while at the same time arguing that their technology will "re-skill" workers in coastal areas formerly employed in fishing (AWS Events, 2019). But fish farming communities, promised the possibilities of industrialised livelihoods via scaled aquafarms off the coast, are still situated ambiguously within the dreams of AI-enabled fish farms. The image of AI-led domestication is not one of permanently inefficient near-shore fish farms, with the ecological intrusions that jeopardise the efficient production of fish. It is eventually to more fully domesticate this process through indoor, on-land fish farms, increasingly automated and discrete from coastal ecologies.

Thus, while the big tech-enabled agricultural landgrab in Africa, like the expansion of big tech fish farms in Chile and Ecuador, point to overtly imperial endeavours, we can also see the foundationally developmental premise behind this in the peripheries of Europe at different green/blue frontiers: sustainable digital tech is about the management of environmental externalities towards enhanced industrial production via "sustainable" calculabilities. These projects even allow these companies to argue that they are more than "net zero," they can be "climate positive," like Green Mountain, while also promising a post-carbon form of economic development.

How do we disrupt the promise of closed-loop ecologies? Max Liboiron proposes models for different ways to consider scientific practice and collaboration under the persistent boot heel of colonial capitalism:

> The temporality of Resource is anticipatory—it makes and even aims to guarantee colonial futures. Crucial to this temporality is the belief that this future can be chosen and that the present can be directed toward it via management practices. As such, Resources eclipse other possible relations with Land both now and in the future. … The landscape cannot support other relations, activities, or futures that might interfere with future use. If a river is for waste assimilation, it can only be a fishing spot if those activities do not preclude its role as a sink. Fostering some futures and eclipsing others is a key technique of the managerial ontologies that characterize Resources and pollution. (2021, p. 64)

Lien also seems aware of this incommensurability, even in the construction of fish as something that can be quantified and made knowable and manageable into the future:

> Many of these [slowed down encounters at field] sites offer the reader a glimpse of live salmon "in-the-making." At other sites, practices can only be inferred in hindsight, for instance, from inscriptions through which salmon are rendered visible in the abstract as well as on paper and on screens, through numbers, images, graphs, or descriptions. These include policy documents, research reports, and websites. Such sites enact salmon too, but differently and allow farmed fish to travel far into the future as well as to many places at once. (2015, p. 17)

This designation that Liboiron makes is thus central to how I understand the resource relations of "sustainability"—if a salmon becomes a vessel for market-driven sustainability, what is the limit of our future and alternative pathways of nature/culture relations? In the commercial sustainability I've outlined above, supported by frequently well-meaning projects and proponents of social (and) scientific research in many cases, nature/culture is strategically aligned in ways that would make the new materialists proud—but within an ecology that is always-already capital, closer to Moore's points about the establishment and production of capitalist ecology (2015, 2017).

While we in some ways arrive at a familiar critique of capitalist systems from an environmental perspective, what I'm proposing here is more an opportunity to think through these knotty political ecologies of capitalist sustainability as they are being increasingly institutionalised and infrastructuralised through cloud-enabled industrial technoscience at the unfolding "frontiers" of green (and blue) capitalism. "Pre-emptive optimisation" of resources for a more calculable planet—mediated through the heavily instrumented fish farm, dependent on computing resources that are inescapably ecological themselves.

Conclusion

Cloud computing is taking on a specific role in the "sustainable" reproduction and harvesting of fish (and other "green" products) in a contemporary "green," digital economy. The infrastructural contradictions of capitalist growth are both being managed in and through digital systems as well as requiring their exponential expansion. This presents fundamental contradictions—as I have shown in other work, the sourcing of renewable electricity for the operations of the "cloud," like the uneven supply of water required to cool servers, frequently reproduces obvious examples of environmental injustice and extractive operations (see Ortar et al., 2023). The relation between cloud infrastructure and the supposedly "sustainable" production of fish protein demonstrates that the rationalities of sustainability ingrained within digital growth depend upon a never-ending industrial mastery by and for capital, and this begins in apparently innocuous attempts to "clean up" certain productive processes. In Lien's framing, for example, domestication for farming is always a process of culturing, as agriculture and aquaculture imagine land- and water-based practices as human productive processes, unpacking how domestication is a material and semiotic process of transforming relations between human society and its "wild" counterparts. But, even at the smaller scale, as Lien acknowledges, this in itself reproduces a colonial ideology of "progression" that leaves such "wild" others as outside of the social fold. Domestication, in its traditional sense, thus depends upon the treatment of animal and/or plant as base resource, biomass which can be continually made and re-made via the rationalities of domestication (e.g. farming). Beyond "taming," it fundamentally denotes a change in human relationality to another thing—one which refers to both potential human needs as well as the social (political economic) processes that entails.

If, as Liboiron asserts, the ideology of "pollution," like the "resource" that affirms the material necessity of external inputs to the system, is foundationally about colonialism in the production of a value order that assumes the capitalist use and exhaustion of land and ecology, then the deepening of these logics in and through "resources" and "sinks," however "green," are as much about organising ecologies in a colonial capitalist framework towards the accumulation of capital. Once we come to this basic premise, our horizons and political orientations towards "sustainability" with AI at the helm become much clearer. Rendering the rift more calculable does not reduce its ecological impacts—it applies the epistemic functions of technoscientific progress to problems of sustaining capitalist growth, however much that may appear in situ as somehow less deleterious and applied towards planetary health.

Competing Interests The author has no conflicts of interest to declare that are relevant to the contents of this chapter.

References

Amazon Web Services. (2019, June 6). *Now Go Build with Werner Vogels – S1E3 Bergen*. YouTube. https://www.youtube.com/watch?v=YZ_qJ5JFD3I

Arboleda, M. (2020). *Planetary mine: Territories of extraction under late capitalism*. Verso.

AWS Events. (2019, December 12). *AWS re:Invent 2019: Deep learning in deep nets: Helping fish farmers feed the world (MLS210-4)* [Video]. YouTube. https://www.youtube.com/watch?v=86Bf34a_d3I

Barney, D. (2022, February 8). Autonomous agriculture? *Heliotrope*. https://www.heliotropejournal.net/helio/autonomous-agriculture

Bauer, S. (2024). Seeing like a model fish: How digital extractions mediate metabolic relations. *Science, Technology, & Human Values, 49*(3), 524–554. https://doi.org/10.1177/01622439241236520

Bridge, G. (2011). Resource geographies 1: Making carbon economies, old and new. *Progress in Human Geography, 35*(6), 820–834. https://doi.org/10.1177/0309132510385524

Brodie, P. (2023). Data infrastructure studies on an unequal planet. *Big Data and Society, 10*(1), 1–14. https://doi.org/10.1177/20539517231182402

Brodie, P. (2024). Smarter, greener extractivism: Digital infrastructure and the harnessing of new resources. *Information, Communication and Society, 28*(6), 1061–1080. https://doi.org/10.1080/1369118X.2024.2341013

Brodie, P., & Barney, D. (2026). Introduction. In P. Brodie & D. Barney (Eds.), *Media rurality*. Duke University Press.

Buck, H. J. (2022). Decarbonization as a service. *Logic(s), 2022*(16). https://logicmag.io/clouds/decarbonization-as-a-service/

Buller, A. (2022). *The value of a whale: On the illusions of green capitalism.* Manchester University Press.

Bumpus, A. G., & Liverman, D. M. (2008). Accumulation by decarbonization and the governance of carbon offsets. *Economic Geography, 84*(2), 127–155. https://doi.org/10.1111/j.1944-8287.2008.tb00401.x

Chaudhary, A. S. (2024). *The exhausted of the earth: Politics in a burning world.* Repeater.

Couldry, N., & Mejias, U. A. (2019). Data colonialism: Rethinking big data's relation to the contemporary subject. *Television & New Media, 20*(4), 336–349. https://doi.org/10.1177/1527476418796632

EcoDataCenter. (2022, October 11). *A new circular data center model creates sustainable and large-scale food production.* EcoDataCenter. https://ecodatacenter.tech/press/a-new-circular-data-center-model-creates-sustainable-and-large-scale-food-production-3229148

EcoDataCenter. (n.d.). *A circular focus in our biggest project yet*. EcoDataCenter – Östersund. https://ecodatacenter.tech/data-center/ecodatacenter-osd

Edwards, P. (2010). *A vast machine: Computer models, climate data, and the politics of global warming*. MIT Press.

Eide. (2023). *Sustainability report 2023.* https://cdn.prod.website-files.com/667bfc675e9e901b48f2a117/66ab40346f4e6f415c936f63_2023%20Sustainability%20report%20EN.pdf

Eide. (2024). *Eide.* https://www.efb.no/en

Filmless. (2024, March 17). *Google X: Tidal vision film* [Video]. YouTube. https://www.youtube.com/watch?v=PsXw9SEKypQ

Frenzel, J., & Ruder, S-L. (2023, March 21). *Can the heat from running computers help grow our food? It's complicated.* The Conversation. https://theconversation.com/can-the-heat-from-running-computers-help-grow-our-food-its-complicated-201064

Gabrys, J. (2017). *Program Earth: Environmental sensing technology and the making of a computational planet*. University of Minnesota Press.

Han, L. Y. (2024). *Deepwater alchemy: Extractive mediation and the taming of the seafloor*. University of Minnesota Press.

Judge, P. (2022, October 11). *EcoDataCenter to reuse heat in fish farms and greenhouses*. Data Centre Dynamics. https://www.datacenterdynamics.com/en/news/ecodatacenter-to-reuse-heat-in-fish-farms-and-greenhouses/

Jue, M. (2021). *Wild blue media: Thinking through seawater*. Duke University Press.

Lally, N., Kay, K., & Thatcher, J. (2022). Computational parasites and hydropower: A political ecology of Bitcoin mining on the Columbia River. *Environment and Planning E: Nature and Space, 5*(1), 18–38. https://doi.org/10.1177/2514848619867608

Liboiron, M. (2021). *Pollution is colonialism*. Duke University Press.

Lien, M. (2015). *Becoming salmon: Aquaculture and the domestication of a fish*. University of California Press.

Lin, C. (2022). How forest became data: The remaking of ground truth in Indonesia. In J. Goldstein & E. Nost (Eds.), *The nature of data: Infrastructures, environments, politics* (pp. 285–302). University of Nebraska Press.

Lippert, I. (2016). Failing the market, failing deliberative democracy: How scaling up corporate carbon reporting proliferates information asymmetries. *Big Data & Society, 3*(2), 1–13. https://doi.org/10.1177/2053951716673390

Marøy, M. J. (2024, May 27). *A glimpse of the watermoon*. Fish Farming Expert. https://www.fishfarmingexpert.com/eide-fjordbruk-floating-closed-containment-watermoon/a-glimpse-of-the-watermoon/1773748

Moore, J. W. (2015). *Capitalism in the web of life: Ecology and the accumulation of capital*. Verso.

Moore, J. W. (2017). Metabolic rift or metabolic shift? Dialectics, nature, and the world-historical method. *Theory and Society, 46*, 285–318. https://doi.org/10.1007/s11186-017-9290-6

Nafus, D. (2023). Unclearing the air: Data's unexpected limitations for environmental advocacy. *Social Studies of Science, 54*(2), 163–183. https://doi.org/10.1177/03063127231201169

Nelson, S., & Bigger, P. (2022). Infrastructural nature. *Progress in Human Geography, 46*(1), 86–107. https://doi.org/10.1177/0309132521993916

Nost, E. (2022). Infrastructuring 'data-driven' environmental governance in Louisiana's coastal restoration plan. *Environment and Planning E: Nature and Space, 5*(1), 104–124. https://doi.org/10.1177/2514848620909727

Nost, E., & Goldstein, J. E. (2022). A political ecology of data. *Environment and Planning E: Nature and Space, 5*(1), 3–17. https://doi.org/10.1177/25148486211043503

Ortar, N., Taylor, A. R. E., Velkova, J., Brodie, P., Johnson, A., Marquet, C., Pollio, A., & Cirolia, L. (2023). Powering 'smart' futures: Data centres and the energy politics of digitalisation. In S. Abram, K. Waltorp, N. Ortar, & S. Pink (Eds.), *Energy futures: Anthropocene challenges, emerging technologies and everyday life* (pp. 125–168). Walter de Gruyter.

Pasek, A. (2019). Managing carbon and data flows: Fungible forms of mediation in the cloud. *Culture Machine, 18.* https://culturemachine.net/vol-18-the-nature-of-data-centers/managing-carbon/

Pasek, A., Lin, C. K., Cooper, Z. G. T., & Kinder, J. (2023). *Digital energetics*. University of Minnesota Press.

Pollet, M. (2023, August 29). On the menu: Norwegian cloud lobster. *Politico.* https://www.politico.eu/article/norway-lobster-water-green-mountain-data-farming/

Pringle, T. P. (2021, May 12). The tech ecosystem and the colony. *Heliotrope.* https://www.heliotropejournal.net/helio/the-tech-ecosystem

Ricaurte, P. (2019). Data epistemologies, the coloniality of power, and resistance. *Television & New Media, 20*(4), 350–365. https://doi.org/10.1177/1527476419831640

Robertson, M. (2012). Measurement and alienation: Making a world of ecosystem services. *Transactions of the Institute of British Geographers, 37*(3), 386–401. https://doi.org/10.1111/j.1475-5661.2011.00476.x

SiliconANGLE theCUBE. (2020, May 11). *Bryton Shang, Aquabyte—CUBE Conversation, May 2020* [Video]. YouTube. https://www.youtube.com/watch?v=K1MldW4ZRXs

TBD Media Group. (2021, July 9). *Green Mountain: The world's greenest data centre*. YouTube. https://www.youtube.com/watch?v=4krpOapkEp0

Velkova, J. (2016). Data that warms: Waste heat, infrastructural convergence and the computation traffic commodity. *Big Data & Society, 3*(2), 1–10. https://doi.org/10.1177/2053951716684144

Vera, L. A., Walker, D., Murphy, M., Mansfield, B., Siad, L. M., Ogden, J., & EDGI. (2019). When data justice and environmental justice meet: formulating a response to extractive logic through environmental data justice. *Information, Communication and Society, 22*(7), 1012–1028. https://doi.org/10.1080/1369118X.2019.1596293

Wang, X. (2020). *Blockchain chicken farm: And other stories of tech in China's countryside*. Farrar.

WA3RM. (2025). *CORALIS*. https://wa3rm.com/partnerships/coralis/

Whitington, J. (2020). Earth's data: Climate change, Thai carbon markets, and the planetary atmosphere. *American Anthropologist, 122*(4), 814–826. https://doi.org/10.1111/aman.13476

Wiessner, M. (2024). The ecologistics of carbon tracking: Environmental accounting software and industrial media practices. *Journal of Environmental Media, 5*(2), 179–199. https://doi.org/10.1386/jem_00113_1

PART II

Promises, Economies, Discourses

CHAPTER 7

The Cruel Optimism of the Sustainable Cloud: Fantasies and Futures of Microsoft Azure

Hamsini Sridharan

Introduction

The cloud has become a near-ubiquitous feature of computing, a seemingly immaterial, infinite condensation of data that serves as the atmospheric infrastructure of artificial intelligence (AI) systems. However, this metaphor is deceptive: cloud computing is relentlessly material in both the environmental and economic senses (Hu, 2015; Monserrate, 2022). With its growth comes the construction of data centers reliant on voracious energy consumption, water extracted to cool servers, and copious waste. This has led to a tension in strategy, as major cloud service providers such as Amazon Web Services, Microsoft Azure, and Google Cloud negotiate between short-term profit and climate change's threats to future profitability. This tension has grown even more acute with the recent advent of compute-intensive generative AI.

H. Sridharan (✉)
University of Southern California, Los Angeles, CA, USA
e-mail: hamsinis@usc.edu

A. Mollen et al. (eds.), *AI Infrastructures and Sustainability*, Palgrave Studies in European Communication Research and Education,
https://doi.org/10.1007/978-3-032-09748-4_7

Tech companies attempt to reconcile economy and environment through corporate sustainability projects; as Hogan (2018) observes, "Big Tech is a main driver of sustainable development worldwide … while also, and invariably, upholding the idea that perpetual growth is possible and economically desirable within these conditions" (p. 632). Sustainability, in this view, is an outgrowth of green capitalism rooted in the discourse of "ecological modernization" developed in the 1980s, which emphasizes the technologically mediated decoupling of environmental impact and resource consumption and faith in "green growth" (Hajer, 1997; Tienhaara, 2014). This is exemplified by the United Nations Brundtland Commission report, which defines "sustainable development" as humanity's ability to "meet the needs of the present without compromising the ability of future generations to meet their own needs," positioning technological innovation as a way to sustain economic growth (World Commission on Environment & Development, 1987). Microsoft, for one, directly quotes this definition in corporate materials (Microsoft, n.d.-c).

In this chapter, I discuss how this imaginary of sustainability shapes cloud infrastructure, focusing on the case of Microsoft Azure. I ask, what fantasies and futures characterize "sustainability" where it meets the greedy materiality of cloud infrastructure and AI? What political possibilities emerge or vanish in these projects?

My analysis is grounded in the infrastructural turn of anthropology and science and technology studies, particularly as it relates to visibility, imagination, and power. Some scholars suggest that invisibility is a defining characteristic of infrastructure (Star, 1999), that infrastructures mediate our relationship to our environment and are accordingly naturalized, disappearing into the background (Edwards, 1997). However, Larkin (2013) argues that invisibility is only one possible condition of infrastructure; oftentimes, infrastructures are strategically rendered spectacular by political actors. Attending to the manipulation of infrastructural (in)visibility can reveal the "sociotechnical imaginaries"—"collectively held, institutionally stabilized, and publicly performed visions of desirable futures"—embedded in infrastructure (Jasanoff & Kim, 2015, p. 4). Indeed, Larkin writes that infrastructures "emerge out of and store within them forms of desire and fantasy" (2013, p. 329). Appel et al. (2018), meanwhile, argue that infrastructures contain promises revealing "aspiration and failure, provision and abjection, and technical progress and its underbelly" (p. 3). The fantasies and futures embedded in infrastructure can be read discursively and aesthetically for their material, political effects.

I focus on Microsoft Azure due to its market share, substantial investment in sustainability, and profusion of materials about its sustainability projects. In 2020, Microsoft announced a set of climate goals that form the backbone of the company's sustainability efforts (Microsoft, 2021, p. 4): becoming "carbon negative" by 2030; protecting ecosystems via the Planetary Computer; reaching "zero waste" by 2030; and becoming "water positive" by 2030. The company also sells Azure cloud products designed to advance other companies' sustainability. Here, I critically examine three projects undertaken with Azure: Microsoft's data center sustainability efforts; its Cloud for Sustainability products; and the Planetary Computer dataset repository. I do so via discourse analysis of online marketing materials and other corporate publications, such as the *We Live in the Cloud* microsite, the Cloud for Sustainability marketing website, and the Planetary Computer repository and associated media. I read materials from these three projects for (1) how they discuss the relationship of economy and environment; (2) what role AI plays; and (3) what political possibilities they encode. By bringing together how Microsoft conceives of its own sustainability, sells sustainability to others, and supports environmental knowledge production and management, I sketch a portrait of how the company renders sustainability infrastructural and positions itself as an essential infrastructure of sustainability globally.

Microsoft's sustainability efforts, I argue, are more than a marketing strategy; the company's faith in the ability of technology, and especially AI, to reconcile capitalism with environmentalism depoliticizes the present in favor of a "sustainable future," exposing a kind of "infrastructural power" (Khalili, 2018; Luitse, 2024) that materially shapes the politics of cloud infrastructure under the aegis of "green data capitalism" (Wiessner et al., 2026). In its data center sustainability efforts, discourses of investment, efficiency, and circularity, backed by AI modeling, seek to decouple environmental impact and business growth by economizing the environment. Cloud for Sustainability marketing, meanwhile, exposes how Microsoft commoditizes sustainability by translating it into a matter of streamlined data analytics, generative and predictive AI, and visions of a datafied natural sublime for companies on endless "sustainability journeys." And the Planetary Computer, in hosting data and applications for free, focalizes environmental knowledge and decision-making at an abstracted planetary scale by foregrounding particular modalities of data and AI analysis. In abstracting and displacing local, material, present environmental impacts to a sublime, global, speculative "green" technofuture, these neoliberal logics of decoupling, commercializing, and scaling do more than greenwash; they actively foreclose other possible political arrangements of computation and environment. Microsoft Azure and its AI tools are positioned as the "solution" to environmental problems—redefined as problems of data—deemphasizing their environmental impact. This reflects the "cruel optimism" (Berlant, 2011) of the fantasy that through technological progress, sustainable cloud infrastructure can reconcile endless economic growth with present and future flourishing in the shadow of the climate crisis.

Cloud Economies and Ecologies

An exploration of its *We Live in the Cloud* virtual data center tour suggests that Microsoft's approach to its own sustainability relies on aspirations of decoupling business growth from resource extraction and consumption through economic logics of investment, efficiency, and circularity. This strategy displaces environmental impact while materially shaping the operations and expansion of cloud infrastructure. In the process, Microsoft positions AI as a mechanism for optimizing sustainability rather than a resource strain.

In April 2021, Microsoft Story Labs launched a 3D interactive microsite called *We Live in the Cloud*, inviting the viewer to "Explore the hidden world of datacenters" (Microsoft Story Labs, 2021). The landing page depicts an animated aerial view of squat buildings, solar panel arrays, and wind turbines surrounded by greenery atop a column in the sky, clouds drifting across the screen. Color-coded cards display information about sustainability, innovation, security, and infrastructure in Azure, with links to *Learn more* indexing a hodgepodge of blog posts, infographics, websites, and videos. An arrow directs the viewer to *Enter The Lobby* before accessing in order: the *Operations Room*, *Mechanical Area*, *Server Room*, *Circular Center*, *Network Room*, and finally, the *Innovation Room*. Some of these spaces, such as the *Circular Center*, represent generic forms in actual data centers; others, such as the *Innovation Room*, are speculative constructs.

Financial logics suffuse Microsoft's sustainability efforts, displacing its environmental impact. Pasek (2019) shows how Microsoft's "fungible mediation" of data center locations, carbon offsets, and renewable energy purchases "translate[s] local relations into generic commodities that can be bought and sold at a distance, obfuscating the question of accountability in favor of the formal logics of accounting" (p. 2). As with carbon, so too with water: beyond efforts to reduce its water consumption, in the virtual tour, Microsoft emphasizes "investments" in water access and replenishment. A 2023 white paper quantifies the company's "water stewardship" using the Volumetric Water Benefit Accounting standard and highlights a "portfolio" of 49 replenishment projects worldwide, from Fargo to Cape Town and beyond (Microsoft, 2023a, p. 4). Impact and investment are reshuffled, water consumed in one location to be replenished elsewhere in future (though the white paper emphasizes that these efforts focus on the most water-stressed areas in which the company operates). As Brain and Lavigne (2024) point out, this displacement is political: for instance, while carbon offsetting is marketed as a way to support conservation, many conservation practices have resulted in dispossession and displacement of indigenous communities. They write, "At their heart, offsetting structures provide ways for wealthy corporations from the Global North to continue their operations, dodge emissions reductions, and push the burden of change and transformation onto the already-marginalized communities least responsible for the crisis" (Brain & Lavigne, 2024, How to measure everything section, para. 5). Meanwhile, the "abstraction of markets" leads to "double counting and corrupt compliance practices" (Brain & Lavigne, 2024, How to make a carbon offset section, para. 7).

Other sections of the tour emphasize efficiency as a decoupling strategy for water usage. A link from the aerial view leads to a blog post that asks, "how can we continue to conserve water while meeting growing customer demand for cloud and AI innovation?" (Walsh, 2024, para. 2). Microsoft's response includes audits "to identify inefficiencies" and "advanced prediction models" to help "anticipate water requirements" (Walsh, 2024, para. 7). Meanwhile, in the *Mechanical Area*, against a backdrop of dun-colored server buildings and wind turbines, a card on *Modern datacenter cooling* explains, "Adiabatic cooling is a highly efficient closed-loop method of temperature control that uses evaporation and outside air to reduce energy usage and water consumption compared to traditional air cooling" (Microsoft Story Labs, 2021). The linked infographic contrasts "modern" cooling to non-modern techniques such as mechanical cooling that use more power and water (Microsoft, 2023b).

Echoing the discourse of ecological modernization, Microsoft deemphasizes the latter; however, a map of cooling methods by region included in the infographic shows that the most resource-intensive cooling methods are still deployed across large swathes of every continent. The infographic indicates that cooling methods are "optimized" by climate, enabling the "minimization" and "maximum utilization" of resources (Microsoft, 2023b). Meanwhile, the heat energy generated by data centers is "pipe[d] to district heating networks to help local communities meet their climate goals," (Microsoft Story Labs, 2021) as with data centers in Finland, exemplifying what Velkova (2016) terms "infrastructural convergence" (p. 2).

The tour also elaborates on Microsoft's zero-waste goal in the model *Circular Center*, where decommissioned data center hardware is routed for disposal. To achieve zero waste, Microsoft has developed a "reverse supply chain model" in which "before an asset is even introduced to Microsoft's supply chain, each part or component already has an optimized disposition plan" (Microsoft Consulting Services, 2021, Building a resilient reverse supply chain model section, para. 3). An "Intelligent Disposition and Routing System" (IDARS) deploys machine learning to sort assets, optimize routes, and provide instructions for disposing of each piece (Borkar, 2022, Plan for every part section, para. 2). Server components that Microsoft deems "valuable," such as processors and memory, are "harvested" for internal reuse, while other hardware is donated to schools or otherwise repurposed (Microsoft Story Labs, 2021). But while Microsoft targets reusing or recycling 90% of its hardware, 10% is still discarded as waste—and data center hardware needs are growing (Borkar, 2022). Another source of circularity can be seen in the funding of the Circular Center program, piloted in Amsterdam and expanded to other locations: the algorithmically managed system was initially funded by internal fees charged to Microsoft business units based on their total carbon emissions (Borkar, 2022). The material circularity of hardware is thus supported by a self-referential circularity of the system, which analyzes Azure supply chain data using Azure-based AI tools and internal financialization of environmental metrics.

Though described in global terms, Microsoft's decoupling strategies disparately impact local environments, demonstrating how "Big Tech has practiced its own kind of climate control, adjusting to local conditions by bending different narratives and imaginaries to stage the next phase of expansion" (Edwards et al., 2024, p. 11). For instance, in a 2019 blog post, Microsoft announced that new data centers in El Mirage and Goodyear, Arizona would be "powered with 100% renewable energy," their sunny climate "making it an ideal location for investing in solar power" (Microsoft, 2019a, para. 4); an investment with First Solar would "provide enough power to cover the energy load for each of our new datacenter campuses" (Microsoft, 2019a, para. 5). Two years later, another post clarifies that the solar plant would offset energy use with Renewable Energy Certificates, not directly supply power to data centers (Walsh, 2021). Meanwhile, as Hao (2024a) reports, the Goodyear data center complex, located in a water-stressed area, was designed to host generative AI behemoth OpenAI, in which Microsoft is a major investor. While the 2019 announcement states that the data center uses outside air cooling instead of water when the temperature drops below 85°F, Hao (2024a) observes that temperatures in the area often exceed that threshold. Even with low-water cooling methods, Microsoft estimates the center will use about 56 million gallons annually—though the company does not publish its actual resource usage (Hao, 2024a). Microsoft has, however, publicized its "investment" in conserving Lake Mead, one of its nearby water replenishment projects (Microsoft, 2019a, para. 8).

Discourses of investment, efficiency, and circularity underlie Microsoft's efforts to decouple business growth from resource usage, rendering environmental impact fungible and optimizable, displacing it across time (usage now, replenishment later) and space (usage here offset there, globally versus locally, closed loops). In the process, Microsoft assumes global environmental stewardship in what Hogan (2018) terms "Big Data Ecologies," operating on a neoliberal logic that "nature will maintain an equilibrium that can be restored if disrupted through both calculable and mappable market-driven assessments and interventions" (p. 635). This balance-sheet approach economizes the environment, making it seem possible—desirable, even—to continue expanding cloud infrastructure. By this logic, if Microsoft can balance out increased resource usage and do more with less, it can justify data center expansion for growing AI demand, displacing the environmental impact of cloud infrastructure while materially expanding it. Cloud ecologies become cloud economy; AI, a tool for optimizing resources rather than depleting them. Meanwhile, in its latest environmental sustainability report, Microsoft's overall emissions increased by 29.1% relative to 2020, likely due to the surge of generative AI; water consumption increased 87% (Microsoft, 2024b).

Selling Sustainability Solutions

Beyond its internal sustainability efforts, Microsoft markets Cloud for Sustainability products. Marketing materials show how Microsoft incorporates generative AI and forecasting models into decontextualized environmental dashboards, selling promises of eliminating data friction and visions of a datafied natural sublime. In the process, Azure makes itself the commercialized infrastructure of sustainability across environmentally destructive industries, undergirding "journeys" towards the ever-approaching, never-present horizon of a sustainable future.

Cloud for Sustainability products, according to the marketing website, allow clients to deploy Azure to standardize environmental monitoring through "data intelligence" for environmental, social, and governance (ESG) reporting; increase the efficiency of their IT infrastructures; and reduce their environmental impact (Microsoft, n.d.-b, Overview section). These "sustainability solutions," as the company calls them, include the Sustainability Manager and an Emissions Impact Dashboard (Microsoft, n.d.-b, Solutions section). Microsoft places particular emphasis on the integration of Copilot, its generative AI chatbot, in these tools. An overview video on the homepage opens with an animation of a darkened Earth in outer space, blue points and lines brightly crisscrossing it to signal cloud connectivity. This transitions to generic shots of office workers into which "nature," in the form of wide-angle, color-saturated images of mountains, lakes, and trees, interjects, followed by an animation of networked icons scrolling against a city sunset. The video then demos employees of the fictional Contoso Coffee using Sustainability Manager and other products, including Copilot, to generate ESG dashboards and reports. Voiceover narration intones, "Now more than ever, organizations are aiming to be more sustainable. They're challenged to get a complete view of their environmental, social, and governance (ESG) data. However, the complexity of this data often slows progress on sustainability goals" (Microsoft, n.d.-b, Watch overview section, 0:02). The video concludes with more shots of "nature" zooming into offices and the image of a glittering, networked planet as the voiceover asserts that these tools give a "clear line of sight into reporting readiness" and a "complete view" of organizations' "sustainability footprint" (Microsoft, n.d.-b, Watch overview section, 4:03). Problems of environmental impact are recast as problems of data to which Azure is the "solution," allowing companies to "overcome ESG data complexity to drive faster insights for reductions and growth" (Microsoft, n.d.-b, Capabilities section). Cloud for Sustainability solutions thus transfigure natural resource usage into data analytics pegged to ESG standards and cleanly visualized in dashboards; this transfiguration is positioned as necessary for visibility into environmental impact.

Microsoft's "solutions" are designed to simplify data collection, processing, analysis, and reporting, enabling companies to simultaneously "reduce" (emissions and other impacts of resource extraction) and "grow" (business)—once again invoking decoupling as sustainability strategy. This is redoubled by the harnessing of AI to "enable new sustainability-based solutions within the emerging climate economy," as the homepage puts it (Microsoft, n.d.-b, Overview section). A linked "guided tour" describes how Evan, the fictional Contoso Chief Sustainability Officer, uses Microsoft Sustainability Manager to calculate the company's imagined carbon footprint by combining and analyzing multiple data sources and "streamlining" emissions calculations (Microsoft, 2020b). Pasek et al. (2023), drawing on Edwards (2013), note that calculating carbon footprint is rife with "data frictions" (p. 3); streamlining strips away this friction while concealing the political choices made in doing so. Indeed, Mattern (2015) observes that in dashboards, "whatever is not readily operationalizable or measurable is simply bracketed out" while the included data, shorn of its politics, becomes "representable, contextualizable, and intelligible," resulting in a "sterilized quasi-transparency" that informs decision-making (Critical mud section, paras. 2–3, 7). Cloud for Sustainability tools are positioned as essential to improving the speed and efficiency of data analysis by eliminating friction, calculating and visualizing environmental impact as a series of decontextualized, optimizable quantities. This constructs a "clear line of sight" and "complete view" of sustainability by bracketing out anything that cannot be datafied and stripping away the messiness of the data that is collected. There is a speculative quality to this marketing; for instance, a feature in Sustainability Manager offers AI-based "what-if analysis" to "forecast the impact of business practice changes on your organization's carbon emissions" (Kareem, 2024, para. 2). In the process, "data governance" (as Microsoft calls it)—rendering unruly, complex data standardizable, centralized, visualizable, and reportable—becomes the modality of environmental governance.

These marketing materials package a sublime, datafied vision of environmental impact that dematerializes the natural world and humans' effect on it. Dashboardification of resource consumption sterilizes environmental "footprint," promising an imaginary of nature untouched by, or resilient to, human impact. Wide-angle images of nature bookending the overview video evoke an aesthetic of the natural sublime into which tiny human figures disappear. This juxtaposition of the natural sublime to what Mosco (2014) calls "the cloud sublime"—"visions contained in the promise of universal knowledge, virtual worlds, and unlimited communication that were once embodied in religion and nature but are now more likely supported by digital technologies" (p. 81)—sells a vision of sustainability as transcending the all-too-human environmental impact of corporations through deracinated data analytics, visualization, and, increasingly, AI.

In this way, Azure accompanies companies on their "sustainability journeys"—pathways towards a future that may or may not be realized. After all, who is buying these solutions? The Cloud for Sustainability website links to industry-specific marketing pages targeting the automotive industry, energy industry, financial services, manufacturing, retail, and building management. The landing page for energy proclaims, "Connectivity and renewables are here to stay," and companies should therefore embrace "innovative technologies to drive efficiency and growth" (Microsoft, n.d.-a, para. 3). It then highlights an estimate by McKinsey & Company that "advanced connectivity" could bring 250 billion USD in value to the oil and gas industry by 2030 (Grijpink et al., 2020, para. 1). A contradiction emerges: that Microsoft's tools (whose own environmental impact is not mentioned) can power the energy transition and help companies reduce emissions while helping oil and gas companies—including Chevron and ExxonMobil—obtain greater value from cloud-optimized drilling. As Hao (2024b) puts it, "There is the tension. On the one hand, AI may be able to help reduce drilling's toll on the environment. On the other hand, it's used for drilling" (para. 13). This has caused turmoil within Microsoft: for years, an employee-led sustainability group has advocated for the company to stop supporting oil companies with specialized cloud computing and AI tools; meanwhile, Microsoft argues that it is helping these companies become more efficient and shift to renewables (Hao, 2024b). The datafied natural sublime of Cloud for Sustainability marketing sells products that become the infrastructure of sustainability across industries—including those most responsible for environmental destruction. In doing so, it sells a vision of a "sustainable future" that masks the rampant unsustainability of the present.

The Gift of Planetary Scale

Finally, Microsoft positions the Planetary Computer as the benevolent cloud infrastructure of environmental knowledge production and management for researchers and policymakers worldwide, promising data, compute, and algorithmic modeling at immense scale, made available through an open data economy. In so doing, it infrastructurally reinforces an abstracted planetary imaginary of AI-mediated environmentalism reliant on remote sensing technologies and mapping.

Introduced in 2020, the Planetary Computer was built on the heels of Microsoft's AI for Earth grant program to provide environmental research and conservation groups with a central platform for hosting data at scale and sharing machine learning tools (Smith, 2020). The homepage (headed *A Planetary Computer for a Sustainable Future*) has a minimalist aesthetic: highly-saturated, colorful satellite images, a simple description of the project, and links to the *Data Catalog*, the *API*, and *Applications* pages (Microsoft, 2020a). The site is expressly geared towards researchers with technical expertise who want to access data and tools as easily as possible.

In a 2019 video as part of Microsoft's *The futurefrom an alternative perspective* series, then-Chief Environmental Officer Lucas Joppa lays out a speculative vision for this resource (Microsoft, 2019b). Dressed in blue and standing in a surrealistic yellow cabin opening on a verdant wood, Joppa argues that "environmental concerns" constitute "the world's biggest" data, compute, and algorithmic challenges (Microsoft, 2019b, 2:48). He continues,

> And that's why we need solutions like artificial intelligence that are capable of being deployed at a planetary scale.... at its core, AI is just an algorithm that solves for an objective function. It solves a problem. And the biggest problem we need to solve right now is how we, as humans, can continue to grow and prosper without destroying the very ecosystems that we all depend on. (Microsoft, 2019b, 2:56)

Posing the problem in this way reflects the "informating of environmentalism," translating the climate crisis into a problem of gathering ever more data—now, a problem for AI to solve (Fortun, 2004; Gabrys, 2016).

The central promises of the Planetary Computer, accordingly, are scale and efficiency—specifically, the availability of compute via Azure and the sheer volume ("petabytes," the website emphasizes) of "global environmental data" (Microsoft, 2020a, para. 1). The description of the *Data Catalog* emphasizes that datasets are available "in consistent, analysis-ready formats," implying that the work of data preparation has already been done, while the API "makes it easy for users to find exactly the data they need" (Microsoft, 2020a, para. 2). In linked technical documentation, the project is described as letting users "leverage the power of the cloud to accelerate environmental sustainability and Earth science" (Microsoft, 2022, para. 1). The implication is that the Planetary Computer speeds up research and conservation by reducing the work involved. In this, like the Cloud for Sustainability tools, it can be read as reducing—or at least, appearing to reduce—data friction. At the same time, Microsoft deemphasizes the material environmental impact of data and computation at such a large scale.

The technical documentation also discusses the Planetary Computer's reliance on open-source tools and standards, emphasizing that data is "made available to users for free" (Microsoft, 2022, para. 2). This, too, is an argument about efficiency, economics, and environment: building on the "incredible ecosystem of tools being developed in the open" enables the API to "streamline and standardize" data (Microsoft, 2022, para. 3); meanwhile, some (but not all) Planetary Computer components are reciprocally made open source. The discourse of "freeness" and "openness" is premised on the assumption that data and tools are, by default, proprietary and costly—implying that the Planetary Computer is a gift to environmentalism. This exemplifies what Aronczyk and Espinoza (2022) describe as "data philanthropy," relying on a philosophy of "shared value" that ultimately sustains tech companies' data-centric business model as much as anything else (p. 185). Indeed, as Lukacz (2024) argues, "data curation practices position Microsoft's computational infrastructure and ML expertise as 'obligatory passage point[s]' (Callon, 1984) between information and decision" (p. 3). On one level, the Planetary Computer is a benevolent contribution to environmental research and conservation; on another, it positions Azure as the necessary cloud infrastructure of that work.

This infrastructural positioning is accompanied by a particular vision of sustainability and environmentalism as necessitating "planetary scale" embedded in the datasets and AI applications the Planetary Computer hosts. Of the more than 100 datasets in the *Data Catalog*, a preponderance contain remote sensing data, particularly from satellites—literally producing an extraterrestrial planetary view. The vast majority are aimed at global mapping and modeling applications using AI. Among the datasets that are not global in scope, all but a few focus on North America or, even more specifically, the United States. Much of the global satellite data comes from U.S. government agencies such as NASA (Landsat) or the European Space Agency's Copernicus program (Sentinel). This reflects the stark skew towards the "Global North" in environmental mapping data observed by Lin (2024)—a discrepancy suggestive of precisely whose view from above constitutes the "planetary." Meanwhile, the applications highlighted on the website, from Esri's ArcGIS for Planetary Computer tools ("free" with Azure and ArcGIS licenses), to the Impact Observatory's Global Land Use and Land Cover Classification map, to Imazon's Deforestation Risk Analysis predictions, also emphasize the use of AI for the mapping and modeling needs of environmental researchers and decision-makers. The planetary imaginary, then, encourages specific approaches to environmental crisis that evoke what Haraway (1988) terms "the god trick," (p. 581) the "view from above" (p. 589) that universalizes specific white, Western, masculinist ways of seeing.

In promotional materials and on the Planetary Computer's website, the environmental impact of the cloud and AI tools themselves are, once again, deemphasized—this time, to position AI as a "planetary scale" solution to the datafied problems of the climate crisis. Joppa concludes the speculative promotional video by declaring, "We have to agree that the objective function for human species on Earth is to minimize our environmental impacts while maximizing the overall global human experience. And the good news is that if we can agree on that, then technology can take us the rest of the way. The future is ours to decide" (Microsoft, 2019b, 8:12). The zoomed-out imaginary of the datafied planet, aided by AI, could empower humans-as-species to decouple environmental resource consumption from "maximizing" the "global human experience"—presumably code for economic prosperity and business growth; this is the future Microsoft wants us to choose.

The Cruel Optimism of the Cloudy Future

Each of the projects discussed above reflects a facet of the economic and environmental sociotechnical imaginary of sustainability embedded in Azure cloud infrastructure: Microsoft's data center sustainability efforts aspire to decouple resource consumption and business growth via logics of investment, efficiency, and circularity; Cloud for Sustainability tools commoditize Azure as the infrastructure of sustainability via dashboards that standardize and decontextualize environmental impact; and the Planetary Computer offers free and open environmental data at immense scale that is nonetheless not without cost. They play with infrastructural (in)visibility in different ways, from the temporal and spatial displacement of data center resource consumption and replenishment, to dashboards that give "clear line of sight" into ESG reporting by dematerializing environmental impact into a datafied natural sublime, to the "view from above" of planetary computing.

All three cases promulgate AI as environmental "solution" by translating environmental problems into problems of data that can be algorithmically modeled. Microsoft deploys AI throughout its data center sustainability efforts, including using predictive weather modeling to optimize water usage and developing the IDARS system for hardware disposal. It incorporates its generative AI chatbot Copilot into ESG reporting tools, which also offer speculative "what-if" analysis for modeling decoupling strategies. The entirety of the Planetary Computer is geared towards AI, with a specific, limiting focus on mapping and modeling remote sensing data. This is reflective of a broad organizational strategy; on Microsoft's main CSR sustainability page, the Chief Sustainability Officer is quoted as saying that AI offers "new opportunities to speed up the availability of climate solutions" (Microsoft, 2024a, para. 6). The page links to a report titled *Accelerating Sustainability with AI: A Playbook*, which argues, "AI is a vital tool to help accelerate the deployment of existing sustainability solutions and the development of new ones—faster, cheaper, and better," in service of a "nature-positive future" (Luers et al., 2023, p. 4).

Microsoft's investments in sustainability are substantial and likely developed in earnest by employees who exhibit a corporate "sustainability ethic" that consists of both "a genuine commitment to solving these diverse problems" and "a belief that only market-based solutions can solve them" (Archer, 2024, p. 17). In an ethnography of workers at a solar energy corporation, Lennon (2024) describes environmental solutionism as "an affective technique that generates the aura of expertise that not only enables corporations to grow their profits and establish their market niche, but also enables employees to perform a humanitarian identity" (p. S140). However, this depoliticizes the environmental problem itself. In this, Microsoft is not alone; Google Cloud and Amazon Web Services similarly embed neoliberal imaginaries of sustainability in cloud infrastructure. As Parikka (2011) observes, such ecological investments do not change the fundamental logics of accumulation; accordingly, "the discourse of sustainability on its own is unsustainable" (p. 17). The effects of this extend far beyond greenwashing, or false marketing. The neoliberal imaginary of sustainability does more than sell cloud computing; it limits imagination and materially shapes cloud infrastructure, foreclosing other possible arrangements of computation and environment.

Microsoft's emphasis on AI's ability to "accelerate" climate solutions evinces a fantasy that technological progress will lead toward ever-more-perfect knowledge and a more sustainable way of being, a mindset that Hong (2020) critiques as the "default to technology," requiring acceptance of capitalist extraction even as it hangs hope on the "next version, the next project, the next invention" (p. 185). In Microsoft's case, faith in technology's ability to reconcile capitalism with environmentalism depoliticizes the present in favor of a "sustainable future." Discourses of this future rely on temporal and spatial displacement, commoditized "journeys," and speculative visions to perpetually defer sustainability. Framing AI as essential to this future subsumes its growing present-day environmental impact to its as-yet unrealized potential. There is a "cruel optimism" (Berlant, 2011) at work in the fantasy attached to cloud infrastructure that unchecked capitalist growth and technological innovation—now via AI—can lead out of the climate crisis rather than deeper in. Infrastructure thus manifests as "concrete instantiations of visions of the future" and "shapes the present through a politics of anticipation" (Gupta, 2018, p. 63).

Read together, these projects of imagination and infrastructure expose the infrastructural power of Microsoft Azure's sustainable cloud politics, power that is aimed at "the (re)production and enforcement of capitalist relations" (Khalili, 2018, p. 915). Luitse (2024) argues that in cloud infrastructures, providers mobilize infrastructural power through vertical integration of services, complementary innovation, and abstraction of technical complexity. Here, I suggest that Microsoft exercises infrastructural power by rendering Azure the datafied infrastructure of sustainability—for itself, for customers across industries, and for environmental knowledge production and decision-making. In doing so, it reflects what Wiessner et al. (2026) call "green data capitalism," which "describes the ways that the traces left by humans and non-humans in interactions with networked systems become valued data for green enterprise" and reproduces power dynamics such as those of the urban/rural divide. This framework combines the technology- and economic growth-centered aspirations of green capitalism with data capitalism, defined as "a system in which the commoditization of our data enables a redistribution of power" that is "weighted toward the actors who have access and the capability to make sense of data" (West, 2019, p. 23). Asymmetries of power emerge in Microsoft's global reach into and across the local communities and ecosystems its data centers impact; the tensions of selling sustainability tools to make environmentally damaging industries such as oil and gas more efficient; and the skew towards the "Global North" in aggregated remote sensing data and environmental mapping tools.

Alternatives to Microsoft's unsustainable sustainability imaginary could exist. What would it look like to foreground place-based accountability for the material impacts of the cloud rather than fungibility, displacement, and abstraction (Pasek, 2019)? To be grounded in relational ways of being in and knowing the environment rather than dematerializing what can be measured, visualized, and financialized from landscapes and concealing or discarding the rest (Mattern, 2015; Pasek et al., 2023)? To acknowledge the limits of the knowledge that emerges from datafication and AI rather than perpetually intensifying dependence on technology (Hong, 2020)? We must (re)politicize the relationship between imagination and infrastructure to confront what is actually sustained in "sustainable" cloud infrastructure.

Competing Interests The author has no conflicts of interest to declare that are relevant to the contents of this chapter.

References

Appel, H., Anand, N., & Gupta, A. (2018). Temporality, politics, and the promise of infrastructure. In N. Anand, A. Gupta, & H. Appel (Eds.), *The promise of infrastructure* (pp. 1–38). Duke University Press Books. https://doi.org/10.1215/9781478002031

Archer, M. (2024). *Unsustainable: Measurement, reporting, and the limits of corporate sustainability*. NYU Press. https://doi.org/10.18574/nyu/9781479822034.001.0001

Aronczyk, M., & Espinoza, M. I. (2022). *A strategic nature: Public relations and the politics of American environmentalism*. Oxford University Press. https://doi.org/10.1093/oso/9780190055349.001.0001

Berlant, L. (2011). *Cruel optimism*. Duke University Press Books. https://doi.org/10.1215/9780822394716

Borkar, R. (2022, March 15). *Learn how Microsoft Circular Centers are scaling cloud supply chain sustainability*. Microsoft Azure Blog. https://azure.microsoft.com/en-us/blog/learn-how-microsoft-circular-centers-are-scaling-cloud-supply-chain-sustainability/

Brain, T., & Lavigne, S. (2024). *All that is air melts into air*. E-Flux Architecture. https://www.e-flux.com/architecture/spatial-computing/592129/all-that-is-air-melts-into-air/

Edwards, D., Cooper, Z. G. T., & Hogan, M. (2024). The making of critical data center studies. *Convergence, 31*(2), 429–446. https://doi.org/10.1177/13548565231224157

Edwards, P. N. (1997). *The closed world: Computers and the politics of discourse in Cold War America*. MIT Press. https://doi.org/10.7551/mitpress/1871.001.0001

Edwards, P. N. (2013). *A vast machine: Computer models, climate data, and the politics of global warming*. MIT Press. https://ebookcentral.proquest.com/lib/socal/detail.action?docID=3339172

Fortun, K. (2004). From Bhopal to the informating of environmentalism: Risk communication in historical perspective. *Osiris, 19*, 283–296. https://doi.org/10.1086/649407

Gabrys, J. (2016). Practicing, materialising and contesting environmental data. *Big Data & Society, 3*(2), 1–7. https://doi.org/10.1177/2053951716673391

Grijpink, F., Katsap, N., Verre, F., & Ward, R. (2020, November 6). *Oil and gas technology: Connectivity for higher performance*. McKinsey & Company. https://www.mckinsey.com/industries/oil-and-gas/our-insights/how-tapping-connectivity-in-oil-and-gas-can-fuel-higher-performance

Gupta, A. (2018). The future in ruins: Thoughts on the temporality of infrastructure. In N. Anand, A. Gupta, & H. Appel (Eds.), *The promise of infrastructure* (pp. 62–79). Duke University Press Books. https://doi.org/10.1215/9781478002031

Hajer, M. A. (1997). *The politics of environmental discourse: Ecological modernization and the policy process*. Oxford University Press. https://doi.org/10.1093/019829333X.003.0002

Hao, K. (2024a, March 1). AI is taking water from the desert. *The Atlantic*. https://www.theatlantic.com/technology/archive/2024/03/ai-water-climate-microsoft/677602/

Hao, K. (2024b, September 13). Microsoft's hypocrisy on AI. *The Atlantic*. https://www.theatlantic.com/technology/archive/2024/09/microsoft-ai-oil-contracts/679804/

Haraway, D. (1988). Situated knowledges: The science question in feminism and the privilege of partial perspective. *Feminist Studies, 14*(3), 575–599. https://doi.org/10.2307/3178066

Hogan, M. (2018). Big data ecologies. *Ephemera, 18*(3), 631–657. http://ephemerajournal.org/sites/default/files/pdfs/contribution/18-3hogan.pdf

Hong, S. (2020). *Technologies of speculation: The limits of knowledge in a data-driven society*. NYU Press. https://doi.org/10.18574/nyu/9781479860234.001.0001

Hu, T.-H. (2015). *A prehistory of the cloud*. MIT Press. https://doi.org/10.7551/mitpress/9780262029513.001.0001

Jasanoff, S., & Kim, S.-H. (Eds.). (2015). *Dreamscapes of modernity: Sociotechnical imaginaries and the fabrication of power*. University of Chicago Press. https://doi.org/10.7208/chicago/9780226276663.001.0001

Kareem, S. M. (2024, April 18). *New AI-powered features for Microsoft Sustainability Manager*. Microsoft Industry. https://www.microsoft.com/en-us/industry/blog/sustainability/2024/04/18/advance-your-carbon-reduction-strategy-with-intelligent-forecasting-and-data-analysis/

Khalili, L. (2018). The infrastructural power of the military: The geoeconomic role of the US Army Corps of Engineers in the Arabian Peninsula. *European Journal of International Relations, 24*(4), 911–933. https://doi.org/10.1177/1354066117742955

Larkin, B. (2013). The politics and poetics of infrastructure. *Annual Review of Anthropology, 42*, 327–343. https://doi.org/10.1146/annurev-anthro-092412-155522

Lennon, M. (2024). The problem with "solutions": Apolitical optimism in the sustainable energy industry. *Current Anthropology*, S130–S154. https://doi.org/10.1086/731293

Lin, C. (2024). Knowing nature through data. In T. Venturini, A. Acker, J.-C. Plantin, & T. Walford (Eds.), *The Sage handbook of data and society* (pp. 207–230). Sage. https://doi.org/10.4135/9781529674699.n13

Luers, A., Dhu, T., Salas, A., Strauss, K., Ferres, J. L., Alissa, H., Alpine, W., Bianchi, G., Gillett, S., Meyer, L., Patron, M., & White, K. (2023). *Accelerating sustainability with AI: A playbook*. Microsoft. https://blogs.microsoft.com/on-the-issues/2023/11/16/accelerating-sustainability-ai-playbook/

Luitse, D. (2024). Platform power in AI: The evolution of cloud infrastructures in the political economy of artificial intelligence. *Internet Policy Review, 13*(2), 1–44. https://policyreview.info/articles/analysis/platform-power-ai-evolution-cloud-infrastructures

Lukacz, P. M. (2024). Imaginaries of democratization and the value of open environmental data: Analysis of Microsoft's planetary computer. *Big Data & Society, 11*(2), 1–14. https://doi.org/10.1177/20539517241242448

Mattern, S. (2015). Mission control: A history of the urban dashboard. *Places*. https://doi.org/10.22269/150309

Microsoft. (2019a, July 30). *Building world-class sustainable datacenters and investing in solar power in Arizona*. Microsoft On the Issues. https://blogs.microsoft.com/on-the-issues/2019/07/30/building-world-class-sustainable-datacenters-and-investing-in-solar-power-in-arizona/

Microsoft. (2019b, December 5). *A planetary computer for Earth* [Video recording]. https://www.youtube.com/watch?v=y9eJMzZEjlc

Microsoft. (2020a). *A planetary computer for a sustainable future*. Retrieved March 15, 2025, from https://planetarycomputer.microsoft.com/

Microsoft. (2020b). *Enable ESG data intelligence guided tour*. Retrieved April 30, 2025, from https://guidedtour.microsoft.com/en-us/guidedtour/sustainability/enable-esg-data-intelligence/1/1

Microsoft. (2021). *2020 environmental sustainability report: A year of action*. https://aka.ms/MSFTSustainabilityReport2020

Microsoft. (2022). *Planetary computer: Documentation*. Retrieved April 30, 2025, from https://planetarycomputer.microsoft.com/docs/overview/about

Microsoft. (2023a). *Water replenishment: Our learnings on the journey to water positive*. https://cdn-dynmedia-1.microsoft.com/is/content/microsoftcorp/microsoft/msc/documents/presentations/CSR/Water-replenishment-learnings-on-journey-to-water.pdf

Microsoft. (2023b). Modern datacenter cooling [Infographic]. https://datacenters.microsoft.com/wp-content/uploads/2023/05/Azure_Modern-Datacenter-Cooling_Infographic.pdf

Microsoft. (2024a). *Advance sustainability*. Retrieved November 20, 2024, from https://www.microsoft.com/en-us/corporate-responsibility/sustainability

Microsoft. (2024b). *How can we advance sustainability? 2024 environmental sustainability report*. https://cdn-dynmedia-1.microsoft.com/is/content/microsoftcorp/microsoft/msc/documents/presentations/CSR/Microsoft-2024-Environmental-Sustainability-Report.pdf

Microsoft. (n.d.-a). *Accelerating the global transition to cleaner energy*. Retrieved April 30, 2025, from https://www.microsoft.com/en-us/sustainability/energy

Microsoft. (n.d.-b). *Microsoft Cloud for sustainability*. Retrieved November 21, 2024, from https://www.microsoft.com/en-us/sustainability/cloud#hero-video

Microsoft. (n.d.-c). *What is sustainability? Definition & importance*. Retrieved March 14, 2025, from https://www.microsoft.com/en-us/sustainability/learning-center/sustainability-definition

Microsoft Consulting Services. (2021, November 2). *Microsoft Circular Centers program achieves 83% reuse, increasing supply chain efficiency and resiliency with Dynamics 365 and Power Platform*. Microsoft Customers Stories. Retrieved

November 18, 2024, from https://customers.microsoft.com/en-us/story/1431789627332547010-microsoftcircular-centers

Microsoft Story Labs. (2021). *We live in the cloud*. Retrieved November 18, 2024, from https://news.microsoft.com/stories/microsoft-datacenter-tour/

Monserrate, S. G. (2022, Winter). *The cloud is material: On the environmental impacts of computation and data storage*. MIT Case Studies in Social and Ethical Responsibilities of Computing. https://doi.org/10.21428/2c646de5.031d4553

Mosco, V. (2014). *To the cloud: Big Data in a turbulent world*. Routledge. https://doi.org/10.4324/9781315631554

Parikka, J. (2011). Introduction: The materiality of media and waste. In J. Parikka (Ed.), *Medianatures: The materiality of information technology and electronic waste*. Open Humanities Press. https://livingbooksaboutlife.org/pdfs/bookarchive/Medianatures.pdf

Pasek, A. (2019). Managing carbon and data flows: Fungible forms of mediation in the cloud. *Culture Machine, 18*. https://culturemachine.net/vol-18-the-nature-of-data-centers/managing-carbon/

Pasek, A., Vaughan, H., & Starosielski, N. (2023). The world wide web of carbon: Toward a relational footprinting of information and communications technology's climate impacts. *Big Data & Society, 10*(1), 1–14. https://doi.org/10.1177/20539517231158994

Smith, B. (2020, April 15). *A healthy society requires a healthy planet*. The Official Microsoft Blog. https://blogs.microsoft.com/blog/2020/04/15/a-healthy-society-requires-a-healthy-planet/

Star, S. L. (1999). The ethnography of infrastructure. *American Behavioral Scientist, 43*(3), 377–391. https://doi.org/10.1177/00027649921955326

Tienhaara, K. (2014). Varieties of green capitalism: Economy and environment in the wake of the global financial crisis. *Environmental Politics, 23*(2), 187–204. https://doi.org/10.1080/09644016.2013.821828

Velkova, J. (2016). Data that warms: Waste heat, infrastructural convergence and the computation traffic commodity. *Big Data & Society, 3*(2), 1–10. https://doi.org/10.1177/2053951716684144

Walsh, N. (2021, June 15). *Expanding cloud services: Microsoft launches its sustainable datacenter region in Arizona*. Microsoft Azure Blog. https://azure.microsoft.com/en-us/blog/expanding-cloud-services-microsoft-launches-its-sustainable-datacenter-region-in-arizona/

Walsh, N. (2024, July 25). *Sustainable by design: Transforming datacenter water efficiency*. The Microsoft Cloud Blog. https://www.microsoft.com/en-us/microsoft-cloud/blog/2024/07/25/sustainable-by-design-transforming-datacenter-water-efficiency/

West, S. M. (2019). Data capitalism: Redefining the logics of surveillance and privacy. *Business & Society, 58*(1), 20–41. https://doi.org/10.1177/0007650317718185

Wiessner, M., Pasek, A., Starosielski, N., & Vaughan, H. (2026). Green data capitalism and its rural extractions. In D. Barney & P. Brodie (Eds.), *Media rurality* (pp. 41-64). Duke University Press. https://www.dukeupress.edu/media-rurality

World Commission on Environment and Development. (1987). *Our common future*. Oxford University Press. https://sustainabledevelopment.un.org/content/documents/5987our-common-future.pdf

CHAPTER 8

Narratives of Indispensability and Infrastructural Solutionism of AI Companies

Salla-Maaria Laaksonen and Meri Frig

Introduction

In summer 2024, Google reported that their energy consumption had risen 50% during the past five years due to the increasing demand caused by AI development, training, and use. The company admitted that this might hinder their goal of reaching net zero emissions by 2030, particularly with the "the uncertainty around the future environmental impact of AI, which is complex and difficult to predict" (Google, 2024, p. 31). This was a surprising "coming out" move for the company, and one of the first

S.-M. Laaksonen (✉) · M. Frig
University of Helsinki, Helsinki, Finland
e-mail: salla.laaksonen@helsinki.fi

M. Frig
e-mail: meri.frig@aalto.fi

M. Frig
Aalto University, Espoo, Finland

A. Mollen et al. (eds.), *AI Infrastructures and Sustainability*, Palgrave Studies in European Communication Research and Education,
https://doi.org/10.1007/978-3-032-09748-4_8

moments when environmental concerns and increasing AI use have been articulated together by the business actors themselves. Instead, discussions on digital technology typically come with techno-optimistic and digital solutionist frames suggesting that technology can help in solving the world's biggest challenges, including the climate crisis (Brenner & Hartl, 2021; Kuntsman & Rattle, 2019; Morozov, 2014). However, increasing concerns have been expressed over the environmental sustainability of digital technology, due to its high energy- and water footprint, and related waste disposal and raw material extraction (Freitag et al., 2021; Istrate et al., 2024; Pasek et al., 2023). Similarly, recent studies have highlighted the substantial environmental costs of AI, in particular generative AI and deploying large-scale AI models (Brevini, 2020; Crawford, 2024; Li et al., 2023; Verdecchia et al., 2023). The majority of the emissions reported by technology companies comes from data centers, with a reported increase of 45% between 2020 and 2022 (World Bank & ITU, 2024).

AI is first and foremost a business project that relies on infrastructural power. Development of AI is largely controlled by big tech companies, who have already accumulated significant societal power as providers of global information and communication infrastructures (Helberger et al., 2018; Kak et al., 2023; Nieborg et al., 2024; Plantin et al., 2018). These multinational digital corporations dominate global markets in digital content distribution, cloud infrastructure, digital search, digital advertising, and digital messaging. Studies in media and communication studies and platform studies have discussed the infrastructural power of the big tech companies over communication flows (e.g., Helberger et al., 2018; Plantin et al., 2018). Through their communication infrastructure design, the companies enable and constrain the styles and means of communication of their users, guided by a deeply embedded capitalistic logic that aims to monetize the social relations they mediate—that is, to connect users with advertisers (Srnicek, 2016; van Dijck, 2013). In addition, some of the companies—most notably Amazon, Google, and Microsoft—also play a more profoundly infrastructural role in the data economy: They provide databases and computing infrastructure that keep our online shops working, trains running, and host the ever-expanding data storage and analytics services for other companies.

In this chapter, we examine what kinds of future-oriented promissory stories the AI and cloud infrastructure industry tells concerning environmental sustainability in their corporate communication in order to reinforce their infrastructural power. Promissory stories are narratives about desired futures that political and economic leaders, such as corporations, rely on to gain legitimacy and mobilize stakeholders (Beckert, 2020). Corporations, furthermore, are recognized as important agential collectives in terms of climate responsibility (e.g., in the United Nations' SDGs), which has led to an increasing focus on environmental issues in the public communication by corporations (e.g., Ihlen, 2009). Such communication can be utilized for ideological persuasion and greenwashing (Mason & Mason, 2012), to postpone dealing with complex issues to an unknown future (Tuan et al., 2024), but also more broadly to garner societal acceptance for the companies and discursively construct desired realities and societal positions (Vaara et al., 2024). At the same time, corporate environmental communication can be viewed as performative and aspirational (e.g., Christensen et al., 2013; Nyberg & Wright, 2016), inviting us to consider its potential impact and the kinds of futures it propagates both inside and outside the company. Nevertheless, corporate communication is strategically employed to pursue specific goals and exert power and influence.

To explore corporate communication around AI infrastructures and sustainability, we turn our empirical gaze to sustainability-related entries in the corporate blogs over a period of 24 years (2000–2024) by five major global digital infrastructure companies: Amazon, Apple, Google, IBM, and Microsoft, all significant providers of cloud infrastructure and artificial intelligence (AI) technologies. We used dictionary-based filtering and corpus linguistics assisted discourse analysis to explore how the companies strategically articulate their technological infrastructure and sustainability together to construct promissory stories towards sustainable futures. Our findings highlight how they amalgamate sustainability issues to construct expanding legitimacy for their infrastructural power and simultaneously hide the increasing concerns over the growing environmental impact of digitalization.

AI Infrastructure Companies and Their Promissory Futures

Scholars have highlighted how the power of platform and AI companies should be understood as infrastructural, networked, and relational, which requires a look beyond individual technologies and actors (Brodie, 2023; Nieborg et al., 2024; Plantin et al., 2018; van der Vlist et al., 2024). Approaching digital technology as an infrastructure also provides conceptual tools to understand its materiality. As Brian Larkin (2013) puts it, infrastructures are material and physical networks that "facilitate the flow of goods, people, or ideas and allow for their exchange over space" (p. 327). While digital infrastructures are the grid of modern society, they become invisible in our everyday relations and assimilate into the background, as infrastructures typically do (Star, 1999). Instead, the infrastructure emerges to us through the matter which it enables to move (Larkin, 2013); in the case of communication infrastructures, we see the content of digital communication, as well as the tools we use to consume it, but the data centers, cables and electricity networks tend to fall out of our sight. As all infrastructures, also infrastructures of AI, are at the same time invisible and opaque.

However, infrastructures are also social constructions that are constantly imagined, shaped, reshaped and made to matter in discourse. As Parks and Starosielski (2015) remind us, media infrastructures are sociotechnical systems that are "material forms as well as discursive constructions" (p. 5). They are material, but also materialized in communication (Cooren, 2018) through policy documents, corporate plans, design schemes, and press coverage. This perspective renders AI not only a business project but also a discursive project, maintained and imagined through social constructions. Overall, the future-oriented stories of the AI industry have been predominantly stories that stress the emerging human-like nature and capabilities of AI and hypothetical future systems (Bory et al., 2024). Another set of more business-oriented stories has, however, circulated around the infrastructures of the data and AI economy, such as data centers and related investments (e.g., Brodie, 2023).

The corporations that own the AI infrastructure also take part in the discursive construction of that infrastructure. Both the inflated public stories around AI as well as the opaqueness of AI infrastructures tend to hide the notion that AI is controlled and dominated by corporate entities (Kak et al., 2023; Plantin et al., 2018), embedded in the cultural circuit of the constantly expanding and concentrating platform capitalism (Narayan, 2022; Srnicek, 2016). Platform capitalism is characterized by data-driven business models, rapid expansion, scalability, speculative financial logics, and weak regulatory mechanisms (Narayan, 2022; Srnicek, 2016). This also renders it as a field of capitalism which is in a state of constant fluctuation, and therefore requires discursive strategies to maintain its appeal, legitimacy, and promissory futures (e.g., Beckert, 2020;

Thrift, 2005). Expectations, discourses and narratives are used in organizations to produce and enact imagined futures and promissory stories (Beckert, 2020, 2021; Haupt, 2021; Mager & Katzenbach, 2021).

Future-oriented discursive work is suggested to be typical to companies in the future-oriented context of technological innovation (Borup et al., 2006; Pollock & Williams, 2010), where future expectations are strongly associated with expectations of market value and business promises (e.g., Beer, 2019; Pollock & Williams, 2010). As Jasanoff (2015) puts it:

> Multinational corporations increasingly act upon imagined understandings of how the world is and ought to be, playing upon the perceived hopes and fears of their customers and clients and thereby propagating notions of technological progress and benefit that cut across. (Jasanoff, 2015, p. 27)

By portraying some future scenarios as more plausible or attractive than others, they help actors momentarily overlook uncertainty in the future (Beckert, 2016) and imply a commitment to a set of particular future possibilities (Berkhout, 2006). These imagined futures are communicated externally in the form of corporate communication, where companies across industries increasingly address questions related to environmental sustainability.

Promissory Stories in Corporate Environmental Communication

Corporations play a central role in the climate crisis by making decisions that affect the climate and natural ecosystems, but also as meaning-makers in the public sphere. Environmental problems such as the climate crisis are considered to present risks but also business opportunities, which is why corporate environmental discourses typically assume compatibility between business interests and the protection of the planet (Nyberg et al., 2022). Consequently, win–win eco-technological frames that emphasize how certain management decisions and ideas benefit business, the planet, and society simultaneously, are prominent in corporate environmental communication (e.g., Frig et al., 2016; Nyberg et al., 2022). Most importantly, corporate environmental communication not only addresses how organizations understand and engage with the natural environment, but need to be analyzed as a practice with performative qualities. This means it not only depicts but also shapes present and future scenarios and sustainability actions (Borup et al., 2006; Nyberg & Wright, 2016), which shifts our attention to what such communication can achieve. It has been argued that corporate environmental communication can be understood as "aspirational talk" that can stimulate action and lead to positive social change (Christensen et al., 2013).

The promissory stories of future states of the world and envisioned courses of action told by organizations, if credible, wield significant influence in the political and economic social order (Beckert, 2020; Pollock & Williams, 2010). The power of promissory stories is rooted in their ability to construct political legitimacy (Beckert, 2020). As Beckert notes, this legitimacy is built on the persuasive power of the narratives rather than any clear foreknowledge of the future. Promissory stories can build legitimacy through reflecting knowledge and conveying "interests, hopes, fantasies, and social norms" (Beckert, 2020, p. 319). Credible and successful promissory stories therefore effectively tap into the aspired realities of stakeholders, and can motivate support and mobilize stakeholders to follow the proposed course of action. By creating expectations about the future and establishing trust in companies' ability to pursue aspired realities, environmental communication can succeed to steer others in ways that suit their goals. For example, corporate environmental communication can be used as a tool to inspire others to achieve common goals, convince investors, and discourage regulatory interference (Frig et al., 2016). Environmental communication is also used to organize and construct the corporation's role and strategy. For example, stated climate targets and other environmental goals can be seen as "commissives" that commit the organization to a course of action (Christensen et al., 2021, p. 411). Therefore, even when there is no certainty of their materialization in the future, the promises and offered future imaginaries themselves organize and constitute behavior.

Despite these future-building capabilities, corporate environmental communication cannot be equated to their environmental action. Companies have also been shown to "cherry pick" what they highlight in their environmental communication (Tuan et al., 2024), promoting their environmental credentials and accomplishments while hiding or downplaying complex and contested topics. Corporate environmental communication is also criticized for ambiguous language, which can be used to display care for the state of the environment without a deep-rooted examination of how the company impacts and engages with its material ecosystem (Frig et al., 2026; Pezzullo, 2024). Promissory stories work to persuade rather than inform, and therefore, can hide more than explain. In this regard, communicating about the AI infrastructure is expected to be a tensioned element for the AI corporations. The infrastructure is at the same time the main tenet of their power and business promise, but also the very thing that embodies the material consequences in terms of sustainability: building AI infrastructures requires land, water, energy, and raw materials (e.g., Brevini, 2020; Brodie, 2023; Crawford, 2024; Pasek et al., 2023).

Materials and Methods

Our empirical data consists of entries in the corporate blogs or news sections (collectively referred to here as blogs) of five major data infrastructure companies: Amazon, Apple, Google, IBM, and Microsoft, that all are significant providers of cloud infrastructure and increasingly AI technologies. Our complete dataset included N = 44,670 posts published between March 2000 and January 2024. As contextual data, we used the fall 2024 versions of the sustainability sections on the companies' websites.

We used dictionary-based filtering to identify blog posts related to environmental sustainability. An initial search with a set of sustainability-related keywords ("climate change", "sustainable", "renewable energy", "emissions", "greenhouse gas", "recycle", 'recycling", "sustainability", "corporate social responsibility", "water usage", "workers", "waste", "sdg", "green") yielded 1048 posts in total. A manual topic verification was conducted by the first author using the blog post titles and intros to include only posts where environmental sustainability was a main topic, resulting in a final dataset of 497 blog posts (151 posts from Amazon, 228 from Google, 48 from IBM, 39 from Apple and 31 from Microsoft, see Fig. 8.1).

Corporate blogs are a form of promotional corporate communication and thus biased towards a positive tone and aim to facilitate an inclusive corporate image (Fieseler et al., 2010). Blogs provide a relatively protected platform for companies to share important information and ideas to stakeholders, yet they do not facilitate dialogue or offer space for criticism. However, they are less formal than corporate annual reporting or official public releases. This makes them prime examples to study how corporations engage in public communication to discursively shape their image and legitimate their actions. The blog posts in our data are typically posted under the authorship of the company name or a senior manager,

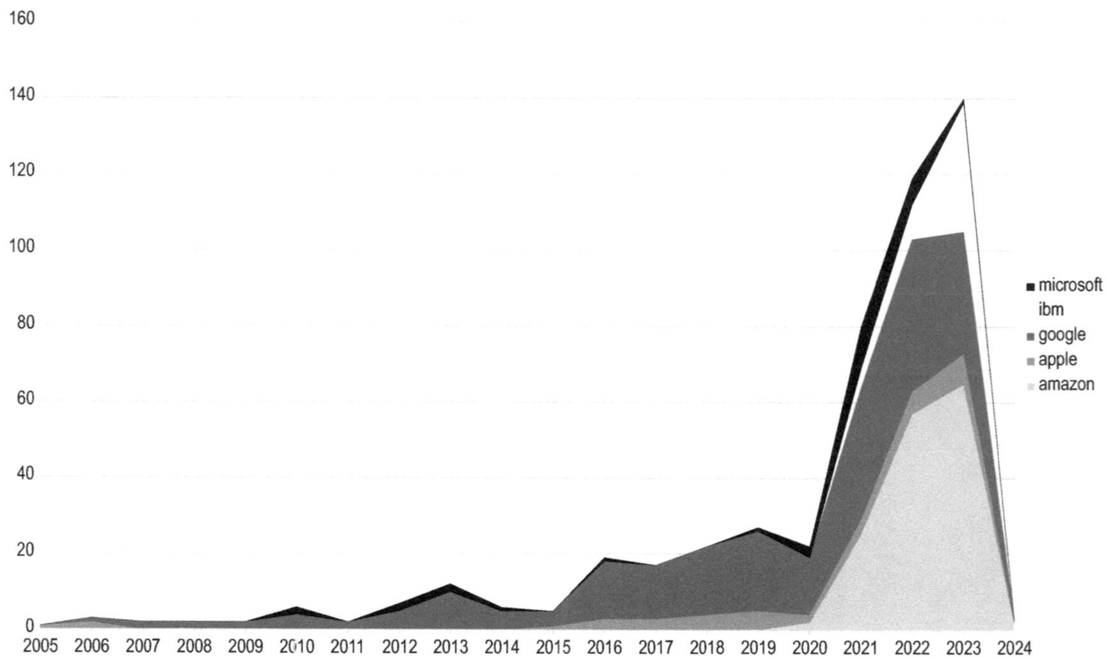

Fig. 8.1 Volume of blog entries per company in the final filtered data (n = 497). Figure produced by authors

but as public corporate communication documents, it can be assumed that the content has been controlled and edited by corporate communications.

We used corpus linguistics assisted discourse analysis to explore how the companies have discursively constructed stories of more sustainable futures. Corpus linguistic protocols and textual data visualizations in Voyant Tools (Sinclair & Rockwell, 2016) were employed to explore the vocabulary used and themes present in the corpus. This method gives us a helicopter view to the data: it allows us to explore the prevalence of main keywords over time, and also to see the sentence or paragraph level context in which these keywords are used. Next, using the central corpus keywords as well as keywords related to infrastructure (such as "data center", "infrastructure", "cloud", "aws", "architecture") as entry points, we used the content view in Voyant Tools to identify and explore passages in which promissory stories were discursively constructed around these keywords. The main approach of our analysis, however, is qualitative, with a focus on the roles narrated for AI infrastructures in the promissory future stories constructed by the companies. In the following findings section, we will first describe the general trends in the corpus and then move on to discuss two main discourses of infrastructural solutionism and AI-powered acceleration.

Findings

First blog posts in our data with environmental sustainability as the main focus were published in 2005 by Apple and 2006 by Google, but overall, the volume of the data is low before 2016. A major rise in environment-related posts is shown in 2021. Overall, Google is the company most vocal in the data, with a steady number of posts from 2016 onwards. The more B2B oriented companies, Amazon and IBM, started communicating about environmental issues only in 2021.

A major focus throughout the years was on the energy solutions for data centers, which consequently are the main element that materializes the infrastructure in the posts (499 mentions in total). Artificial intelligence or AI as a term emerged in March 2018 (see Fig. 2a). Before that, machine learning, deep learning, or other specific techniques were referred to. The analysis of the corpus keywords (Fig. 2a, b) hints towards the observation that questions related to renewable energy have been considered "solved" during the study period (probably with carbon offsetting, see e.g., Brodie, 2023), and the companies' focus has been diverted to AI solutions and related opportunities.

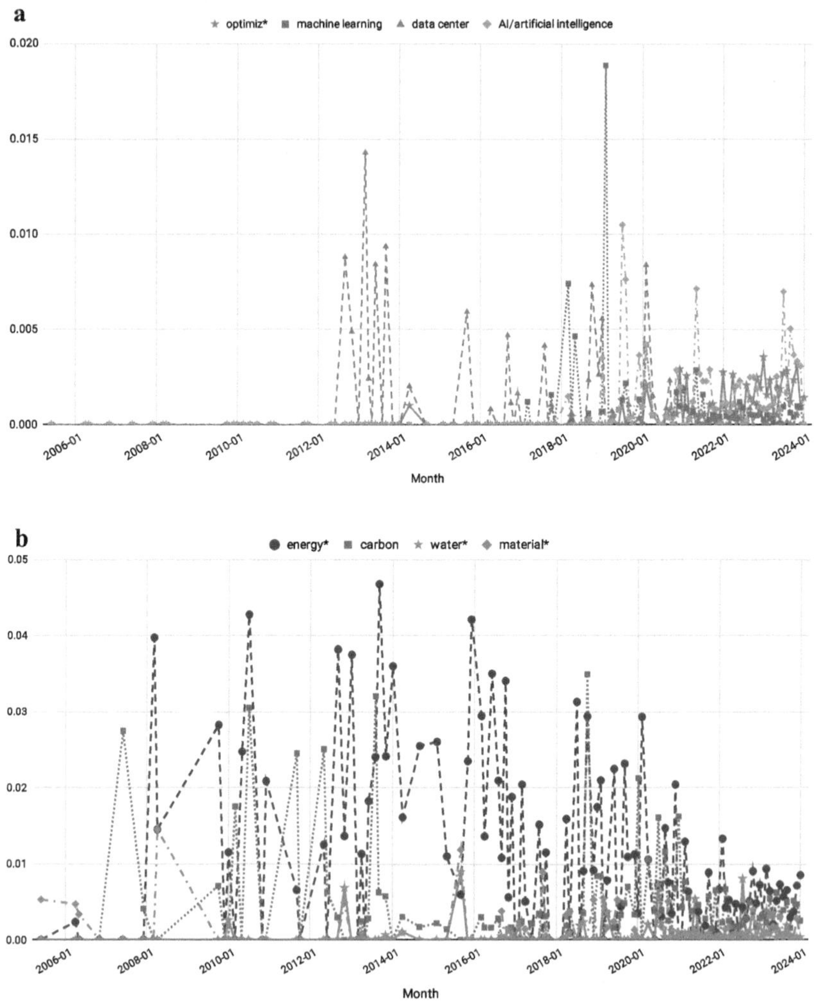

Fig. 8.2 Relative prevalence of selected keywords in the corpus over time, **a** data center, machine learning, artificial intelligence, **b** energy, carbon, water, material. Figures produced by authors

Environmental sustainability was predominantly approached through the emissions resulting from energy use, while other material aspects received less attention if any (see Fig. 2b). Renewable energy projects, both purchasing and investing, were heavily accentuated by the data center providers Amazon, Google, and Microsoft. As a major consumer product manufacturer, Apple frequently discussed the sustainability of its products and supply chains, ranging from energy and materials to recycling programs. Amazon and IBM both published several posts that instruct their customers to optimize their cloud processes for sustainability. Apple and Google also discussed the sustainability of their offices and office buildings, from energy use to food waste, with a general tone of technological sublime that portrays the buildings as technological achievements:

> With 17 megawatts of rooftop solar, Apple Park will run one of the largest on-site solar energy installations in the world. (Apple, 2017, para. 3)

In general, problems and challenges, when presented, were presented on a global scale, which consequently allowed the companies to present solutions to global problems. "[G]lobally only about 1 percent of our energy comes from solar", reminded Google in June 2016, and proceeded to promote Project Sunroof, a Google initiative that allows users to analyze their roof location, shape and local weather patterns using Google Earth imagery to "create a personalized solar plan" (Google Project Sunroof, n.d.). Strikingly, in the blog posts, there was no questioning of the increasing energy demand and intensification of digital activities, no question about reduction or limits—just a promissory story of digital technology that allows us to get all new shiny things without abandoning anything: "How immersive commerce can drive your sustainability goals while making your merch look fabulous" asks Amazon in December 2022 (Amazon, 2022, title). The future world promised to us by digital infrastructure companies is a world of abundance:

> Imagine a world of abundance—a world where products are infinitely recycled and the design process itself begins with considering the health and well-being of people and the environment. Imagine those products flowing through an economy that is both profitable and stems depletion of raw materials. That's the world we want for all of us, and Google is working with the experts who are getting us there. (Google, 2018a, para. 1)

Overall, future-orientation was very prominent in the discourses the companies mobilize. In terms of mission statements and slogans, sustainability is constructed as a central concern for the companies and a part of everything they do. For example, in their 2024 sustainability vision, Meta (2024, heading 3) declared they are "in the business of building better realities—and not just virtual ones" whereas Apple recurrently repeated it slogan saying "more than 100,000 employees are dedicated to making the best products on earth, and to leaving the world better than we found it" (e.g., Apple, 2016, para. 12). In the following, we will focus in depth on the grandiose roles given to the digital infrastructure and AI solutions in fulfilling these future visions.

Infrastructural Solutionism

Promissory stories aim to alleviate stakeholder uncertainty about the future (Beckert, 2020). In our data, this was visible particularly in narratives of technological solutions to global sustainability issues, which were envisioned and advocated by companies. In the corporate blog discourse, the complex issues of climate crisis and technological development amalgamate to an optimistic and techno-solutionist future narrative. In their promissory stories, the companies frequently connected sustainability questions to their overall success and business prospects. Consequently, technologies that they offer are presented as both a means and an end, as typical to technosolutionism (e.g., Morozov, 2014):

> Our vision is simple: we want a circular Google within a sustainable world. The challenges to making this vision a reality are as daunting as they are exciting. It demands that we redefine how systems work—from what we value and the choices we make, to the assumptions and industrial processes that have been standard practice across our economy for decades. (Google, 2019a, paras. 5–6)

In this promissory discourse the services and infrastructures offered by the companies are positioned as essential tools in the sustainability transition. This story is constructed across various blog post types: general sustainability updates, product releases, reporting on corporate social responsibility activities, and even positional texts directed to policy makers. These stories generate an optimistic future fantasy, with innovative and transformative business moves waiting ahead for all stakeholders. The inherent uncertainty introduced by climate change is confronted with certainty constructed by highlighting the technological magic related to the digital infrastructure:

> Entire sectors … are rethinking their approach to resource use and the value that Microsoft technology will play in helping them transform their approach to business. … We have an amazing opportunity in front of us to tap into the culture of innovation and the power of cloud computing, devices and our partner ecosystem to enable a transition to a new way of thinking and interacting with our planet's resources. (Microsoft, 2014, para. 7–8)

These posts propagate *infrastructural solutionism*: data and computing infrastructures were discursively constructed as environmentally friendly solutions. The companies frequently depict how their technologies and infrastructure help other actors to be more sustainable, often accompanied with data-based arguments showing the scale of energy or cost savings achieved by, for example, moving "to the cloud". For instance, Amazon published a series of posts talking about their cloud customers who improved the efficiency of their operations and thus reduced energy consumption. These actors ranged from retailers and energy technology pioneer companies to transport and agriculture businesses. Digital infrastructures, thus, have solutionist power across fields, and they are always compatible with other existing business goals:

> Today, the talented people of IBM are using our cutting-edge technologies, including hybrid cloud and AI, to keep transforming not only our own operations for increased sustainability, but also the operations of our clients and partners. (IBM, 2023a, para. 3)

Infrastructures were also narrated to be prime solutions for key actors in sustainability: intelligent data infrastructures help sustainability experts and climate scientists to do their work. Amazon and Google also reported on specific systems designed to help in the generation of sustainability-related knowledge and monitoring issues related to environmental risks. When publicizing these projects, the companies highlighted how their infrastructures, the data they host, and machine learning systems help the world to make sense about climate issues and other environmental concerns, which makes their infrastructures essential for knowledge production. This discourse connects to the broader data analytics imaginary (Beer, 2017): it is panoramic, prophetic, revealing and smart. Further, it puts forth the idea that the mere availability of information is a major factor in advancing climate goals globally, which fits well with the existing business promises of Google, in particular:

> It's just one way that we're helping organizations make sense of data and identify opportunities for change. Positive environmental impact is possible if we give people access to information. By filling in gaps in knowledge, we can help people and policymakers take actions that create change on a global scale. Ultimately, we hope Google can provide a platform for our users to change the world. Twenty years after our founding, we've only just begun. (Google, 2018b, para. 10)

Simultaneously, these stories legitimize the infrastructures by tying them together with actors and practices that are already sustainable, thus building authority for the companies and their infrastructure in the environmental realm. The innovations described, however, were mostly applications based on the existing systems, with no requirement to rethink the business model. Instead, they supported the infrastructural power of the companies by spreading their influence into new areas in everyday life and transforming their infrastructure also to be the infrastructure that enables eco-conscious choices for various stakeholders. Therefore, these solutions offered yet another way to legitimize the digital infrastructures owned by the technology companies as well as their expansion and power.

AI-Powered Sustainable Acceleration

When AI emerged as a specific term in 2018, it seamlessly fit into the existing promissory and solutionist story, but also expanded it. AI—typically used without explaining further what kind of AI—was touted as a means to improve efficiency and productivity, which are tightly woven with sustainability. AI helps, powers, empowers, improves, and accelerates. Consequently, the solutionist discourses became characterized with an overarching logic of progression and growth. The future path is, thus, marked with *sustainable acceleration* made possible by digital technology infrastructures. The examples from Google and IBM below highlight the promissory acceleration but also the amalgamation of profitability and sustainability:

> According to research we published this week with Ellen MacArthur Foundation and McKinsey & Company, AI can not only accelerate the shift to a more sustainable future, but also generate new value. Already, AI is helping businesses quickly make sense of data and make complex decisions. (Google, 2019a, b, para. 4)

> Creating a balanced sustainability/profitability roadmap is a powerful first step to driving organizations forward during the age of AI. (IBM, 2023d, para. 8)

The corporate discourse highlighted two key processes allowed and enhanced by data analytics and AI technologies: *automation* and *optimization*. These processes were presented as the one-size-fits-all solution across industries: be it bioreactors, steel and cement production, delivering parcels, or waste management. These two AI-enabled processes allow the simultaneous minimizing of environmental impact and expanding operations and economy, thus building on the same dual capability as infrastructural solutionism. As providers of automation and optimization, the companies highlighted their infrastructural knowledge: existing expertise related to data curation, machine learning and designing systems is transferred to the AI era, as shown in a blog post by IBM:

> This emerging area balances asset reliability and use optimization ... with sustainability, such as improvements in the areas of energy and water efficiency, waste management, and environment monitoring and management. ... Fortunately for utility companies, innovators like IBM have been developing tools to help businesses minimize their environmental impact and expand operations with efficiency. (IBM, 2023b, para. 4)

Like infrastructures, AI was presented as a tool for sustainability, but issues related to its sustainability were very rarely mentioned. Instead, it was presented as a solution that also makes *itself* and the infrastructure sustainable by increasing the efficiency of, for example, data centers and electricity networks:

> Thanks to advances in artificial intelligence and chip design, our data centers are seven times more energy efficient today than they were five years ago. (Google, 2019, para. 3)

> Smart grid technology—an integral part of energy's digital transformation—promises to modernize the traditional electrical system with an infusion of digital intelligence that helps energy providers transition to clean energy and reduce carbon emissions. (IBM, 2023c, para. 1)

The promissory stories related to AI are prime examples of stories that present business interests and planetary benefits as mutually compatible (e.g., Nyberg et al., 2022). They are stories that many stakeholders want to hear, as they give the permission to keep pursuing existing goals and plans without radical changes while still being sustainable. Therefore, they have high potential to be plausible promissory stories—which consequently are performative in the sense that they provide legitimate reasons for increasing AI adoption.

Conclusion

In this chapter, we used corporate blogs by five major AI and cloud infrastructure providers to examine how the companies constructed future-oriented promissory stories to showcase the importance of their infrastructure in the sustainability transition. Our findings highlight how digital infrastructure companies discursively built the relationship between their technologies and sustainability transition by framing digital infrastructures and AI as indispensable tools needed to strive towards greener societies. Unsurprisingly, digital technology was depicted as a solution which enables, simultaneously, achieving business profitability and sustainability. AI, in particular, is depicted as a means to even solve the existing problems—otherwise rarely mentioned—related to the sustainability of the digital infrastructure. This promissory story was stable across the data, and also reflects previous studies looking at the strategic blending of digital technologies and visions for better worlds (e.g., Haupt, 2021; Morozov, 2014; Srnicek, 2016).

Our analysis shows how in the context of the climate crisis, the technology companies colonize the novel area of rising public concern, sustainability, to bolster the power of their infrastructures (also Sharon & Gellert, 2023). By communicating that their infrastructures are relevant for the future and the sustainability transition, they effectively mobilize the sustainability question to legitimize their infrastructures. As the companies tell stories about plausible and attractive futures afforded by their technologies, they construct certainty into the uncertain future to convince stakeholders. Promissory stories, indeed, are only effective if stakeholders believe in them and take part in the futures they propose (Beckert, 2020). We suggest that in the middle of the so-called tech-lash, increasing demands for the responsibility of technology companies more generally, the industry desperately needs legitimate future visions. The criticism targeted towards the companies indicates an exhaustion of their technological promise (Beckert, 2020), but sustainability provides fresh ground to seize in order to overcome this exhaustion. In terms of promissory legitimacy, sustainability issues are especially effective: virtually all actors are struggling to meet their climate goals, and technology companies are one of the few actors who are seemingly able to provide plausible projections and action paths towards those goals.

At the same time, the technology companies remain, perhaps strategically, silent about the materiality of their infrastructures and the related immediate environmental consequences of their operations: constantly and rapidly expanding digital consumption and the natural resources it needs (e.g., Pasek et al., 2023). While the seemingly invisible media infrastructures can be materialized and made visible in communication (Cooren, 2018), we have drawn attention to corporate communication as a means of obscuring the materialization of these infrastructures. In their corporate environmental communication, the corporations reproduce top-level techno-optimistic visions where digital technology is touted as an essential solution to the sustainability crisis and promote incremental sustainability-related innovations in their services. None of the companies propose solutions that require fundamental shifts to their business models. Rather, they focus on enacting future visions with joint responsibility that distracts the gaze away from their own operations and impact.

Future-oriented discourse can contribute to organizations' discursive legitimation as it equips organizations with expert authority and presents them as socially indispensable (Géring et al., 2023); it legitimizes their actions in the present and claims their social importance in the future. As Nyberg and Wright (2016, p. 633) state, "Corporate claims surrounding climate change are performative in that they change the present and, at the same time, colonize the future through acting upon particular conceptualizations of climate change". In the light of our data, these conceptualizations are heavily built on technological solutionism and reserve the role of a valuable social actor to the technology companies designing and providing these technologies. In their future aspirations, digital technology companies are leading the path to a sustainable future *ahead* of other actors, seeking to fill the space of social imagination (Mager & Katzenbach, 2021) with technology-heavy futures.

Notably, people consider businesses to be most trusted to integrate innovations into society and expected to steer societies towards a better future (Edelman Trust Report, 2024). At the same time, it remains an open question how genuinely interested the companies are in ethical development. At best, corporate environmental discourse could be performative in the sense that it would guide the company's actions or promote activism outside the company (Christensen et al., 2013). With the profoundly opaque AI and cloud industry it is extremely hard to evaluate what is the case (Brevini, 2020). While there is increasing granular and measured information over the emissions caused by the production, maintenance, and use of digital technologies, the information remains scattered and top-level. Companies emphasize their green-ness in their communication, but some global players do not communicate about their environmental impact and goals at all—including the generative AI company OpenAI. Currently, with accelerating interest in AI, the environmental cost of this hype has not reached the overarching attention it requires.

Competing Interests The authors have no conflicts of interest to declare that are relevant to the contents of this chapter.

References

Apple. (2016, August 17). *Apple announces environmental progress in China & applauds supplier commitment to clean energy*. Apple Newsroom. https://www.apple.com//newsroom/2016/08/apple-announces-environmental-progress-in-china/

Apple. (2017, April 17). *Apple celebrates Earth Day with new initiatives and stories of innovation*. Apple Newsroom. https://www.apple.com//newsroom/2017/04/apple-celebrates-earth-day/

AWS. (2022, December 22). *How immersive commerce can drive your sustainability goals while making your merch look fabulous*. AWS Blog. https://aws.amazon.com/blogs/industries/how-immersive-commerce-can-drive-your-sustainability-goals-while-making-your-merch-look-fabulous/

Beckert, J. (2016). *Imagined futures: Fictional expectations and capitalist dynamics*. Harvard University Press.

Beckert, J. (2020). The exhausted futures of neoliberalism: From promissory legitimacy to social anomy. *Journal of Cultural Economy, 13*(3), 318–330. https://doi.org/10.1080/17530350.2019.1574867

Beckert, J. (2021). The firm as an engine of imagination: Organizational prospection and the making of economic futures. *Organization Theory, 2*(2), 1–21. https://doi.org/10.1177/26317877211005773

Beer, D. (2017). Envisioning the power of data analytics. *Information, Communication & Society, 21*(3), 1–15. https://doi.org/10.1080/1369118X.2017.1289232

Beer, D. (2019). *The data gaze: Capitalism, power and perception*. Sage.

Berkhout, F. (2006). Normative expectations in systems innovation. *Technology Analysis & Strategic Management, 18*(3–4), 299–311. https://doi.org/10.1080/09537320600777010

Borup, M., Brown, N., Konrad, K., & van Lente, H. (2006). The sociology of expectations in science and technology. *Technology Analysis & Strategic Management, 18*(3–4), 285–298. https://doi.org/10.1080/09537320600777002

Bory, P., Natale, S., & Katzenbach, C. (2024). Strong and weak AI narratives: An analytical framework. *AI and Society*, 1–11. https://doi.org/10.1007/S00146-024-02087-8

Brenner, B., & Hartl, B. (2021). The perceived relationship between digitalization and ecological, economic, and social sustainability. *Journal of Cleaner Production, 315*, article 128128. https://doi.org/10.1016/j.jclepro.2021.128128

Brevini, B. (2020). Black boxes, not green: Mythologizing artificial intelligence and omitting the environment. *Big Data & Society, 7*(2), 1–5. https://doi.org/10.1177/2053951720935141

Brodie, P. (2023). Data infrastructure studies on an unequal planet. *Big Data & Society, 10*(1). https://doi.org/10.1177/20539517231182402

Christensen, L. T., Morsing, M., & Thyssen, O. (2013). CSR as aspirational talk. *Organization, 20*(3), 372–393. https://doi.org/10.1177/1350508413478310

Christensen, L. T., Morsing, M., & Thyssen, O. (2021). Talk–action dynamics: Modalities of aspirational talk. *Organization Studies, 42*(3), 407–427. https://doi.org/10.1177/0170840619896267

Cooren, F. (2018). Materializing communication: Making the case for a relational ontology. *Journal of Communication, 68*(2), 278–288. https://doi.org/10.1093/joc/jqx014

Crawford, K. (2024). Generative AI's environmental costs are soaring—And mostly secret. *Nature, 626*, 693. https://doi.org/10.1038/D41586-024-00478-X

Edelman Trust Report. (2024). *2024 Edelman Trust Barometer*. https://www.edelman.com/trust/2024/trust-barometer

Fieseler, C., Fleck, M., & Meckel, M. (2010). Corporate social responsibility in the blogosphere. *Journal of Business Ethics, 91*, 599–614. https://doi.org/10.1007/s10551-009-0135-8

Freitag, C., Berners-Lee, M., Widdicks, K., Knowles, B., Blair, G., & Friday, A. (2021). The real climate and transformative impact of ICT: A critique of estimates, trends, and regulations. *Patterns, 2*(9), Article 100340. https://doi.org/10.1016/j.patter.2021.100340

Frig, M., Dovbysh, O., & Laaksonen, S-M. (2026). Greening the platforms or organizational bullshit? A typology of empty and misleading environmental communication by global platform companies. In S.-M. Laaksonen, M. Pantti, & O. Dovbysh (Eds.), *Platforms and the planet: Big Tech, digital platforms and environmental responsibility*. Emerald Publishing.

Frig, M., Fougère, M., Liljander, V., & Polsa, P. (2016). Business infomediary representations of corporate responsibility. *Journal of Business Ethics, 151*(2), 337–351. http://www.jstor.org/stable/45022671

Géring, Z., Tamássy, R., Király, G., & Rakovics, M. (2023). The portrayal of the future as legitimacy construction: Discursive strategies in highly ranked business schools' external communication. *Higher Education, 85*(4), 775–793. https://doi.org/10.1007/s10734-022-00865-1

Google. (2018a, April 17). *Designing for human and environmental health*. Google The Keyword blog. https://blog.google/outreach-initiatives/environment/designing-human-and-environmental-health/

Google. (2018b, September 14). *The path to a sustainable future begins with informed decisions*. Google The Keyword blog. https://blog.google/outreach-initiatives/sustainability/path-sustainable-future-begins-informed-decisions/

Google. (2019a, June 18). *A circular Google in a sustainable world*. Google The Keyword blog. https://blog.google/outreach-initiatives/sustainability/circular-google-sustainable-world/

Google. (2019b, June 4). *100 percent renewable energy, for the second year in a row*. Google The Keyword blog. https://blog.google/outreach-initiatives/sustainability/100-percent-renewable-energy-second-year-row/

Google. (2024). *Environmental Report 2024*. https://www.gstatic.com/gumdrop/sustainability/google-2024-environmental-report.pdf

Google Project Sunroof. (n.d.). *Project Sunroof*. Retrieved May 1, 2025, from https://sunroof.withgoogle.com/

Haupt, J. (2021). Facebook futures: Mark Zuckerberg's discursive construction of a better world. *New Media & Society, 23*(2), 237–257. https://doi.org/10.1177/1461444820929315

Helberger, N., Pierson, J., & Poell, T. (2018). Governing online platforms: From contested to cooperative responsibility. *The Information Society, 34*(1), 1–14. https://doi.org/10.1080/01972243.2017.1391913

IBM. (2023a, April 10). *IBM's enduring commitment to environmental leadership*. IBM Blog. https://www.ibm.com/blog/ibms-enduring-commitment-to-environmental-leadership/&

IBM. (2023b, February 7). *Why is more sustainable asset management for utilities important?* IBM Think. https://www.ibm.com/think/insights/sustainability-utilities

IBM. (2023c, July 24). *Optimizing energy production with the latest smart grid technologies*. IBM Think. https://www.ibm.com/think/topics/smart-grid

IBM. (2023d, July 5). *Sustainability in the Age of AI*. IBM Think. https://www.ibm.com/think/insights/sustainability-ai-impact

Ihlen, O. (2009). Business and climate change: The climate response of the world's 30 largest corporations. *Environmental Communication, 3*(2), 244–262. https://doi.org/10.1080/17524030902916632

Istrate, R., Tulus, V., Grass, R. N., Vanbever, L., Stark, W. J., & Guillén-Gosálbez, G. (2024). The environmental sustainability of digital content consumption. *Nature Communications, 15*(1), 1–11. https://doi.org/10.1038/s41467-024-47621-w

Jasanoff, S. (2015). Future imperfect: Science, technology and the imaginations of modernity. In S. Jasanoff & S. Kim (Eds.), *Dreamscapes of modernity: Sociotechnical imaginaries and the fabrication of power* (pp. 1–33). University of Chicago Press.

Kak, A., Myers West, S., & Whittaker, M. (2023, December 5). Make no mistake—AI is owned by Big Tech. *MIT Technology Review*. https://www.technologyreview.com/2023/12/05/1084393/make-no-mistake-ai-is-owned-by-big-tech

Kuntsman, A., & Rattle, I. (2019). Towards a paradigmatic shift in sustainability studies: A systematic review of peer reviewed literature and future agenda setting to consider environmental (un)sustainability of digital communication. *Environmental Communication, 13*(5), 567–581. https://doi.org/10.1080/17524032.2019.1596144

Larkin, B. (2013). The politics and poetics of infrastructure. *Annual Review of Anthropology, 42*(1), 327–343. https://doi.org/10.1146/annurev-anthro-092412-155522

Li, P., Yang, J., Islam, M., & Ren, S. (2023). *Making AI less "thirsty": Uncovering and addressing the secret water footprint of AI models*. ArXiv. https://doi.org/10.48550/arXiv.2304.03271

Mager, A., & Katzenbach, C. (2021). Future imaginaries in the making and governing of digital technology: Multiple, contested, commodified. *New*

Media & Society, 23(2), 223–236. https://doi.org/10.1177/1461444820929321

Mason, M., & Mason, R. (2012). Communicating a green corporate perspective: Ideological persuasion in the corporate environmental report. *Journal of Business and Technical Communication, 26*(4), 479–506. https://doi.org/10.1177/1050651912448872

Meta. (2024). *Homepage—Meta Sustainability.* https://sustainability.atmeta.com/

Microsoft. (2014, April 21). *Innovating toward greater sustainability—Earth Day 2014.* Microsoft Corporate Blogs. https://blogs.microsoft.com/blog/2014/04/22/innovating-toward-greater-sustainability-earth-day-2014/

Morozov, E. (2014). *To save everything, click here: The folly of technological solutionism.* Public Affairs.

Narayan, D. (2022). Platform capitalism and cloud infrastructure: Theorizing a hyper-scalable computing regime. *Environment and Planning A, 54*(5), 911–929. https://doi.org/10.1177/0308518X221094028

Nieborg, D., Poell, T., Caplan, R., & van Dijck, J. (2024). Introduction to the special issue on locating and theorising platform power. *Internet Policy Review, 13*(2), 1–17. https://doi.org/10.14763/2024.2.1781

Nyberg, D., Ferns, G., Vachhani, S., & Wright, C. (2022). Climate change, business, and society: Building relevance in time and space. *Business & Society, 61*(5), 1322–1352. https://doi.org/10.1177/00076503221077452

Nyberg, D., & Wright, C. (2016). Performative and political: Corporate constructions of climate change risk. *Organization, 23*(5), 617–638. https://doi.org/10.1177/1350508415572038

Parks, L., & Starosielski, N. (2015). Introduction. In L. Parks & N. Starosielski (Eds.), *Signal traffic: Critical studies of media infrastructures* (pp. 1–28). University of Illinois Press. https://doi.org/10.5406/j.ctt155jmd9.4

Pasek, A., Vaughan, H., & Starosielski, N. (2023). The world wide web of carbon: Toward a relational footprinting of information and communications technology's climate impacts. *Big Data and Society, 10*(1), 1–14. https://doi.org/10.1177/20539517231158994

Pezzullo, P. C. (2024). On environmental communication as a care discipline. *Environmental Communication, 18*(1–2), 1–7. https://doi.org/10.1080/17524032.2023.2300361

Plantin, J.-C., Lagoze, C., Edwards, P., & Sandvig, C. (2018). Infrastructure studies meet platform studies in the age of Google and Facebook. *New Media & Society, 20*(1), 293–310. https://doi.org/10.1177/1461444816661553

Pollock, N., & Williams, R. (2010). The business of expectations: How promissory organizations shape technology and innovation. *Social Studies of Science, 40*(4), 525–548. https://doi.org/10.1177/0306312710362275

Sharon, T., & Gellert, R. (2023). Regulating Big Tech expansionism? Sphere transgressions and the limits of Europe's digital regulatory strategy. *Information, Communication & Society, 27*(15), 1–18. https://doi.org/10.1080/1369118X.2023.2246526

Sinclair, S., & Rockwell, G. (2016). *Voyant tools*. https://voyant-tools.org/

Srnicek, N. (2016). *Platform capitalism*. Polity Press.

Star, S. L. (1999). The ethnography of infrastructure. *American Behavioral Scientist, 43*(3), 377–391. https://doi.org/10.1177/00027649921955326

Thrift, N. (2005). *Knowing capitalism*. Sage. https://doi.org/10.1111/j.1468-2257.2006.00344_2.x

Tuan, A., Corciolani, M., & Giuliani, E. (2024). Being reassuring about the past while promising a better future: How companies frame temporal focus in social responsibility reporting. *Business & Society, 63*(3), 626–667. https://doi.org/10.1177/00076503231182627

Vaara, E., Aranda, A., & Etchanchu, H. (2024). Discursive legitimation: An integrative theoretical framework and agenda for future research. *Journal of Management, 50*(6), 2343–2373. https://doi.org/10.1177/01492063241230511

van der Vlist, F., Helmond, A., & Ferrari, F. (2024). Big AI: Cloud infrastructure dependence and the industrialisation of artificial intelligence. *Big Data and Society, 11*(1), 1–16. https://doi.org/10.1177/20539517241232630/

van Dijck, J. (2013). *The culture of connectivity: A critical history of social media*. Oxford University Press. https://doi.org/10.1093/ACPROF:OSO/9780199970773.001.0001

Verdecchia, R., Sallou, J., & Cruz, L. (2023). A systematic review of Green AI. *WIREs Data Mining and Knowledge Discovery, 13*(4). https://doi.org/10.1002/widm.1507

World Bank & International Telecommunication Union (ITU). (2024). *Measuring the emissions & energy footprint of the ICT sector: Implications for climate action*. https://www.itu.int/hub/publication/d-ind-clim-2023-01/

CHAPTER 9

Alliance or Self-Reliance in New Geopolitical Technospheres—AI Infrastructures in Poland

Małgorzata Winiarska-Brodowska

Introduction

In uncertain times, sustainability (including of Artificial Intelligence [AI] infrastructures) is seen as "a bulwark against emerging geopolitical risks" (Kononenko & Noonan, 2022, p. 1). For example, "in trade and energy, dependence on imported carbon (especially from Russia) is seen as a security liability" (Kononenko & Noonan, 2022, p. 1). Instead of seeing sustainable development as a response to global challenges, Kononenko and Noonan (2022) refer to the notion of the "nationalisation" of sustainability to indicate that governments "may pursue sustainability based on their own national threat assessments" (p. 1). That is, sustainability is shaped by national priorities rather than being pursued as a universal solution to global systemic challenges. Many issues surrounding sustainability, e.g., digital threats, have become embedded in national security policies worldwide, whilst at the same time countries are striving for resource independence. Poland is no exception here—increasing the

M. Winiarska-Brodowska (✉)
Jagiellonian University, Kraków, Poland
e-mail: malgorzata.brodowska@uj.edu.pl

A. Mollen et al. (eds.), *AI Infrastructures and Sustainability*, Palgrave Studies in European Communication Research and Education,
https://doi.org/10.1007/978-3-032-09748-4_9

resilience in the public and private, as well as in military and civilian information systems and attaining the capability to effectively prevent, combat and respond to cyber threats is among the guidelines of the *National Security Strategy* of the Republic of Poland (2020, p. 20). Indeed, even prior to the war in Ukraine, reducing reliance on energy and essential raw materials was increasingly recognized by many international actors as a key strategic objective, including Poland, where, for example, it is present in the *Energy Policy of Poland until 2040* (Ministry of Climate & Environment, 2021, pp. 15–19), in which the optimal use of own energy resources is described.

Taking the above into account, the understanding of AI infrastructures in the context of this chapter, which highlights Polish news media's coverage of AI infrastructures and sustainability, presenting findings from a qualitative analysis that explores emerging themes in articles from one of the country's leading quality newspapers, follows Crawford's (2021) concept of AI infrastructure—a hybrid, which is "complex, cross-breeding corporate and state logics, exceeding traditional state border and governance limits" (p. 208). Crawford explores AI in the widest sense, and the economic, political, cultural, and historical forces that shape it. As Crawford (2021) suggests,

> once we connect AI within these broader structures and social systems, we can escape the notion that artificial intelligence is a purely technical domain. At a fundamental level, AI is technical and social practices, institutions and infrastructures, politics and culture. (p. 8)

And sustainability is understood as a concept rooted in self-reliance (Kurtz, 2022, p. 239), with the goal of a self-reliant community assumed to be not (just) achieving complete self-sufficiency in isolation, but first utilizing local resources while recognizing the complex global interdependences. By doing so, the community in question is imagined to be able to actively engage in trade for goods that cannot be locally produced, fostering sustainable relationships.

Ensuring autonomy in the digital space is one of the key challenges of modern times. AI is promoted as a critical driver of technological advancement in many parts of the world—with the US, China and the European Union (EU) leading engagement—influencing many different sectors and spheres of life. The EU's championing of digital sovereignty (Celeste,

2021; Floridi, 2020; Pohle & Thiel, 2020) provides not only for regulatory solutions (European Parliament & the Council of the European Union, 2024) or political initiatives (such as the AI Action Summit, 2025) and *AI Continent Action Plan 2025* (European Commission, 2025b)), but is also investing in AI infrastructures. Experts point out the need for cultivating the domestic digital technology industry (e.g. Kissinger et al., 2024, p. 124). European AI actors such as Mistral AI are recognising the need to build data centres and ensure there is enough electricity for the scale of AI development:

> The access to infrastructure is important, if you don't have this, you cannot build large language models. We could train the first ones on [the EU supercomputer] Leonardo. We were lucky enough not being blocked access to computing, but this will come for other companies. The volumes that are needed for AI are incredible. (Kroet, 2024, para. 4)

In 2024, the European Commission approved seven AI factories, proposed by the European High Performance Computing Joint Undertaking (EuroHPC JU, 2024), an entity leading the way in European supercomputing. Two sites out of the seven proposed new AI factories are politically important for Poland: the first one is Kajaani, Finland: "LUMI AIF" at CSC, where along with Denmark and Norway, three Central and Eastern European (CEE) countries—Czechia, Estonia, and Poland have joined the initiative; and Stuttgart, Germany: "Hammer-HAI" at the University of Stuttgart (being in the immediate vicinity of Poland). As per the announcement, the hosting sites will deploy brand-new, world-class AI-optimised supercomputers. The EU is also following the dominant mantra that more computing is needed and is cheering AI innovation (Haeck, 2025b). This approach should be debated especially from a sustainability perspective. Both EU-level policy and current national policies in member states are very much steered towards making more computing necessary in many spheres of social life and government action. This has a significant impact for Central and Eastern Europe, and Poland in particular. Joining the AI factories initiative means direct participation in the creation of innovative solutions which can be used within the country's policies. Both for Poland and the European Union it is also important that supercomputing can be shared in collaboration with neighbouring countries which experience similar geopolitical challenges, with the simultaneous support of wider EU structures, thus ensuring its anchoring in European politics. The AI factory in Finland will feature an experimental platform, providing cutting-edge infrastructure for developing and testing innovative AI models and applications, and fostering collaboration across Europe (European Commission, 2024b). From a geopolitical perspective, it is worth noting that none of the data centres will be situated in the CEE countries for now.[1] Yet, building resilient infrastructure in the CEE region is essential for long-term peace. Investments in infrastructure not only constitute an opportunity for the development of a country, largely through the use of local resources, but is also deemed to symbolically mark the country's importance in the international arena.

Poland has been preparing for the strategic adoption of AI, which the EU has called for through initiatives in a range of areas, such as e-government, healthcare, mobility, and education. For the EU, "these sectors are identified as among the most ready for large-scale AI deployment, with applications ranging from autonomous vehicles and smart traffic systems to AI-driven healthcare solutions and education technologies" (European Commission, 2024a, para. 1). The EU is pushing forward with AI implementation because it sees AI as a strategic necessity—AI plays a crucial role in shaping global power dynamics. Poland, as one of the leaders in CEE governments' AI readiness index, seems to be well prepared to implement AI within public services (Thormundsson, 2024), as well as in other sectors (Digital Poland, 2024).

These preparations are taking place in a moment of geopolitical turbulence. When it comes to geopolitical issues, it is worth paying attention to the remark made by Kissinger et al. (2024) that: "Europe faces the choice of whether to act as an ally to one side or the other in each major technological sphere—shaping its course by establishing a special relationship—or as a balancer between sides" (p. 125). They also explain that,

[1] Even though Poland, for example, has places with great potential for the development of AI infrastructures, such as Kraków, Poznań or Warszawa. [When this publication was being finalized it was announced that PIAST AI Factory in Poznan would join the second wave of AI Factories. Later, in October 2025 it was also announced that Gaia AI Factory would be established in Kraków. Both centers will cooperate with the Finnish LUMI AI Factory].

> here, the preferences of the traditional EU states and the newer Central and Eastern European entrants may differ, reflecting varying geopolitical and economic situations. Thus far, historic global powers such as France and Germany have prized independence and the freedom to maneuver in their technology policy. However, peripheral European states with recent and direct experience of foreign threats – such as post-Soviet Baltic and Central European states – have shown greater readiness to identify with a US-led "technosphere". (Kissinger et al., 2024, p. 125)

For example, Google and Microsoft have become the main partners of the Polish National Cloud, a company created by the Polish Development Fund and the bank, PKO BP, to manage data centres located in Poland. As Polish journalists have emphasized in their articles on the partnership, sovereignty was the primary motivation for building the company: "It was to be managed by Polish companies so that this business would maintain its sovereign character. Today, sovereignty means the Google Cloud or Microsoft Azure platform"[2] (Czubkowska, 2024, para. 21). However, international relationships may be dynamic—for example, on the one hand the Polish-US collaboration is strengthened by Microsoft's plans to invest an additional 700 million USD in Poland to improve Polish cybersecurity in cooperation with the country's armed forces (Koper & Florkiewicz, 2025). On the other hand, the dynamics may change, if only due to the fact that the United States recently introduced regulations that affect the export of advanced semiconductors for artificial intelligence to Central and Eastern European countries, including Poland (Haeck, 2025a). When discussing geopolitical tensions, it is also important to remember that the concept of self-reliance (Kurtz, 2022), as described above, is not only about being able to become completely self-sustaining and exclusive, as the usage of reliance indicates an emphasis on interdependence vis-à-vis independence, underlining complex, intricate networks of dependence. AI development depends on transnational access to computing power, data, talent, and global collaboration. Even states promoting independence in AI development still rely on international research, supply chains, and technological exchanges, facing a dilemma on how to balance gains from technological advancement with the risks of dependence.

[2] All quotes here and in the part concerning research results are translated by author [MWB].

In the CEE region, these transnational dynamics are particularly relevant. Even though the region has benefitted from access to EU funds for developing digital infrastructure, CEE countries face challenges due to a historically lower level of technological development (Tutak & Brodny, 2024), as well as challenges such as political instability and regulatory uncertainties (Żuk & Żuk, 2024). With regards to AI systems, Skubis et al. (2024) have explored how AI technologies enhance urban efficiency, sustainability, and livability through practical applications in, inter alia, traffic management, healthcare, energy efficiency, and environmental management in Poland, while Dworzecki and Nowicka (2021) have explored how the security of citizens, human rights and sustainable development change at the nexus of AI and ICT-enhanced solutions. However, the scientific literature on Poland that includes a specific geopolitical perspective on AI infrastructure development and questions of sustainability is limited. This chapter aims to contribute to these publications by focusing on the ways AI systems development is discussed in the Polish media. Newspapers are the undisputed leader in creating opinion in Poland (data for the last decade: PBC, 2024a, p. 3) and they contribute to defining the role that AI systems might have in the country. The chapter places a particular focus on Polish news media coverage of AI infrastructures and sustainability and presents results of a qualitative analysis that discusses the emerging themes in articles of one of the leading quality newspapers.

Background: Polish Digitalisation Strategy in the Context of Geopolitical Developments in the CEE Region

The media debate about AI and sustainability can be seen as part of the process of developing the document on *Polish Digitalisation Strategy to 2035*. The strategy was announced at the end of 2024 by the Polish Digital Affairs Minister and referred to three pillars: (1) improving digital competences on a national scale, (2) protecting minors and (3) battling disinformation. These pillars are seen by experts as important in the context of the geopolitical threats from Russia and Belarus—see *Raport Zespołu* (Ministerstwo Sprawiedliwości, 2025). In relation to disinformation issues and cybersecurity different Polish media also frequently report on and include official statements, e.g.

> Poland is the most attacked country in the European Union: Poland is in a hybrid war with Russia. The most common area of attack is of course critical infrastructure – the Polish Deputy Prime Minister and Minister of Digital Affairs emphasized. (Bielicka, 2025, para. 1)

Besides emphasizing security issues, the *Polish Digitalisation Strategy* is also a strategy that promotes fair digital transformation—as stated on the government website (Ministerstwo Cyfryzacji, 2024a) presenting the *State Digitalization Strategy. Draft for public consultation* (2024b): "a developing digital state must take care of the climate, the rights of platform workers and support for people whose jobs are threatened by technology. It cannot also think that technology alone will solve all problems" (para. 6). The national media coverage that I analyse in this chapter provides a broader context and explains the complexity of the issues being addressed by this national policy development process. The media and other organisations have made the case that it is important to realize that technology alone is not the solution, as exemplified by an approach presented by one of the biggest AI oriented non-profit organizations in Poland—the Digital Poland Foundation. This foundation mainly brings together Polish and international companies located in Poland, but is also open to local governments, academic centres, research institutions and non-profit organizations. It supports building a complete ecosystem necessary for the development of digital innovations. Contributing to the process of digital transformation in the region, it has created a series of publications titled *Digital Champions CEE*—which offers an annual ranking of the 100 biggest tech companies in the CEE region. The foundation claims this is the most comprehensive and transparent study of its kind. The goal of the ranking is to integrate and promote the CEE region, showcase best practices for scaling businesses, inspire entrepreneurs to build digital companies and decision-makers to create smart public policies. Every year, the Foundation also publishes a *Technology in the service of society* report (Digital Poland, 2022), and the 2023 edition focused on AI related topics, with reference to the UN Sustainable Development Goals (SDG) (Digital Poland, 2023). In the context of AI development in Poland the references to the SDG are important; especially matters which are discussed in this chapter, including: the building of resilient infrastructure, promoting inclusive and sustainable industrialization and fostering innovation in peaceful and inclusive societies, which provide access to justice for all and build strong, effective and accountable institutions. The 2023 *Technology in the service of society* report stated that "the use of new technologies is to be a response to challenges emerging on a global scale: climate change, depletion of natural resources, social polarization of views and growing economic inequality" (Digital Poland, 2023, p. 19). However, the report also mentioned the "intended or unintended consequences of AI that will cause widespread harm to people, the economy, and the environment" (Digital Poland, 2023, 76). In the 2022 edition devoted to SDG/ESG, the organisation published the results of a survey it had conducted regarding the public awareness of the possibilities of new technologies. The report pointed out that "80% of Polish society believes that new technologies and digitalization can help solve the most important problems facing Poland. Poles also believe that digitalization and new technologies can help minimize our negative impact on the environment (93%)" (Digital Poland, 2022, p. 7); moreover, "as many as 81% of people with higher education believe that, among other things, 5G networks and artificial intelligence can contribute to better use of natural resources (vs. 62% with primary education)" (Digital Poland, 2022, p. 7). The research results were then commented on by experts in report, e.g.,

> the results of the study mainly show that the deficits in Poles' awareness of digitalization and new technologies result largely from the way in which the benefits are communicated to them. The language of state strategies and the media puts forward theses that almost everyone can accept, as long as they are general and contain such broad and vague words as 'state', 'support', 'better', 'more', 'solve'. Where we talk about specifics, the result is worse, because social awareness is lower and probably also marked by specific fears. (Digital Poland, 2022, p. 46)

The work of this organisation contributed to raising social awareness on the role of new technologies and digitalization in people's lives and shed light on how they can contribute to country's robustness and much needed resilience in uncertain times and geopolitical challenges.

Methodological Considerations

Taking the above discussions as a background, for this chapter I performed a qualitative analysis of the news media reporting on AI infrastructures and sustainability in Poland. Thematic analysis (TA) is referred to as possibly the most widely used qualitative method of data analysis and constitutes the essential starting point of virtually all qualitative data analysis (Herzog et al., 2019, p. 385). TA has similarities to qualitative content analysis (QCA) (Kuckartz & Rädiker, 2023; Mayring, 2022; Schreier, 2012; Schreier et al., 2019), however, whilst QCA "emerged from quantitative content analysis and is solely focused on description; as such, it is suited for the analysis of large data sets" (Herzog et al., 2019, pp. 387–388), TA involves interpretation and can be used for small and medium-sized datasets, like that presented in this research. In this study, the process of identification of themes, the selection of related statements in the data (extracts from articles) and their interpretation adhere to the categories of transparency and reflexivity described by Herzog et al. (2019, p. 390), which are as follows: outlining the method of analysis, distinguishing data set, elaboration on data gathering and explaining methodological decisions (see the following paragraphs), complying with ethical standards, a critical reflection on data analysis, demonstrating illustrative examples, and including extracts from the qualitative data (displayed in a part presenting research results).

The texts analysed in this chapter were published between January 2022 and December 2024 in one of the most influential and widely read quality newspapers in Poland, *Gazeta Wyborcza*. This data collection timespan starts with the year when ChatGPT was launched (2022) and the use of AI quickly gained attention and was widely discussed in the media. It is also worth noting that the indicated time frame overlaps with the war in Ukraine and also with the change of power in Poland, when, after eight years of Law and Justice rule, Donald Tusk took power in 2023, forming a government of Civic Coalition, Poland 2025, Polish People's Party and New Left.

According to Polish Reading Research statistics (PBC, 2022; PBC, 2024b, p. 3) *Gazeta Wyborcza* had the highest sales results during the years analysed (2022–2024). It is also one of the most influential, opinion-forming Polish media outlets (see IMM, 2023a, 2023b, 2024a, 2024b). To gather data, I used the search term "AI infrastructure" to identify relevant pieces (mainly longer articles and interviews) that referred to the Polish context and in relation to sustainability issues. I identified 46 items to include in the thematic analysis, bearing in mind that the choice of the term brings limitations—such a broad term may encompass varied elements (e.g. hardware, software, data centres, cloud computing as well as legislative and policy frameworks), what may cause some research challenges and risks related to overlooking specific aspects of infrastructure relevant to the research focus. Each text was manually coded in order to identify emerging themes. When constructing themes, the subthemes were deliberately not taken into account in order to maintain clarity as complicated thematic structures may contradict the perspicuity. When reviewing the themes some were grouped together and renamed if there was considerable overlap and/or similarity.

The analysed articles were written mainly by Polish journalists, from both local and national bureaus of the paper. Some articles were written by foreign journalists and translated into Polish—for instance a text was translated from *Le Figaro* which is a part of the Leading European Newspaper Alliance (LENA), the largest media network in Europe promoting quality journalism (Woitier, 2023). Other texts were created as part of the "PULSE" project, a European initiative supporting international journalistic cooperation (Cieśliński, 2024c) or the "Let's Choose Our Europe" project, which is co-financed by the European Union through the European Parliament's Communication Grants Programme (Cieśliński, 2024b). There were also pieces within the *Polish Scientists Report* series of articles, in which representatives of the world of science talk about their latest achievements, discoveries, experiments and inventions that are changing the world. Not only were contributions from Polish scholars featured, but there were also texts presenting ideas of well-known specialists in the field of AI, such as Kate Crawford (a researcher of artificial intelligence and its political and social implications working at the University of Southern California in Los Angeles, at Microsoft Research in New York, and at the Chair of Artificial Intelligence and Justice at the École Normale Supérieure in Paris), and Kevin Kelly (a creator and the first editor-in-chief of the online service Wired, about new technologies, and author of books devoted to AI).

Research Results

I identified three emerging themes from the analysis: (1) the theme of geopolitics and challenges for Poland, and specifically a military dimension, (2) the theme of innovation, resilient infrastructure and strong and effective institutions and (3) the theme of labour problems.

Geopolitics: AI Infrastructure, Sustainability and Global Power Dynamics

The geopolitical landscape has shaped the discourse around AI and sustainability (in the sense of self-reliance) in Poland, particularly in the context of the ongoing war in Ukraine, which has served as a testing ground for advanced AI applications in military contexts. Companies such as Palantir, Microsoft, and Google have collaborated with Ukrainian forces using experimentally different AI systems, illustrating the dual-use nature of AI technologies that can be harnessed for both military and civilian purposes.

The significance of AI infrastructure was underlined by the media coverage especially in the context of geopolitics and security issues (particularly critical infrastructure) in Europe. The media texts concerned Europe as a whole, as well as Poland and Ukraine. Looking to the east of the Polish border, media coverage notices the actions taken by the United States. Two quotes from the article regarding operating AI on the frontline in Ukraine can serve as an example here. First: "In 2024 the involvement of American technology companies in Ukraine's defence machine has become so obvious that *Time* magazine devoted its cover to the topic" (Mazzini, 2024, para. 34). As Meisner and Takahashi (2013) point out "among magazines very few have the iconic global status and recognition of *Time*, historically the most widely read and influential weekly news magazine" (p. 256). In this way, the cover story gains importance and is widely discussed. The second quote comes from the same *Gazeta Wyborcza* article: "Overseas companies have turned Ukraine into their artificial intelligence laboratory" (Mazzini, 2024, para. 34). The word "laboratory" evokes associations with science and research which are still given relatively high trust and are positively perceived—a large majority of Europeans believe in the benefits of science (cf. European Commission, 2025a) and Americans' support for science and technology has been consistently quite positive for at least four decades (Southwell &

White, 2022). However, it is important to remember that laboratories are also where failures happen and it means their testing is done in a context where, if it fails, it does not directly impact US military or civilians.

The war in Ukraine dominated many of the analysed texts. They predominantly present the Polish perspective, both by focusing on specific events or individuals (e.g. "He tracks Russian convoys. And maybe more? I met a Pole operating AI on the front in Ukraine", Mazzini, 2024) as well as by providing in-depth analyses and presenting an issue within a broader context, often connecting it to larger social, political, or economic factors, as for instance when discussing climate neutrality goals (which has a distinct meaning in the context of cooperation between Poland and the US). The US perspective was mentioned earlier in this text with the quote from Kissinger et al. (2024), and it is worth referring to the article that described the problems of American Big Tech (which is involved not only in Ukraine but also in Poland fighting disinformation, protecting critical infrastructure and using artificial intelligence for civilian and military cybersecurity) meeting its climate goals as their CO_2 emissions are rising rapidly due to the development of artificial intelligence, which consumes a lot of energy. "Microsoft may fail to achieve negative CO_2 emissions by 2030, as the US IT giant had previously planned. [Similarly,—MWB] Google planned to achieve climate neutrality by 2030" (Kublik, 2024, para. 4). The development of artificial intelligence entails the expansion of data centres that have a huge demand for energy that is not met by new sources of renewable energy. These issues were also considered in an interview of a Polish journalist with Kate Crawford (Cieśliński, 2024a). Nevertheless, the majority of the analysed texts touched on geopolitics and the US role in the CEE, while the ecological aspects were much underrepresented in the study. The geopolitical dimension was also highlighted by concerns with the entry of Chinese companies onto the market, as illustrated by this quote: "the growing Chinese technological power will be a huge challenge for us. And then the difficulties we had with Facebook or Instagram may turn out to be a pleasant memory" (Pikuła, 2022, para. 26).

The national security perspective in the context of self-reliance seems to grow in importance during the period of analysis, too. The articles in *Gazeta* generally assess the EU's involvement in AI related research and innovation as insufficient. For example, the journalist Cieśliński (2024b) writes in an article titled *Europe must double its spending on research and innovation to catch up with the US and China. Independent experts report* that: "if Europe does not become a leader in these key areas [semiconductors, digital communications and artificial intelligence - MWB], it will become dependent on others, which will limit its ability to solve the most pressing problems of its own citizens" (para. 8). He also mentions that the expert report—an in-depth analysis of the effectiveness of the Horizon Europe framework programme for research and innovation—also includes a number of recommendations, and that the programme is of great importance for the competitiveness, security and sustainable development of the EU.

Concerns with the consequences and social costs of AI systems in public spaces, public administration and consumer services and products were also raised by a Polish scientist, who wrote that "some systems, for example, by means of fraud or spreading false information, could influence consumer decisions, political decisions, social behaviours or health decisions" (Muzyka, 2023, para. 28). However, great hopes are placed in EU regulations in this context. Particularly when "AI could quickly become a stake in economic and military competition, especially given China's ambitions. Technical and ethical questions about AI now also have geopolitical dimensions" (Woitier, 2023, para. 6).

The spread of false information mentioned above is in line with global trends anticipated for the coming years. The World Economic Forum Global Risks Perception surveys of 2023–2024 and 2024–2025 (WEF, 2024, 2025) point at misinformation and disinformation as the most severe problems. As the 2024–2025 report stated:

> the role of technology in geopolitical tensions also concerns respondents... There are many ways in which a proliferation of false or misleading content is complicating the geopolitical environment. It is a leading mechanism for foreign entities to affect voter intentions; it can sow doubt among the general public worldwide about what is happening in conflict zones; or it can be used to tarnish the image of products or services from another country. (WEF, 2025, p. 8)

The examples mentioned so far take on particular importance in the context of external attempts to destabilize the situation in Europe. Equally, the concept of self-reliance, especially in the national context increases in priority. The quotes above show how prominent the issues of innovation, resilient infrastructure, and strong and effective institutions are becoming in Poland.

Approaching the Change—Smooth AI Adaptation at the Local Level While Striving for Strong National Institutions

The studied texts show relatively unproblematic local AI adaptation and infrastructure development on the one hand, and some institutional challenges at the national level on the other hand. Several analysed articles described the development of cities and regions in the context of development of AI infrastructure. For example, there are detailed portrayals of the Polish Silicon Valley; describing Wrocław as "an ideal place to establish startups and develop innovations" (Niebał, 2022, para. 1). Or, when the media described an infrastructure project named "Construction of the Artificial Intelligence Application Laboratory in Imaging Diagnostics", where scientists wanted to obtain data for training databases for artificial intelligence algorithms, among others, from hospitals in the Częstochowa region of Poland:

> The laboratory will be established in specially rebuilt and adapted for this purpose premises of the Faculty of Science, Natural Sciences and Technology of Jan Dlugosz University. It is a long-term project. Thanks to the new infrastructure, interesting ideas, important research works with a strong emphasis on innovation and on the transfer of technology to the socio-economic environment of the region will be created. (Strąk, 2024, para. 4 and 10)

As well as Wrocław and Częstochowa other cities can also profit from AI infrastructures—Łódź with improved road infrastructure solutions, Szczecin through promoting ecological means of transport (bicycle infrastructure), and Radom, where, thanks to cooperation with the University of Radom on the use of artificial intelligence in public services: "AI will help city officials in many matters: data analysis, warning against disasters, traffic control, designing urban infrastructure, improving air quality. It will also help improve communication with residents, medical services, the recruitment process for schools and public safety" (Rusek, 2024, para 3).

Using and developing AI requires also requires changing institutions and even entire organizational structures at the national level. The articles in *Gazeta* forward the argument that it is not possible to perfect AI without changing the infrastructure around it—as Kevin Kelly argued at the Masters&Robots event in Warsaw, "to harness the power of AI, we will need to learn new ways of thinking" (Breczko, 2024, para 1). Adaptation takes time, and this time allows society to adapt and respond to challenges. The reporting emphasizes how politicians need to approach AI in a responsible way, assuring support and anticipating the long-term effects of change. The relevant institutions should be provided with stability and financing, which unfortunately has not always been the case. The Polish situation is described by Sosnowska and Czubkowska (2024) in the article titled: *We have people, we have no money. So what should the Polish AI champion be made of?* The authors report on the activities of the Polish government, which in their eyes do not seem to be particularly spectacular. Although the Minister of Digital Affairs assures that he is lobbying for the creation of a special government fund for the development of AI, so far only an advisory group has been established, and it is headed by a person who "praises China's path of building technology and slams Europe for its regulations" (Sosnowska & Czubkowska, 2024, para. 24).

The articles also paid attention to ongoing changes in institutions in Poland, such as IDEAS NCBR, a research organization dealing with the development of AI systems in Poland. The organization was created in 2021 by the National Centre for Research and Development and is described as "one of several European institutes with enormous potential to place Poland among the leading countries developing artificial intelligence" (Korcz, 2024, para. 9). The Centre is internationally recognized and supported by many well-known institutions and scientists, which is of significance in the context of AI development depending on access to computing power, data, talent, and most of all global collaboration. Potential instability within this institution could disrupt its operations and hinder its effectiveness, and according to the concept of self-reliance, the capabilities of institutions should be strengthened, while maintaining global cooperation. Among others, it was also stressed by Korcz (2024) that the lack of long-term stability at the institution brings difficulties in attracting the best talent to Poland (this issue will be further discussed in the next section). The picture emerging from the analysed articles is ambiguous; on the one hand, it presents examples of well-functioning institutions and AI infrastructures that are being developed at the local level, but on the other hand, it shows changes at the national level that require further refinement and finding the best formula for their functioning.

Labour—Brain Drain, Low Wages and Digital Well-Being

The analysed articles also bring up how the lack of long-term stability influences the economic situation of young Poles. Several articles underline the brain drain in the country and hold it up to scrutiny, for example: "IDEAS NCBR was a real alternative for young, talented and ambitious IT specialists, giving them the opportunity to develop their scientific passions in Poland" (Korcz, 2024, para. 14). Without the appropriate conditions for scientific work in the country young people will look for them abroad. And as Kosiński, a Polish social psychologist and data scientist working at Stanford University underlines: "Talent is the 'oil' of the AI era. What matters is the capital of ideas that initiate the development of this technology" (Duszczyk, 2025, para. 21).

Another interesting aspect related to labour is described by Pikuła (2022). He refers in his article to the responsibility concerning digitalization and the usage of AI, which has been shifted to the users themselves. He pointed out that this "shifting of responsibility is very class-based, because there are people who have more competences, more resources to deal with the policies of large corporations, but there are also those who cannot cope, and very often these people are perceived negatively" (Pikuła, 2022, para. 20). He explains in the piece that the assumption that everyone should take care of their own digital well-being is cruelly unfair: "it is difficult to take care of conscious content consumption when you have to work two jobs" (para. 20). In CEE, including Poland, the percentage of employees working two jobs is higher than in Western Europe, and the labour market data does not inspire optimism over any change to that status quo in the short term (Statista Research Department, 2025). Additionally, according to Eurostat (2024), Poland has one of the longest working weeks in the European Union (39.3 in 2023 with the EU average being 36.1).

Lastly, the analysed texts also emphasized the huge amount of hidden labour that usually comes from the peripheries and is used for mass labelling and data checking:

> In many ways, the planet's AI infrastructure is simply a giant mining industry for the 21st century. Everyone has probably heard that it is constantly extracting colossal amounts of data from all of us, but not necessarily that it is perpetuating quite traditional forms of mining. And the IT industry's demand for rare earth minerals, oil and coal, and water to cool data centers is huge - but the industry itself does not bear the real costs of

> extraction. AI also exploits huge amounts of poorly paid labour to perform all the tasks it cannot do itself, especially training models and cleaning data. (Cieśliński, 2024a, para. 18–19)

Whereas this perspective was not brought up in relation to Poland particularly, the articles in *Gazeta* emphasized how AI systems are subject to the logic of capital, police control and militarization, and distorted working conditions—they increase, for example, surveillance and control by bosses, and enable increasingly precise management of employees' time (Cieśliński, 2024a). The third emerging theme focuses on labour showing different aspects of this issue—brain drain, low wages, digital well-being and responsibility—in which effective but also fair and inclusive institutions play an important role.

Conclusions

The chapter presents the Polish context of AI infrastructures and sustainability, discussing emerging themes identified in the study which concern the economic as well as social dimensions of geopolitics. The military and economic dimensions were most visible in the articles, indicating the importance of the ongoing war in Ukraine as a wider context. However these dimensions were also present in texts discussing issues such as cybersecurity, information flow and infrastructure in Poland—in line with the concept of self-reliance, but nevertheless recognizing the complex global interdependencies and recognizing opportunities for potential alliances. The media coverage suggests that effective and resilient institutions are indispensable for the proper functioning of the state, while also highlighting that social dimensions boil down to labour-related issues.

In line with the strategic adoption of AI in the EU in key areas such as e-government, healthcare, mobility, and education—which belong to sectors identified as among those which are the most ready for large-scale AI deployment—the analysed articles presented AI infrastructures in Poland and their development in the areas of military, public administration and research. In an overwhelming majority of these, the advancements were seen as desired and positive, which is of great importance in the geopolitical context in CEE.

Media reporting and the themes that emerge may contribute to public discussions and in consequence to important changes. Local and national media that explain the complexity of the issues being addressed, and which through debate actively take part in political processes, can motivate and urge decision-makers to create smart public policies (approaching AI in a responsible way) and contribute to considerations at higher levels of government responsible for establishing regulations (anticipating the long-term effects of AI-related change). Therefore the media debate surrounding AI and sustainability in Poland can be seen as beneficial, for instance, to the process of developing the document on *Polish Digitalisation Strategy to 2035*. Media debates on AI infrastructure and sustainability are important, an example of which is Poland. We are currently witnessing the making of technospheres that are of significance, especially on a geopolitical level.

Competing Interests The author has no conflicts of interest to declare that are relevant to the contents of this chapter.

References

AI Action Summit. (2025). https://www.elysee.fr/en/sommet-pour-l-action-sur-l-ia

Bielicka, M. (2025). Wicepremier Gawkowski w Poznaniu: Polska jest najbardziej atakowanym państwem Unii Europejskiej [Deputy Prime Minister Gawkowski in Poznan: Poland is the most attacked country in the European Union]. *Gazeta Wyborcza*. https://poznan.wyborcza.pl/poznan/7,36001,31823198,wicepremier-gawkowski-na-cyberbezpieczenstwo-potrzebne-sa-w.html

Breczko, B. (2024, November 7). Żeby wykorzystać możliwości AI, będziemy musieli nauczyć się nowych sposobów myślenia [To harness the power of AI, we will need to learn new ways of thinking]. *Gazeta Wyborcza*. https://wyborcza.biz/biznes/7,177150,31439530,zeby-wykorzystac-mozliwosci-ai-bedziemy-musieli-nauczyc-sie.html

Celeste, E. (2021). Digital sovereignty in the EU: Challenges and future perspectives. In F. Fabbrini, E. Celeste & J. Quinn (Eds.), *Data protection beyond borders: Transatlantic perspectives on extraterritoriality and sovereignty* (pp. 211–228). Hart. https://doi.org/10.5040/9781509940691.ch-013

Cieśliński, P. (2024a, May 24). *Trzeba ponownie uruchamiać elektrownie węglowe i gazowe, żeby zasilić ChatGPT [Coal and gas power plants need to be restarted to power ChatGPT]*. Gazeta Wyborcza. https://wyborcza.pl/magazyn/7,124059,30992533,trzeba-ponownie-uruchamiac-elektrownie-weglowe-i-gazowe-zeby.html

Cieśliński, P. (2024b, November 22). Europa musi podwoić wydatki na badania i innowacje, żeby dogonić USA i Chiny. Raport niezależnych ekspertów [Europe must double its spending on research and innovation to catch up with the US and China. Independent experts report]. *Gazeta Wyborcza*. https://wyborcza.pl/7,75400,31482076,europa-musi-podwoic-wydatki-na-badania-i-innowacje-zeby-dogonic.html

Cieśliński, P. (2024c, October 2). Europa budzi się do walki o kosmos. Oby tylko zdążyła [Europe is waking up to the fight for space. If only it had time]. *Gazeta Wyborcza*. https://wyborcza.pl/7,75400,31352204,europa-budzi-sie-do-walki-o-kosmos-oby-tylko-zdazyla.html

Crawford, K. (2021). *Atlas of AI. Power, politics and the planetary costs of artificial intelligence*. Yale University Press. https://www.jstor.org/stable/j.ctv1ghv45t

Czubkowska, S. (2024, June 24). Big techy, wielkie interesy i wielki lobbing. Oto pięć strategii, dzięki którym spółki technologiczne owijają sobie rządy wokół palca [Big Tech, Big Business and Big Lobbying. Here are five strategies that allow technology companies to wrap governments around their finger]. *Gazeta Wyborcza*. https://wyborcza.biz/biznes/7,177150,31081770,big-techy-wielkie-interesy-i-wielki-lobbing-oto-piec-strategii.html

Digital Poland. (2022). *Technology in the service of society. Will Poles become society 5.0? Edition 2022*. https://digitalpoland.org/en/publications/download?id=ce836f49-8a43-4305-a3b6-b929c59ba433

Digital Poland. (2023). *Technology in the service of society. Will Poles become society 5.0? Edition 2023*. https://digitalpoland.org/en/publications/download?id=5b0d59ab-761e-4617-b2cd-a0f184cd60aa

Digital Poland. (2024). *Digital champions CEE*. https://digitalpoland.org/en/publications/download?id=05ffe50a-f7b3-4ab0-b129-afb1be31845d

Duszczyk, M. (2025). *Polskiego uczonego nazywają "Oppenheimerem AI". Ostrzega: AI może zagrozić demokracji [Polish scientist called "Oppenheimer AI". He warns: AI could threaten democracy]*. Rzeczpospolita. https://www.msn.com/pl-pl/technologia/sztuczna-inteligencja/polskiego-uczonego-nazywaj%C4%85-oppenheimerem-ai-ostrzega-ai-mo%C5%BCe-zagrozi%C4%87-demokracji/ar-AA1BiMvD

Dworzecki, J., & Nowicka, I. (2021). Artificial Intelligence (AI) and ICT-enhanced solutions in the activities of police formations in Poland. In A. Visvizi & M. Bodziany (Eds.), *Artificial Intelligence and its contexts. Advanced sciences and technologies for security applications* (pp. 161–181). Springer. https://doi.org/10.1007/978-3-030-88972-2_11

European Commission. (2024a). *EU study calls for strategic AI adoption to transform public sector services. Shaping Europe's digital future*. https://digital-strategy.ec.europa.eu/en/library/eu-study-calls-strategic-ai-adoption-transform-public-sector-services

European Commission. (2024b, December 10). *Seven consortia selected to establish AI factories which will boost AI innovation in the EU* [Press release]. https://ec.europa.eu/commission/presscorner/api/files/document/print/en/ip_24_6302/IP_24_6302_EN.pdf
European Commission. (2025a). *European citizens' knowledge and attitudes towards science and technology*. https://europa.eu/eurobarometer/surveys/detail/3227
European Commission. (2025b). *Shaping Europe's leadership in artificial intelligence with the AI continent action plan*. https://commission.europa.eu/topics/eu-competitiveness/ai-continent_en
EuroHPC JU. (2024). *Selection of the first seven AI factories to drive Europe's leadership in AI*. https://eurohpc-ju.europa.eu/selection-first-seven-ai-factories-drive-europes-leadership-ai-2024-12-10_en
European Parliament & the Council of the European Union. (2024). *Regulation - EU - 2024/1689 - EN - EUR-Lex*. https://eur-lex.europa.eu/eli/reg/2024/1689/oj/eng
Eurostat. (2024). *Actual and usual hours of work*. https://ec.europa.eu/eurostat/statistics-explained/index.php?title=Actual_and_usual_hours_of_work
Floridi, L. (2020). The fight for digital sovereignty: What it is, and why it matters, especially for the EU. *Philosophy & Technology, 33*, 369–378. https://doi.org/10.1007/s13347-020-00423-6
Haeck, P. (2025a, January 21). Poland fumes over US block on AI chips. *POLITICO*. https://www.politico.eu/article/poland-fumes-us-block-joe-biden-ai-chips-cap-export/
Haeck, P. (2025b, February 10). The EU's new AI mantra: We're open for business. *POLITICO*. https://www.politico.eu/article/eu-ai-mantra-action-summit-artificial-intelligence-europe-tech-economy-founders/
Herzog, C., Handke, C., & Hitters, E. (2019). Analysing talk and text II: Thematic analysis. In H. van den Bulck, M. Puppis, K. Donders & L. van Audenhove (Eds.), *The Palgrave handbook of methods for media policy research* (pp. 385–402). Palgrave Macmillan. https://doi.org/10.1007/978-3-030-16065-4_22
IMM. (2023a). *Gazeta Wyborcza najbardziej opiniotwórczym medium w Polsce. Na podium także RMF FM oraz Onet [Gazeta Wyborcza is the most opinion-forming media in Poland. On the podium also RMF FM and Onet]* (Najbardziej opiniotwórcze media marca 2023). https://www.imm.com.pl/gazeta-wyborcza-najbardziej-opiniotworczym-medium-w-polsce-na-podium-takze-rmf-fm-oraz-onet/
IMM. (2023b). *Gazeta Wyborcza z tytułem najbardziej opiniotwórczego medium w kraju. Na drugim miejscu Onet, podium zamyka Rzeczpospolita [Gazeta Wyborcza with the title of the most opinion-forming media in the country. Onet in second place, Rzeczpospolita rounds off the podium]* (Najbardziej

opiniotwórcze media września 2023). https://www.imm.com.pl/gazeta-wyborcza-z-tytulem-najbardziej-opiniotworczego-medium-w-kraju-na-drugim-miejscu-onet-podium-zamyka-rzeczpospolita/

IMM. (2024a). *Gazeta Wyborcza na czele najbardziej opiniotwórczych mediów w lipcu. Na podium także TVN24 i Rzeczpospolita [Gazeta Wyborcza at the forefront of the most opinion-forming media in July. TVN24 and Rzeczpospolita also on the podium]* (Najbardziej opiniotwórcze media lipka 2024). https://www.imm.com.pl/gazeta-wyborcza-na-czele-najbardziej-opiniotworczych-mediow-w-lipcu-na-podium-takze-tvn24-i-rzeczpospolita/

IMM. (2024b). *Gazeta Wyborcza opiniotwórczym liderem. W czołówce również Rzeczpospolita i Onet [Gazeta Wyborcza is the opinion leader. Also in the lead are Rzeczpospolita and Onet]* (Najbardziej opiniotwórcze media września 2024). https://www.imm.com.pl/gazeta-wyborcza-opiniotworczym-liderem-w-czolowce-rowniez-rzeczpospolita-i-onet/

Kissinger, H., Schmidt, E., & Huttenlocher, D. (2024). *The age of AI. And our human future.* John Murray Press. https://ageofaibook.com/

Kononenko, V., & Noonan, E. (2022). *Sustainability in the age of geopolitics.* European Parliament. https://www.europarl.europa.eu/RegData/etudes/ATAG/2022/679092/EPRS_ATA(2022)679092_EN.pdf

Koper A., & Florkiewicz P. (2025, February 17). *Microsoft to invest $700 million to boost Poland's cybersecurity.* Reuters. https://www.reuters.com/technology/microsoft-invest-700-mln-poland-says-polish-pm-2025-02-17/

Korcz, M. (2024, October 1). Kolejne apele do premiera. "IDEAS dawał młodym szansę rozwijania pasji naukowych w Polsce" [Further appeals to the Prime Minister. "IDEAS gave young people a chance to develop their scientific passions in Poland"]. *Gazeta Wyborcza.* https://wyborcza.biz/biznes/7,177150,31349588,do-tuska-splywaja-kolejne-apele-ideas-dawal-mlodym-szanse.html

Kroet, C. (2024, June 14). *Mistral AI warns of lack of data centres and training capacity in Europe.* Euronews. https://www.euronews.com/next/2024/06/14/mistal-ai-warns-of-lack-of-data-centres-training-capacity-in-europe

Kublik, A. (2024, July 30). Sztuczna i energożerna - rozwój AI pompuje emisje gazów cieplarnianych [Artificial and energy-hungry - AI development pumps up greenhouse gas emissions]. *Gazeta Wyborcza.* https://wyborcza.biz/biznes/7,177150,31184647,sztuczna-i-energozerna-rozwoj-ai-pompuje-emisje-gazow-cieplarnianych.html

Kuckartz, U., & Rädiker, S. (2023). *Qualitative content analysis. Methods, practice and software.* Sage. https://us.sagepub.com/en-us/nam/qualitative-content-analysis/book282907

Kurtz, L. (2022). Sustainable development. In L. Kurtz (Ed.), *Encyclopedia of violence, peace, & conflict* (pp. 239–251).

Mayring, P. (2022). *Qualitative content analysis. A step-by-step guide*. Sage. https://us.sagepub.com/en-us/nam/qualitative-content-analysis/book269922

Mazzini, M. (2024, September 20). *Namierza rosyjskie konwoje. Czy tylko? Spotkałem Polaka obsługującego AI na froncie w Ukrainie [He tracks Russian convoys. And maybe more? I met a Pole operating AI on the front in Ukraine]*. Gazeta Wyborcza. https://wyborcza.pl/magazyn/7,124059,31314214,namierza-rosyjskie-konwoje-czy-tylko-spotkalem-polaka-obslugujacego.html

Meisner, M. S., & Takahashi, B. (2013). The nature of time: How the covers of the world's most widely read weekly news magazine visualize environmental affairs. *Environmental Communication, 7*(2), 255–276. https://doi.org/10.1080/17524032.2013.772908

Ministerstwo Cyfryzacji. (2024a). *Strategia Cyfryzacji Polski do 2035 roku [Digitalization Strategy of Poland until 2035]*. https://www.gov.pl/web/cyfryzacja/strategia-cyfryzacji-polski-do-2035-roku

Ministerstwo Cyfryzacji. (2024b). *Strategia Cyfryzacji Państwa. Projekt do konsultacji społecznych [State Digitalization Strategy. Draft for public consultation]*. https://www.gov.pl/web/cyfryzacja/strategia-cyfryzacji-polski-do-2035-roku

Ministerstwo Sprawiedliwości. (2025, January 10). *Raport Zespołu ds. Dezinformacji Komisji ds. badania wpływów rosyjskich i białoruskich na bezpieczeństwo wewnętrzne i interesy Rzeczypospolitej Polskiej w latach 2004–2024 [Report of the Disinformation Team of the Commission for the study of Russian and Belarusian influence on the internal security and interests of the Republic of Poland in the years 2004–2024]*. https://www.gov.pl/web/sprawiedliwosc/raport-zespolu-ds-dezinformacji-komisji-ds-badania-wplywow-rosyjskich-i-bialoruskich

Ministry of Climate and Environment. (2021). *Energy Policy of Poland until 2040 (EPP2040)*. https://www.gov.pl/web/climate/energy-policy-of-poland-until-2040-epp2040

Muzyka, K. (2023, November 9). Prawnik z PAN: Śledzę, jak rozwój sztucznej inteligencji wpływa na regulacje prawne [PAN layer: I follow how the development of artificial intelligence affects legal regulations]. *Gazeta Wyborcza*. https://wyborcza.pl/7,75400,30380268,prawnik-kiedy-ai-wnosi-przeciwko-tobie-pozew-czyli-prawo-a.html

National security strategy of the Republic of Poland. (2020). https://www.bbn.gov.pl/ftp/dokumenty/National_Security_Strategy_of_the_Republic_of_Poland_2020.pdf

Niebał, I. (2022, December 20). Rozwiązania branży IT z Wrocławia napędzają cały świat. "Najwięcej projektów realizuje się na rynkach najbogatszych" [IT industry solutions from Wrocław drive the whole world. "The largest number of projects are being implemented in the richest markets"]. *Gazeta*

Wyborcza. https://wroclaw.wyborcza.pl/wroclaw/7,35771,29266299,najwiecej-projektow-realizuje-sie-na-rynkach-najbogatszych.html

PBC. (2024a). *Raport AUDYT PBC (dawniej ZKDP) Rozpowszechnianie Tytułów Prasowych w II kwartale 2024 r. [AUDYT PBC (formerly ZKDP) Report Distribution of Press Titles in Q2 2024]*. https://www.pbc.pl/wp-content/uploads/2024/08/Raport_Audyt_PBC_2024_II_Kwartal.pdf

PBC. (2024b). *Wyniki Audytu Prasa+ [Results of the Press+Audit]*. https://www.pbc.pl/wyniki-prasa-plus/

PBC. (2022). *Raport AUDYT PBC (dawniej ZKDP) Rozpowszechnianie Tytułów Prasowych w 2022 r. [AUDIT PBC (formerly ZKDP) report Distribution of Press Titles in 2022]*. https://www.pbc.pl/wp-content/uploads/2023/03/Raport_Audyt_PBC_2022.pdf

Pikuła, R. (2022, June 12). Ktoś z was zjadł psie ciasteczka, czyli jakich narracji uczą nas technologiczni giganci? [Someone ate dog cookies, or what narratives are tech giants teaching us?]. *Gazeta Wyborcza*. https://wyborcza.biz/biznes/7,177150,28444360,jak-rozmawiac-o-technologii-by-miec-nad-nia-kontrole.html

Pohle, J., & Thiel, T. (2020). Digital sovereignty. *Internet Policy Review*, *9*(4), 1–19. https://doi.org/10.14763/2020.4.1532

Rusek, M. (2024, March 13). *Sztuczna inteligencja pomoże urzędnikom z Radomia [AI will help officials from Radom]*. Gazeta Wyborcza. https://radom.wyborcza.pl/radom/7,48201,30793741,sztuczna-inteligencja-pomoze-urzednikom-z-radomia-poprawic-jakosc.html

Schreier, M. (2012). *Qualitative content analysis in practice*. Sage. https://methods.sagepub.com/book/mono/qualitative-content-analysis-in-practice/toc

Schreier, M., Stamann, C., Janssen, M., Dahl, T., & Whittal, A. (2019). Qualitative content analysis: Conceptualizations and challenges in research practice – introduction to the FQS special issue "Qualitative content analysis I." *Forum: Qualitative Social Research*, *20*(3), Article 38. https://doi.org/10.17169/fqs-20.3.3393

Skubis, I., Wolniak, R., & Grebski, W. W. (2024). AI and human-centric approach in smart cities management: Case studies from Silesian and Lesser Poland Voivodships. *Sustainability*, *16*(18), Article 8279. https://doi.org/10.3390/su16188279

Sosnowska, J., & Czubkowska, S. (2024). Mamy ludzi, nie mamy pieniędzy. Z czego ma więc powstać polski czempion AI? [We have people, we have no money. So what should the Polish AI champion be made of?] *Gazeta Wyborcza*. https://wyborcza.biz/biznes/7,177150,30630219,jak-wyhodowac-polskiego-czempiona-ai.html

Southwell, B., & White, K. (2022). *Science and technology: Public perceptions, awareness, and information sources*. National Science Foundation. https://ncses.nsf.gov/pubs/nsb20227/public-perceptions-of-science-and-technology

Statista Research Department. (2025, April 30). *Labor market in Central and Eastern Europe (CEE) - statistics & facts*. Statista. https://www.statista.com/topics/12036/labor-market-in-cee/#topicOverview

Strąk, B. (2024, December 8). Ponad 6 mln zł na budowę w Częstochowie laboratorium do badania zastosowań sztucznej inteligencji. "Nie chodzi o naukę dla nauki" [Over PLN 6 million for the construction of a laboratory in Częstochowa for research on artificial intelligence applications. "It's not about science for science's sake"]. *Gazeta Wyborcza*. https://czestochowa.wyborcza.pl/czestochowa/7,48725,31522349,ponad-6-mln-zl-na-budowe-w-czestochowie-laboratorium-do-badania.html

Thormundsson, B. (2024). *Top 20 Eastern European AI-ready countries 2022*. Statista. https://www.statista.com/statistics/1231719/eastern-europe-government-artificial-intelligence-readiness-index/

Tutak, M., & Brodny, J. (2024). Technological progress in central and Eastern Europe: Digitalization and business innovation leaders and outsiders. *Journal of Open Innovation: Technology, Market, and Complexity*, *10*(4), Article 100404. https://doi.org/10.1016/j.joitmc.2024.100404

WEF. (2024). *Global risks report*. https://www.weforum.org/publications/global-risks-report-2024/

WEF. (2025). *Global risks report*. https://www.weforum.org/publications/global-risks-report-2025/

Woitier, C. (2023, May 10). Jaka AI jest w porządku, a jaka będzie zakazana? UE chce regulacji jeszcze w tym roku [LE FIGARO] [What AI is OK and what will be banned? EU wants regulation this year [LE FIGARO]]. *Gazeta Wyborcza*. https://wyborcza.pl/7,179012,29745944,europa-chce-byc-pionierem-w-regulowaniu-sztucznej-inteligencji.html

Żuk, P., & Żuk, P. (2024). The role of trust, information and legal stability in the development of renewable energy: The analysis of non-economic factors affecting entrepreneurs' investments in green energy in Poland. *Environment, Development and Sustainability*, *26*, 18499–18534. https://doi.org/10.1007/s10668-023-03400-z

CHAPTER 10

Discursive Infrastructuring of AI in Russia: Yandex's Sustainability Reporting

Olga Dovbysh

Introduction

In February 2025, director of AI development at Yandex, Aleksander Krainov, claimed that Russia was lacking computing facilities and would soon lack the electricity to educate new AI models: "if you want to build a large data center now, not only will it take you a year to power it with power, ... you won't be given as much as you need" (Aryalina & Milkin, 2025, para 2). The growing infrastructural challenge for AI in Russia is a real future: as of April 2024, 225 Russian data centres utilized approximately 1% of the national energy system, with expected growth of 30%–40% annually (Aryalina & Milkin, 2025). Though there is an energy surplus in the country, the demand for and distribution of energy are highly unequal. There are currently energy deficits in the capital agglomerations of Moscow and St. Petersburg and surpluses in other regions (Aryalina & Milkin, 2025; see also Velkova in this volume on energy deficits).

O. Dovbysh (✉)
University of Helsinki, Helsinki, Finland
e-mail: olga.dovbysh@helsinki.fi

A. Mollen et al. (eds.), *AI Infrastructures and Sustainability*, Palgrave Studies in European Communication Research and Education,
https://doi.org/10.1007/978-3-032-09748-4_10

The rapidly expanding influence of artificial intelligence around the globe makes it a pivotal force in our transforming world. Simultaneously, the growing energy and resource requirements of AI raise concerns about the sustainability of its infrastructures (Hogan, 2022; Milmo, 2024). On top of this, escalating geopolitical tensions in Eurasia and other parts of the world have resulted in an intensification of security and sovereignty discourses in discussions surrounding digital technologies and AI (Baur, 2024). How do the challenges of sustainability and growing sovereignty concerns regarding AI infrastructures manifest in contemporary Russia—an authoritarian country at war?

Krainov's statement is one of the few from Russian AI developers highlighting AI's materiality and its resource dependence, contrasting mainstream techno-populist narratives that frame technological advancements as meeting population needs and fostering national pride (Solovyeva & Yablokov, 2024). The Russian president envisions AI as crucial for the country's "scientific, technological, and ideological" sovereignty (Muhametshina, 2024, para 3) amidst "restricting access to AI technologies due to unfair competition from unfriendly foreign states"(President of Russia, 2024, New challenges section) shaping the symbolic framing of AI development. The Federal Project "Artificial Intelligence" and the National Project "Data Economy and Digital Transformation of the State," running until 2030, aim to build a national AI ecosystem with significant infrastructural expansion. The state supports universities and research centres in AI development,[1] with authorities expecting AI to significantly contribute to GDP growth (Petrova, 2024). Sanctions and the withdrawal of companies from the Russian market following the Ukraine invasion pose additional challenges to the AI industry and its infrastructure.

These circumstances make Russia a unique case for examining what drives the sustainability of AI infrastructures in tech companies operating in non-Western and non-democratic contexts. Relying on approaches in science and technology studies and infrastructure studies, considering media infrastructures as complex and layered sociotechnical issues with far-reaching consequences (Parks & Starosielski, 2015; Plantin & Punathambekar, 2019; Velkova & Plantin, 2023), as well as on an infrastructural perspective on digital sovereignty (Musiani, 2022; Williams

[1] State investments for the period 2025–2027 will be around 26.49 billion roubles.

et al., 2024), this chapter aims to elucidate the discursive construction of the sustainability of AI infrastructures by Yandex, a leading Russian tech company and a developer of AI and AI models.

Given the constraints of access to empirical data in restricted regimes (Gel'man, 2023), the chapter focuses on an investigation of the company's sustainability reporting. As data, corporate sustainability reports are a form of CSR (corporate social responsibility) communication through which companies report their activities and, at the same time, construct, negotiate, and modify what a socially responsible organization means (Christensen & Cheney, 2011). More broadly, reporting is utilized to garner societal acceptance for companies and to discursively construct desired realities and societal roles (Berger & Luckmann, 1966).

Along with their Western counterparts, the practices of sustainability or ESG reporting have been adopted by leading non-Western companies. In Russia, although non-financial reporting is not mandatory, the number of companies publishing these reports has grown since 2001. By 2023, 270 companies in Russia (both national and transnational) had started to provide reports on their non-financial information. In many cases, companies started ESG reporting because of the opportunities to attract Western investors who did not want to support "brown" businesses. After Russia's invasion of Ukraine and subsequent sanctions, concerns arose about Russian companies' motives for continuing ESG reporting. However, reporting persisted due to interest from new international partners like BRICS countries and Asia–Pacific and Latin American markets (Zavrazhneva, 2024). Additionally, Russia's 2023 climate doctrine aiming for carbon neutrality by 2060, further drives companies' focus on sustainable development (Zavrazhneva, 2024).

Approaching infrastructures as both material and symbolic forms, the study presented in this chapter revealed four main discourses through which Yandex constructs and stabilizes the sustainability of AI infrastructures in its sustainability reporting. The study also elucidates how ideas of sovereignty emerge in these discourses visualizing AI infrastructures.

Discursive Constructioning of AI Infrastructures

From a structuralist perspective, the AI technology stack at large includes infrastructure, models, and applications, along with the respective providers of these components (van der Vlist et al., 2024). The core

AI infrastructure encompasses both cloud software and hardware platforms (van der Vlist et al., 2024). Critical AI studies recognize contested and debated boundaries of AI, which are also dependent on who defines them (Crawford, 2021). As such, a more critical understanding of AI defines it as "an assemblage of technological arrangements and sociotechnical practices, as concept, ideology, and dispositif" (Raley & Rhee, 2023, pp. 188–189). Following this vein and Parks and Starosielski's definition of media infrastructures (2015), I understand AI infrastructures as situated sociotechnical systems that are designed and configured to support the operation and maintenance of AI models and applications.

Discursive work is an important element of the social construction of public understanding of a technology or a service (Gillespie, 2010). Through this work, companies or other involved stakeholders make claims about "what these technologies are and are not, and what should and should not be expected of them" (Gillespie, 2010, p. 359). AI infrastructures can also be seen as both material and symbolic (Bowker & Star, 2000) or as "material forms as well as discursive constructions" (Parks & Starosielski, 2015, p. 5). As Bowker and Star (2000, p. 292) put it: "The medium of an information system is not just wires and plugs, bits and bytes, but also conventions of representations, information both formal and empirical."

The ways infrastructures are designed, regulated, collectively imagined, and repetitively used have far-reaching consequences (Parks & Starosielski, 2015). In this regard, Yandex's sustainability reporting can be studied as the company's discursive work of the social construction of AI and its infrastructures.

AI infrastructures can be understood as boundary objects that "have different meanings in different social worlds" but are "robust enough to maintain a common identity across sites" (Bowker & Star, 2000, p. 297). This addresses the strong relationality of infrastructure as a concept—it is not comprised of static and isolated objects but is something that is produced and reproduced through practices and are inevitably connected to social structures (Star, 1999). The development of powerful media infrastructures has everywhere formed the material and ideological foundation for producing new social forms and defining the terms of citizenship (Plantin & Punathambekar, 2019). In this logic, Yandex's sustainability reporting is utilized in this research to sort out the company's own ideologies as well as state ideologies in the process of the symbolic making of AI infrastructure and its sustainability in Russia.

Yandex, the State, and AI

Yandex, a multinational corporation, specializes in internet-related products and services, primarily in Russia and other CIS countries. Founded in 1997 in Moscow, Yandex is often compared to Google due to its wide range of offerings, including a dominant search engine, online advertising, e-commerce, transportation services, and cloud computing. Today, Yandex encompasses over 90 digital services and products, including Yandex Search, cloud storage, a mail service, and more. The company also offers material services like food delivery (Yandex.Lavka), IoT products, smart devices, ride-hailing, carsharing, delivery services, and an e-commerce platform (Yandex.Market). It is a key player in the RuNet.

Since President Dmitry Medvedev's 2009 declaration of Yandex as a national asset, Yandex has faced growing scrutiny from the Russian state (Kravets-Meinke, 2024). This led to the 2016 *On news aggregators* law requiring platforms like Yandex. News to exclude officially unregistered news sites (Wijermars, 2021). In 2019, legislation limiting foreign ownership of Russian internet companies enabled government intervention in Yandex's operations (Kravets-Meinke, 2024).

Over the years, Yandex leaders have increasingly balanced service delivery with the constraints of a tightening authoritarian climate. Solovyeva and Bristow (2024, p.) claim that Yandex leaders strategically decided to stay beyond politics by constructing corporate sovereignty, through political compromise, and by focusing on business growth. Depoliticization at Yandex was justified by a care ethics forming a safety cocoon where employees felt secure and protected. However, it also led to growing conformity with Russian state politics and the depoliticization of organizational communication (Solovyeva & Bristow, 2024).

Following Russia's invasion of Ukraine, Yandex faced new challenges, including compliance with state legislation, international sanctions, and media criticism. Yandex.News contributed to pro-state war coverage by indexing only state-owned media (Kravets-Meinke, 2024). In 2022, Yandex sold Yandex.News and Yandex.Zen to the state controlled VK Group, which further consolidated state media control. Simultaneously, the company went through a series of crises including personal sanctions on the company's top managers. Moreover, hundreds of employees and a number of senior leaders resigned or left the country in protest against the war (Solovyeva & Bristow, 2024). In 2024, the company underwent significant upheaval and restructuring, selling assets located in Russia to a consortium of Russian buyers and reorganizing non-Russian assets as Nebius Group, led by Arkady Volozh, former CEO and co-founder of Yandex.

Yandex is currently a leading company in AI development, including AI models and infrastructure like cloud services (Rozhkov, 2024). At least 17 Yandex services, including the virtual assistant Alisa, use the YandexGPT model. In 2022, Yandex uploaded its megamodel YaLM (Yet another Language Model) as open source. Beyond generative neural networks, Yandex's AI advancements include computer vision and unmanned transport.

Yandex launched its cloud computing platform, Yandex.Cloud, in 2018. By 2023, Yandex.Cloud had over 32,000 clients and was a national leader in cloud computing (Rozhkov, 2024). With the rapid growth of Russia's cloud market following the exit of foreign players post-Ukraine invasion, Yandex has invested heavily to compete with rivals like Rostelekom, Selectel, Cloud.ru, and VK Cloud. Yandex owns four data centres: two in the Moscow region, one in the Vladimir region, and one in the Ryazan region. Before restructuring, Yandex also owned a data centre in Mäntsälä, Finland, now owned by Nebius Group.

Approaches to Discursive Infrastructuring

Methodologically, this study relies on a conceptual approach of discursive infrastructuring that foregrounds the role of discourse as a constitutive element of sociotechnical infrastructures (Bennani-Taylor, 2024). The approach, synthetizing tools from the theoretical domains of infrastructure studies and Foucauldian discourse analysis, stems from the idea of the textual, or discursive, production of infrastructure (Aspria et al., 2016), especially given the contested and yet not conventionalized understanding of AI and its infrastructures. Stressing the relational and temporal dimensions of infrastructure, Bennani-Taylor (2024, p. 3) defines infrastructuring as "processes which attempt to fix a material-symbolic assemblage within a particular social order." As such, the discursive processes of infrastructuring "attempt to stabilise AI as an assemblage comprising specific ideologies, materialities, and relationships of power" (Bennani-Taylor, 2024, p. 3). Within the framework of discursive infrastructuring, I consider Yandex sustainability reports an infrastructuring discourse that is simultaneously developed through and demonstrated by analysis of these documents.

In her approach, Bennani-Taylor combines Foucauldian discourse analysis with an ethnographic method for analysing infrastructure (Star, 1999). As I study not only text but also visual imageries in comics, I compliment this approach with visual discourse analysis that claims it is possible to think of visuality as a sort of discourse. Besides text, discourses can be articulated through all sorts visual and verbal images and texts, specialized or not, and also through the practices that those languages permit (Rose, 2001).

A Foucauldian understanding of discourse considers it "a specific ensemble of ideas, concepts, and categorizations that are produced, reproduced, and transformed in a particular set of practices and through which meaning is given to physical and social realities" (Hajer, 1995, p. 44). Foucault considered discourse as a form of discipline: discourse is powerful because it disciplines subjects into certain ways of thinking and acting. Also, power and knowledge are tightly interrelated in discourses. This is how Foucault (1995, p. 27) puts it: "power and knowledge directly imply one another; ... there is no power relation without the correlative constitution of a field of knowledge, nor any knowledge that does not presuppose and constitute at the same time power relations."

Following this logic, the analysis should go beyond interpreting what is said in the text in order "to excavate the implicit visions of AI embedded within the document, and the social and historical contexts they are tied to" (Bennani-Taylor, 2024, p. 5). Excavation of AI infrastructure discourses in Yandex's sustainability reporting allows for tracing of how and to what extent the discursive making of sustainable AI infrastructures is moulded by the country's political and social peculiarities.

Also, discursive infrastructuring borrows from Star's seminal techniques for "reading infrastructure," such as "the identification of master narratives" and "surfacing invisible work" (Star, 1999, pp. 384–385). The former technique pays attention to what has been made other or unnamed, including creating global actors to represent a plurality of perspectives, personification, passive voice, the deletion of modalities, and "turning a diverse set of activities and interests into one actor with a presumably monolithic agenda" (Star, 1999, p. 385). The latter refers to tracing the hidden processes and the "articulation work" that enables them (Star, 1999, p. 385).

Yandex is among the few Russian internet companies reporting on non-financial performance. The company started to publish sustainability reports in 2020, a year after VKontakte, which was the first in the sector. Its latest sustainability report was published in June 2024 in three formats—a traditional pdf document available for reading online and downloading in Russian and English (Yandex, 2023a), a short web version with the most important highlights of the report (Yandex, 2023b), and comics entitled *9 stories about people and technologies* (Yandex, 2023c). Besides text, all three formats include images, such as photos (or photo-like images generated by neural networks), and drawings.

The comics consist of nine separate stories, each illustrated in a distinct visual style and featuring the name or pseudonym of the illustrator. These stories, which depict technology-driven solutions for societal or environmental issues, are based on topics from the main report. However, the selection process for these topics remains unclear, and there is no information on the illustrators' level of creative freedom from company direction. This chapter focuses on stories 1, 3, 6, and 8, which are more explicitly related to AI. Table 10.1 provides brief descriptions of these stories.

All three formats—the pdf report, highlights, and comics—formed the data sample for this study. Also, I used data from additional Yandex documents about data centres and cloud services, mentioned in the report as hyperlinks. During the first familiarization stage, I carefully read all the materials (including visual ones) to immerse myself in the sources and tentatively marked key themes in them (Rose, 2001) while paying attention to elements that indicate "master narratives" (Star, 1999, p. 384). Then, I returned to the materials again and again with a more critical gaze to support the previous steps with a so-called "interdiscursive analysis"

Table 10.1 Selected stories from the comics

Number	*Title*	*Topic*
1	Nature, education and health in the cloud	The help of Yandex Cloud for research purposes
3	Ecological, technological market	Environment-friendly packages, the use of neural networks and robots for better user experience with Yandex Market (marketplace)
6	AI assistant and education	Free YandexGPT-based AI assistant helps secondary school students prepare for graduation exams (Yandex Uchebnik)
8	Protecting users and data	Security technologies

(Fairclough, 2010, p. 238) that connects analysis of the text with analysis of social practices. In particular, I was attentive to the usage of words and phrases, the communities addressed or imagined, assumed interpretations made in the materials, as well as the production of the text and access to it.

Previous research has addressed the peculiarity of sustainability reporting as a genre of corporate communication that aims to help stakeholders (from investors to consumers and civil society organizations) evaluate the sustainability of companies but that might result in bias in accounts of environmental and social impacts (Frig et al., 2025). As such, the report's genre should be taken into account—it conditions the structure and tonality of the narration. In this regard, the visual forms (comics, images) allow for deeper delving and tracing hidden processes and the "articulation work."

Findings: Yandex Sustainability Report and Comics as Infrastructuring Discourses

The analysis revealed four main discourses that I loosely divide into two groups. The first group (discourses 1 and 2) contributes to the discursive understanding of sustainable AI and its applications as infrastructure within a given (imagined) social context. The second group (discourses 3 and 4) constructs the vision of AI infrastructures within the company's narratives about AI and sustainability. Below I critically discuss these discourses in relation to the ideas of digital sovereignty I consider an integral element of them.

Digital sovereignty has become a powerful political discourse around the world to enforce national laws and justify governmental interventions in the digital sphere to protect "vital goods" ranging from security to prosperity, cultural norms, diversity, and media control (Heidebrecht, 2024). In the case of Russia, digital sovereignty is mainly related to the country's long-term efforts to establish a "sovereign internet" (Budnitsky & Jia, 2018; Litvinenko, 2021). Being interwoven with political-economic agendas, infrastructural discourses reflect larger collective imaginaries. Ideas of digital sovereignty and global leadership germinate in the company's sustainability reporting in imagining AI infrastructure as an impregnable fortress that holds its ground under the onslaught of enemies. Yandex thus supports the national plan for locally owned, controlled, and operated innovation ecosystems ensuring digital sovereignty – and AI sovereignty as part of it.

Discourse 1 "AI for People to Control Nature"

Discourse 1 reflects the construction of AI as a tool in the hands of powerful people (Yandex employees and users). The evidence of this discourse can be read in different parts of the report where AI is used to trace, study, and control natural objects (climate regimes, animals, weather) even though it requires resources and produces greenhouses gases (GHGs)—and in that sense mirroring discussions from Europe and the US (see Sridharan and Brodie in this volume). Thus, the report claims that

> digital technologies play an important role in solving complex climate problems. Yandex services, for example, analyze meteorological data and climate phenomena [and] build and visualize climate forecasts, thereby helping scientists study the possibilities of combating climate change and businesses to choose strategies for adaptation to their consequences. (Yandex 2023a, p. 87)

In the next paragraph, the report admits that "the operation of any digital service is associated with processes that result in greenhouse gas emissions, and we strive to study them" and that "more than half of Yandex's total carbon footprint comes from electricity consumption by data centres" (Yandex, 2023a, p. 87). These statements construct the idea that despite negative environmental impacts, natural resources are essential for creating value for people. This aligns with Western tech companies' sustainability discourse, where digital technology development is viewed as a solution-centric approach to societal issues (Kuntsman & Rattle, 2019).

Comic 1 develops this idea further. In the comic, the El Niño climate phenomenon is illustrated as an angry red bull waking up from a volcano. A person standing on the roof of a house in a village at the foot of the volcano asks him: "What are you going to do to us? We knew you'd come." The bull growls: "But how?" Then an explanation is given: "There's a city, and in it a building, and in it a data centre, and in it a server cluster, and in it a Yandex neural network that calculates in advance when and where you'll appear." The next picture shows a gender-neutral

Fig. 10.1 Screenshot of comic 1 *Nature, Education and Health in the Cloud* (Yandex, 2023c)

person throwing up their hands in bewilderment: “I’m afraid you won’t understand, you’re just a cloud of ash. It’s a wonder you can even talk” (Fig. 10.1).

The comic’s narrative mirrors the Russian fairy tale structure where a villain threatens a community’s peaceful life (Propp, 1971). The hero, a main actor in Propp’s classification thwarting the villain, is depicted as a non-human, non-material neural network. Its location is described in a typical fairy tale manner, keeping the most important thing (like Koshchei’s death) under protective layers. Humans play a secondary role in the confrontation between the El Niño villain and the Yandex neural network, reduced to communicating with the villain. El Niño, an environmental phenomenon, is portrayed as an aggressive entity to be defeated. The winning strategy involves predicting and nullifying its impact. Initially, the human dispatcher communicates with El Niño, but by the comic’s end, they strip its agency away (“you won’t understand, you’re just a cloud of ash”). This strategy highlights humans, empowered by AI, as nature’s host.

This discourse stabilizes AI as an empowering tool of control, which also contributes to the idea of sovereignty. Digital sovereignty depends on locally owned, controlled, and operated innovation ecosystems and is able to increase the state’s technical and economic independence and autonomy (Musiani, 2022). This discourse expands sovereignty towards control of planetary influences through the AI tools provided by Yandex. As mentioned earlier, similar approaches attempting at interconnecting both sovereignty discourses and the use of AI for forecasting weather extremes (among other examples of managing the climate crisis) can be observed in the European Union and beyond. Whereas Europe builds on European sovereignty through interstate cooperation and transnational networks of cooperation in building AI infrastructures (see introduction in this volume), the Yandex sustainability reporting exemplifies similar ambitions albeit with different execution. Overall, negative consequences in the form of greenhouse gas emissions are represented as unpleasant but inevitable and therefore acceptable components of the greater goal of sovereignty.

Discourse 2 "AI of Generation and Class Gaps"

Discourse 2 reflects the discursive construction of AI as a boundary object (dis)connecting different social worlds of actors where younger, well-educated people of an upper-middle class are seen as the main social group practising and benefiting from AI.

Comic 6 addresses the gap illustrating a father who does not understand what his son is doing on the computer and how AI can be used in education, in particular in preparation for the secondary school graduation exam. The father is visualized as a person belonging to a particular social group—he is wearing *tel'nyashka*, a horizontally striped undershirt worn by Russian military personnel and has a tattoo on his left arm, which visualizes him as a person with a military background. Being in his 40s, he doesn't understand the usefulness of AI, saying, "I do not understand this generation. When I was his age, I played GTA" (Fig. 10.2).

This comic draws symbolic borders between people of different age, education, and occupation and their engagement with AI. A similar generational gap is present in comic 3.

The sustainability report stresses the importance of young people for technological development: "We love working with young people, in whom we see great potential for the development of the technology industry" (Yandex, 2023a, p. 37). Also, the report mentions the lack

Fig. 10.2 Screenshot of comic 6 *AI Assistant and Education* (Yandex, 2023c)

of specialists as the main obstacle for AI development and criticizes the state education system for its inability to solve this problem: "the educational system risks adapting too slowly to new trends in technological development" (Yandex, 2023a, p. 46). The report mentions numerous activities and initiatives from school through university that Yandex offers in parallel with or as part of the state education system. In this manner, Yandex elaborates an educational infrastructure to (re)produce IT specialists and future workers.

This discourse is engaged with digital sovereignty through the idea of reproducing IT workforces. On the other hand, the discourse also indicates the "beyond the politics" approach of Yandex towards its technologies and engaged communities. In the case of Yandex, depoliticization takes the form of imagining its own universe—"the illusion of a politically neutral mini-state within Russia" (Solovyeva & Bristow, 2024, p. 8). In doing so, the report, highlights, and comics discursively stabilize AI within the social group of young, educated, white people of middle or upper-middle class, living in the larger cities of Russia. This group does not represent Russia's population at large. Moreover, it is precisely members of this group who left Russia en masse after the invasion of Ukraine in February 2022 and the military mobilization in Russia in September 2022 (Kostenko et al., 2023). Similar to stabilizing AI in other national contexts (Bennani-Taylor, 2024), Yandex constructs it as bonded with notions of progress and modernity.

Discourse 3 "Leadership by Infrastructure Sustainability"

Topical discussions of AI infrastructure in the report are divided into two parts. First, it is mentioned in the subchapter *Energy Efficiency* where the discussion revolves around the data centre and its PUE (power usage effectiveness) index; second, in the subchapter *Carbon Footprint* where Scope 1 and Scope 2 are assessed and discussed. The comics and the report highlights do not address these topics.

The success of the Yandex data centre's energy efficiency is constructed in relation to its world counterparts with statements like "4.5 times lower additional energy consumption for servicing server equipment in 2023 than the world average" (Yandex, 2023a, p. 76), or "The average annual PUE value of the largest data centers in Russia ... was 1.13 ..., which is comparable with the indicators of world industry leaders and 28% better than the world average, which in 2023 was 1.58" (Yandex, 2023a, p. 77), or "Yandex's Chervonenkis is the TOP-4 most powerful commercial supercomputer in Europe" (Yandex, 2023a, p. 78). The report thus not only illustrates the energy sustainability of the Yandex data centres (master narrative) but also sets a relativist way of assessing this efficiency (better than the world or Europe). Also, it does invisible work of claiming Yandex as part of European IT sector and the company that obtains leading position among European and Western companies in AI development and infrastructure sustainability.

Discourse 4 "Securitizing the Infrastructure"

Discussion of security issues is a significant part of the sustainability report, constituting security as part of the sustainability ethos. The report stresses the growing importance of security and the need to increase its effectiveness: "In 2023, we expanded our team—the number of employees responsible for digital security increased by a third. This is due to both business growth and the desire to protect our infrastructure and services even more effectively" (Yandex, 2023a, p. 62). In the report, infrastructure security is constituted by the physical security of data centres and the security of cloud services.

The description of the physical security measures of data centres creates an image of an impregnable fortress: access to the data centres is "strictly regulated—you can't go inside without a pre-approved application." (Yandex, 2023d, p. 4).[2] The level of control inside the data centres is such that even those who have access are controlled: "All cloud service objects (server racks, boxes, equipment diagnostic zones) are constantly under video surveillance, and camera recordings are stored on the company's servers for at least three months" (Yandex, 2023d, p. 4). Security protocols cover unused equipment too: "broken equipment is stored in special safe packages [and] is not replaced or removed from the premises without a special request … Broken equipment is destroyed within the data centers" (Yandex, 2023d, p. 4). The described practices symbolically illustrate that the "fortress's" control of objects continues even after their "death".

The metaphor of Yandex digital infrastructure as a fortress can also be seen in the comic 8, *Protecting Users and Data*, where scammers

[2] A separate report about the security of Yandex.Cloud. A hyperlink to this report is provided in the section on security in the sustainability report.

Fig. 10.3 Screenshot of comic 8 *Protecting Users and Data* (Yandex, 2023c)

illustrated as aggressive black devils try to circumvent Yandex security technologies. Yandex security is illustrated as a wall made of labelled bricks that the devils try to ruin (Fig. 10.3). At the end of the comic, the wall remains unbroken—the fortress did not fall.

This discourse stabilizes data centres and cloud services as objects of the company's and the nation's security. Technological sovereignty is here imagined as securitization practices protecting against the external foes.

Conclusions: Sustainability of AI Infrastructure in the Context of an Authoritarian Regime

This study elaborates the emerging problem of the sustainability of digital infrastructures with the rapid growth of AI and AI-driven models. Despite growing awareness of the negative impacts on both the planet and societies, many countries have doubled down on security- and sovereignty-driven discourses in their pursuit of global leadership in AI and digital technologies (Baur, 2024; Rone, 2024). In the European context, imaginaries of data and infrastructure are coupled with politicized concepts of control, territoriality, and sovereignty (Baur, 2024). Both within countries and across borders, AI infrastructures – whether material (like data centres) or immaterial (like cloud services)—create new power dynamics and dependencies and challenge the traditional view of sustainability as simply environmental, social, and economic (Dillard et al., 2008).

In authoritarian contexts, sustainability narratives take on additional dimensions as they intersect with discourses of national self-sufficiency and sovereignty (Glasze et al., 2023). This chapter has explored the interwovenness of sustainability and digital sovereignty from the perspective of digital infrastructures. Operating under an authoritarian regime and being under partial state control through ownership structure, Yandex echoes a state-led narrative of AI as part of state ambitions for technological and ideological sovereignty. AI and AI-driven services are constructed as infrastructuring entities that can ensure control over natural and planetary events as well as the (re)production of a community of professionals and practitioners. At the same time, the study proves the apolitical stance of Yandex (Solovyeva & Bristow, 2024) in sustainability discourses: AI and its infrastructures are getting constructed along the ideas of progress, modernization, and westernization "on the ground"—in the everyday practices of its customers and employees. As such, the objects of AI infrastructure (mainly data centres and cloud services) are visualized as simultaneously the object of the company's security and objects of pride in comparison to global and European competitors.

Competing Interests This research has been conducted as part of the project: "FLOWISION: Best from both worlds – enhancing energy transition in Russia and Finland by making resource flows visible," funded by the Kone Foundation. See https://flowision.fi.

References

Aryalina, M., & Milkin, V. (2025, February 21). Российским дата-центрам не хватает электричества на обучение новых ИИ-моделей. *Vedomosti*. https://www.vedomosti.ru/business/articles/2025/02/21/1093517-rossiiskim-data-tsentram-ne-hvataet-elektrichestva

Aspria, M., de Mul, M., Adams, S., & Bal, R. (2016). Of blooming flowers and multiple sockets: The role of metaphors in the politics of infrastructural work. *Science & Technology Studies*, *29*(3), 68–87. hdl.handle.net/1765/93300

Baur, A. (2024). European dreams of the cloud: Imagining innovation and political control. *Geopolitics, 29*(3), 796–820. https://doi.org/10.1080/14650045.2022.2151902

Bennani-Taylor, S. (2024). Infrastructuring AI: The stabilization of 'artificial intelligence' in and beyond national AI strategies. *First Monday*, *29*(2). https://doi.org/10.5210/fm.v29i2.13568

Berger, P. L., & Luckmann, T. (1966). *The social construction of reality.* Doubleday.

Bowker, G. C., & Star, S. L. (2000). *Sorting things out: Classification and its consequences.* MIT press. https://doi.org/10.7551/mitpress/6352.001.0001

Budnitsky, S., & Jia, L. (2018). Branding internet sovereignty: Digital media and the Chinese-Russian cyberalliance. *European Journal of Cultural Studies, 21*(5), 594–613. https://doi.org/10.1177/1367549417751151

Christensen, L. T., & Cheney, G. (2011). Interrogating the communicative dimensions of corporate social responsibility. In Ø. Ihlen, J. F. Bartlett & S. May (Eds.), *The handbook of communication and corporate social responsibility* (pp. 491–504). Wiley. https://doi.org/10.1002/9781118083246.ch24

Crawford, K. (2021). *The atlas of AI: Power, politics, and the planetary costs of artificial intelligence*. Yale University Press. https://yalebooks.yale.edu/book/9780300264630/atlas-of-ai/

Dillard, J., Dujon, V., & King, M. C. (Eds.). (2008). *Understanding the social dimension of sustainability*. Routledge.

Fairclough N. (2010). *Critical discourse analysis: The critical study of language* (2nd ed.). Longman.

Foucault, M. (1995). *Discipline and punish: The birth of the prison* (A. Sheridan, Trans., 2nd ed.). Vintage Books.

Glasze, G., Cattaruzza, A., Douzet, F., Dammann, F., Bertran, M.-G., Bômont, C., Braun, M., Danet, D., Desforges, A., Géry, A., Grumbach, S., Hummel, P., Limonier, K., Münßinger, M., Nicolai, F., Pétiniaud, L., Winkler, J., & Zanin, C. (2023). Contested spatialities of digital sovereignty. *Geopolitics, 28*(2), 919–958. https://doi.org/10.1080/14650045.2022.2050070

Gel'man, V. (2023). Exogenous shock and Russian studies. *Post-Soviet Affairs, 39*(1–2), 1–9. https://doi.org/10.1080/1060586X.2022.2148814

Gillespie, T. (2010). The politics of 'platforms.' *New Media & Society, 12*(3), 347–364. https://doi.org/10.1177/1461444809342738

Hajer, M. A. (1995). *The politics of environmental discourse: Ecological modernization and the policy process*. Oxford University Press.

Heidebrecht, S. (2024). From market liberalism to public intervention: Digital sovereignty and changing European union digital single market governance. *JCMS: Journal of Common Market Studies, 62*(1), 205–223. https://doi.org/10.1111/jcms.13488

Hogan, M. (2022). Data center. In L. A. Schintler & C. L. McNeely (Eds.), *Encylopedia of big data*. Springer.

Kostenko, N., Kamalov, E., Sergeeva, I., & Zavadskaya, M. (2023). *The Russian rhizome: A social portrait of new immigrants*. Re: Russia. https://re-russia.net/en/expertise/045/

Kravets-Meinke, D. (2024). The sad fate of Yandex: From independent tech startup to Kremlin propaganda tool. *ZOiS Spotlight*. https://www.zois-berlin.de/en/publications/zois-spotlight/the-sad-fate-of-yandex-from-independent-tech-startup-to-kremlin-propaganda-tool

Kuntsman, A., & Rattle, I. (2019). Towards a paradigmatic shift in sustainability studies: A systematic review of peer reviewed literature and future agenda setting to consider environmental (un)sustainability of digital communication. *Environmental Communication, 13*(5), 567–581. https://doi.org/10.1080/17524032.2019.1596144

Litvinenko, A. (2021). Re-defining borders online: Russia's strategic narrative on internet sovereignty. *Media and Communication, 9*, 5–15. https://doi.org/10.17645/mac.v9i4.4292

Milmo, D. (2024, July 2). Google's emissions climb nearly 50% in five years due to AI energy demand. *The Guardian*. https://www.theguardian.com/technology/article/2024/jul/02/google-ai-emissions

Muhametshina, E. (2024, December 11). Что говорил Владимир Путин о развитии искусственного интеллекта. *Vedomosti*. https://www.vedomosti.ru/politics/articles/2024/12/11/1080816-chto-govoril-putin-o-razvitii-iskusstvennogo-intellekta

Musiani, F. (2022). Infrastructuring digital sovereignty: A research agenda for an infrastructure-based sociology of digital self-determination practices. *Information, Communication & Society, 25*(6), 785–800. https://doi.org/10.1080/1369118X.2022.2049850

Parks, L., & Starosielski, N. (2015). Introduction. In Parks, L., & Starosielski, N. (Eds.), *Signal traffic: Critical studies of media infrastructures* (pp. 1–28). University of Illinois Press. https://www.press.uillinois.edu/books/?id=p080876

Petrova, V. (2024, December 16). *САПФИР блеснет интеллектом*. Kommersant. https://www.kommersant.ru/doc/7380894

Plantin, J. C., & Punathambekar, A. (2019). Digital media infrastructures: Pipes, platforms, and politics. *Media, Culture & Society, 41*(2), 163–174. https://doi.org/10.1177/0163443718818376

President of Russia. (2024). *National strategy for the development of artificial intelligence for the period up to 2030*. http://www.kremlin.ru/acts/bank/44731/page/1

Propp, V. J. (1971). *Morphology of the folktale*. University of Texas Press.

Raley, R., & Rhee, J. (2023). Critical AI: A field in formation. *American Literature, 95*(2), 185–204. https://doi.org/10.1215/00029831-10575021

Rone, J. (2024). 'The sovereign cloud' in Europe: Diverging nation state preferences and disputed institutional competences in the context of limited technological capabilities. *Journal of European Public Policy, 31*(8), 2343–2369. https://doi.org/10.1080/13501763.2024.2348618

Rose, G. (2001). *Visual methodologies: An introduction to the interpretation of visual materials*. SAGE.

Rozhkov, R. (2024, September 25). Yandex Cloud за два года инвестирует в развитие платформы 42 млрд рублей. *Forbes*. https://www.forbes.ru/tekhnologii/521857-yandex-cloud-za-dva-goda-investiruet-v-razvitie-platformy-42-mlrd-rublej

Solovyeva, O., & Bristow, A. (2024). Business beyond politics? A-political corporate leadership in authoritarian Russia. In *The Routledge critical companion to leadership studies* (pp. 361–373). Routledge. https://doi.org/10.4324/9781003363125

Solovyeva, O., & Yablokov, I. (2024). Putin's technological deluge: Techno-populism, anti-Westernism, and the strive for global leadership. *Communist and Post-Communist Studies, 58*(2), 28–47. https://doi.org/10.1525/cpcs.2024.2308299

Star, S. L. (1999). The ethnography of infrastructure. *American Behavioral Scientist, 43*(3), 377–391. https://doi.org/10.1177/00027649921955326

Van Der Vlist, F., Helmond, A., & Ferrari, F. (2024). Big AI: Cloud infrastructure dependence and the industrialisation of artificial intelligence. *Big Data & Society, 11*(1). https://doi.org/10.1177/20539517241232630

Velkova, J., & Plantin, J. C. (2023). Data centers and the infrastructural temporalities of digital media: An introduction. *New Media & Society, 25*(2), 273–286. https://doi.org/10.1177/14614448221149945

Wijermars, M. (2021). Russia's law "On news aggregators": Control the news feed, control the news? *Journalism, 22*(12), 2938–2954. https://doi.org/10.1177/1464884921990917

Williams, R., Silvast, A., & Musiani, F. (2024). Governance by information infrastructures: Origins and evolution of the concept. *First Monday*, *29*(10). https://doi.org/10.5210/fm.v29i10.13794

Yandex. (2023a). *Yandex sustainability progress report*. https://sustainability.yandex.ru/download-center

Yandex. (2023b). *Sustainable development in Yandex*. https://sustainability.yandex.ru/2023-highlights/

Yandex. (2023c). *9 stories about people and technologies*. https://sustainability.yandex.ru/2023-highlights/comics

Yandex. (2023d). *Security in Yandex.Cloud*. https://storage.yandexcloud.net/yc-compliance/security-in-yandex-cloud-2023-09-12.pdf

Zavrazhneva, A. (2024, August 14). *How non-financial reporting is developing in Russia today.* RBC Trends. https://trends.rbc.ru/trends/green/66bc74ea9a7947e83f4d2445?from=copy

CHAPTER 11

Entangled Sustainabilities: News Media Partnerships and Generative AI Market Power

Anne Mollen

Generative AI's Strategic News Partnerships

Generative AI applications have led to significant turmoil in the digital industries since the launch of ChatGPT in November 2022. Recognising the new field of economic expansion, big tech companies have since heavily invested in AI technology (Morris & Uddin, 2025) through more investment in their own generative AI developments, partnerships with generative AI providers or in most cases both. Generative AI providers have also actively sought deeper integration with major digital technology companies, as seen in Microsoft's collaborations with OpenAI or the French company Mistral AI.

Incentives to seek deeper integration with big tech corporations, such as the infamous GAMAM (Google, Apple, Meta, Amazon, Microsoft),

A. Mollen (✉)
University of Münster, Münster, Germany
e-mail: anne.mollen@uni-muenster.de

A. Mollen et al. (eds.), *AI Infrastructures and Sustainability*, Palgrave Studies in European Communication Research and Education,
https://doi.org/10.1007/978-3-032-09748-4_11

include access to computing power, training data and product implementation opportunities. Accordingly, observers in the field have recognised that data, capital, ecosystems and expertise are key for manifesting market power in the generative AI industry (Mozilla Foundation, 2024), which explains the competitive advantage for the already dominant big technology corporations (Vipra & Korinek, 2023).

An infrastructural perspective can help cast light on the role played by the generative AI production chain and its importance for market concentration in matters of sustainability. Massive data centres, immense large language model (LLM) architectures, vast data sets, facilities for energy production and the like are becoming key infrastructures undergirding generative AI development while at the same time manifesting market power. In their materiality, these infrastructures imply far-reaching risks to sustainability—from huge resource demands to ethical implications and unequal distribution of economic gains from generative AI, to name just a few.

This chapter provides a political economy perspective on market concentration in the generative AI industry with a focus on sustainability. It does so by investigating recently established collaborations between generative AI providers and news media as well as publishing houses, who are consequently becoming part of generative AI infrastructures, analysing such partnerships through the lens of sustainability. By considering sustainability as encompassing social, economic and ecological dimensions, a focus on their interrelation provides a necessary perspective on the sustainability implications of generative AI systems far beyond generative AI providers.

A Political Economy and Sustainability Perspective on Generative AI

Recent partnerships, mergers and acquisitions between tech companies in relation to generative AI have become a focus of attention for competition authorities (Vestager et al., 2024). Less attention has been paid to partnerships between news media publishers and generative AI organisations, even though most generative AI providers are heavily investing in them. OpenAI can be considered the frontrunner in this development, having started to secure news media partnerships since around July 2023, starting with key industry actors like the Associated Press and continuing to secure new collaborations on a global scale, such as most recently at the time of writing with *The Guardian* (February 2025). While initial partnerships like the one between OpenAI and Axel Springer were met with widespread public interest, being marketed as "the first of its kind" (OpenAI, 2023b, para. 4) global news media partnership "to deepen beneficial use of AI in journalism" (OpenAI, 2023b, title), such partnerships are now becoming industry standard.

Much of the scholarly debate in media and communication studies has so far focused on the shifts in, for instance, journalistic production through the application of generative AI technologies (Cools & Diakopoulos, 2024). The economic dimension of a stronger integration of generative AI with news media has largely remained unconsidered. This is surprising since these partnerships embody a current shift in the relationship between big tech and news production entities.

While big tech corporations have traditionally highlighted their role as neutral platforms (Gillespie, 2010) that simply provide distribution channels for news media content and cannot be held accountable for the content they circulate, the sheer numbers of such newly formed partnerships make it apparent that authoritative news media content is becoming increasingly important for generative AI providers. At the same time, major news media organisations are filing lawsuits against generative AI providers, claiming copyright infringements over the use of their material for training generative AI systems (New York Times, 2023) and attempts at developing generative AI products in-house (Roth & Kennemer, 2024). We are thus currently observing a shifting actor landscape at the intersection of generative AI and news media, with a strong inclination towards economic and competition objectives, which raises questions from an infrastructural perspective.

Analysts emphasise that the generative AI industry is prone to market concentration (Vipra & Korinek, 2023) due to the technology's reliance on digital infrastructures such as data and technical systems (Mozilla Foundation, 2024), giving the already dominant tech companies a heavy competitive advantage. Further, the technology's preconditions create very high entry barriers for other potential competitors (Gray Widder et al., 2023). Considering big tech dominance in the generative AI industry, it thus seems astonishing that Microsoft CEO Satya Nadella framed generative AI as a disruption to the concentrated platform and search engine industry, and that journalists should accordingly welcome AI:

> Let's face it, there's a real aggregation power in a few places, right? Search is one. News feeds is another. Both of these things could be up for disruption.... What happens to the information ecosystem when there's high concentration is deterioration. (Nadella cited in Manancourt, 2024, para. 4)

Confronted with such claims, it becomes important to investigate the role of media and publishing houses in generative AI infrastructures and market concentration processes, since they imply far-reaching consequences for how generative AI is used to generate knowledge about the world and consequently for what role it will play within democratic public spheres and opinion-making.

Investigations into market concentration, specifically focusing on ownership and the monopolistic tendencies in the news and cultural production industries, have a long tradition within media and communication research (Baker, 2006). Political economy perspectives on media and communication have highlighted the importance of the political, societal and democratic implications of a concentrated media market (Downing, 2011; McChesney, 2008). While media concentration in pre-digital landscapes could usually be grouped into different types of media concentration (e.g. vertical, horizontal, diagonal and conglomerates; Knoche, 2021), such assessments have become much more complex in digital media ecosystems. With platformization, we are now observing media concentration as entanglements of "large corporate ecosystems" (Poell, 2020, p. 652) that dominate not only content production or distribution, but also hardware production, data aggregation, advertising businesses and the like. Sociologist Philipp Staab (2024) even claims that in contemporary digital capitalism, tech firms do not dominate markets but instead form proprietary markets constituted through unprecedented and abundant forms of control within such markets.

Considering the corporate entanglements among generative AI infrastructures, questions on the role of news media partnerships in the market power of dominant generative AI providers are currently left unanswered. Such questions matter from a sustainability perspective, since economic concentration and power always relate to questions of economic exploitation and equal distribution of capabilities for human welfare (Sen, 2008), as politically institutionalised within the UN Sustainable Development Goals (United Nations, 2015). When understood as intra- and intergenerational justice (UN WCED, 1987), a connection between sustainability and critical political economy approaches to media concentration is thus easily drawn, because

> critical political economy continues to be centrally concerned with the relations between the organization of culture and communications and the constitution of the good society grounded in social justice and democratic practice. (Wasko et al., 2011, p. 2)

Matters of economic concentration in the generative AI industry go beyond high market entrance barriers and unjust distribution of profit. With generative AI being increasingly positioned as an epistemic technology (Alvarado, 2023), used to search for information and know about the world, concentration in the generative AI industry goes to the heart of equal access to and distribution of knowledge, political opinion-making and democratic practice. Because generative AI increasingly seems to rely on traditional journalistic news media content to fulfil its role as an epistemic technology and an alternative to search engines and news feeds, the role of news media should be examined from a combined political economy and sustainability perspective. Such a joint approach provides added analytical value by connecting often-separated economic, social and environmental sustainability concerns in relation to generative AI and grounding these within the economic rationales of generative AI businesses.

While, for instance, environmental concerns about extremely resource-intensive large language models as the basis for generative AI applications are widely discussed (Bender et al., 2021; Li et al., 2023; Strubell et al., 2020) a critical political economy connects environmental concerns to matters of economic concentration in the generative AI industry, opening perspectives on, for example, how dominant generative AI providers set environmentally harmful industry standards. The analysis of generative AI and news media partnerships presented below thus allows us to conceptualise responsibility for the sustainability risks of generative AI applications well beyond the engineering stage. The analysis raises concerns about the role of news media and publishing houses in manifestations of economic power with certain generative AI providers and how this might align with principles of social, economic and environmental justice.

Integrating News Media into Generative AI Infrastructures

Investigating generative AI infrastructures is key for understanding market concentration in the generative AI industry. Along the generative AI value chain, ownership and access to infrastructure establish high entry barriers, preventing competitors from entering the market while at the same time manifesting market power for those who are already key market actors (Mozilla Foundation, 2024).

A closer look at what constitutes infrastructure helps provide a more detailed description of generative AI infrastructures. To briefly summarise recent approaches, infrastructures need to be acknowledged for their materiality and their purpose of allowing the distribution and transportation of forms of matter, as noted by anthropologist Brian Larkin (2013, p. 329). Parks and Starosielski specify that media and communication infrastructures "support the distribution of audiovisual signal traffic" (2015, p. 4)—referring to the undersea cables, data submission networks, copper lines and so on that enable the transmission of data, media content or interpersonal communication. At the same time, this materiality always emerges from relational settings (Star & Ruhleder, 1996), implying that many actors are entangled with the materiality of generative AI and should be acknowledged in any infrastructural analysis (Mollen & Kannengießer, 2025).

When understanding generative AI as communicative agents (Guzman & Lewis, 2020), an infrastructural perspective acknowledges the materiality of different elements along the generative AI value chain that contribute to the agent's ability to assume the role of interactant within communicative encounters (Mollen & Kannengießer, 2026), allowing examination of how it is shaped by diverse actors. An infrastructural perspective thus requires a detailed look at generative AI's technological set-up, not to reveal how the technology works in a practical sense, but rather to investigate the political rationalities and market dynamics implied in infrastructures as the backends of contemporary media (Parks et al., 2023).

What constitutes generative AI can be observed along its value chain, responding to recent calls that "it is becoming increasingly important to understand the value chains of AI in the digital platform economy for strategic, political, and economic reasons" (van der Vlist et al., 2024, p. 2). One common way of dissecting the value chain of generative AI can be drawn from commonly applied lifecycle analyses in machine learning (ML) research, where Luccioni et al. (2022) have identified raw material extraction, material manufacturing, equipment manufacturing, system development and training, system deployment, and disposal/end of life as key stages along the generative AI value chain. This distinction resonates with concerns about accumulation of power with existing big technology companies in the generative AI industry. Here, big tech's dominant position in hardware development, computing power and energy supply, their in-house expertise in building and developing new ML technologies, and their access to unique training data and eventually their ability to deploy and integrate generative AI technologies into their vast product ecosystems are all prerequisites for their competitive advantage.

Accordingly, since late 2022, major technology companies as well as smaller generative AI providers have engaged in mergers and partnerships along these infrastructures, in the form of partnerships to ensure generative AI integration into a vast array of products (e.g., Mistral AI and SAP, BNP Paribas, Capgemini, etc.; Sun, 2024), access to computing power (e.g., OpenAI and Microsoft or Anthropic and AWS; Hartmans, 2023; OpenAI, 2023a), training data (e.g., SAP partnerships about business data with Aleph Alpha, Anthropic and Cohere; SAP News, 2023), or hardware (e.g. Adobe and NVIDIA). Such partnerships are being established systematically and strategically across the industry. Especially interesting from a media and communication perspective are partnerships between generative AI developers and news media and publishing houses.

One key framing of such partnerships is the access to journalistic content as training data, since it is widely recognised that journalistic content is essential for generating well-formulated generative AI outputs (Schaul et al., 2022). However, a more systematic investigation seems called for, as these strategic partnerships demonstrate a fundamental shift in the actor constellations within the generative AI, news media and publishing industries. These are worth investigating from a critical political economy and media concentration perspective.

Analysing Changing Actor Constellations in the Generative AI and News Media Industries

Starting from the observation that an infrastructural perspective is essential for understanding market concentration in the generative AI industry, this chapter investigates how partnerships between news media or publishing houses and generative AI providers are positioned within generative AI infrastructures. While journalistic content as training data is one aspect to consider, access to reliable journalistic content on current affairs can also be significant for the deployment stage of generative AI products. Considering that generative AI chatbots are heavily marketed as information resources and an epistemic technology (Alvarado, 2023) that could potentially disrupt the information ecosystem, questions of media concentration align closely with questions of market concentration.

This chapter thus responds to recent criticisms of infrastructural approaches and their failure to acknowledge the materiality of media and communication technologies that underpins long-established critical political economy approaches to media and communication (Hesmondhalgh, 2021). Instead, this investigation builds on the observation that current actor constellations in the generative AI and news media industry are changing. From one angle, news media are becoming relevant actors within the generative AI industry. From a different angle, generative AI providers and their systems are gaining relevance within the news media industry. In any case, the shifting constellations at the intersection of generative AI and the news media industry can be empirically assessed.

The analysis of actors and their control and ownership of markets (vertical and horizontal), as well as of mergers, takeovers and strategic alliances, has long been a feasible way to analyse processes of concentration in the media industry (Knoche, 2021). Accordingly, this chapter asks how strategic partnerships between generative AI providers and news media/publishing houses form new actor constellations and how they relate to matters of media and market concentration. The emerging actor constellations will be investigated for their implications for economic, social and environmental sustainability. The infrastructural perspective towards market and media concentration not only allows for the analysis of sustainability implications, since they manifest within generative AI infrastructures, but equally centres the responsibility of actors in shaping generative AI infrastructures and their sustainability implications.

To investigate the changing actor constellations and the type of relation they establish, this study relies on a qualitative network analysis of generative AI and news media actors and their positioning towards each other and the narrative framings and ascriptions of relevance of these relationships (Hollstein & Straus, 2006). The analysis is based on a document sample collected from the websites of generative AI providers and technology reporting about mergers and partnerships between generative AI providers and news media. Overall, 36 documents were collected from generative AI organisation blogs or press releases and tech reporting, ranging in date from November 2022 to September 2024. The material was coded with qualitative coding software to systematise actors, their relations and the ascriptions of relevance through a focus on norms and values.

Analysis reveals emerging and shifting relations between generative AI organisations and news media companies that are formalised in different ways and in different positionalities. The types of relation range from strategic *partnerships* between news media and generative AI organisations, to *oppositional positionings* in the course of legal disputes, to *explorations* or more concrete *negotiations* of possible collaborations. Such relations are variously manifested in corporate agreements and formalised ways of cooperating, through lawsuits or blocking access to news media websites by generative AI providers, to consultation processes on possible partnerships. The analysis thus shows that new constellations of actors emerge at the intersection of generative AI organisations and the news media industry, with different rationales implied. The following sections will focus on what these rationales mean from a sustainability perspective.

Embedding Journalism in the Generative AI Value Chain: Economic Sustainability

The relevance of an economic perspective emerges quite clearly across the material. The analysis exemplifies that the newly emerging relations between generative AI providers and news media, both cooperative as well as antagonistic, are supported by a rationale of fostering market power. OpenAI emerges as the dominant actor able to secure the most partnerships with news media organisations. At the same time, they and their close partner Microsoft are also the object of oppositional relations, as demonstrated through news media organisations engaging in lawsuits against both companies. OpenAI is thus not only the frontrunner in terms of technological advancements bringing generative AI applications to the market, but equally in shaping emerging business relations with news media partners, as shown in Fig. 11.1.

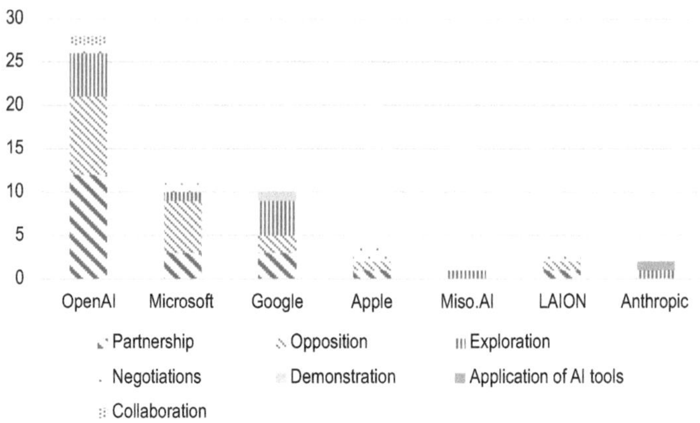

Fig. 11.1 Newly reported relations between generative AI providers and news media

Other generative AI providers such as Apple or Google are trying to follow the OpenAI partnership strategy, but their newly established relationships with news media organisations largely remain on the level of negotiations and explorations without securing any specific deals. This lack of emerging partnerships for generative AI providers other than OpenAI does not seem to be primarily a financial issue. For example, as some of the documents in the sample rumour, Apple seems to have offered around 50 million dollars for multiyear partnerships with news media publishers, whereas OpenAI presumably offers between one and five million dollars per year to publishers for allowing them to access their news media content. While *new revenue models* emerge as the most important category in the documents when analysing the relevance that news media organisations ascribe to their partnerships with generative AI organisations, these new revenue streams do not seem to stem from direct payments but rather through increasing *outreach and audience engagement* via generative AI outputs, as this quote from one of the documents demonstrates:

> "We believe that people searching with AI models will be one of the fundamental ways that people navigate the web in the future," said Nicholas Thompson, The Atlantic's CEO. "We're delighted to partner

> with OpenAI, to make The Atlantic's reporting and stories more discoverable to their millions of users, and to have a voice in shaping how news is surfaced on their platforms." (OpenAI, 2024c, para. 3)

When looking at the results of the analyses from an infrastructural perspective, the analysed documents ascribe particular relevance to partnerships between news media publishers and generative AI organisations in relation to training data and the deployment phase. However, having access to training data through partnerships with news media organisations emerges much less prominently than might be expected. Only five documents in the sample mention explicitly that newly formed partnerships will guarantee access to high-quality training data for generative AI providers. Instead, the *ascription of relevance* as well as the *norms* associated with the emerging relations in the material highlight much more prominently that partnerships matter specifically for the deployment phase of generative AI output. Having access to quality news media content that is *reliable*, *trustworthy*, *current* and *authoritative*—to name just a few of the norms associated with journalistic content in the sample—emerges as one of the most relevant aspects in the partnerships between news media and generative AI providers:

> Through this partnership, OpenAI has permission to display content from News Corp mastheads in response to user questions and to enhance its products, with the ultimate objective of providing people the ability to make informed choices based on reliable information and news sources. (OpenAI, 2024b, para. 1)

These examples exemplify how news media content emerges as a key value for generative AI providers in their deployment phase, since value is drawn from outputting reliable and accurate information to their users.

Accordingly, very few generative AI providers seem to have become successful in positioning themselves as news distributors through their partnerships with news media organisations. Publishers at the same time engage in these partnerships in hopes of new revenue opportunities. Those generative AI providers who secure partnerships can further manifest their position along the generative AI value chain regarding access to reliable and factual training data and information output, which the technologies struggle with. Partnerships with news media organisations thus should be considered for their impact on economic sustainability—since they play a significant role in market power and concentration in the generative AI industry and potentially raise market entry barriers. With OpenAI as the frontrunner in securing such partnerships, current developments point towards a deepening of inequalities on the generative AI market and thus towards negative effects on economic sustainability. This further underlines the need for critical perspectives on shifting relations in an industry that increasingly shapes how we create and perceive knowledge about the world.

Dominant Language and Knowledge Infrastructures: Social Sustainability

Integrating news media into the generative AI value chain has strong implications for matters of social sustainability. Securing strategic partnerships with news publishers does not only strengthen the economic advantage for already dominant generative AI providers – depending on whether generative AI organisations will be successful in positioning themselves as another gateway for accessing news content, it will also affect matters of information access, diversity of opinions and worldviews (Kuai et al., 2025), and thus matter significantly for political opinion-making and foundational democratic principles. Algorithmic fairness and bias in data sets have become a well-established topic in ML-oriented research (Barocas et al., 2019; Mittelstadt et al., 2016), which has identified discrimination against individuals (Wachter, 2022) or the promotion of certain cultural values while neglecting others (Birhane et al., 2022) as potential problems. When integrated along the generative AI value chain, news media equally play a role in the promulgation of fair representations and diversity of opinion in the outputs of generative AI applications.

It is obvious that many dominant generative AI applications are built upon an Anglo-American bias that might lead to epistemic injustices through their widespread application in forms of knowledge production (Luo & Puett, 2024). These injustices specifically disadvantage the Global South (the Majority World), both in the application of generative AI tools (Muzanenhamo & Power, 2024) as well as in representations of cultural and knowledge repositories (Kraft & Soulier, 2024). One outcome is a lack of adequate representation by generative AI of smaller languages and their associated cultural heritage, a fact also reflected in many initiatives to build generative AI tools for specific languages—ranging from European LLMs on quite a substantial scale to much smaller initiatives for Sub-Saharan languages (OpenEuroLLM, 2025; Lelapa AI, n.d.).

Partnerships between generative AI organisations and news publishers equally reflect a bias towards US-based knowledge repositories. In the sample analysed for this study, 29 US-based outlets are mentioned by name, with many more US outlets taking part in the mentioned partnership deals as part of larger cooperative ventures between multi-outlet publishing houses and generative AI providers. They are contrasted by only six outlets from Spain, France and Germany being explicitly mentioned, and no African, Asian, South American or other news media being considered in such partnerships.[1] This strong inclination only further manifests bias towards English-speaking and US-based outlets and bodies of knowledge. Considering that generative AI organisations attempt to position themselves as new gateways for information retrieval, this striking imbalance restricts information on current news items, even though OpenAI likes to present their international partnership as a globally reflective outreach:

> In partnership with Le Monde and Prisa Media, our goal is to enable ChatGPT users around the world to connect with the news in new ways that are interactive and insightful. (OpenAI, 2024a, para. 3)

News media partnerships are especially relevant for prompts addressing current events, which are not reflected in the training data used during the development process of AI systems. For current news, generative AI organisations instead search for recent information and then convert and re-assemble found text on an issue into new summarised outputs. Seeing as many attribution problems can be observed even among existing partnerships (Jaźwińska & Chandrasekar, 2025), it is to be feared that bias in such partnerships towards US media further endangers the representation of cultural diversity and heritage across the globe. Accordingly, concentration in news media partnerships might endanger Sustainable Development Goal 16 on "Strong Institutions" with its subgoal of ensuring

[1] For an updated list of partnerships between news media and generative AI organisations, see the *Platforms and Publishers: AI Partnership Tracker*, https://petebrown.quarto.pub/pnp-ai-partnerships/

"public access to information and protect fundamental freedoms, in accordance with national legislation and international agreements" (United Nations, 2015, p. 28).

In a concentrated generative AI marketplace, a few corporations have the power to position themselves as central gatekeepers that can promise revenues to news media outlets through their growing user base. They also exercise gatekeeping power in selecting those news media outlets and content that they consider valuable and relevant. In a concentrated market place, it is unreasonable to assume that diversity of opinions, perspectives, topics and knowledge repositories will emerge out of industry logic. Instead, diversity of perspectives and adherence to democratic principles of opinion-making seem like subjects for further media regulation that will increasingly also need to consider generative AI as a sphere of action. The founding principles of a Global News Media Trust, announced at the 2025 Paris AI Action summit, exemplify the need for coordinated action to "enable news content creators—particularly those producing content in the Global Majority—to be paid for content essential to training AI large language models (LLMs) and to foster linguistic diversity in the development of AI technology" (IFPIM, 2025, para. 1). More research on the consequences of unbalanced partnerships needs to provide further insights—especially considering current geopolitical shifts and ruptures, to target questions of diversity of opinion, equality and fair representation through generative AI.

Partnerships in Context: Environmental Sustainability

Engaging in strategic cooperation with news publishers allows generative AI providers to extend their market power, especially in relation to training data and the output phase of their generative AI systems. In other words, such partnerships are becoming a strategic asset that all dominant generative AI providers actively seek, while only the dominant actors seem to be successful in securing them, most notably OpenAI. This development has an effect on environmental sustainability since it further strengthens the position of generative AI providers that currently establish highly resource-intensive generative AI models without concern for environmental impacts, while also making news media distribution through generative AI interfaces increasingly resource-intensive.

Research into ML is continuously demonstrating the substantial energy, water and other resource demands of generative AI systems

(Bender et al., 2021; Luccioni et al., 2022; Strubell et al., 2020), largely due to their massive model architectures, training data and extensive inference numbers. These resource demands have been continuously growing according to a "bigger is better" mantra (Bender et al., 2021; Rohde et al., 2024) that is only slowly starting to be challenged. The dominant position of big AI companies (van der Vlist et al., 2024), an extension of the already powerful big tech companies, means that a few select key players exert market power in the generative AI industry.

This market power implies a dominant role in establishing industry standards, or at least tendencies. Regarding environmental sustainability, such market tendencies include the "bigger is better" ethos as well as a lack of information about the environmental impacts of generative AI systems. At the same time, the growing energy demand is becoming an obvious concern so that big tech companies position questions of energy access as a key political and industrial issue. From an industry perspective, this trend is resulting in big tech companies invoking a presumed inevitability of AI, thus legitimising their non-compliance with self-set emission targets. In addition, these firms are re-establishing energy sources like nuclear power through company-run reactors as well as encouraging the reactivation of decommissioned nuclear plants through deals with external partners. While major generative AI providers like OpenAI, Microsoft, Google or Meta further push for highly automated solutions in their products, this results in substantially more hardware, greater demands on energy and water, and the need for more data centres to be built.

Partnerships between publishing houses and big AI organisations further strengthen this market power by advancing their dominant position along the generative AI value chain with regard to training data and generative AI deployment. Accordingly, news media publishers should reflect their role in promoting and perpetuating environmentally harmful industry standards. In particular, if news media organisations have formulated sustainability principles, these should be considered when closing deals with generative AI providers. So far, oppositional positions of news media organisations in the sample vis-à-vis generative AI organisations do not refer to environmental sustainability concerns over generative AI, but primarily towards copyright infringements over protected news media material and the undermining of the media business model through unlawful foundations in the generative AI industry. As news outlets like the *New York Daily News*, *Chicago Tribune* and others involved in a joint lawsuit reported,

> This lawsuit is about how Microsoft and OpenAI are not entitled to use copyrighted newspaper content to build their new trillion-dollar enterprises without paying for that content. (David, 2024, para. 4)

If news media position themselves in opposition to generative AI organisations, their main concerns so far thus address impacts on their direct business and revenue models, which they see threatened by copyright infringements. They do not reflect their role in the wider ecosystem of generative AI market power, at least not in the public-facing statements that this sample relies on.

A more interesting and subtle development instead is the self-reliance of news media organisations on their outputs and the positioning of generative technologies as a simple tool to be implemented, rather than considering generative AI providers as organisational actors that they must engage with. In the sample analysed, a small number of major outlets like the *New York Times*, the *Financial Times*, *Forbes* and several tech magazines describe their self-reliant implementation of generative AI tools for users to engage with their content:

> The Financial Times has a new generative AI chatbot called Ask FT that can answer questions its subscribers ask. Similar to generalized AI bots (like ChatGPT, Copilot, or Gemini), users can expect a curated natural language answer to whatever they want to know. (Roth & Kennemer, 2024, para. 1)

Instead of engaging in partnerships, such self-reliant implementations of generative AI might be a way to counter further accumulation of power in the big tech industry. However, it seems that self-hosted generative AI applications will be seen as an addition to partnerships—the *Financial Times* is self-hosting as well as engaging in partnerships. From an environmental perspective, self-hosting of generative AI applications as a way for audiences to engage with a news outlet's content might be a way to counter environmentally harmful big AI practices – even though self-hosted AI applications consume more energy than their non-AI counterparts.

Conclusion

Market power in the generative AI industry is key to understanding how environmentally, socially and economically harmful industry standards are being established and manifested. The sustainability of generative AI then becomes a much broader issue to consider, when all sustainability dimensions are recognised for their interrelation. An open letter by news organisations on copyright infringements in the generative AI industry considers these interrelations and their wider effects, which here are closely interlinked with questions of media diversity:

> Such practices undermine the media industry's core business models, which are predicated on readership and viewership (such as subscriptions), licensing, and advertising.... In addition to violating copyright law, the resulting impact is to meaningfully reduce media diversity and undermine the financial viability of companies to invest in media coverage, further reducing the public's access to high-quality and trustworthy information. (David, 2023, para. 5)

The changing actor constellations between news media and generative AI organisations thus open a space for investigation that concerns matters of sustainability in relation to generative AI infrastructures and media concentration that go far beyond the environmental concerns raised by generative AI. In an answer to calls for connecting infrastructural perspectives with political economy perspectives (Hesmondhalgh, 2021), this chapter has demonstrated how isolated ecological sustainability perspectives on generative AI remain limited in scope. Narrow concerns about the energy consumption of generative AI applications fail to see how implications interrelate along the generative AI value chain.

A political economy perspective on media concentration at the intersection of generative AI and news outlets instead shows how market power manifests along the infrastructures of generative AI – and how this sheds new light on partnerships between news media and generative AI providers. These partnerships need to be considered for their extremely far-reaching impacts on information access, epistemologies and constitutions of public spheres, in which generative AI will increasingly play a key role. There is a seminal shift underway which requires media and communication research to not only consider how industry practices in journalism change through the application of generative AI in newsrooms, but equally to understand the epistemic role of machines as communicators. Some news media have already positioned themselves in opposition to generative AI organisations on the basis of wider industry concerns such as media diversity, quality of content, revenue streams and copyright. Nevertheless, this field of inquiry needs to be further broadened to acknowledge the social and environmental justice role of news media in generative AI infrastructures, as well as the democratic implications of generative AI itself.

Overall, this analysis reflects that many more actors than generative AI providers are responsible for the social, economic and ecological sustainability implications of generative AI. News media organisations should regard cooperation with generative AI organisations not only as a matter of securing new revenue opportunities but also in light of their entangled sustainability implications. At the same time, market concentration in the generative AI industry has been shown to be deeply entangled with justice and environmental implications, which not only opens new research perspectives but also prompts new regulatory responses.

Competing Interests The author has no conflicts of interest to declare that are relevant to the contents of this chapter.

References

Alvarado, R. (2023). AI as an epistemic technology. *Science and Engineering Ethics*, *29*(5), Article 32. https://doi.org/10.1007/s11948-023-00451-3

Baker, C. E. (2006). Media concentration and democracy: Why ownership matters. *Cambridge University Press*. https://doi.org/10.1017/CBO9780511810992

Barocas, S., Hardt, M., & Narayanan, A. (2019). *Fairness and machine learning: Limitations and opportunities*. https://fairmlbook.org/

Bender, E. M., Gebru, T., McMillan-Major, A., & Shmitchell, S. (2021). On the dangers of stochastic parrots: Can language models be too big? In *Proceedings of the 2021 ACM Conference on Fairness, Accountability, and Transparency* (pp. 610–623). https://doi.org/10.1145/3442188.3445922

Birhane, A., Kalluri, P., Card, D., Agnew, W., Dotan, R., & Bao, M. (2022). The values encoded in machine learning research. In *2022 ACM Conference on Fairness, Accountability, and Transparency* (pp.173–184). https://doi.org/10.1145/3531146.3533083

Cools, H., & Diakopoulos, N. (2024). Uses of generative AI in the newsroom: Mapping journalists' perceptions of perils and possibilities. *Journalism Practice*, 1–19. https://doi.org/10.1080/17512786.2024.2394558

David, E. (2023, August 10). News outlets demand new rules for AI training data. *The Verge*. https://www.theverge.com/2023/8/10/23827316/news-transparency-copyright-generative-ai

David, E. (2024, April 30). New York Daily News, Chicago Tribune and other sue OpenAI and microsoft. *The Verge*. https://www.theverge.com/2024/4/30/24145603/ai-openai-microsoft-new-york-daily-news-sue-copyright

Downing, J. D. H. (2011). Media ownership, concentration, and control: The evolution of debate. In J. Wasko, G. Murdock & H. Sousa (Eds.), *The handbook of political economy of communications* (1st ed., pp. 140–168). Wiley. https://doi.org/10.1002/9781444395402.ch7

Gillespie, T. (2010). The politics of 'platforms.' *New Media & Society, 12*(3), 347–364. https://doi.org/10.1177/1461444809342738

Gray Widder, D., West, S., & Whittaker, M. (2023). Open (for business): Big tech, concentrated power, and the political economy of OpenAI. *SSRN Electronic Journal*. https://doi.org/10.2139/ssrn.4543807

Guzman, A. L., & Lewis, S. C. (2020). Artificial intelligence and communication: A human–machine communication research agenda. *New Media & Society, 22*(1), 70–86. https://doi.org/10.1177/1461444819858691

Hartmans, A. (2023, September 25). Amazon is investing up to $4 billion in OpenAI rival Anthropic. *TIME*. https://time.com/6317366/amazon-anthropic-ai-deal/

Hesmondhalgh, D. (2021). The infrastructural turn in media and internet research. In P. McDonald (Ed.), *The Routledge companion to media industries* (1st ed., pp. 132–142). Routledge. https://doi.org/10.4324/9780429275340-13

Hollstein, B., & Straus, F. (2006). *Qualitative Netzwerkanalyse*. VS. https://doi.org/10.1007/978-3-531-90074-2

IFPIM. (2025, February 10). *New partnership launched to ensure linguistic diversity and broad journalistic content for AI models*. https://ifpim.org/resources/new-partnership-launched-to-ensure-linguistic-diversity-and-broad-journalistic-content-for-ai-models/

Jaźwińska, K., & Chandrasekar, A. (2025). AI search has a citation problem. *Columbia Journalism Review*. https://www.cjr.org/tow_center/we-compared-eight-ai-search-engines-theyre-all-bad-at-citing-news.php

Knoche, M. (2021). Media concentration: A critical political economy perspective. *tripleC: Communication, Capitalism & Critique. Open Access Journal for a Global Sustainable Information Society, 19*(2), 371–391. https://doi.org/10.31269/triplec.v19i2.1298

Kraft, A., & Soulier, E. (2024). Knowledge-enhanced language models are not bias-proof: Situated knowledge and epistemic injustice in AI. In *The 2024 ACM Conference on Fairness, Accountability, and Transparency* (pp. 1433–1445). https://doi.org/10.1145/3630106.3658981

Kuai, J., Brantner, C., Karlsson, M., Van Couvering, E., & Romano, S. (2025). AI chatbot accountability in the age of algorithmic gatekeeping: Comparing generative search engine political information retrieval across five languages. *New Media & Society*. Online First. https://doi.org/10.1177/14614448251321162

Larkin, B. (2013). The politics and poetics of infrastructure. *Annual Review of Anthropology, 42*(1), 327–343. https://doi.org/10.1146/annurev-anthro-092412-155522

Lelapa AI. (n.d.). Meet Vulavula. *Lelapa AI products*. https://lelapa.ai/products/vulavula/

Li, P., Yang, J., Islam, M. A., & Ren, S. (2023). Making AI less "thirsty": Uncovering and addressing the secret water footprint of AI models. https://doi.org/10.48550/ARXIV.2304.03271

Luccioni, A. S., Viguier, S., & Ligozat, A.-L. (2022). Estimating the carbon footprint of BLOOM, a 176B-parameter language model. https://arxiv.org/abs/2211.02001

Luo, Q., & Puett, M. (2024). Anglo-American bias could make generative AI an invisible intellectual cage. *Nature*, *629*(8014), Article 1004. https://doi.org/10.1038/d41586-024-01573-9

Manancourt, V. (2024, January 15). Microsoft CEO: Journalists should welcome AI. *POLITICO*. https://www.politico.eu/article/microsoft-ceo-journalists-should-welcome-ai/

McChesney, R. W. (2008). *The political economy of media: Enduring issues, emerging dilemmas*. Monthly Review Press.

Mittelstadt, B. D., Allo, P., Taddeo, M., Wachter, S., & Floridi, L. (2016). The ethics of algorithms: Mapping the debate. *Big Data & Society*, *3*(2). https://doi.org/10.1177/2053951716679679

Mollen, A., & Kannengießer, S. (2025). Shaping AI (more) sustainably. Socio-technological perspectives on AI infrastructures. In T. Kox, A. Ullrich & H. Zech (Eds.), *Uncertain journeys into digital futures: Inter- and trans-disciplinary research for mitigating wicked societal and environmental problems* (pp. 207–218). Nomos. https://doi.org/10.5771/9783748947585

Mollen, A. & Kannengießer, S. (2026). The material condition: A practice theory-oriented infrastructural turn to the ethics of human-AI communication. *Human-Machine Communication*, 12.

Morris, S., & Uddin, R. (2025, February 7). Big tech lines up over $300bn in AI spending for 2025. *Financial Times*. https://www.ft.com/content/634b7ec5-10c3-44d3-ae49-2a5b9ad566fa

Mozilla Foundation. (2024). *Accelerating progress toward trustworthy AI*. [White paper] https://foundation.mozilla.org/en/research/library/accelerating-progress-toward-trustworthy-ai/whitepaper/

Muzanenhamo, P., & Power, S. B. (2024). ChatGPT and accounting in African contexts: Amplifying epistemic injustice. *Critical Perspectives on Accounting*, *99*, Article 102735. https://doi.org/10.1016/j.cpa.2024.102735

New York Times. (2023, December 27). The Times sues OpenAI and Microsoft over A.I. use of copyrighted work. *New York Times*. https://www.nytimes.com/2023/12/27/business/media/new-york-times-open-ai-microsoft-lawsuit.html

OpenAI. (2023a, January 23). OpenAI and Microsoft extend partnership. *OpenAI News*. https://openai.com/index/openai-and-microsoft-extend-partnership/

OpenAI. (2023b, December 13). Partnership with Axel Springer to deepen beneficial use of AI in journalism. *OpenAI News*. https://openai.com/blog/axel-springer-partnership

OpenAI. (2024a, March 13). Global news partnerships: Le Monde and Prisa Media. *OpenAI News*. https://openai.com/index/global-news-partnerships-le-monde-and-prisa-media/

OpenAI. (2024b, May 22). A landmark multi-year global partnership with News Corp. *OpenAI News*. https://openai.com/index/news-corp-and-openai-sign-landmark-multi-year-global-partnership/

OpenAI. (2024c, May 29). A content and product partnership with The Atlantic. *OpenAI News*. https://openai.com/index/enhancing-news-in-chatgpt-with-the-atlantic/

OpenEuroLLM (2025, February 3). OpenLLMs for transparent AI in Europe. *OpenEuroLLM blog*. https://openeurollm.eu/blog/launch-press-release

Parks, L., & Starosielski, N. (Eds.). (2015). *Signal traffic: Critical studies of media infrastructures*. University of Illinois Press. https://doi.org/10.5406/illinois/9780252039362.001.0001

Parks, L., Velkova, J., & de Ridder, S. (2023). Media backends: Digital infrastructures and sociotechnical relations. *University of Illinois Press*. https://doi.org/10.5622/illinois/9780252045349.001.0001

Poell, T. (2020). Three challenges for media studies in the age of platforms. *Television & New Media*, *21*(6), 650–657. https://doi.org/10.1177/1527476420918833

Rohde, F., Wagner, J., Meyer, A., Reinhard, P., Voss, M., Petschow, U., & Mollen, A. (2024). Broadening the perspective for sustainable artificial intelligence: Sustainability criteria and indicators for artificial intelligence systems. *Current Opinion in Environmental Sustainability*, *66*, Article 101411. https://doi.org/10.1016/j.cosust.2023.101411

Roth, E., & Kennemer, Q. (2024, March 23). Financial Times tests an AI chatbot trained on decades of its own articles. *The Verge*. https://www.theverge.com/2024/3/23/24106296/ask-ft-generative-ai-chatbot-answers-tool

SAP News. (2023, July 20). SAP invests in three leading generative AI companies: Aleph Alpha, Anthropic, and Cohere. *SAP News Center.* https://news.sap.com/2023/07/generative-ai-investments-aleph-alpha-anthropic-cohere/

Schaul, K., Yu Chen, S., & Tiku, N. (2022, April 19). Inside the secret list of websites that make AI like ChatGPT sound smart. *Washington Post.* https://www.washingtonpost.com/technology/interactive/2023/ai-chatbot-learning/

Sen, A. (2008). *Commodities and capabilities (13th imprint).* Oxford University Press.

Staab, P. (2024). Markets and power in digital capitalism. *Manchester University Press.* https://doi.org/10.7765/9781526172174

Star, S. L., & Ruhleder, K. (1996). Steps toward an ecology of infrastructure: Design and access for large information spaces. *Information Systems Research, 7*(1), 111–134. https://doi.org/10.1287/isre.7.1.111

Strubell, E., Ganesh, A., & McCallum, A. (2020). Energy and policy considerations for modern deep learning research. *Proceedings of the AAAI Conference on Artificial Intelligence, 34*(9), 13693–13696. https://doi.org/10.1609/aaai.v34i09.7123

Sun, W. (2024, June 5). SAP and Mistral AI announce partnership to deliver leading large language models for business. *SAP News Center.* https://news.sap.com/2024/06/sap-mistral-ai-leading-llm-maker-partnership/

UN WCED. (1987). *Our common future.* World Commission on Environment and Development. https://sustainabledevelopment.un.org/content/documents/5987our-common-future.pdf

United Nations. (2015). *Transforming our world: The 2030 Agenda for Sustainable Development.* https://sdgs.un.org/sites/default/files/publications/21252030%20Agenda%20for%20Sustainable%20Development%20web.pdf

van der Vlist, F., Helmond, A., & Ferrari, F. (2024). Big AI: Cloud infrastructure dependence and the industrialisation of artificial intelligence. *Big Data & Society, 11*(1). https://doi.org/10.1177/20539517241232630

Vestager, M., Cardell, S., Kanter, J., & Khan, L. M. (2024). *Joint statement on competition in generative AI foundation models and AI products.* European Commission Competition & Markets Authority. https://competition-policy.ec.europa.eu/document/download/79948846-4605-4c3a-94a6-044e344acc33_en?filename=20240723_competition_in_generative_AI_joint_statement_COMP-CMA-DOJ-FTC.pdf

Vipra, J., & Korinek, A. (2023). *Market concentration implications of foundation models: The invisible hand of ChatGPT.* Center on Regulation and Markets Working Paper #9. Brookings. https://www.brookings.edu/wp-content/uploads/2023/09/market-concentration-implications-of-foundation-models-final-1.pdf

Wachter, S. (2022). The theory of artificial immutability: Protecting algorithmic groups under anti-discrimination law. *SSRN Electronic Journal*. https://doi.org/10.2139/ssrn.4099100

Wasko, J., Murdock, G., & Sousa, H. (Eds.). (2011). *The handbook of political economy of communications* (1st ed.). Wiley. https://doi.org/10.1002/9781444395402

PART III

Futures, Politics, Governance

CHAPTER 12

Not Seeing the Data for the Trees: How Ecological Metaphors Matter in Academic Discourse on Platforms and AI

Gerwin van Schie and Inte Gloerich

Introduction

Trees and plants have been a rich source of metaphors for various kinds of writers throughout history. Philosophy and literature are full of roots, branches, and stems (Wampole, 2016) and knowledge organization and visualization has been regularly portrayed as being shaped like trees at least since the Middle Ages (Lima, 2014; Rieppel, 2010). Furthermore, and very relevant to this chapter, the fields of computation and technology are rife with terms related to ecologies and the various natural elements that help sustain life (Peters, 2015; Scarano et al., 2024).

G. van Schie (✉)
Utrecht University, Utrecht, Netherlands
e-mail: G.A.vanSchie@uu.nl

I. Gloerich
Amsterdam University of Applied Sciences, Amsterdam, Netherlands
e-mail: i.gloerich@hva.nl

A. Mollen et al. (eds.), *AI Infrastructures and Sustainability*, Palgrave Studies in European Communication Research and Education,
https://doi.org/10.1007/978-3-032-09748-4_12

Especially in the context of complex and seemingly immaterial technologies like platforms and AI, metaphors abound that are employed to explain, visualise, or convey key functionalities and use cases. As performative language, metaphors *do* things in the world (Austin, 1962), they "take action" (Carbonell et al., 2016, p. 145) and create "patterns of thinking that repeat themselves subconsciously" (Wampole, 2021, p. 52), all the while performing societal norms, ideologies, and worldviews and influence technological development, policy-making, and popular uptake. Since metaphors that invoke nature and ecology are not only employed in marketing strategies of polluting industry (Smith, 1998) but also by academics studying contemporary media and technology, understanding the political implications of these metaphors is key.

In this chapter, we will, therefore, take a critical look at botanical and ecological metaphors employed in a few key publications on platformization and AI. Special attention will be given to José van Dijck's article titled *Seeing the Forest for the Trees* (2021), in which the image of a tree is employed as a metaphor to think about potential avenues to regulate platform companies, and the book *The Platform Society* (van Dijck et al., 2018), in which an ecological understanding of platform companies and technologies is operationalized. These works have been chosen for their explicit use of botanical and ecological metaphors in the study of platforms and AI, and their big influence on the field of platform studies. Specifically, we trace how the used metaphors offer a foundation for the naturalisation of the use of AI by platforms. We show that such ecological metaphors naturalise platforms and the knowledge processes and infrastructures that AI builds on. Responding to Wyatt's (2021) call to media researchers to "deconstruct the metaphors of the powerful" and to propose alternatives, we investigate the unwanted effects of the use of tree-based AI metaphors in academic research. We join her call for the development of critical, clear, and evocative alternatives and contribute with a proposal of our own. Not only will this study, therefore, question the metaphorical roots of platforms studies as a field, it will also serve as an encouragement for other researchers to both further develop this line of inquiry, and remain critical of the use of natural and ecological metaphors in their own writing.

We will start by tracing a small history of the abundant use of ecological metaphors in the history of media studies. We then point to platform studies as a contemporary site in which this legacy is continued. Contemporary tech platforms are a primary site of AI development, both as a provider of data to train models on, and as a location to employ those models in various processes, ranging from recommendation systems to content moderation and generation. Metaphors that aim to convey key aspects of these systems, processes, and relations, impact the way AI is understood in platform studies. Platform scholars Helmond and van der Vlist recently advocated "for the continued integration of the platform metaphor with conceptual frameworks like 'ecosystems'" as a way to account for the evolving nature of the platform landscape and as a way to anticipate "emerging future platforms, such as the impending "AI platform shift" (Helmond & van der Vlist, 2024, p. 35). With this chapter, we aim to provide a counter argument to this call by revealing the sociopolitical implications of this metaphor for imagining environmentally sustainable futures of and with platforms and AI.

Studying Metaphors

In their influential book on metaphors, Lakoff and Johnson explain how "[t]*he essence of metaphor is understanding and experiencing one kind of thing in terms of another*" (Lakoff & Johnson, 1980, p. 5, emphasis in original). The resulting use of language is therefore always more than mere wordplay or poetry. Metaphors structure our thoughts and experience and are therefore always "metaphorical concepts" (Lakoff & Johnson, 1980, p. 6). Such metaphorical concepts are generally used to highlight particular qualities of a concept or idea, and in doing so, they necessarily downplay other aspects of their referent. The choice for a particular metaphor is, therefore, not accidental, but often driven by the intentions, politics and/or ideology of the person communicating or culture in which the communication is being done. As shown by Anaïs Augé (2023), debates around climate change are rife with metaphors, ranging from thinking about the earth as a building that's on fire, to climate science as a fake religion, all depending on what side of the debate the communicators are on. However, for metaphors that are normalised and have become part of everyday language, these intentions and purposes move into the background while the metaphors inconspicuously continue to carry forward "implicit presuppositions" (Deleuze & Guattari, 2021, p. 91) that structure meanings and experiences related to the things they describe. As such, they impact actual attitudes, actions, and sociopolitical realities, generally in support of established lines of power and the normative dynamics that constitute societies (Austin, 1962;

Tseng, 2010; Wyatt, 2021). For example, the metaphor of "the cloud" for the data centres and server farms fundamental in platform services portrays these buildings and the devices in them as immaterial while hiding the far-reaching sociopolitical and environmental impacts they have (Peters, 2015). Anything from policy making around platform technologies to personal data practices is impacted by the image the ephemeral cloud. Our job in the broad field of cultural studies and critical data studies is to investigate the meanings metaphors convey and which meanings they hide, as well as what attitudes and actions they afford (Wyatt, 2021).

Methodologically, we are inspired by Christy Wampoles, "ecocritical metaphorology" (2021, p. 52) as a way to focus on the translational, political, and ideological work done by figurative speech that involves words related to nature, plants, flowers, and trees, to "help us understand the extent to which metaphorical thinking facilitates or hinders our efforts to 'save the planet'" (Wampole, 2021, p. 53). This approach builds on the work of Hans Blumenberg, who suggested "metaphorology" as a method "to burrow down to the substructure of thought" (Blumenberg, 2010, p. 6). Literature scholar Christy Wampole used this method to study various botanical metaphors in continental philosophy in her 2016 book on "rootedness", in which she shows the various implications of thinking through root metaphors (Wampole, 2016). More recently, however, she has commented that such methods might also be incredibly useful to study more everyday uses of ecological metaphors, in particular in "the kinds of language production that precipitate changes in behaviour and policy" as "it could reveal the unconscious patterns in the way people think and talk about the environment and climate change" (Wampole, 2021, pp. 52, 54). By applying this approach to the language used in academic writing about platforms and AI, we aim to uncover some of the unintended byproducts of using ecological and botanical metaphors as explanatory frameworks. We will therefore focus most of our attention to the connotative aspects of the used metaphors; in other words, rather than looking at the literal function of the metaphor in the explanation of the author, we are most interested in what other meanings are invoked simultaneously. By extending the metaphor further than originally intended, we aim to problematize common ecological metaphors in light of environmental destruction and climate change.

Understanding Media as Ecology

The academic comparison of technologies with living beings—and their development with evolution—goes as far back as what many consider the start of a philosophy of technology. In his 1877 book, titled *Grundlinien einer Philosophie der Technik*, philosopher Ernst Kapp, develops an understanding of tools and machines as organs of living organisms. Technological tools, as organs, only get their meaning and purpose in relation to the humans that use them, or, as Kapp explains: "The root of a tree, cut off from the trunk, ceases to be a root; it is, in this extragenetic isolation, just another piece of wood" (Kapp et al., 2018, p. 41). Kapp used many comparisons with nature to explain his theories, he did, however, never lose sight of the metaphorical nature of his comparisons: "Tools and machines neither grow on trees nor fall like manna from heaven; instead, they exist 'because we have made them ourselves'" (Kapp et al., 2018, p. 126). Furthermore, while much of the work by Kapp has now been refuted, his idea of technologies as artificial organs clearly lived on in the work of media scholars like Marshall McLuhan, who considered media "the extensions of man" (McLuhan, 1994).

Apart from reflecting on the relation between individual technologies and people, McLuhan, in tandem with his contemporary Neil Postman, developed an understanding of media as an environment. This so-called environmental understanding of media has been one of the leading paradigms of media studies roughly since the 1960's and 1970's. This understanding can be noticed by the abundant use of words like "ecology" in past and present studies of media (Grønning, 2020; Lum, 2000; Scolari, 2012). Media ecologies come into being through interacting media systems, a process in which the words used to give meaning to these interactions bring about particular ecologies (Fuller, 2005). In addition, various media scholars have broadened understandings of media ecologies by not only engaging with media technologies as ecology, but simultaneously understanding nature as a medium, an approach that opens up possibilities for "all environments to benefit from a critical understanding of mediation" (Starosielski, 2019, p. 2). While separating nature and culture has its own problematic implications (Haraway, 1997), we argue that there is an ideological difference between a philosophical argument for understanding forests as a medium, and naturalizing platforms and AI through ecological metaphors. Where the former might help highlighting the ways contemporary nature is socio-politically charged, the latter runs the risk of obscuring and naturalizing the human-made decisions, infrastructures, and politics that help shape our contemporary colonial, capitalist and environmentally destructive technologies.

Platforms as Ecologies, The Platform Society as a Tree

In contemporary platform studies, words like "platform ecology" and "AI ecosystem" are common ways to understand the various interrelations and dependencies between tech companies, material infrastructure, and cultural production (see for example, Sheikh et al., 2023; van Dijck et al., 2018). While these environmental understandings have been operationalized to study media in terms of their material impact on the environment (Maxwell & Miller, 2012) and in terms of their cultural meaning—see, for example, John Durham Peters' work on the metaphor of the "cloud", the work by Jussi Parikka on insect and virus metaphors in cultures of computation (Durham Peters, 2015; Parikka, 2010)—we argue that we need more critical work on the botanical, arboreal, and environmental metaphors that guide our understanding of digital platforms in light of environmental sustainability causes, in part because, as we will show, critical media scholars also employ such metaphors themselves.

To show the apparently self-evidentiary nature of understanding media systems as an ecology, and platforms as trees, we will now delve deeper in some of the work produced by what could be called the "Amsterdam School of platform studies" (Christofari, 2023). We will focus in particular on the work of one of its foundational members, José van Dijck, who has been writing about big tech for roughly two decades. In an earlier Dutch version of the influential book titled *The Platform Society: Public Values in a Connective World* (van Dijck et al., 2023), written for a general public that includes policy makers, the authors make explicit that the metaphor of "the ecosystem of connective platforms" is meant to convey the "high degree of interconnectedness and mutual entanglement of all online platforms through shared mechanisms" (van Dijck et al., 2016, p. 20, translation by the authors). In the later English version of this book, catered more to academics, at the first mention of the word "platform ecology", the authors acknowledge the metaphorical nature of this term, but the footnote is dedicated to explaining the "platform" metaphor, seemingly foregoing the explanation of "ecology" as a metaphor itself (van Dijck et al., 2018, p. 4).

Van Dijck et al. (2018) cast the platform society as an ecosystem or ecology to be able to investigate the sociopolitical and economic influence on public life of their intricate connections. They write that while the platform ecosystem seems neutral "it is not neutral, on the contrary, the ideological tenets inscribed in the ecosystem's architecture put a formidable stamp on what constitutes public value and whose interests are served" (p. 22). Later, van Dijck (2021) adds the more detailed metaphor of the tree, with its roots, trunk, and branches, to represent the relationships and power dynamics between different components of the platform society. By proposing this new metaphor, van Dijck (2021) makes four key contributions: explaining the hierarchies that make up the complex and often blackboxed systems of the platform society; drawing attention to the dynamics that keep these hierarchies in place; helping to "redraft compartmentalized governance frameworks into a more holistic approach" (p. 2802); and, highlighting key points at which governance, regulation, and policymaking could intervene to support public values. For example, the metaphor of the tree serves to highlight that while we see, experience, and interact with certain parts of what makes up the platform society, other parts—represented by the roots of the tree—remain out of our direct view. This underground space is populated by protocols, cables, precious metals, chips, and data centres, i.e. many of the infrastructural prerequisites for having platforms at all (van Dijck, 2021). Likewise, to much of the functioning of AI—such as the recommendation of content—platforms play the role of infrastructures. Like infrastructures are known to do (Star & Ruhleder, 1996), the roots of the platform tree are often taken for granted or seem to be incapable of being changed by virtue of the size and importance of the tree that relies on them. The metaphor of the tree also brings into focus how different part of the 'platform tree' relate to each other through hierarchies and interdependencies. Not only do the trunk and the branches of the platform tree rely on the protocological and material infrastructures of the roots, but the apps and platforms that serve specific sectors like healthcare, mobility, and news—represented by the branches of the tree—rely on the intermediaries that dominate the trunk of the tree. Many of these intermediaries fall under the control of the powerful corporate GAFAM umbrella. It is easy to see how a news outlet depends on the algorithmic search dynamics of Google or the social features of Facebook and its subsidiaries to reach audiences. The trunk thus holds significant power over what the branches can do. However, like the life-giving process of photosynthesis that the leaves on a tree's branches perform, the platform tree's branches also provide a life-giving supply of data that sustains both its trunk and its roots. These same data make possible various AI-based processes that increasingly pervade platform functionality. While power hierarchies exist in the platform tree—and the power of the centralised GAFAM trunk cannot be underestimated—each part of the tree supports the health of the tree as a hole (van Dijck, 2021).

Van Dijck (2021) argues that platforms are also like trees because they "constitute 'living' dynamic systems, always morphing and hence co-shaping [their] species" (p. 2805). Often, regulatory frameworks address aspects of platformisation in isolation or within national boundaries, and as a result platform companies have been able to route around many obstacles regulatory bodies put in their way. Like a tree whose new branches peak through the holes in a fence meant to limit its growth, platforms mutate to find their way around regulations that would impede the continuation of their power. For van Dijck (2021), the metaphor of the platformisation tree facilitates the creation of new platform imaginaries that serve people and societies instead of the centralised power of corporations. By adding the tree to the already available natural metaphors to describe platforms, the term ecosystem can now be understood in two distinctive ways that pertain to slightly different scales. First, we can consider specific platforms or platform companies as an ecology or ecosystem. Here the metaphor is used to describe the environment created within the confines of an application or the confines of the software and/or hardware of one specific company. Second, we can use the word ecosystem or ecology to describe the environment in which platforms exist and do their work. Within this understanding platforms become species that compete for the available resources. This latter understanding can be seen within media studies in general and platform studies in particular by occasional references to concepts like, for example "evolution", when discussing a development history of a particular app or company (Helmond et al., 2019; Scolari, 2013), or the idea of the "invasive species" when discussing how a relatively new application or technology disrupts the established media landscape (Lai & Flensburg, 2021). While using different, albeit natural words, these instances draw on the same ecological metaphor. After all, the ideas of evolution, the idea of a tree, and the idea of the invasive species implies a process of homeostasis, of an environment or ecology that is in a constant search of an equilibrium between its inhabitants (Helmond & van der Vlist, 2024).

This shows how widespread thinking and writing about platforms and companies as living entities has become.

While the metaphor of the tree makes the organizational structure of the platform society apparent and the insights gathered from it are critical for developing responses and policies that reassert and protect public values, we argue that the metaphor has other effects as well. By using the tree and ecological metaphors, the way platforms are structured and interrelated is discursively naturalized and portrayed as—to a degree—autonomous from human intentions and interventions. This presents a discrepancy with the environmental impact of technological development throughout human history and has become especially pronounced in the context of digital platforms (see e.g. Crawford, 2021; Velkova, 2016, 2021), and the enormous amounts of waste generated by our electronic devices at the end of their life cycle (Wan, 2021). We should be, therefore, be cautious to equate AI and platform infrastructure with nature and ecology. This is the dimension of our critique and call for alternatives.

What Remains Hidden Within the Tree and Ecology Metaphors

One way of showing the more problematic aspects of understanding platform dynamics in terms of an ecology is by diving into the metaphor more deeply. If we extend the metaphor of the tree and think of all that is hidden in its abstracted image, we might start to think of the bugs living in the tree as the large but invisible teams of content moderators that must perform emotionally taxing labour in poor conditions. We might think of the bees that pollinate the tree as the click workers, gig workers, and everyday users that move from platform to platform and consciously or unconsciously produce supplies of data to be capitalised upon by platform and AI companies. Yet, these fundamental aspects of what sustains the health of the tree and the ongoing platformisation of society remain out of view of the tree metaphor understood as fundamentally consisting of three layers: the roots, the trunk, and the branches. Like with an actual tree, platforms cannot exist without being entangled into an intricate network of other living and changing beings. Emphasising this entanglement and shape-shifting capacity in a metaphor for platformisation is fundamental to bring into light the politics of the choices that led to its current shape as well as its potential for being radically reimagined.

The tree of platformisation highlights the power of established infrastructures and platform companies. However, in the process, this power is flattened: no dissent or difference seems possible. Extending the natural metaphor to include a bigger picture runs the risk of presenting platformisation as a natural equilibrium. Not everything that takes place in and among platforms sustains them or the networks they are part of. Bugs do not call to mind dissent, yet, platforms are continuously host to activities that go against the grain, call for change, or hijack their system for ulterior ends. Anything from activists finding their way around content moderation to third parties using data illegitimately could fall under this banner. Simply put, platforms are spaces of contestation, of activism, of tactical use (Milan & Treré, 2019), rather than equilibriums. Presenting them as natural systems, as ecological phenomena, hides the struggle it takes—for good or for bad—to keep them running. In other words: "it casts humans as mere components of a quasi-biological system that they cannot control, and does not seem to offer any obvious point of departure for theorizing human agency and intention in the creation and usage of technologies" (Heise, 2002, p. 158). Envisioning platformisation as a tree, positions these platforms as almost unavoidable, and homogenizes the plurality of approaches that people have towards embedding technologies in their lives.

More fundamentally, the metaphor of the tree—or other natural metaphors for that matter—presents platforms and platformisation not as consisting of designed elements but rather as naturally occurring phenomena. Although a tree is constantly changing and responding to its environment, what eludes the metaphor is that these changes are politically, economically, and ideologically informed. There is no grand design that determines the shape of the entire platform tree, but each element is the result of situated decisions that benefit particular stakeholders and work at the detriment of others. This means that, given other sociopolitical and ideological contexts and concerns, platformisation could take on very different shapes that are not well represented by the metaphor of the tree with its inherently centralised trunk. Moreover, the power of the trunk of the tree—dominated by the companies that make up GAFAM—is reinforced by the metaphor. This is partly by design. Van Dijck (2021) uses the tree metaphor exactly because it shows so clearly that power is, in fact, centralised with GAFAM. However, at the same time, the metaphor naturalises the idea that the shape of a network of platforms contains this point of centralisation. If platformed society is like a tree, it is hard to come up with a relational network that is not centralised into some form of roots-trunk-branches structure. Federated networks like Mastodon or distributed databases like blockchains simply have no place in this metaphor. Yet, they too are or could be (part of) platforms, albeit reimagined ones.

There is a kind of evolutionary directionality hidden within the metaphor of the tree. The roots, trunk, and branches of a tree make up one species; an acorn tree's trunk grows an acorn tree's branches, a willow's roots are connected to a willow's trunk. The tree metaphor implies a logical and natural organization of the relationship between the material base (roots), the few large software platforms with near-monopolies (trunk), and the many applications that run on this infrastructure (branches and leaves). It equates the bugs living in the trees and the bees pollinating its flowers to the click workers, platform moderators, and users sustaining the tree. However, no part of this way of organizing platforms and companies is predestined: these roots don't naturally lead to this trunk, and this trunk does not necessarily lead to these branches. The protocological and material roots of the platform tree are not tied to a specific species of above-ground platform. Mastodon uses several of the same "roots" as a platform like Instagram does, such as the general internet protocol suite and the hardware people use to access these different platforms. An alternative metaphor should thus be able to capture the divergent uses and connections of different elements of platformisation.

The aforementioned examples of forms of critique and resistance still give the impression that these initiatives, together with the established platforms, somehow exist in an ecology. However, this metaphor also naturalizes several important forces as if they are laws of nature, such as the regulatory and political framework, the geopolitical situation, and the various historical forms of inequality through which platforms and their infrastructure operate. By envisioning platforms as trees in an ecology "[t]echnologies are seen as independent forces shaping society regardless of social, cultural and power-related factors" (Ruotsalainen & Heinonen, 2015, p. 5). Technologies have "built-in power relations" (Ruotsalainen & Heinonen, 2015, p. 5). In addition, some the meanings attached to ecologies, such as the idea of evolution, often mistakenly believed to equate to "survival of the fittest", fit well with several tropes attached to capitalism and neoliberalism. These political and economical systems, are, however, not laws of nature, like, for example, gravity.

Instead, they are human made systems that we can change if we collectively want them to. Describing the development of platforms in terms of "evolution" (Helmond et al., 2019; Scolari, 2013) treats individual platforms as living organisms and creates the feeling that their changes over time are the result of random mutations rather than deliberate design. Furthermore, when a platform "ecology" is believed to be governed by a principle of "survival of the fittest" the precarity of workers might be seen as inevitable, rather than logical result of design decisions. To avoid these problematic ways of thinking, we might have to move away from ecological and natural metaphors to describe BigTech. In the next, section we will discuss a potential alternative.

Conclusion: Towards Alternative Metaphors

Like Leonelli (2016), Amoore (2018), and Wyatt (2021), we propose to move beyond the critique of existing metaphors into a proposal for alternatives. Given the human-made nature of AI, platforms and the material infrastructures of which they are a part, and given the performativity of metaphors, we feel that we should actively seek metaphors that reflect artificial and constructed characteristics of technologies and companies. Ideally such metaphors should also connect well with existing environmentally critical discourse. Inspired by Susan Leigh Star's (quoted in Englehardt, 2015) move from the metaphor of computers as information highways to sewers and Cohn's (2023) likening of AI to a colon because of the "huge amount of waste that AI and all backends generate" (n.p.), we too propose that thinking about data infrastructures, platform companies and AI as part of a sewage system brings into focus critical aspects of their organization. This metaphor has specific implications for thinking about (1) media content of platform companies, (2) AI and platform companies as public utility, and (3) alternative platform futures. Below we will delve a bit deeper into the implications for thinking about AI infrastructures as a sewage system.

Thinking about AI infrastructure as a sewage system turns its core product into excrement or waste. While this might currently feel like a rhetorical leap, references to data as a waste product have been part of critical data studies literature since its very inception. Most notably, Rob Kitchin considers much data to be "exhaust data" (2014, pp. 6–8) that is never created with the intention to be captured. He calls for an awareness of these data being epistemologically "messy and dirty" (Kitchin, 2014,

p. 29). This way of thinking is not only present in critical data scholarship but also in the common phrase in data science practice of data "cleaning" (Rawson & Muñoz, 2019).

The metaphor of platform infrastructure as a sewage system might help in thinking about AI platforms as a public utility, and its management a matter of public health. Lack of regulation and oversight might turn potentially fertile material into toxic waste polluting our living environment. Its management should, therefore, "be subject to the same scrutiny as utility providers" (Mollen et al., 2024, p. 3) and adhere to public values (van Dijck et al., 2018). We have shown that, while alive and constantly mutating, trees also convey a sense of inherent centralised control and attempts at achieving homeostasis. Imagining the infrastructure that platforms, algorithms, and AI make up as a sewage system instead allows for an even more fluid image in which anyone wishing to build their own systems based on shared protocols and infrastructure has the agency to do so. Like people capturing rainwater to use as water to flush a toilet or to sprinkle a garden in times of drought, the image of platforms as a sewage system brings into view the many alternatives that already exist or those that could tap into the public backbone in the future. This approach might create a much-needed bridge between academic debates on platforms and algorithmic governance, and their infrastructural and environmental dimensions.

In conclusion, in this article we have shown how the use of ecological metaphors to explain platforms and AI does carry problematic ideological implications. Based on our ecocritical metaphorology, we have suggested the alternative metaphor of the sewage system in order to highlight three key dimensions of platformisation: it calls attention to that which is produced and transported in the sewage system and as a result to those that produce it as key points of focus for critical investigations; it potentially presents AI and their platforms as public infrastructures that demand publicly organised maintenance; and it offers an imaginary that is inherently modular and adaptable by anyone. Finally, we believe that ecocritical metaphorology is an important new methodology for scholars in the humanities. While discourse around emerging technologies is heavily influenced by corporate demands, it is our responsibility to create critical, yet evocative alternatives.

Acknowledgements For this work, Gerwin van Schie was partly funded by a Spinoza grant of the Dutch Research Council (NWO), awarded in 2021 to José van Dijck, Professor of Media and Digital Society at Utrecht University. He also extends his gratitude to the colleagues of Tema Genus, part of the Department of Thematic Studies of Linköping University for their hospitality during multiple visits in the academic year 2023–2024, which allowed him to write this chapter.

Competing Interests The authors have no conflicts of interest to declare that are relevant to the contents of this chapter.

References

Amoore, L. (2018). Cloud geographies: Computing, data, sovereignty. *Progress in Human Geography, 42*(1), 4–24. https://doi.org/10.1177/0309132516662147

Augé, A. (2023). *Metaphor and argumentation in climate crisis discourse.* Routledge. https://www.routledge.com/Metaphor-and-Argumentation-in-Climate-Crisis-Discourse/Auge/p/book/9781032379807

Austin, J. L. (1962). *How to do things with words.* Oxford University Press.

Blumenberg, H. (2010). *Paradigms for a metaphorology.* Cornell University Press.

Carbonell, J., Sánchez-Esguevillas, A., & Carro. B. (2016). The role of metaphors in the development of technologies. The case of the artificial intelligence. *Futures, 84*(2016), 145–153. https://doi.org/10.1016/j.futures.2016.03.019

Christofari, G. (2023). *The politics of platformization: Amsterdam dialogues on platform theory.* Institute of Network Cultures. https://networkcultures.org/wp-content/uploads/2023/02/PoliticsofPlatformization_INC2023_TOD48.pdf

Cohn, J. (2023). Eugenictech: Three perspectives on the (b)anality of AI. In L. Parks, J. Velkova, & S. de Ridder (Eds.), *Media backends: Digital infrastructures & sociotechnical relations* (pp. 62–79). University of Illinois Press. https://www.jstor.org/stable/10.5406/jj.10405519.7

Crawford, K. (2021). The atlas of AI: Power, politics, and the planetary costs of artificial intelligence. *Yale University Press.* https://doi.org/10.2307/j.ctv1ghv45t

Deleuze, G., & Guattari, F. (2021). *A thousand plateaus.* Bloomsbury Academic.

Englehardt, A. (2015). Infrastructural inquiries: Interview with Lisa Parks. *Machinic.* https://machinic.info/Parks

Fuller, M. (2005). *Media ecologies: Materialist energies in art and technoculture.* The MIT Press.

Grønning, A. (2020). Ecologies of connecting across generations. In A. N. Markham & K. Tiidenberg (Eds.), *Metaphors of internet: Ways of being in the age of ubiquity* (pp. 97–106). Peter Lang Publishing.

Haraway, D. (1997). *Modest_Witness@Second_Millennium.FemaleMan©Meets_OncoMouseTM: Feminism and technoscience*. Routledge.
Heise, U. K. (2002). Unnatural ecologies: The metaphor of the environment in media theory. *Configurations, 10*(1), 149–168. https://doi.org/10.1353/con.2003.0006
Helmond, A., Nieborg, D. B., & van der Vlist, F. N. (2019). Facebook's evolution: Development of a platform-as-infrastructure. *Internet Histories, 3*(2), 123–146. https://doi.org/10.1080/24701475.2019.1593667
Helmond, A., & van der Vlist, F. N. (2024). Platform: A tapestry of meanings and metaphors. In J. Farkas & M. Maloney (Eds.), *Digital media metaphors* (1st ed., pp. 24–38). Routledge. https://doi.org/10.4324/978 1032674612-4
Kapp, E., Wolfe, L. K., & Zielinski, S. (2018). *Elements of a philosophy of technology: On the evolutionary history of culture*. In J. W. Kirkwood & L. Weatherby (Eds.), University of Minnesota Press. https://doi.org/10.5749/j.ctv7n0cpf
Kitchin, R. (2014). *The data revolution: Big data, open data, data infrastructures and their consequences*. Sage.
Lakoff, G., & Johnson, M. (1980). *Metaphors we live by*. University of Chicago Press.
Lai, S. S., & Flensburg, S. (2021). Invasive species of the app ecosystem: Exploring the political economy of mobile communication. *International Journal of Communication, 15*(2021), 2301–2318. https://ijoc.org/index.php/ijoc/article/view/16906
Leonelli, S. (2016). *Data-centric biology: A philosophical study*. The University of Chicago Press.
Lima, M. (2014). *Book of trees: Visualizing branches of knowledge*. Princeton Architectural Press.
Lum, C. M. K. (2000). Introduction: The intellectual roots of media ecology. *New Jersey Journal of Communication, 8*(1), 1–7. https://doi.org/10.1080/15456870009367375
McLuhan, M. (1994). *Understanding media: The extensions of man*. MIT Press.
Milan, S., & Treré, E. (2019). Big data from the south(s): Beyond data universalism. *Television & New Media, 20*(4), 319–335. https://doi.org/10.1177/1527476419837739
Maxwell, R., & Miller, T. (2012). *Greening the media*. Oxford University Press.
Mollen, A., Keilbach, J., Brodie, P., Jancovic, M., Helmond, A., Crosera, A., Velkova, J., Ochner, V., Maxigas, M., & Jansen, F. (2024). Governing digital infrastructures for a secure and sustainable future. *SSRN Electronic Journal*. https://doi.org/10.2139/ssrn.4879449
Parikka, J. (2010). *Insect media: An archaeology of animals and technology*. University of Minnesota Press.

Peters, J. D. (2015). *The marvelous clouds: Toward a philosophy of elemental media*. University of Chicago Press.

Rawson, K., & Muñoz, T. (2019). Against cleaning. In M. K. Gold & L. F. Klein (Eds.), *Debates in the digital humanities* (pp. 279–292). University of Minnesota Press. https://doi.org/10.5749/j.ctvg251hk

Rieppel, O. (2010). The series, the network, and the tree: Changing metaphors of order in nature. *Biology & Philosophy, 25*(4), 475–496. https://doi.org/10.1007/s10539-010-9216-4

Ruotsalainen, J., & Heinonen, S. (2015). Media ecology and the future ecosystemic society. *European Journal of Futures Research, 3*(2015), Article 9. https://doi.org/10.1007/s40309-015-0068-7

Scarano, F. R., Aguiar, A. C. F., Holz, V. L., de Macedo, A. L., Lombardi, A., Santos, L. D., & Koch, F. (2024). Plant-life vocabulary as metaphors for post-normal planetary challenges. *Theoretical and Experimental Plant Physiology, 36*(3), 399–409. https://doi.org/10.1007/s40626-024-00333-4

Scolari, C. A. (2012). Media ecology: Exploring the metaphor to expand the theory. *Communication Theory, 22*(2), 204–225. https://doi.org/10.1111/j.1468-2885.2012.01404.x

Scolari, C. A. (2013). Media evolution: Emergence, dominance, survival and extinction in the media ecology. *International Journal of Communication, 7*(2013), 1418-–1441. https://ijoc.org/index.php/ijoc/article/view/1919

Sheikh, H., Prins, C., & Schrijvers, E. (2023). Mission AI: The new system technology. *Springer*. https://doi.org/10.1007/978-3-031-21448-6

Smith, T. M. (1998). *The myth of green marketing: Tending our goats at the edge of apocalypse*. University of Toronto Press.

Star, S. L., & Ruhleder, K. (1996). Steps toward an ecology of infrastructure: Design and access for large information spaces. *Information Systems Research, 7*(1), 111–134, https://dl.acm.org/doi/pdf/10.1145/192844.193021

Starosielski, N. (2019). The elements of media studies. *Media+Environment, 1*(1), 1–6. https://doi.org/10.1525/001c.10780

Tseng, M. (2010). The performative potential of metaphor. *Semiotica, 2010*(180), 115–145. https://doi.org/10.1515/semi.2010.033

van Dijck, J. (2021). Seeing the forest for the trees: Visualizing platformization and its governance. *New Media & Society, 23*(9), 2801–2819. https://doi.org/10.1177/1461444820940293

van Dijck, J., Poell, T., & de Waal, M. (2016). *De platformsamenleving*. Strijd om publieke waarden in een online wereld.

van Dijck, J., Poell, T., & de Waal, M. (2018). The platform society: Public values in a connective world. *Oxford University Press*. https://doi.org/10.1093/oso/9780190889760.001.0001

Velkova, J. (2016). Data that warms: Waste heat, infrastructural convergence and the computation traffic commodity. *Big Data & Society, 3*(2), 1–10. https://doi.org/10.1177/2053951716684144

Velkova, J. (2021). Thermopolitics of data: Cloud infrastructures and energy futures. *Cultural Studies, 35*(4–5), 663–683. https://doi.org/10.1080/09502386.2021.1895243

Wan, E. (2021). Laboring in electronic and digital waste infrastructures: Colonial temporalities of violence in Asia. *International Journal of Communication, 15*(2021), 2631–2651. https://ijoc.org/index.php/ijoc/article/view/13971

Wampole, C. (2016). Rootedness: The ramifications of a metaphor. *University of Chicago Press*. https://doi.org/10.7208/chicago/9780226317793.001.0001

Wampole, C. (2021). An ecocritical metaphorology. *Contemporary French and francophone studies, 25*(1), 52–59. https://doi.org/10.1080/17409292.2021.1865056

Wyatt, S. (2021). Metaphors in critical internet and digital media studies. *New media & Society, 23*(2), 406–416. https://journals.sagepub.com/doi/full/10.1177/1461444820929324

CHAPTER 13

Responsiveness and AI in Environmental Governance: Infrastructures, Power, and Institutional Capacity

Jędrzej Niklas

Introduction

As AI and data-driven technologies become central to environmental governance, they are often portrayed as transformative tools for tackling pressing ecological challenges. Media narratives and policy frameworks highlight AI applications such as wildfire detection, energy grid optimization, and satellite-based deforestation monitoring, framing these innovations as key to addressing climate change, biodiversity loss, and other sustainability threats (Joppa, 2017; Kloppenburg et al., 2022; Turnbull et al., 2023). Political discourse similarly echoes this enthusiasm: the European Union's "twin transition", for instance, envisions digital innovation as a catalyst for green solutions (Kovacic et al., 2024).

J. Niklas (✉)
University of Cambridge, Cambridge, UK
e-mail: jn488@cam.ac.uk

Polish Academy of Sciences, Warsaw, Poland

A. Mollen et al. (eds.), *AI Infrastructures and Sustainability*, Palgrave Studies in European Communication Research and Education,
https://doi.org/10.1007/978-3-032-09748-4_13

Yet, this optimistic narrative of "green AI" merits closer scrutiny. While AI can enhance environmental monitoring and resource management, scholars caution that it may also reinforce technocratic governance models, sideline local knowledge, and privilege market-driven indicators over democratic, context-sensitive approaches (Bakker & Ritts, 2018; Gabrys et al., 2022; Nost & Goldstein, 2022; van Wynsberghe, 2021). These critiques help situate AI systems within a broader political context. At the same time, they raise important questions about the extent to which these technologies genuinely contribute to fulfilling socio-ecological promises.

Therefore, this chapter directly connects AI to ongoing discussions on environmental governance and sustainability. Environmental governance, broadly defined here as the regulatory processes, mechanisms, and institutions through which political actors influence environmental actions and outcomes (Lemos & Agrawal, 2006), has evolved from traditional state-centric policies to more diverse, multi-actor arrangements (Agrawal et al., 2022). While this shift allows for greater participation and innovation, it also exposes tensions between conservation goals, economic structures, and social inequalities. Increasingly, governance approaches emphasize sustainability, recognizing that challenges like climate change, deforestation, and biodiversity loss require systemic interventions that address interlinked economic, social, and political dynamics (Agrawal et al., 2022). AI's role in this space thus poses a dual challenge: how do AI-based systems relate to these ambitious sustainability objectives, and to what extent can they genuinely contribute to these goals in an equitable, context-sensitive manner?

To explore these questions, this chapter proposes two key moves. First, it treats AI systems and data-driven technologies as *public digital infrastructures*, that is, as large-scale socio-technical systems grounded in material resources, policy frameworks, and institutional capacities (Goldstein & Mazzucato et al., 2024; Nost, 2022). This framing builds on recent scholarship that understands digital infrastructures such as identity, payments, and data-sharing not simply as technical platforms, but as collectively shaped systems whose publicness emerges from their embedding within state institutions, their orientation towards delivering public value, and their governance through principles of universality, participation, and accountability (Eaves et al., 2025). Moving beyond common critiques of AI, such as calls for transparency or technocratic control, this infrastructural perspective draws attention to who funds and maintains these systems, what standards they operate under, and whose values guide their development. In doing so, it underscores the political nature of AI and reveals why "green AI" is not merely a matter of efficiency or innovation but also of power, governance, and public accountability.

Second, the chapter introduces responsiveness as a framework for understanding the integration of AI into environmental governance, particularly in support of sustainability goals. Rather than focusing solely on inclusion or procedural participation, responsiveness here implies an openness to social mobilization and a robust institutional capacity for decisive action. Drawing on strands of the Responsible Innovation literature (Stilgoe et al., 2013) alongside critical perspectives (Pellizzoni, 2020), this approach emphasizes two intertwined dimensions: empathetic perception—the willingness to incorporate multiple voices, challenge entrenched assumptions, and enable grassroots energy to shape AI-based infrastructural priorities, and resolute engagement—the capacity of public institutions to mobilize legal, financial, and administrative resources to enact large-scale changes.

The remainder of this chapter is structured as follows. First, I develop the notion of AI systems as public digital infrastructure and consider how this perspective situates AI within broader governance structures. Second, I outline responsiveness—through the twin pillars of empathetic perception and resolute engagement—as a lens for rethinking how AI can be harnessed or repurposed for environmental governance and sustainability. Finally, I ground this framework in a case study of Poland's forestry sector, where data-driven tools and emerging AI applications intersect with tensions over centralised decision-making, local agency, transparency, and power. This empirical example reveals both the potential and the challenges of making AI-driven governance truly responsive, equitable, and oriented toward long-term ecological resilience.

AI and Data Systems as Infrastructures in Environmental Governance

In this section, AI and large data systems, which play a crucial role in achieving ecological and environmental goals, are not treated merely as collections of algorithms or digital services but as infrastructures in their own right. Drawing on the work of Bowker and Star (1999), Star and Bowker (2010), infrastructure encompasses not only physical networks such as railways and roads or digital assets like servers and protocols but also the underlying layers of standards, classifications, and social practices that determine how technology functions and who has access to it. Crucially, infrastructure often remains invisible, seamlessly integrated into daily operations until it fails or is critically examined for the ways it reinforces particular power structures and values (Star & Bowker, 2010).

Adopting an infrastructural perspective on AI and data systems allows for a shift in focus beyond the technical mechanics of specific algorithms—for instance, their role in deforestation monitoring or climate modelling—toward the broader socio-technical systems that sustain them. This approach highlights who funds and maintains these infrastructures, what standards are embedded within them, and who ultimately benefits from the knowledge they produce. In the environmental domain, such "knowledge infrastructures" (Edwards, 2017) serve not only to monitor environmental conditions—tracking air quality, biodiversity, or carbon fluxes—but also to model ecological change and construct a form of environmental memory. These systems facilitate the accumulation of long-term datasets, providing the basis for policy decisions informed by historical trends in climate change and biodiversity loss. The continuity and integrity of these datasets rely on stable funding, institutional priorities, and governance structures (Edwards, 2017). Interruptions—whether financial, political, or technical—expose the vulnerabilities of these infrastructures, highlighting that data is a product of ongoing maintenance efforts (often described as "invisible work") and governance choices (Star & Bowker, 2010). This includes both technical upkeep—such as server operations, sensor calibration, and software updates—and institutional processes, like negotiating data standards and regulatory frameworks. Neglecting these aspects can impede coordination between environmental agencies and compromise predictive models, weakening responses to ecological disruptions.

From the perspective of the political ecology of data (Goldstein & Nost, 2022; Nost & Goldstein, 2022), development of environmental data infrastructures is driven by unequal power dynamics, as governments and corporations with significant financial and technical resources define priorities, set classification standards, and dictate the direction of AI applications in environmental governance. As a result, data infrastructures shape not just what is monitored but also what is made visible and actionable in environmental decision-making, determining which ecosystems are closely observed, regulated, or intervened upon, while others remain outside the scope of governance frameworks (Bakker & Ritts, 2018; Kloppenburg et al., 2022; Turnbull et al., 2023).

Crucially, AI systems and data infrastructures are material in their own right, meaning they do not simply document environmental change but actively reshape ecosystems and landscapes. Processes such as digital mapping, algorithmic resource management, and automated regulation enforcement not only influence land use, conservation practices, and ecological restoration but also generate tangible environmental consequences (Goldstein & Nost, 2022). The operation of these infrastructures also requires significant energy, water, and raw materials—from the electricity needed to power and cool data centres processing climate models to the extraction of rare earth metals essential for computational hardware (Lehuedé, 2024).

At the same time, research on public policy highlights how digital infrastructures designed for social and state functions—such as digital identity systems, electronic payment networks, and data-sharing platforms—are increasingly central to economic governance, resource management, and environmental regulation (Eaves et al., 2025; Mazzucato et al., 2024; Nagar & Eaves, 2024). These infrastructures not only enable administrative functions but also shape how environmental and ecological priorities are implemented. This raises important questions about what qualifies as public infrastructure, how it should be designed, and what principles should guide its development to serve the common good, particularly in relation to long-term ecological sustainability and governance.

Considering these insights, the design and governance of infrastructure cannot be reduced solely to considerations of technical efficiency; rather, it requires reflection on its attributes (such as interoperability and openness) and its broader functions (such as supporting economic development and environmental governance goals). This perspective underscores the importance of diverse stakeholder engagement, the necessity of social participation, and the pursuit of long-term public value. Scholars further emphasize that democratising infrastructure—by expanding access, ensuring transparency, and fostering co-creation—can be a crucial mechanism for addressing both social and environmental challenges (van Veelen et al., 2021). The directionality and purpose of these infrastructures are crucial, as they determine whether digital systems serve climate resilience, environmental governance, and economic inclusion or instead reinforce existing inequalities (Eaves et al., 2025). For this reason, public digital infrastructure is not only a matter of operational efficiency but also of transparency, shared accountability, and a commitment to a sustainable (and even explicitly ecological) approach to technological development.

However, ensuring that these infrastructures align with broader social and environmental goals is particularly critical in the environmental domain, where public and collective interests are at stake (Edwards, 2017; Nost, 2022). These infrastructures not only influence ecological governance but also shape the distribution of resources and the ability of communities to respond to environmental crises. To fully grasp these challenges, both an analytical and political lens is needed to examine how AI infrastructures integrate into governance and whether they contribute to systemic transformation. Beyond technical assessments, a political language is required to articulate how AI infrastructures can serve collective interests. One way to develop such a language is through the concept of responsiveness, which the next section explores as a framework for bridging these dimensions.

Responsiveness as a Transformative Approach: Empathetic Perception and Resolute Engagement

Responsiveness has its roots in discussions on Responsible Innovation (RI) (Stilgoe et al., 2013) and environmental governance (Mustalahti, 2018; Pellizzoni, 2004). In these fields, it is generally understood as the ability to continuously address emerging problems, societal voices, and ethical concerns. Put simply, these perspectives frame responsiveness as the capacity to recognise diverse needs and perspectives and respond to them in ways that match the scale of social or environmental challenges. It is often linked to participation, transparency, and inclusivity. At first glance, this may appear as just another set of consultation procedures, particularly in the context of RI, where responsiveness is often framed alongside anticipation, reflexivity, and inclusion (Stilgoe et al., 2013). However, Pellizzoni (2020) critiques this version of responsiveness, arguing that it fails to challenge deeper power structures and instead remains confined to procedural adjustments rather than substantive change. He calls for a more radical openness that not only acknowledges social demands but also allows for fundamental transformations in governance structures. Additionally, literature on political theory highlights the importance of strong institutions and their capacity to respond effectively to social and environmental demands. In the context of a responsive state (Fineman, 2008), scholars emphasise the active role of public institutions as resource mobilisers, ensuring that they have the authority and capability to implement long-term policies. Others (Mustalahti et al., 2020) stress the need to equip local communities with the necessary resources and capacities to engage meaningfully in environmental governance. These perspectives point to a broader reflection on the goals and operational mechanisms of public infrastructures, particularly in managing environmental resources and governance structures.

This section builds on existing discussions of responsiveness, recognising that it already serves as a useful starting point in debates about technology, innovation, and computer science. However, these perspectives often require reorganisation to better address deeper power structures and systemic transformations. In this light, I propose a more transformative understanding of responsiveness, cantered around two key dimensions: empathetic perception—a radical openness to social perspectives—and resolute engagement—a commitment to mobilising public resources for systemic change. Together, these elements frame the integration of AI and data in environmental governance not as a procedural exercise in stakeholder inclusion but as a dynamic process of political, social, and technological transformation.

Empathetic perception requires a fundamental openness to social visions, alternative definitions of environmental and social problems, and contestation of the status quo. Existing approaches to responsiveness do not necessarily generate the collective energy required for significant change. A transformative approach goes further, fostering social mobilisation—the ability of communities to cultivate a shared sense of purpose and commitment. At the core of this concept is a fundamental openness to contestation and the redefinition of issues. As Pellizzoni (2004, 2020) argues, institutions and public leaders must be willing to reassess their assumptions in response to grassroots movements, activist organisations, local communities, and independent experts. Protests against resource exploitation or grassroots campaigns for biodiversity protection are not disruptions but essential drivers of environmental re-politicisation (Accetti, 2021). Such mobilisation can expose gaps in existing assumptions and challenges the depoliticised framing of AI as a neutral tool. Instead, it highlights the need to reconsider AI infrastructure priorities in light of social contestation and ecological justice. Rather than centring exclusively on market efficiency, this perspective invites a broader reflection on how AI can serve the common good, foster climate solidarity, and uphold interspecies justice as part of a renewed political engagement with environmental governance. Therefore responsiveness is not merely about "gathering opinions" but about recognising moments of disruption as valuable and creative opportunities for rethinking dominant paradigms.

The second pillar, resolute engagement refers to the ability of public institutions to translate social visions into concrete programmes and investments. Bottom-up pressure or civic enthusiasm alone is insufficient when funding, regulatory, or coordination mechanisms are lacking. According to Fineman's (2008) theory of the "responsive state," public authorities must be strong and proactive enough to protect the common good from competing interests and address social inequalities through robust institutional capacities and resource allocation. Institutional mobilisation involves not only ensuring sufficient budgets and personnel but also establishing stable legal frameworks. For instance, if AI is to be employed in monitoring CO_2 emissions, significant investment in data infrastructure, interagency cooperation, and legislative measures mandating reporting and enforcement mechanisms are required. This represents a fundamentally different scale of action than simply optimising existing procedures (Eckersley, 2004; Tompkins & Adger, 2005). Institutions must also be capable of responding swiftly in crisis situations (such as natural disasters, illegal deforestation, or environmental contamination), necessitating procedural flexibility and a well-coordinated executive apparatus. Resolute engagement, therefore, is not merely about executing decisions but about shaping and maintaining the conditions under which digital environmental infrastructures serve broader societal goals rather than being dictated solely by profit motives or short-term political considerations.

In this framework, both empathetic perception and resolute engagement operate in tandem for AI and data systems to genuinely function as public infrastructures serving the environment. Where communal energy exists and where the state (or other public entities) is prepared to leverage its resources and authority, the possibility for deep transformation arises. This vision contrasts with liberal approaches, where public participation is often limited to consultation, and state intervention remains minimal. Responsiveness in this sense entails a feedback loop between "raising a voice" (through contestation, demands, or social analysis) and concrete policy steps that incorporate these demands into practice or long-term strategies. However, this process requires institutions with adequate infrastructure, resources, and political will, while also ensuring that society has space for genuine mobilisation.

The subsequent sections of this chapter will illustrate how this vision of responsiveness plays out in the specific context of Poland's forestry sector. This analysis will also examine the potential and challenges of implementing transformative responsiveness in practice, particularly in the face of the complex dynamics associated with AI and data systems in ecosystem management.

Empirical Focus: Polish Forestry and its Public Digital Infrastructure

The Polish forestry sector offers a particularly compelling example of how data systems and AI tools function as public infrastructures shaping environmental governance. Forests cover approximately 30% of Poland's territory, with nearly 80% managed by the State Forests (SF, pol. *Lasy Państwowe*). This powerful institution, which combines characteristics of both a government agency and a state-owned enterprise, employs over 25,000 people and maintains significant financial and organisational autonomy (Niedziałkowski & Putkowska-Smoter, 2021). Officially overseen by the Ministry of Climate and Environment, SF in practice operates with its own budgets, research centres, and detailed internal regulations. The scale and consequences of SF's operations make it a particularly significant site for the integration of data technologies in environmental governance. These digital infrastructures are not new additions but continue a long historical tradition of forestry management in Poland, where systematic data collection and state oversight have shaped practices over decades. Understanding how digital systems—from databases to AI-driven forest monitoring algorithms—are designed, maintained, and deployed provides insights into their role in supporting environmental objectives, including climate adaptation and sustainable development.

Adopting an infrastructural perspective (Edwards, 2017; Star & Bowker, 2010) allows us to see Polish forestry not just as a collection of individual technologies such as drones, sensors, or AI applications that model wildfire risks, but as an integrated system that determines how knowledge is produced, shared, and applied in environmental governance. This system encompasses hardware components (servers, networks, field sensors), institutional structures (hierarchical governance, legal frameworks, financial priorities), and social practices (classification systems, data collection procedures, organisational culture). Such forest "knowledge infrastructures," (Edwards, 2017) enable long-term forest monitoring, timber harvesting planning, and the designation of protected areas. While often "invisible" in daily operations, these systems become highly significant when conflicts arise over data access, concerns emerge about the marginalization of specific ecological indicators, or questions are raised about decision-making transparency. At the same time, their maintenance requires significant institutional effort. The SF invest heavily in sustaining these infrastructures, employing dedicated IT and data management units responsible for system upkeep, security, and continuous development. This specialized labour—spanning database administration, software engineering, and regulatory compliance—ensures that the technological backbone of forest governance remains operational and adaptable to new environmental and policy challenges.

Forests play a fundamental role in sustainability debates, serving as critical sites for discussions on climate policy, biodiversity conservation, and resource management. Globally, forests are central to strategies addressing carbon sequestration, ecosystem resilience, and socio-economic development, while in Poland, they occupy a particularly significant position within national sustainability policies. The data systems used to monitor forest health, track logging volumes, and assess environmental changes are key instruments in shaping these policies, directly influencing governance decisions. However, tensions have emerged regarding whose interests these infrastructures ultimately serve. Over the past decades, disputes over large-scale logging, such as in the Białowieża Forest, have raised questions about whether the State Forests' technological and organisational capacities align with broader social and ecological priorities—or, conversely, reinforce a more technocratic, production-focused paradigm (Blicharska & Van Herzele, 2015; Niedziałkowski & Chmielewski, 2023). In this sense, the forestry sector provides a revealing example of how data-driven infrastructures can both enable and constrain more inclusive, sustainability-oriented governance.

In this section, I examine how specific digital infrastructures—including the State Forests Information System (SILP) and the Forest Data Bank—are integrated into governance logics, analysing this process through the lens of responsiveness. This perspective helps to illuminate the tensions between reinforcing centralised control and expanding collaboration with diverse actors. SF's digital tools can either consolidate bureaucratic authority or open pathways for more inclusive and ecologically sound forest management, depending on how they are designed and implemented. By tracing these dynamics, this analysis highlights both the constraints and possibilities embedded in AI-driven and data-intensive forestry governance.

This analysis draws on a thematic analysis of 37 semi-structured interviews with key stakeholders involved in forest governance, technology implementation, and policy contestation. The respondents included representatives from eight environmental and digital rights NGOs (NGO), seven public institutions (PI), three IT companies (IT), five frontline foresters (FF), five State Forests administrators and managers (SFM), and nine experts from academia, forestry, and IT (EXP). These interviews, conducted in a structured yet flexible format, allowed for an in-depth exploration of emergent themes while ensuring coverage of core governance and technological issues. This diverse set of perspectives provided critical insights into how digital infrastructures shape decision-making, transparency, and power dynamics in forestry governance.

Thematic analysis followed Braun and Clarke's (2006) six-step approach, starting with data familiarisation, initial coding, pattern identification, and theme refinement. The coding framework combined deductive codes, based on socio-technical infrastructure literature, with inductive codes emerging from the interviews. Key themes included the role of digital tools in decision-making, tensions between centralisation and local autonomy, transparency in data governance, and the contested meanings of sustainability in forestry management. To ensure sensitivity to sectoral and positional differences, Charmaz's (2014) constructivist grounded theory guided iterative coding, capturing contextual variations in stakeholder narratives and highlighting power dynamics embedded in technological systems.

This combination of thematic analysis and constructivist grounded theory enabled a systematic yet open-ended engagement with the data, revealing tensions between centralized control and participatory governance. These methods provide insight into the complexity and relational character of public forestry infrastructures in Poland, highlighting the intersections of digital governance, institutional power, and environmental politics.

Empathetic Perception: Openness, Contestation, and Data Infrastructures

Empathetic perception in forest governance extends beyond merely defining which socio-ecological challenges matter; it also involves an openness to critique, collaboration, and unexpected perspectives. In Poland, however, the SF continue to operate through a highly specialised, top-down model that offers minimal space for broader community or ecological frames of reference. While forestry officials and data experts collect extensive metrics, the assumptions underlying these measurements—what constitutes a "key indicator" or a "forest problem"—are largely dictated by hierarchical standards favouring economic and managerial goals.

This approach has historically shaped Polish forestry governance, restricting the scope of recognized issues and formalizing them through rigid procedures. As one civil society representative explained:

> There's no real space for negotiation. Forest management is framed as a technical issue, and decisions are made behind closed doors. Communities and activists are left to react rather than participate. (NGO5)

What is at stake goes beyond basic consultation or transparency: it concerns the infrastructural design that moulds knowledge and decisions. Star and Bowker (2010) remind us that infrastructures typically remain hidden in everyday practice, yet they profoundly affect which issues and viewpoints gain traction. A telling illustration in Polish forestry is the Forest Data Bank. Established in the 2010s to unify data from over 300 forestry districts, it serves as a key platform for making forestry data accessible to both the public and other institutions, such as local governments. The system integrates voluminous information on tree stands, logging volumes, and pest control measures, providing a centralised repository for monitoring and decision-making. One State Forests forester noted:

> It's a tool that shows a lot and helps us manage forests effectively. It's built to integrate massive amounts of information in one place. (SFM4)

One of its original developers noted that a crucial decision during its construction was making the data open access—a choice that was not self-evident. "There were real concerns," he recalled. "Many foresters, recalling the large protests of the 1990s, worried that open data could fuel conflicts rather than support better governance" (EXP1).

Despite its technical merits, the Bank primarily centres on economic and operational measures—timber production, pest mitigation, and similar metrics—while factors such as local biodiversity or cultural values receive considerably less emphasis. As one NGO leader put it:

> These systems are designed for foresters, not for communities. They open the door just enough to say they're being transparent, but not enough for anyone to walk through. (NGO7)

Nonetheless, civil society groups have increasingly sought to reclaim or rework official data in ways that amplify alternative perspectives. A prominent example is the Logging Map, an NGO-driven initiative that repackages raw statistics from the Forest Data Bank into user-friendly visualisations of planned cutting sites. By highlighting local effects and potential ecological losses, activists aim to broaden the conversation around what forests represent and who decides their fate. One activist remarked:

> The map wasn't just data, it was a way to connect people to these decisions... it gave them a voice. (NGO3)

Such instances reveal the contested nature of forest data infrastructures. Although the SF do release certain datasets, they maintain control over the classification systems and indicators that define "proper" forestry management. Civic actors can creatively reinterpret these data flows but face inherent limits in reshaping core metrics of success. As another NGO representative observed:

> The problem isn't access to data; it's what they do with it. They're happy to show you the numbers, but don't expect them to act on what you say. (NGO5)

These remarks underscore the complexity of "listening" in environmental governance. Institutional inertia often intertwines with grassroots resistance: activists may highlight alternative knowledge—emphasising biodiversity or local livelihoods—yet the deeper logic of data categorisation remains anchored in existing protocols. Although recent years have witnessed stronger public debate and novel narratives around forest stewardship, the fundamental priorities and data structures within the State Forests have changed only marginally.

Ultimately, this dynamic reveals how the openness crucial to empathetic perception can be both fostered and constrained by infrastructural design. Even sophisticated tools, praised for operational efficiency, may struggle to accommodate diverse social values or adapt metrics without a more extensive shift in governance norms. While activist movements have persistently challenged forestry policies in Poland, their efforts have rarely translated into substantive institutional changes. The SF remain a dominant and highly resistant actor, shaping decision-making processes in ways that limit external influence. In practice, empathetic perception in Polish forestry remains contested—shaped by institutional rigidity on one side and grassroots challenges on the other, illustrating that truly inclusive forest governance hinges on the capacity and willingness of data infrastructures to absorb alternative voices and disrupt entrenched power asymmetries.

Resolute Engagement: Capacity, Autonomy, and Governance Priorities

While empathetic perception speaks to an institution's openness to alternative perspectives, resolute engagement highlights its ability to mobilise resources and implement decisions once key issues are identified. In Polish forestry, this capacity is epitomized by the SF—an organisation whose robust technological investments and organizational autonomy underscore both the power and the limitations of centralised action.

The SF stand among Poland's largest public entities, overseeing roughly 80% of the country's forested area with a workforce exceeding 25,000. This scale, comparable to major financial institutions in terms of headcount and assets, endows SF with substantial organisational heft. One senior representative underscored this scope:

> It's impressive when you consider the scope. Our size is on par with a major bank... 25,000 employees, 8 million hectares under supervision. (SFM4)

Substantial budgets and extensive data systems reinforce this stature. Yet maintaining these infrastructures requires continuous effort, with thousands of employees engaged daily in data collection and system upkeep. This often-overlooked labour ensures that forestry data remains up to date and actionable. As one specialist involved in system maintenance remarked:

> People often focus on the outputs, maps, reports, statistics, but behind that, there's a huge amount of work. Thousands of foresters, administrators, and IT staff input data every day to keep the system running. (EXP3)

This capacity emerged partly from institutional evolution. Rooted in the socialist era of the 1970s and restructured amid the 1990s' political and economic reforms, the SF pioneered the State Forests Information System (SFIS), a national platform for integrating forestry data. According to one IT expert:

> Building the system in the '90s was quite an adventure, a genuine transformation. We had Western funding, extensive testing, and somehow we pieced it all together into something that worked. (SFM2)

A distinctive feature of SF has been its unusual autonomy. Freed from certain budgetary constraints and able to direct resources internally, the organisation developed advanced IT infrastructures and even acquired a technology firm to reduce reliance on external contractors. One forester described:

> Keeping IT operations in-house gives us more flexibility to adapt systems to our needs. It's about ensuring the technology works for us, not the other way around. (FF2)

This independence, however, also shapes how effectively the SF can respond to pluralistic environmental or social concerns. Critics argue that the same autonomy that drives bold investments can insulate SF from external scrutiny. As one environmental advocate remarked:

> They're big, well-financed, and can do impressive things, but they're also hard to move or question. They might gather data, but whose priorities are those data serving? (NGO2)

A telling example of how strong institutional capacity can yield immediate benefits is SF's wildfire detection and response system. By merging real-time data from observation towers, drones, and machine-learning algorithms, it rapidly alerts firefighting units to newly detected hot spots. An expert commented:

> The crucial part is the direct link between information and action. It's not just a screenful of data, there are people out there ready to respond. (EXP6)

Hailed as one of the most advanced systems in Europe, it underscores that even the best technologies rely on organisational structures (trained staff, established procedures, and reliable funding) to be effective. As one forester explained:

> You can't just throw technology at a problem and hope it works. It needs a foundation, trained personnel, solid processes, stable budgets. (EXP6)

Yet this same capacity does not necessarily translate into strong engagement with longer-term ecological concerns. While SF excels at crisis response or resource extraction goals, critics point to its limited commitment to biodiversity or broader sustainability metrics. An NGO leader noted:

> They excel at emergency response, but if you look at protecting habitats or limiting timber extraction, they lag behind. It's not just about technology—it's about where their priorities lie. (NGO6)

These examples illustrate how resolute engagement can be selective. Crises that align with SF's core functions, like firefighting, prompt rapid mobilisation, whereas slower-moving ecological or social issues may remain under-resourced or overshadowed by production-oriented goals. In turn, the high level of institutional autonomy and historical entrenchment can amplify this selective capacity, making it harder for external voices (e.g., local communities, NGOs) to prompt meaningful policy changes.

Overall, this tension illuminates the complexities of "resolute engagement" in Polish forestry. While resource abundance and formidable infrastructures can facilitate swift and effective interventions, they also risk reinforcing pre-existing hierarchies if institutional culture is not receptive to diverse societal demands. As the next section explores, bridging the gap between such high-level capacity and inclusive, ecologically minded governance remains a critical challenge.

Conclusion: Responsiveness, Public Infrastructures, and the Scale of Transformative Action

This chapter has proposed responsiveness as a way to analyse and potentially reorient the role of AI and data-driven tools in environmental governance. Rather than prescribing a fixed institutional model, responsiveness serves as a conceptual device for examining the reciprocal relationship between openness to social critique (empathetic perception) and the capacity to mobilise resources on a large scale (resolute engagement). While the chapter has primarily drawn conceptual insights from the Polish forestry context, the institutional dynamics it explores—around bureaucratic resistance, civic contestation, and infrastructural dependencies—are not unique. Similar questions of responsiveness, public value, and democratic oversight arise in other domains where AI is introduced into public governance.

A key insight is that public digital infrastructures, including AI applications, can facilitate both democratic processes and ambitious, large-scale action—but only when organisational capacity and societal input are mutually reinforcing (Edwards, 2017). Responsiveness highlights a feedback loop: robust infrastructures and institutional budgets may enable decisive action, yet without sustained civic engagement and critical reflection, they risk entrenching top-down priorities. Conversely, local contestation and democratic mobilization can expand policy horizons, but without institutional momentum and resource flows, such calls for change may dissipate or remain symbolic. This interplay between democratisation and centralisation underscores a persistent tension in environmental governance: how to harness large-scale bureaucratic strength for genuinely inclusive, socio-ecological goals.

A further insight concerns the material and organisational dimensions of large-scale environmental interventions. High-level policies, data systems, and AI-driven analytics require not only visionary ideas but also stable funding, dedicated personnel, and political backing. Rather than treating these technologies as standalone solutions, responsiveness situates them within existing organisations and infrastructures. AI tools do not function in isolation; they interact with human expertise, institutional frameworks, and material infrastructures. These interactions are crucial, shaping both the potential and the limitations of AI in addressing environmental challenges. A responsive approach calls for a deeper understanding of these dependencies, ensuring that AI complements rather than displaces the systemic capacities required for sustainable governance.

Additionally, the sustainability potential of AI hinges on continuous dialogue between diverse social actors—foresters, local communities, researchers, and policymakers—and the ability to convert these insights into concrete action. Public digital infrastructures can act as both enablers and gatekeepers of sustainable governance. On the one hand, well-funded, centralised systems may expand AI's reach, enabling broad-scale monitoring, real-time data analysis, and more agile responses to environmental threats (Eaves et al., 2025). On the other hand, such centralised power may hamper democratic oversight or marginalize alternative ways of defining and pursuing sustainability. Responsiveness thus highlights the balancing act between building institutional strength (such as the resources to deploy AI extensively) and maintaining the openness necessary for genuine participation and ecological integrity. This dynamic underscores responsiveness as a valuable framework for understanding—and potentially reshaping—the integration of AI and data infrastructures in long-term environmental governance.

At the same time, a focus on macro-level capacity inevitably bypasses some nuances of local experience. While responsiveness sheds light on systemic dynamics, it may not fully capture the complexities of on-the-ground struggles—especially those tied to place-based cultural values or the micro-politics of community organising. Furthermore, responsiveness does not automatically resolve the challenges posed by entrenched institutional power. Large bureaucratic infrastructures, such as those governing forestry, are often resistant to change, making it difficult for grassroots movements to achieve lasting influence. Further research or complementary theoretical lenses could deepen our understanding of how small-scale, everyday initiatives intersect with these rigid governance structures and where real opportunities for institutional responsiveness might emerge.

In adopting responsiveness, this chapter does not offer a definitive solution to the entwined challenges of climate change, biodiversity loss, and social equity. Instead, it provides a language for recognising the interplay between critical dialogue and institutional capacity in shaping data and AI integration into governance. Responsiveness is not a panacea—it remains an abstract framework and does not guarantee an even distribution of power across all stakeholders. However, it clarifies the often-invisible processes—such as resource allocation, infrastructural maintenance, and political commitment—that underpin large-scale change.

Ultimately, if public digital infrastructures are to serve socio-ecological ends, their design and deployment must enable both participation and decisive action. Responsiveness highlights how these dual imperatives can support one another, provided institutions are willing to revise entrenched priorities in response to new data, public critique, and shifting political landscapes. Whether in forestry or other domains, a sustainable future depends on harnessing large systems' capacity for change while ensuring that local knowledge and societal voices remain integral. By embedding AI and data systems within a responsive governance framework, we gain a more material, institutional perspective on transformation—one that underscores how technology's real potential lies in its alignment with inclusive decision-making structures and collective aspirations for ecological well-being.

Competing Interests The author has no conflicts of interest to declare that are relevant to the contents of this chapter.

References

Accetti, C. I. (2021). Repoliticizing environmentalism: Beyond technocracy and populism. *Critical Review, 33*(1), 47–73. https://doi.org/10.1080/08913811.2021.1908023

Agrawal, A., Brandhorst, S., Jain, M., Liao, C., Pradhan, N., & Solomon, D. (2022). From environmental governance to governance for sustainability. *One Earth, 5*(6), 615–621. https://doi.org/10.1016/j.oneear.2022.05.014

Bakker, K., & Ritts, M. (2018). Smart earth: A meta-review and implications for environmental governance. *Global Environmental Change, 52*, 201–211. https://doi.org/10.1016/j.gloenvcha.2018.07.011

Blicharska, M., & Van Herzele, A. (2015). What a forest? Whose forest? Struggles over concepts and meanings in the debate about the conservation of the Białowieża Forest in Poland. *Forest Policy and Economics, 57*, 22–30. https://doi.org/10.1016/j.forpol.2015.04.003

Bowker, G. C., & Star, S. L. (1999). *Sorting things out: Classification and its consequences.* MIT Press.

Braun, V., & Clarke, V. (2006). Using thematic analysis in psychology. *Qualitative Research in Psychology, 3*(2), 77–101. https://doi.org/10.1191/1478088706qp063oa

Charmaz, K. (2014). Grounded theory in global perspective: Reviews by international researchers. *Qualitative Inquiry, 20*(9), 1074–1084. https://doi.org/10.1177/1077800414545235

Eaves, D., Mazzucato, M., & Pagliarini, G. (2025). *Leveraging digital public infrastructures for the common good to promote inclusive and sustainable economic development in Brazil.* UCL Institute for Innovation and Public Purpose. Working Paper Series (IIPP WP 2024–19). https://www.ucl.ac.uk/bartlett/public-purpose/wp2024-19

Eckersley, R. (2004). *The green state: Rethinking democracy and sovereignty.* MIT Press.

Edwards, P. N. (2017). Knowledge infrastructures for the Anthropocene. *The Anthropocene Review, 4*(1), 34–43. https://doi.org/10.1177/2053019616679854

Fineman, M. A. (2008). The vulnerable subject: Anchoring equality in the human condition. *Yale Journal of Law and Feminism, 20*, 23.

Gabrys, J., Westerlaken, M., Urzedo, D., Ritts, M., & Simlai, T. (2022). Reworking the political in digital forests: The cosmopolitics of socio-technical worlds. *Progress in Environmental Geography, 1*(1–4), 58–83. https://doi.org/10.1177/27539687221117836

Goldstein, J. E., & Nost, E. (Eds.). (2022). *The nature of data.* University of Nebraska Press.

Joppa, L. N. (2017). The case for technology investments in the environment. *Nature, 21/28.* https://www.nature.com/articles/d41586-017-08675-7

Kloppenburg, S., Gupta, A., Kruk, S. R. L., Makris, S., Bergsvik, R., Korenhof, P., Solman, H., & Toonen, H. M. (2022). Scrutinizing environmental governance in a digital age: New ways of seeing, participating, and intervening. *One Earth, 5*(3), 232–241. https://doi.org/10.1016/j.oneear.2022.02.004

Kovacic, Z., García Casañas, C., Argüelles, L., Yáñez Serrano, P., Ribera-Fumaz, R., Prause, L., & March, H. (2024). The twin green and digital transition: High-level policy or science fiction? *Environment and Planning E: Nature and Space*, 28(1). https://doi.org/10.1177/25148486241258046

Lehuedé, S. (2024). An elemental ethics for artificial intelligence: Water as resistance within AI's value chain. *AI & Society, 40*, 1761–1774. https://doi.org/10.1007/s00146-024-01922-2

Lemos, M. C., & Agrawal, A. (2006). Environmental governance. *Annual Review of Environment and Resources, 31*(1), 297–325. https://doi.org/10.1146/annurev.energy.31.042605.135621

Mazzucato, M., Eaves, D., & Vasconcellos, B. (2024). Digital public infrastructure and public value: What is 'public' about DPI? UCL Institute for Innovation and Public Purpose. Working Paper Series (IIPP WP 2024–05). https://www.ucl.ac.uk/bartlett/public-purpose/wp2024-05

Mustalahti, I. (2018). The responsive bioeconomy: The need for inclusion of citizens and environmental capability in the forest based bioeconomy. *Journal of Cleaner Production, 172*, 3781–3790. https://doi.org/10.1016/j.jclepro.2017.06.132

Mustalahti, I., Gutiérrez-Zamora, V., Hyle, M., Devkota, B. P., & Tokola, N. (2020). Responsibilization in natural resources governance: A romantic doxa? *Forest Policy and Economics, 111*, Article 102033. https://doi.org/10.1016/j.forpol.2019.102033

Nagar, S., & Eaves, D. (2024). Interactions between artificial intelligence and digital public infrastructure: Concepts, benefits, and challenges. *arXiv*. https://doi.org/10.48550/arXiv.2412.05761

Niedziałkowski, K., & Chmielewski, P. (2023). Challenging the dominant path of forest policy? Bottom-up, citizen forest management initiatives in a top-down governance context in Poland. *Forest Policy and Economics, 154*, Article 103009. https://doi.org/10.1016/j.forpol.2023.103009

Niedziałkowski, K., & Putkowska-Smoter, R. (2021). What is the role of the government in wildlife policy? Evolutionary governance perspective. *Politics and Governance, 9*(2), 428–438. https://doi.org/10.17645/pag.v9i2.4106

Nost, E. (2022). Infrastructuring "data-driven" environmental governance in Louisiana's coastal restoration plan. *Environment and Planning E: Nature and Space, 5*(1), 104–124. https://doi.org/10.1177/2514848620909727

Nost, E., & Goldstein, J. E. (2022). A political ecology of data. *Environment and Planning E: Nature and Space, 5*(1), 3–17. https://doi.org/10.1177/25148486211043503

Pellizzoni, L. (2004). Responsibility and environmental governance. *Environmental Politics, 13*(3), 541–565. https://doi.org/10.1080/0964401042000229034

Pellizzoni, L. (2020). Responsibility. In A. Kalfagianni, D. A. Fuchs, & A. Hayden (Eds.), *Routledge handbook of global sustainability governance* (pp. 129–140). Routledge. https://www.taylorfrancis.com/books/9781315170237

Star, S. L., & Bowker, G. C. (2010). How to Infrastructure. In L. Lievrouw & S. Livingstone (Eds.), *Handbook of new media: Social shaping and social consequences of ICTs, updated students edition* (pp. 230–245). SAGE. https://doi.org/10.4135/9781446211304.n13

Stilgoe, J., Owen, R., & Macnaghten, P. (2013). Developing a framework for responsible innovation. *Research Policy, 42*(9), 1568–1580. https://doi.org/10.1016/j.respol.2013.05.008

Tompkins, E. L., & Adger, W. N. (2005). Defining response capacity to enhance climate change policy. *Environmental Science & Policy, 8*(6), 562–571. https://doi.org/10.1016/j.envsci.2005.06.012

Turnbull, J., Searle, A., Hartman Davies, O., Dodsworth, J., Chasseray-Peraldi, P., Von Essen, E., & Anderson-Elliott, H. (2023). Digital ecologies: Materialities, encounters, governance. *Progress in Environmental Geography, 2*(1–2), 3–32. https://doi.org/10.1177/27539687221145698

van Veelen, B., Rella, L., Taylor Aiken, G., Judson, E., Gambino, E., Jenss, A., Parashar, A., & Pinker, A. (2021). Interventions on democratizing infrastructure. *Political Geography, 87*, Article 102378. https://doi.org/10.1016/j.polgeo.2021.102378

van Wynsberghe, A. (2021). Sustainable AI: AI for sustainability and the sustainability of AI. *AI and Ethics, 1*(3), 213–218. https://doi.org/10.1007/s43681-021-00043-6

CHAPTER 14

AI Infrastructures, Total Mobilisation and Decomputing

Dan McQuillan

Infrastructural Violence

This chapter defines contemporary AI as systems based on artificial neural networks (Nielsen, 2015), and its infrastructures as datasets, models, computer chips and, in particular, data centres. The advent of generative AI has thrust these infrastructures into popular awareness, in particular because of their seemingly insatiable demand for energy. All AI burns a large amount of electricity when it is trained (optimised) and then some more each time it is queried (makes inferences). While the companies themselves remain tight-lipped about the energy consumption of specific AI models, some overall parameters can be deduced about the data centres that house all the computing power for AI and other internet services. A report from Berkeley estimated that the energy demand of US data centres will have risen from roughly 2% of total US power consumption in 2018 to 12% by 2028, with the growth driven by GPU-based servers and the demand for generative AI (Shehabi et al., 2024).

D. McQuillan (✉)
Goldsmiths, University of London, London, UK
e-mail: d.mcquillan@gold.ac.uk

A. Mollen et al. (eds.), *AI Infrastructures and Sustainability*, Palgrave Studies in European Communication Research and Education,
https://doi.org/10.1007/978-3-032-09748-4_14

In Ireland, whose tax breaks have made it a dumping ground for Big Tech's data centres, the industry is already consuming one-fifth of the country's electricity and is absorbing all of the additional wind energy generation that Ireland has managed to bring online (Daly, 2024). Cloud companies seem aware that carbon emissions from data centres are a PR liability and have made efforts over recent years to portray their efforts as "green tech" through the use of renewable energy and under the cover of carbon offsets. However, this way of papering over the cracks has been blown away by the energy demands of generative AI, and both Microsoft (Rathi & Bass, 2024) and Google (Rahman-Jones, 2024) have confessed an inability to meet their own climate targets. The gap between AI's demands and the grid infrastructure means that the impact is broader than can be measured in Megawatt-hours. In west London, a hold was put on building much needed new housing because data centres were already using up the grid capacity (Hammond & Morris, 2022), At the same time as the UK was experiencing energy shortages and inflated prices, with millions of households in fuel poverty (Bolton et al., 2025) a consortium of data centre operators lobbied the government for priority for energy usage in the event of power cuts (Hurst, 2022) As data centres and AI become more central to the country's strategic and growth ambitions, the UK government will find itself choosing between an industry it recently reclassified as "critical national infrastructure" (Loughran, 2024) and the winter survival chances of the old, the disabled and other marginalised parts of the population.

The AI apparatus also demands vast quantities of human energy in order to sustain the illusion that it is adding something novel to the world. The take-off of contemporary AI was made possible by the outsourcing of vast quantities of data labelling to create ImageNet, a set of millions of images sorted into thousands of categories (Russakovsky et al., 2015). Virtual labour meant that a task of previously infeasible scale could be done cheaply by thousands of anonymous and unacknowledged workers (Paullada et al., 2021). The arrival of the transformer models that power generative AI shifted the locus of that labour to sanitising toxic text sourced from an unfiltered trawl of the internet, a traumatising task which was delegated to workers in the Global South (Perrigo, 2023). ChatGPT introduced the extra step of Reinforcement Learning from Human Feedback (Lambert et al., 2022) which rewards people for training a model to emulate creative writing or coding, but only so that the AI can later be used to substitute for similarly skilled workers in real jobs (Eloundou et al., 2023). However complex its algorithms, AI lacks contextual understanding, relationality or adaptiveness. In order for AI to pose as a real life solution, the people around it will always have to backfill the ways its emulations fall short (Germain, 2024). All AI systems invisibilise the labour needed to compensate for their lack of common sense, and the callousness and collateral damage by which this debt is generated surely means Big Tech should be in the dock for reparations.

AI's extractiveness is justified by the benefits it's claimed it will bring. However, there's an ever widening gap between AI's computational demands and its ability to do something useful in the real world. Artificial neural networks are, fundamentally, giant pattern-finding mechanisms that optimise the correlation between the training data and their outputs. There's no understanding involved, so AI is always faking it even when it happens to hit on the right answer. This is true of both generative and predictive forms of the technology. The confabulations (Nelson, 2024) or so-called "hallucinations" of Large Language Models are paradigmatic examples of this, and recent claims that it can evade this by adding intermediary "reasoning" were debunked almost as soon as they were out of the gate (Mirzadeh et al., 2024). Moreover, the extra steps added by these models increase the computed inferences by hundreds or thousands of times, burning more energy as they go. And yet, despite its escalating resource use and the intractability of its tendency to get things wrong, each new AI model is used to legitimate an even deeper intrusion into decision-making that has real consequences for people's lives. AI is illegitimately presented as the answer to problems with society's existing infrastructures. AI won't lead to a revolution in cancer care (Bawden et al., 2024) or erase educational gaps via the introduction of super-intelligent virtual tutors, but it has already succeeded in diverting attention from the lack of funding for healthcare and education systems (Williamson, 2024). In the field of social relations, AI is becoming an engine of precaritisation and deprivation, undermining key workers from care staff to nurses on the basis that they can be replaced by its synthetic substitutes (Zeff, 2024). Given the definition of structural violence as ways in which institutions or social structures harm people through preventing them from meeting their fundamental needs (Galtung, 1969), it's clear that AI has become a form of infrastructural violence.

Scale

The single word used inside the industry to legitimise AI's vast intake of electrical energy and human labour is "scale". Neural networks were originally consigned to irrelevance because of the vast pools of data and computing power required to grind out a useful model. This all changed in 2012, when the convergence of the ImageNet dataset and the computing power of GPU microprocessors enabled convolutional neural networks to beat all previous benchmarks (Krizhevsky et al., 2012). There's a collective belief in the industry that every significant development since then has involved scaling up the size of the datasets and the "compute", the number of floating-point operations (FLOP) needed to train a model. The breakthrough image classification algorithm AlexNet required 10^{17} FLOP, but the transformer-based architectures of generative AI have multiplied this by many factors of 10, with Large Language Models like ChatGPT requiring 10^{24} operations and recent models from Meta and Alphabet reaching 10^{25}—that's 10 followed 25 zeroes. This rate of growth outpaces expansion of any other tech "revolution", from mobile phone adoption to genome sequencing (Sevilla & Roldán, 2024). Such is the faith in the effectiveness of scaling that many in the industry refer to it in terms of a physical law. Some researchers predict the arrival, by the year 2030, of models that need 10^{29} FLOP to be trained (Sevilla et al., 2024). To put that into perspective, it would require spending hundreds of billions of dollars on expanding AI infrastructure, while optimising a single model would require training runs of several months and the use of millions of high-end GPU chips. The energy required would be so vast that demand would have to be spread across different national grids so as not to completely overload them. The vision of AI which is being driven forward into material reality is of a planetary-scale machine.

The activity of scaling imbues the AI industry with a form of self-reinforcing virtue (Hanna & Park, 2020). By doing something that is "big" it can make claims about solutions that not only incorporate economies of scale but are sufficiently powerful to dissolve previously unsurmountable barriers (Ye, 2020). It's scale that attracts the impatient flows of venture capital, and it's scale that underpins the assertion that this is all something so new and important that previous rules and regulations don't apply. These are the same narratives that enabled entities like Uber and Deliveroo to normalise sweatshop levels of precarity under the deregulating glamour of machine learning algorithms (Narayan,

2022). What contemporary AI adds is the narrative of AGI, or Artificial General Intelligence, which is usually defined as general-purpose AI that can do all cognitive tasks a human can do, and may exceed human cognition altogether. Scale is a vision of unrestricted and infinite growth based on identifying previously unrealised forms of enclosure, but it is also a claim to forms of knowledge that will reach beyond human understanding (McQuillan, 2017). The belief in AGI is kept alive by the increasing performance of AI on the industry's self-defined metrics (Bommasani et al., 2022) slathered with mind-boggling volumes of hype. The commitment to scaling and the attendant opportunity to fantasise about emerging signs of mind-like reasoning (Bubeck et al., 2023) sustain the narrative that AI is deserving of all the material and human resources that can be thrown at it, because the power of AI to generate solutions is key to the future of both the planet and the human race itself.

In the imaginary of AI believers there are no social, environmental or planetary limits. When former Google CEO Eric Schmidt was challenged about AI's energy requirements, his response was to argue for going further and faster on the basis that it's already too late to reverse climate change and only AI itself can provide us with a way to overcome it (Schmidt, 2024). While this class of viewpoint endorses the goal of AGI, it also rationalises the adoption of AI's foundationally flawed technologies across industrial production and administrative tasks in the name of a mythic efficiency. The velocity with which the whole AI enterprise seems to be heading for the outer envelope of resource limitations hasn't, so far, interrupted the inflow of increasing amounts of capital, from investments in data centres to financial speculation on the GPU chips themselves (Kinder, 2024). On one level, this reflects the speculative dynamics of the stockmarket which will seize any opportunity for arbitrage (Callanan et al., 2024), but it's overlaid by the unwavering faith in AI expressed by national governments and entities like the EU (Voss, 2022). The overarching logic of AI metrics, like that of GDP, is growth, irrespective of whether this leads to social benefit and despite the collateral damage caused along the way. Scaling is the AI version of the growth ideology which has driven the capitalist economy since its emergence and provided the rationale for colonial expansionism. It's clear that basing our economic ideas about growth on a narrow set of measures that make no distinction between constructive or destructive externalities is what's propelled us to the point of irreversible climate change. AI's infrastructural acceleration is simply the next iteration.

Total Mobilisation

How are we to understand the commitment to the scaling of AI infrastructure despite such obvious environmental and social harms? I suggest that the convergence of forces around AI infrastructure can be understood as a form of "total mobilisation", a term which Ernst Jünger, writing in the aftermath of his experiences in World War I, used to characterise the channelling of the entire material and energy resources of a nation into a new technological order driven by a will to power. His argument was that "the Great War was fought not only between two groups of nations but also between two epochs" (Jünger, 2017, p. 37) where the new paradigm of total mobilisation is "driven relentlessly to seize matter, movement and force through the formalism of technoscience" (Costea & Amiridis, 2017, p. 482). In Jünger's conceptualisation, the mobilisation of all sources of material and human energy is a response to permanent insecurity, the sense that national life is besieged by potential risks which need to be resolved or eliminated. The state, in his view, is thus called on to secure whatever is necessary to ensure existential security. "The task of total mobilization is the conversion of life itself into energy, as it manifests itself in business, technology, and transport, in the whirring of wheels, or in fire and movement on the battlefield" (Jünger, 2017, p. 150). In our time, AI is positioned as a form of technoscientific power which presents urgent issues of existential risk. At the first level the risk is AI itself, in the form of the fantasies about the emergence of a hostile AGI. However, the more significant shift is the way states see the risk as missing out on a new epoch where AI's alleged powers are the source of economic and geopolitical strength. The very generalisability of AI manifests the integration of forces that Jünger foresaw in his visions of total mobilisation; "The organising force and the grip of industry, the work force of the mass, the national enrolment of finance, the superiority of science and its intimate binding to life itself, the development of culture as a whole—who could enumerate all that will be made to come together?" (Jünger, 1930a, as cited in Costea & Amiridis, 2017). Arguments for the unconstrained expansion of AI infrastructure can be understood through the lens of total mobilisation because they are driven by uncannily similar beliefs and commitments. Total mobilisation legitimates a new form of political order formed by crossing a threshold which crystallises organised destruction and organised production into a new normality, a vision of power through unlimited progress and the "extension of the perspective of utility into the infinite" (Jünger, 1930b, as cited in Costea & Amiridis, 2017).

Jünger centred his notion of total mobilisation around the vitalism of conflict. The dynamic of conflict, as opposed to mere competition, is becoming increasingly apparent as an intrinsic aspect of AI and its material infrastructures. Whilst the original breakthroughs in deep learning took place when the public rhetoric of Silicon Valley centered on tech's potential for democratisation, AI is now mired in the USA-China Cold War and is very visibly entangled with the military-industrial complex. Hostile competition with China was a key factor in legislation such as the CHIPS Act which authorised approximately 280 billion USD to fund semiconductor research and manufacturing in the USA, with a particular focus on the most advanced GPUs for AI that are more or less the exclusive product of Taiwan's TSMC corporation (Miller, 2024). This was combined with a slew of export bans on US-made semiconductors and equipment to China. We are seeing increasingly open and indeed strident commitments by AI companies to the development and support of military applications (Abraham, 2024), frequently justified by the idea of global rivalry with China (Morozov, 2023). Even OpenAI, which was explicitly founded to ensure the "safe and beneficial" development of AGI for humanity as a whole, joined in the business of military contracts and weapons development (O'Donnell, 2024). Seen from the perspective of total mobilisation, this is not really a change per se but the visible expression of an underlying order which Jünger labelled "the age of work". For Jünger the essence of total mobilisation is the mode of ordering "through which the widely ramified and richly veined currents of modern life can be marshalled, with a single flick of the switch, into military energy" (Jünger, 1930b, as cited in Costea & Amiridis, 2017) and he would be entirely unfazed by the deployment of various kinds of AI in the Gaza genocide (Reiff, 2023). It's not so much that AI and its infrastructures become bent towards the potential for military confrontation, but rather that the logic of total mobilisation is one born from the industrial nature of modern warfare, which carries outwards to become the infrastructural logic of society during so-called peacetime.

> Thus the image of war as armed action is flowing increasingly into the intensified image of a gigantic work process. Alongside the armies meeting on the battlefields, there arise the modern armies of logistics, of alimentation, of the arms industry – the army of work in general.... This absolute

> channelling of potential energy, which transformed industrial states into volcanic forges, is perhaps the starkest indication of the dawn of the age of work. (Jünger, 1930b, as cited in Costea & Amiridis, 2017)

Understanding the growth of AI infrastructure through the paradigm of total mobilisation isn't merely a way to express its voracious demands for energy or its intimate relation to militarised conflict, but a warning about its epochal goals. AI has emerged at a pivotal moment when neoliberalism is breaking down under the strain of a number of self-generated crises, from austerity to climate change. Whilst AI is often seized on as a form of case-by-case technosolutionism, as a high-tech fix that can be used to paper over underlying structural deficits, the drive of AI-as-total-mobilisation is a response of a different order. Seen through Jünger's eyes, the push for transcendence through AI is a form of nihilism. Jünger's commitment was to what Nietzsche would characterise as an active nihilism, not the passive exhaustion of the spirit's power but the outgrowing of values that held things back, and which must now be destroyed so as to clear the way for new ones. Running through Jünger's concept of total mobilisation is a

> profound ambivalence characterizing nihilism, and by extension the machine, in Nietzsche's thought. While on the one hand it degrades life, deprives it of any higher meaning and reduces it to a function of utility, on the other hand its fullest realization is the ground from which a new vitality can spring. (Bousquet, 2016, p. 22)

Reading AI infrastructures in this way, the demand isn't simply the seizure of gigawatts of energy or the depletion of water resources from regions at risk of desertification, but for an apparatus of alignment with a Nietzschean will to power. The purpose of mobilising all available energies is quite explicitly the severing of society from its previous moorings. This is where the lineaments of AI infrastructure fuse with the ambition of today's totalitarian political forces to move beyond the liberal rules-based order. As Jünger wrote, "In technology we recognize the most effective and incontestable means of total revolution. We know that the sphere of destruction possesses a secret center from which the seemingly chaotic process of the subjugation of the old forces accomplishes itself" (Jünger, 1981, as cited in Bousquet, 2016). Moreover, and completely in line with the various neofascist populisms of the present day, total mobilisation is tied to the reemergence of racial supremacy. “We observe that a new humanity is moving to this crucial center stage. The phase of destruction will be replaced by a real and visible order, if that race which understands the new language as elementary language, and not in the sense of mere intellect, progress, utility and convenience, achieves dominion [Herrschaft]” (Jünger, 1981, as cited in Bousquet, 2016).

White Supremacy

Whether or not Jünger’s thought forms an explicit part of Silicon Valley imaginaries, we can observe a lot in the discourse that aligns with total mobilisation. In particular, the ideas of “effective altruism”, the notion that AGI is just around the corner and that the most beneficial thing one can do for humanity is to make sure it is achieved as soon as possible (Gebru, 2022), and “longtermism”, where the future of humanity is imagined as up to 10^{54} virtual consciousnesses inhabiting computational hardware (Torres, 2021). The latter figure represents the vast majority of humans who will ever have lived, meaning that this future morally outweighs any collateral suffering caused in the here and now. Effective altruism and longtermism echo total mobilisation in being ideologies of transcendence whose existential significance means that an unlimited share of global resources should be put behind their realisation. Rather than staying confined to nerdish online discussion boards, these ideas were boosted by cryptocurrency-funded think tanks (Bordelon, 2024) into policy circles in Washington (Bordelon, 2023) and London (Clarke, 2023), helping to redpill the UK government agenda away from ethical harms to the more apocalyptic vision of AI Safety and its obsession with emergent superintelligence. Another influential strand which feeds into total mobilisation is accelerationism, a commitment to the radical intensification of technological change and capitalist growth with the deliberate aim of disruption and limit-breaking as a way to induce irreversible social change. The current of accelerationism that’s active in and around AI is an explicitly far right project drawing its ideas from the so-called Dark Enlightenment and the ideology of neoreaction (Haider, 2017), as espoused by commentators like Curtis Yarvin. Among adherents of neoreactionary ideology are highly influential Silicon Valley figures like Peter Thiel, co-founder of Palantir and sometime advisor to Donald Trump. The neoreactionary movement has been actively attempting to establish prototype “network states” (Srinivasan, 2022) either from scratch by buying land or by taking over San Francisco (Duran, 2024a), but has recently reached a plane of global influence through its fusion with Trump's MAGA movement, exemplified by Thiel protégé and Trump Vice-President J.D. Vance (Duran, 2024b). Neoreactionary talking points are now shaping the future of our social and material infrastructures.

This chapter argues that the current expansion of AI infrastructures is symptomatic of total mobilisation and its authoritarian politics. Whatever the growing awareness of AI's environmental harms, it should be clear that the dynamics of total mobilisation won't be interrupted by well-meaning appeals to limit carbon emissions. The ideologies that drive contemporary mobilisation draw equally from strands of climate denialism and from beliefs that only AGI can solve climate change anyway. Likewise, the agendas formed by the fusion of neoreaction and populist politics won't be perturbed by the idea of everyday suffering for masses of ordinary people. Both AI and AGI have mathematical and ideological precursors in Victorian eugenics, the pseudo-scientific rationalisation for British imperialism and its global extractivism (Clayton, 2020). Discussions about the application of AI to social questions are increasingly combined with openly eugenicist logics (Toorn & Soldatić, 2024), whether it's the idea that shoddy and second-best AI healthcare is "good enough" for the poor or the Global South, or the notion that AI-driven education complements innate biological hierarchies of intelligence (Williamson, 2021). Forms of supremacism are conformal with the operations of AI itself, which operates in social contexts so as to essentialise difference and intensify forms of ordering that designate some lives as relatively disposable (McQuillan, 2022). Structures of resource flow, from mineral extraction to electricity grids, are aligning with social ideologies that valorise an elite minority as the historical agents whose grasp of a uniquely powerful technology will lead the world system to the next level (Andreessen, 2023). Thus, the acceleration in AI infrastructure and its very tangible resource demands can be understood as a dimension of a more technopolitical phase shift, one which mobilises material, social and affective resource to consolidate hierarchies of power based on claims to racial and biological superiority. The question for the rest of us is how to respond to the infrastructures of computational supremacism.

Decomputing

This chapter proposes that resistance to the total mobilisation and supremacist politics materialised in AI takes the form of "decomputing". Decomputing starts by opposing the need for hyperscale data centres. It does so on the basis of the environmental harms they cause and because they host AI's precaritising and immiserating computations. By acknowledging that environmental damage and structural violence are intrinsic to AI, decomputing challenges the inevitability of more AI on both ecological and social grounds. The ever-expanding data centre estate represents not only the enclosure of land, water and energy but the forced advance of AI into every aspect of our lives, from the minutiae of everyday experience to the administrative apparatus of the state. Decomputing identifies the material infrastructure of AI as that which props up its predictive preemptions and powers the conversion of our daily interactions into data points for paranoid risk calculations. The data centre's windowless warehouses and evaporative cooling towers are engines that consume natural resources to produce not only CO_2 emissions, but alienation and precarity. However, data centres are also the Achilles' heel of the emerging techno-authoritarian order, and a popular front to resist their expansion would bring together social movements whose concerns range from climate change to energy poverty to labour justice. Decomputing draws attention to data centres as both a pedagogic and organisational opportunity, where assembling in opposition to their expansion is also a chance to raise consciousness regarding the infrastructural intersectionality of different struggles.

Decomputing is a pivot away from the environmental and social harms of AI and the supremacist agendas that drive them. It identifies a rejection of scale as a way to mitigate harms and a heuristic for alternative ways forward. Decomputing opposes scale as a form of growth ideology, and the corporate and state commitments to AI as the latest drivers of unconstrained growth. Decomputing thus implies an engagement with the principles of degrowth. The idea of degrowth is not only a direct challenge to AI's runaway extractivism but to the world view that underpins it, one that is prepared to externalise no end of environmental and social harms in the pursuit of wealth and power for a minority. Degrowth isn't simply a form of refusal but a process that "strengthens social justice and self-determination and strives for a good life for all under the conditions of this changed metabolism" and "redesigns its institutions and infrastructure so that they are not dependent on growth and continuous expansion for their functioning" (Schmelzer et al., 2022, as cited in Meyers, 2023). While degrowth begins with tactics that interrupt extractivism in the here and now, its focus is on the question of what replaces it; on the reconstruction of social and productive relationships and on a more collective stewardship of land and resources. Decomputing as degrowth applies a direct brake to the firestorm of total mobilisation around AI and its out-of-control infrastructures.

Decomputing also opposes scale as a means of enforcing automatisation. As Ivan Illich argues, tools transform from means to ends when their scale, size, or structure requires people to adapt to them, rather than enhancing people's autonomy and capacity. Scaling in this sense is the means by which something which is presented as a tool, like AI, becomes instead a system, a further enmeshment of lived experience and technical means in a mutually configuring apparatus. In this sense, AI is an intensification of the institutional, bureaucratic and market structures which strip agency from workers and communities and place it instead in opaque and abstract mechanisms. The problems we face are not ones of data governance, but the fact that our lives are so datafied in the first place. Decomputing, by contrast, is the de-automatisation of social relations and the disentangling of important decisions from AI's reductive outputs. It's the process of developing alternative forms of organisation and decision-making that draw instead on reflective judgement (Weizenbaum, 1984) and situated responsibility (Haraway, 1988). Decomputing is thus as much about deprogramming society from its technogenic certainties as it is about decarbonising its computational infrastructures. It is a deliberate turn away from a framework of efficiency and optimisation to "matters of care" (Bellacasa, 2017), taking our mutual vulnerabilities and dependencies as the ontological grounding for social production that emphasises balance, moderation and reciprocity. It is also, therefore, a way to wrest social and institutional praxis away from the kinds of thoughtlessness (Arendt, 2022) and utilitarian cruelty that is openly advocated for by adherents of neoreactionary technopolitics.

Decomputing counters total mobilisation and the untrammeled power of techno-authoritarians with the assertion that technologies like AI should be subject to social sanction. In other words, as was widely argued in the 1970s and 1980s, technologies that are likely to have a widespread impact on society should be subjected to critical interrogation before their widespread adoption. As the development of AI has demonstrated, existing regulatory mechanisms can't be trusted to sufficiently resist the influence of Big Tech in this regard. This applies even in the EU, where some compliance with a rules-based order is still performed, let alone in the USA, where regulatory capture by Big Tech has extended to state capture in open alliance with political forces from the far right. Decomputing takes instead a prefigurative approach to technopolitics, in that its practice enacts the forms of empowerment and sustainable relations that it seeks to bring about. The primary organisational forms of decomputing are therefore the kinds of assemblies described elsewhere as workers' and people's councils (McQuillan, 2022), that is, collectivities that are firmly rooted in local and professional contexts and in varieties of lived experience. The specific groups that will seek to carry forward decomputing will be as varied as their contexts, from healthcare or social work professionals to parent-teacher associations to trade unions. These may take on specific forms, such as the technology networks established in London in the mid-1980s which aimed to "bring together the 'untapped skill, creativity and sheer enthusiasm' in local communities with the 'reservoir of scientific and innovation knowledge' in the polytechnics" (Smith, 2014, p. 17). Whatever their context, they will need to develop criteria for critically assessing tools, especially those with the potential to become systems in themselves.

Fortunately, the task of devising criteria for socially and environmentally appropriate technologies doesn't have to start from scratch. The work of Ivan Illich in *Tools for Conviviality* is one possible starting point (Illich, 1975). Illich was concerned that the growth of industrial society was exceeding a number of natural scales in ways that were destructive and unsustainable and, by catalysing a movement toward total mobilisation, AI's infrastructures are certainly doing their bit to fulfill these dire predictions. Illich proposed convivial tools as a counterpoint to destructive technics. He defined convivial tools as those that enabled the exercise of autonomy and creativity, rather than the conditioned responses demanded by manipulative systems. The *Matrix of Convivial Technologies* (MCT) extends Illich's ideas by specifying an array of dimensions against which conviviality can be assessed, including accessibility (who can build or use it?), relatedness (how does it affect relations between people?) and bio-interaction (how does the tech interact with living organisms and ecologies?) (Vetter, 2018). In the context of decomputing, the MCT will benefit from approaches like frugal computing (Vanderbauwhede, 2023) and permacomputing (Permacomputing, 2024) which have already started to align computation within planetary and social limits. Adding to the MCT, we could say that appropriate tools are those that are not scalable because, like the act of care itself, they are always rooted in specificity and context. Rather than scaling, alternative tools tackle widespread needs by multiplying and federating.

Decomputing is the development of a counter-power to the technopolitical apparatus of AI and its totalising transformations. The stance of decomputing is that AI brings with it forms of environmental and social violence and cannot contribute to sustainable relations. Decomputing also highlights the role of scale and the way a belief in infinite growth drives AI infrastructures to become a form of total mobilisation. This, in turn, nests seamlessly within a wider will to power that manifests as far right politics and nihilistic imaginaries. What decomputing offers in contrast is one pathway to societies built on relations of care, whose attributes aren't abstraction and manipulation but mutual aid and solidarity. In doing so, decomputing resists growth by putting forward positive alternatives. It also identifies the crucial role of de-automatisation; the recognition that autonomy, agency and collective self-determination are in inverse proportion to the degree to which human relations are skewed by algorithmic ordering. Decomputing is the prefigurative decoupling of advanced computation from social goals; it is the reassertion of the need for convivial technologies and the construction of forms of collective social power that can bring them into being. As well as being a programme of social reconstruction, decomputing is a necessary form of social self-defence. The uncontested elevation of AI has contributed to the general strengthening of white supremacy and to the instrumenting of an administrative coup by those who subscribe to such ideologies (Natanson et al., 2025). The establishment of structures like workers' and people's councils to steward tech development and deployment according to collectively agreed social values is a technopolitical buttress against similar attempts to take control of society's future direction. A world reconfigured around degrowth, care and collective agency may seem improbable, but the alternative is the current technocratic trajectory which leads to widespread forms of collapse. We will be a step closer to sustainability when the vast shells of former AI data centres have been returned to common ownership and replaced by fields, playgrounds and community-run workshops for conversion and repair.

Competing Interests The support of the Economic and Social Research Council (ESRC) is gratefully acknowledged. Grant Ref ES/W002639/1.

References

Abraham, Y. (2024). "Order from Amazon": Tech giants storing mass data for Israel's war. *+972 Magazine*. https://www.972mag.com/cloud-israeli-army-gaza-amazon-google-microsoft/

Andreessen, M. (2023). *The techno-optimist manifesto*. https://a16z.com/the-techno-optimist-manifesto/

Arendt, H. (2022). *Eichmann in Jerusalem: A report on the banality of evil*. Penguin Classics. https://www.penguin.co.uk/books/62456/eichmann-in-jerusalem-by-arendt-hannah/9780241552292

Bawden, A. (2024, July 10). NHS urged to prioritise cancer care basics over tech and AI "magic bullets". *The Guardian*. https://www.theguardian.com/society/article/2024/jul/08/nhs-cancer-care-basics-over-tech-ai-magic-bullets

Bolton, P., Kennedy, S., & Hinson, S. (2025). *Fuel poverty in the UK*. UK Parliament. https://commonslibrary.parliament.uk/research-briefings/cbp-8730/

Bommasani, R., Hudson, D. A., Adeli, E., Altman, R., Arora, S., Arx, S. von, Bernstein, M. S., Bohg, J., Bosselut, A., Brunskill, E., Brynjolfsson, E., Buch, S., Card, D., Castellon, R., Chatterji, N., Chen, A., Creel, K., Davis, J. Q., Demszky, D.,... Liang, P. (2022). On the opportunities and risks of foundation models. *arXiv*. https://doi.org/10.48550/arXiv.2108.07258

Bordelon, B. (2023, October 13). How a billionaire-backed network of AI advisers took over Washington. *POLITICO*. https://www.politico.com/news/2023/10/13/open-philanthropy-funding-ai-policy-00121362

Bordelon, B. (2024, March 26). The little-known AI group that got $660 million. *POLITICO*. https://www.politico.com/news/2024/03/25/a-665m-crypto-war-chest-roils-ai-safety-fight-00148621

Bousquet, A. (2016). Ernst Jünger and the problem of nihilism in the age of total war. *Thesis Eleven, 132*(1), 17–38. https://doi.org/10.1177/0725513615619501

Bubeck, S., Chandrasekaran, V., Eldan, R., Gehrke, J., Horvitz, E., Kamar, E., Lee, P., Lee, Y. T., Li, Y., Lundberg, S., Nori, H., Palangi, H., Ribeiro, M. T., & Zhang, Y. (2023). Sparks of artificial general intelligence: Early experiments with GPT-4. *arXiv*. https://doi.org/10.48550/arXiv.2303.12712

Callanan, N., Tan, G., Vossos, T., Arroyo, C., & Milton, I. J. (2024, November 17). Wall Street's elites are piling into a massive AI gamble. *Bloomberg*. https://www.bloomberg.com/news/articles/2024-11-17/ai-s-1-trillion-hysteria-offers-fat-payday-for-wall-street-bankers

Clarke, L. (2023, September 14). How Silicon Valley doomers are shaping Rishi Sunak's AI plans. *POLITICO.* https://www.politico.eu/article/rishi-sunak-artificial-intelligence-pivot-safety-summit-united-kingdom-silicon-valley-effective-altruism/
Clayton, A. (2020, October 27). How eugenics shaped statistics. *Nautilus.* http://nautil.us/issue/92/frontiers/how-eugenics-shaped-statistics
Costea, B., & Amiridis, K. (2017). Ernst Jünger, total mobilisation and the work of war. *Organization, 24*(4), 475–490. https://doi.org/10.1177/1350508417699619
Daly, H. (2024). *Data centres in the context of Ireland's carbon budget*. University College Cork. https://www.ucc.ie/en/epmg/news/data-centres-in-the-context-of-irelands-carbon-budget.html
de la Bellacasa, M. P. (2017). *Matters of care* (3rd ed.). University of Minnesota Press. https://www.upress.umn.edu/9781517900656/matters-of-care/
Duran, G. (2024a, April 26). The tech baron seeking to purge San Francisco of "blues". *The New Republic.* https://newrepublic.com/article/180487/balaji-srinivasan-network-state-plutocrat
Duran, G. (2024b, July 22). Where J.D. Vance gets his weird, terrifying techno-authoritarian ideas. *The New Republic.* https://newrepublic.com/article/183971/jd-vance-weird-terrifying-techno-authoritarian-ideas
Eloundou, T., Manning, S., Mishkin, P., & Rock, D. (2023). GPTs are GPTs: An early look at the labor market impact potential of large language models. *arXiv.* https://doi.org/10.48550/arXiv.2303.10130
Galtung, J. (1969). Violence, peace, and peace research. *Journal of Peace Research, 6*(3), 167–191. https://doi.org/10.1177/002234336900600301
Gebru, T. (2022, November 30). Effective altruism is pushing a dangerous brand of "AI safety". *Wired.* https://www.wired.com/story/effective-altruism-artificial-intelligence-sam-bankman-fried/
Germain, T. (2024). *AI took their jobs. Now they get paid to make it sound human.* BBC Future. https://www.bbc.com/future/article/20240612-the-people-making-ai-sound-more-human
Haider, S. (2017). The darkness at the end of the tunnel: Artificial intelligence and neoreaction. *Viewpoint Magazine.* https://viewpointmag.com/2017/03/28/the-darkness-at-the-end-of-the-tunnel-artificial-intelligence-and-neoreaction/
Hammond, G., & Morris, S. (2022, July 28). West London faces new homes ban as electricity grid hits capacity. *Financial Times.* https://www.ft.com/content/519f701f-6a05-4cf4-bc46-22cf10c7c2c0
Hanna, A., & Park, T. M. (2020). Against scale: Provocations and resistances to scale thinking. *arXiv.* https://doi.org/10.48550/arXiv.2010.08850

Haraway, D. (1988). Situated knowledges: The science question in feminism and the privilege of partial perspective. *Feminist Studies, 14*(3), 575–599. https://doi.org/10.2307/3178066

Hurst, A. (2022, September e). UK data centres at risk of outages this winter. *Information Age*. https://www.information-age.com/uk-data-centres-at-risk-of-outages-this-winter-20169/

Illich, I. (1975). *Tools for Conviviality*. Fontana. https://archive.org/details/illich-conviviality

Jünger, E. (2017). *The worker: Dominion and form* (L. P. Hemming, Ed.; B. Costea, Trans.). Northwestern University Press. https://books.google.co.uk/books?id=KBeHAQAACAAJ

Kinder, T. (2024, November 4). Wall Street frenzy creates $11bn debt market for AI groups buying Nvidia chips. *Financial Times*. https://www.ft.com/content/41bfacb8-4d1e-4f25-bc60-75bf557f1f21

Krizhevsky, A., Sutskever, I., & Hinton, G. E. (2012). ImageNet classification with deep convolutional neural networks. In *Proceedings of the 25th International Conference on Neural Information Processing Systems - Volume 1* (pp. 1097–1105). https://doi.org/10.1145/3065386

Lambert, N., Castricato, L., Werra, L. von, & Havrilla, A. (2022, December 9). Illustrating Reinforcement Learning from Human Feedback (RLHF). *Hugging Face Blog*. https://huggingface.co/blog/rlhf

Loughran, J. (2024, September 12). UK elevates data centres to critical infrastructure status for stronger cyber defences. *Engineering and Technology Magazine*. https://eandt.theiet.org/2024/09/12/uk-elevates-data-centres-critical-infrastructure-status-stronger-cyber-defences

McQuillan, D. (2017). Data science as machinic neoplatonism. *Philosophy & Technology, 31*(2), 253–272. https://doi.org/10.1007/s13347-017-0273-3

McQuillan, D. (2022). *Resisting AI: An anti-fascist approach to artificial intelligence*. Bristol University Press. https://bristoluniversitypress.co.uk/resisting-ai

Meyers, M. (2023). *A degrowth perspective on artificial intelligence – Analysing the appropriateness of machine learning to a degrowth context* [Master's thesis, ETH Zürich]. *ETH Zürich Research Collection*. https://doi.org/10.3929/ethz-b-000622669

Miller, C. (2024, April 25). The Chips Act has been surprisingly successful so far. *Financial Times*. https://www.ft.com/content/26756186-99e5-448f-a451-f5e307b13723

Mirzadeh, I., Alizadeh, K., Shahrokhi, H., Tuzel, O., Bengio, S., & Farajtabar, M. (2024). GSM-symbolic: Understanding the limitations of mathematical reasoning in large language models. *arXiv*. https://doi.org/10.48550/arXiv.2410.05229

Morozov, E. (2023, May). AI: The key battleground for Cold War 2.0? *Le Monde diplomatique*. https://mondediplo.com/2023/05/02china

Narayan, D. (2022). Platform capitalism and cloud infrastructure: Theorizing a hyper-scalable computing regime. *Environment and Planning a: Economy and Space, 54*(5), 911–929. https://doi.org/10.1177/0308518X221094028

Natanson, H., Vynck, G. D., Dwoskin, E., & Douglas-Gabriel, D. (2025, February 6). Elon Musk's DOGE is feeding sensitive federal data into AI to target cuts. *The Washington Post*. https://www.washingtonpost.com/nation/2025/02/06/elon-musk-doge-ai-department-education/

Nelson, R. (2024). On confabulation. *AI Log*. https://www.ailog.blog/p/on-confabulation

Nielsen, M. A. (2015). *Neural networks and deep learning*. http://neuralnetworksanddeeplearning.com

O'Donnell, J. (2024, December 4). OpenAI's new defense contract completes its military pivot. *MIT Technology Review*. https://www.technologyreview.com/2024/12/04/1107897/openais-new-defense-contract-completes-its-military-pivot/

Paullada, A., Raji, I. D., Bender, E. M., Denton, E., & Hanna, A. (2021). Data and its (dis)contents: A survey of dataset development and use in machine learning research. *Patterns*, *2*(11), Article 100336. https://doi.org/10.1016/j.patter.2021.100336

Permacomputing. (2024). *Permacomputing/ principles*. https://permacomputing.net/Principles/

Perrigo, B. (2023, January 18). Exclusive: The $2 per hour workers who made ChatGPT safer. *TIME*. https://time.com/6247678/openai-chatgpt-kenya-workers/

Rahman-Jones, I. (2024, July 3). AI means Google's greenhouse gas emissions up 48% in 5 years. *BBC News*. https://www.bbc.com/news/articles/c51yvz51k2xo

Rathi, A., & Bass, D. (2024, May 15). Microsoft's AI push imperils climate goal as carbon emissions jump 30%. *Yahoo Finance*. https://finance.yahoo.com/news/microsoft-ai-push-imperils-climate-160020868.html

Reiff, B. (2023, November 30). "A mass assassination factory": Inside Israel's calculated bombing of Gaza. *+972 Magazine*. https://www.972mag.com/mass-assassination-factory-israel-calculated-bombing-gaza/

Russakovsky, O., Deng, J., Su, H., Krause, J., Satheesh, S., Ma, S., Huang, Z., Karpathy, A., Khosla, A., Bernstein, M., Berg, A. C., & Fei-Fei, L. (2015). ImageNet large scale visual recognition challenge. *International Journal of Computer Vision, 115*(3), 211–252. https://doi.org/10.1007/s11263-015-0816-y

Schmidt, E. (2024, October 1). *Fireside - Eric Schmidt*. [Video]. YouTube. https://www.youtube.com/watch?v=oC46CzxT750

Sevilla, J., Besiroglu, T., Cottier, B., You, J., Roldán, E., Villalobos, P., & Erdil, E. (2024, August 20). Can AI scaling continue through 2030? *Epoch AI*. https://epoch.ai/blog/can-ai-scaling-continue-through-2030

Sevilla, J., & Roldán, E. (2024, May 28). Training compute of frontier AI models grows by 4–5x per year. *Epoch AI*. https://epoch.ai/blog/training-compute-of-frontier-ai-models-grows-by-4-5x-per-year

Shehabi, A., Smith, S. J., Hubbard, A., Newkirk, A., Lei, N., Siddik, M. A., Holecek, B., Koomey, J. G., Masanet, E. R., & Sartor, D. A. (2024). *2024 United States data center energy usage report*. Lawrence Berkeley National Laboratory. https://eta-publications.lbl.gov/sites/default/files/2024-12/lbnl-2024-united-states-data-center-energy-usage-report.pdf

Smith, A. (2014). Socially useful production. *STEPS Working Paper 58*. https://steps-centre.org/publication/socially-useful-production/

Srinivasan, B. (2022). *The network state: How to start a new country*. Amazon Kindle. https://www.amazon.co.uk/Network-State-How-Start-Country-ebook/dp/B09VPKZR3G

van Toorn, G., & Soldatić, K. (2024). Disablism, racism and the spectre of eugenics in digital welfare. *Journal of Sociology, 60*(3), 523–539. https://doi.org/10.1177/14407833241244828

Torres, É. P. (2021, October 19). Why longtermism is the world's most dangerous secular credo. *Aeon*. https://aeon.co/essays/why-longtermism-is-the-worlds-most-dangerous-secular-credo

Vanderbauwhede, W. (2023). Frugal computing – on the need for low-carbon and sustainable computing and the path towards zero-carbon computing. *arXiv*. https://doi.org/10.48550/arXiv.2303.06642

Vetter, A. (2018). The matrix of convivial technology – assessing technologies for degrowth. *Journal of Cleaner Production, 197*, 1778–1786. https://doi.org/10.1016/j.jclepro.2017.02.195

Voss, A. (2022). *REPORT on artificial intelligence in a digital age A9–0088/2022 European Parliament*. European Parliament. https://www.europarl.europa.eu/doceo/document/A-9-2022-0088_EN.html

Weizenbaum, J. (1984). *Computer power and human reason*. Penguin UK. https://archive.org/details/computerpowerhum0000weiz_v1p2

Williamson, B. (2021, September 8). New biological data and knowledge in education. *code acts in education*. https://codeactsineducation.wordpress.com/2021/09/08/new-biological-data-knowledge-education/

Williamson, B. (2024, August 29). Automated austerity schooling. *code acts in education*. https://codeactsineducation.wordpress.com/2024/08/29/automated-austerity-schooling/

Ye, K. (2020). Silicon Valley and the English language. In *Affecting technologies, machining intelligences*. https://web.archive.org/web/20210325143231/https://book.affecting-technologies.org/silicon-valley-and-the-english-language/
Zeff, M. (2024, March 19). Nvidia wants to replace nurses with AI for $9 an hour. *Gizmodo*. https://gizmodo.com/nvidia-wants-replace-nurses-with-ai-1851347917

CHAPTER 15

More Compute for a Burning Planet? A Scarcity Approach to AI Infrastructures

Fieke Jansen and Niels ten Oever

Introduction

The advent of Generative AI products like ChatGPT or Bard requires a lot of computing power and exacerbates data centres' environmental impact. For example, Microsoft's water consumption for cooling its data centres has dramatically risen from 4.2 million m^3 in 2020 to 6.4 million m^3 in 2022 (Microsoft, 2024). This rise can partly be attributed to the increased computing power and cooling needed to run ChatGPT, which is hosted on Microsoft Azure. Concerns about the climate and ecological impacts of the technology industry predate Generative AI, as witnessed in the growing academic interest in theorising about the materiality and environmental costs of the internet and the cloud (Edwards et al., 2024; Hesmondhalgh, 2021). Scholars have quantified energy consumption and

F. Jansen (✉) · N. Oever
University of Amsterdam, Amsterdam, Netherlands
e-mail: fieke@criticalinfralab.net

N. Oever
e-mail: niels@criticalinfralab.net

A. Mollen et al. (eds.), *AI Infrastructures and Sustainability*, Palgrave Studies in European Communication Research and Education,
https://doi.org/10.1007/978-3-032-09748-4_15

carbon emissions of AI models (Bender et al., 2021; Hao, 2019), water needs to run data centres (Hogan, 2015), and the impact of AI on different earth systems throughout the entire hardware lifecycle (Falk et al., 2024). Falk et al. (2024) show how environmental harms are disproportionately felt in the Global South, while economic benefits are primarily concentrated in the West. In this chapter, we build on this body of work that foregrounds the unsustainable nature of AI to explore how the governance of its infrastructures needs to be reconfigured for society to stay within the planetary boundaries. We are particularly interested in AI infrastructure, as like all other infrastructures, data centres shape the distribution of social and economic activity in a certain way (Bowker & Star, 2008), centralising power in the hands of a few companies and facilitating the free flow of capital while externalising social and environmental costs to society.

In the current AI landscape, environmental concerns occupy a marginal position in policy debates. When governance frameworks address AI's environmental harms, they are narrow in scope, focusing on reducing carbon emissions and energy use, and not the neoliberal calculus of extraction and commodification that underpins this industry, which is inherently at odds with ecological integrity and environmental justice. To explore the reconfiguration of AI governance, we move beyond a critique of what is, "the sum of all environmental harms associated with AI infrastructures" and "the limits of current governance frameworks", to what could be, emancipatory alternatives that go beyond the status quo, by asking experts to design AI infrastructures in scarcity. In our research, we used the term scarcity to counterpose the dominant values that underpin AI development, that of unbridled growth and abundance of resources, in the race for technological hegemony. By combining participatory action research with the method of defamiliarisation in the context of Europe, we show that when experts centre scarcity in governance approaches to AI, the demands change from narrow sustainability efforts to the desire to structurally reconfigure the technology industry. Here, the state is seen as the primary power holder that can operate on the scale needed to limit the environmental externalities of neoliberalism and provide public interest solutions. This imagined state is a normative answer to the status quo of political governance in European democracies. A critique on the current market-state entanglements and interstate competition for AI hegemony, which we observed in full force while participating in the 2025 AI Action

Summit in Paris, where political and industrial leaders pushed for investment in and deregulation of the AI industry, and public interest was reduced to open source.

In this chapter, we use the term Europe to refer to the European project, and while the political and economic integration among European countries is not without strife, the AI strategy of the EU remains uncontested. We will first lay out recent academic debates on infrastructures, materiality, and technology governance, then introduce our methods. Next, we will present our findings and conclude with a discussion on the state's role in AI infrastructure governance. Our core argument is that in re-imagining AI infrastructure governance, participants articulate the need for a completely different state. This imagined state echoes a certain nostalgia for the Western European welfare state, where citizens trust in the competency of the state to ensure that social, environmental, and human rights are protected. This imagined state opposes the state and the market entanglements of contemporary statecraft and is seen as an actor that can act at scale and operate from a rational and democratically established rule-based order to prioritise societal wellbeing over capital accumulation and securitisation.

Infrastructure, Power, and the Shaping of Sustainability Approaches

This chapter takes an infrastructural perspective on the relationship between AI, governance, and the environment. Infrastructure studies allow scholars to engage with the materiality of infrastructure, and move beyond the cultural imagination of AI as immaterial and the carbon tunnel of sustainable AI to account for its operational and embodied harms. The term operational harms captures pollution and resource consumption related to the running of AI infrastructure, particularly data centres, and the term embodied harms is used to account for harms in the mining, manufacturing, transport, and disposal of hardware (Chen & Burrington, 2023; Maphosa et al., 2023; Sutherland, 2022). The focus on infrastructure as an object for AI governance builds on Balayn and Gürses's (2024) argument that contemporary AI governance regimes are inadequate as they focus on services and products and not the engineering environments that produce them. AI-based services, they argue, are likely produced and delivered through computational infrastructures, made up of agile production environments, clouds, and end devices, owned by a few companies (Balayn & Gürses, 2024). Governing AI to account for environmental harms should therefore not look at the individual model, but the infrastructures that enable this kind of computation. Therefore, we locate the study of AI governance in infrastructure studies, specifically in two key debates in the field: how power is embedded and enacted through infrastructure (ten Oever, 2023) and how engaging with the materiality of media brings environmental questions into a relational understanding of digital infrastructures (Edwards et al., 2024). Integrating environmental considerations into debates on AI infrastructure allows us to engage with questions of power, shed light on the limits of contemporary AI governance approaches, and develop emancipatory futures.

Infrastructure scholars started engaging with questions of power by acknowledging that large-scale systems shape the distribution of social and economic activity by enabling certain practices and restricting others (Bowker & Star, 2008). As such, this chapter starts from the observation that infrastructures are inherently political. They are historically determined and embed and enact particular economic and political interests, making it pertinent to understand who has the power to shape infrastructures, under what conditions, for which purpose, and at what cost. Scholars remind us that infrastructures do not materialise out of nowhere; they are the result of local practices influenced by the norms, values, and practices set by global systems (Brodie & Velkova, 2021; Galloway, 2012; Hesmondhalgh, 2021). In a case study on Ericsson's Vaudreuil-Dorion data centre, Brodie and Velkova (2021) observe that digital infrastructures carry the promise of economic growth and prosperity, which entices the state to create a favourable tax, development, and political climate to attract this industry. However, the economic temporality of the digital, that of financial speculation, and changing corporate strategy, make infrastructures soft, malleable, and disposable. The Vaudreuil-Dorion data centre site and many others (Lehuedé, 2021; Rone, 2024) remind us that digital infrastructure is highly speculative real estate used for financial speculation and capital accumulation.

The political economy of these infrastructures foregrounds that the governance of these industrial sites is shaped through a shared belief system (Maxigas & ten Oever, 2023; ten Oever, 2023), the neoliberal epoch of open market and free flow of capital combined with the belief that progress and economic growth are dependent on technological innovation and dominance. Globally, this is fuelling a geopolitical race for hegemony, where AI is the latest incarnation of this interstate competition. Locally, data centres have become contested infrastructural sites, making conflict between local interest and global norms and values visible. At the local level, citizens feel excluded from the decision-making process around infrastructure (Rone, 2024), local social and economic activity lose out while global technology companies are given preferential access to the electricity grid (Velkova, 2024), and pollution and waste from manufacturing and discarding of hardware accumulates largely in the Global South hidden out of view of those in power (Chen & Burrington, 2023; Maphosa et al., 2023). Critical media scholars argue that AI will perpetuate and intensify these dynamics as it requires significant computing power, data, and expert knowledge, further increasing global dependency on a few technology companies who are building resource-intensive computational infrastructures. In this chapter, we will contribute to these debates on infrastructure and power by making familiar objects unfamiliar, decentring the dominant worldview in the analysis of data centres, to argue that in Europe, it is not market power that people oppose but the state-market entanglements.

Digital infrastructures have long been represented as immaterial in the cultural imagination (Ensmenger, 2021; Frenzel, 2023; Starosielski, 2015), erasing the connection between their environmental and human costs and placing them outside the realm of traditional governance mechanisms. In the turn to infrastructure, a growing body of media studies scholarship has established that computing infrastructures are very much material and come with a range of environmental harm. Data centres gobble up a significant amount of water and electricity (Hogan, 2015; Velkova, 2024), are based on the exploitation of natural and human resources (Starosielski & Walker, 2016), and have significant pollution associated with the mining, manufacturing, transport, disposal of hardware (Bridges, 2023), and carbon footprint with its operations (Pasek et al., 2023). In response to discussions on the material impact of its infrastructure, the technology industry has positioned the internet, cloud, and AI as indispensable to social and economic wellbeing and argues that while it has a direct negative impact on the environment, it has and will significantly contribute to the decarbonisation of other industries (Jansen, 2025; Sridharan, 2025). This positioning drives a narrow sustainability agenda that mobilizes discourses of efficiency to align environmental goals with economic imperatives (Sridharan, 2025). A proposition which finds political traction with the European Commission and some of its member states, who want to ensure that Europe does not lose out in the race for AI hegemony and are in search of quick sustainability fixes that do not set limits on their economies. Furthermore, the industry downplays its environmental impact by emphasising that its energy consumption has been moderate in comparison to the growth of computing power (Edwards et al., 2024; Jansen, 2025). The flawed logic that sustainability through efficiency gains is possible in a capitalist system (Alcott, 2005) reinforces the perception of technological exceptionalism. These dynamics reinforce the idea that the technology industry operates outside the realm of traditional governance mechanisms.

Ensmenger argues that "the computer industry has largely succeeded in declaring itself outside of this history, and therefore independent of the political, social, and environmental controls that have been developed to constrain and mediate industrialization" (Ensmenger, 2021, p. 7). These dynamics matter in discussions around the climate crisis and ecological degradation, as the self-declaration of the independence of cyberspace (Barlow, 1996) permeated a belief that the state had no sovereignty over new technological developments and that technology companies and engineers are the primary power-holders, making corporations responsible for how we define sustainability and understand environmental wellbeing. While this notion of an absent state is historically incorrect—the state has intrinsically been involved in the development of the internet, the cloud, and now AI through centuries of public policy (Holt, 2024), public investments (Mazzucato, 2011), and more recently through deregulation and liberalisation (Rone, 2024)—it is local struggle against the arrival and expansion of data centres (Hogan, 2015; Lehuedé, 2021; Rone, 2024) that demands the state to act. In the Dutch context, protests against the development of hyperscale data centres operated by Big Tech companies were directed at the state. Citizens contested allocation of water and renewable energy sources to data centres over the needs of households and other industries and opposed the political vacuum in which citizen voices were not heard (Jansen, 2022; Rone, 2024). In response to the protest, Meta halted its plans to build in the village of Zeewolde, a development which is still considered a local win over global capital, but, in reality, displaced the problem to other territories as it did not stop data centre construction, it merely halted it in the Netherlands. The aftermath of Zeewolde made us interested in re-imagining AI infrastructure governance beyond conflict around individual data centres to address the economic and political relations that are embedded and enacted through infrastructures. Designing in scarcity is our attempt to challenge the economic logic of the Big Tech industry, which can be characterised as predatory capitalism, where AI is the latest incarnation in a long line of interstate competition and capital accumulation.

Methods

To explore governance approaches that keep AI developments within planetary boundaries, we engaged in a thematic analysis to capture the values, principles, and actors that experts believe should ensure sustainable AI infrastructures by combining participatory action research with the methods of defamiliarisation. Participatory action research is in line with the objective of critical social science, which views the role of academia to expose and explain power structures and relationships to alleviate unnecessary and unwanted suffering (Fay, 1987). This method allows for the co-creation of knowledge on a specific topic through collaborative brainstorming, conversation, and ideation to identify pathways for social change (Greenwood & Levin, 2007; Grønhaug & Olson, 1999). Often used to gain insight into the experiences and needs of impacted communities, we use this method to have academics, civil society organisations, and policymakers jointly try to understand the world, learn together, and articulate shared demands to keep AI developments within planetary boundaries. Participatory action research is layered with the method of defamiliarisation, which originates from literary and critical theory. An approach used to make the familiar unfamiliar and challenge everyday automated perceptions about an object or situation (Bell et al., 2005; Kaomea, 2003). Specifically, the method of critical defamiliarisation, which juxtaposes what could be against what is, aims to allow participants to bring new normative questions to the fore and "search for emancipatory alternatives to transcend the status quo" (Gunderson, 2020: 89). We applied defamiliarisation to the participatory action workshop by asking participants to design AI infrastructure in scarcity. This act of defamiliarisation opens up space to move beyond a critique that is the sum of all environmental harms associated with AI infrastructures to a more conscious articulation of the underlying historically, geographically, and culturally determined worldviews that shape their relationship to data centres and society and imagine different futures.

The sample for this chapter is three participatory action research workshops with a total of 80 participants. These workshops are part of a larger and ongoing research project into the governance of data centres in Europe. The twin transition, including the AI act, local protests against data centre development in the Netherlands, Ireland, and Spain, soaring energy prices since Russia's full-scale invasion of Ukraine in 2022, and congestion in electricity networks, makes Europe an interesting region to study the governance of AI infrastructures. The first workshop took place in July 2023 as part of a week-long retreat organised by the critical infrastructure lab, Green Web Foundation, and Share Foundation (Jansen et al., 2023). The retreat brought together 25 European academics and civil society organisers interested in infrastructure governance. The second workshop took place at Privacy Camp, in January 2024, and brought together academics, civil society organisers, and policymakers who actively engage in the Brussels policy space and are interested in digital rights issues (Jansen & Cath, 2024). There were three parallel tracks and around 40 people joined our workshop *Down with Data Centres; developing critical policy for environmentally sustainable tech in Europe*. The third workshop, *Rethinking Data Centers in the Age of Scarcity*, was a dedicated event organised at the University of Amsterdam, that brought together 16 academics, civil society practitioners, and policymakers from Western Europe working on and interested in data centre governance. All participants were either from Europe or deeply familiar with the policy landscape of Europe.

Each workshop was tailored to the specific location and group; one started with an outdoor exercise and another with a detailed mapping of social and environmental harms of internet infrastructures. Still, the insights of the workshops are comparable as the participants had a similar profile, all interested in digital rights and the environment, and the workshops had a similar approach, structure, and guiding question, "How can we govern data centres in scarcity?" We designed and facilitated the workshops. Each workshop started with an exercise aimed at identifying the knowledge level of the participants and providing everyone with the opportunity to speak and share their expertise. This was followed by a brief level-setting part, where experts, including one of the authors, would provide insights on harms associated with data centres and frameworks to situate these harms in broader environmental, economic, and political developments. The act of defamiliarisation related to our main research question, "How do we keep infrastructural developments within planetary boundaries?" or, said differently, "How can we design data centre governance in scarcity?" We closed each workshop by briefly summarising the key points made on designing in scarcity and asked if participants had something to add as a way to validate our findings. When participants struggled to start their brainstorming on "designing in scarcity", we introduced the case of Meta's data centre in the village of Zeewolde and asked how they would distribute the finite amount of renewable energy, would they allocate it to a hyperscale data centre that will be the backbone of the metaverse or to a hospital or a local community. This line of questioning was enough to start a lively discussion. The workshop discussions were documented through self-documentation, where participants took notes of the conversation on flip-charts, and by us taking notes of each sub-group report on how they would design in scarcity.

Findings: Emancipatory AI Infrastructure Governance Futures

The overwhelming feeling that emerged from the workshops is that there are no sustainable AI infrastructures. The technology industry is viewed as the driver of unbridled growth of the AI market while externalising its environment and social cost upon society under a vague promise of progress. In this section, we analyse the emancipatory futures proposed in the workshop to show how designing in scarcity is about governance. Participants' sustainability demands target the state as a power holder, oppose the current focus on efficiency gains by the market, object to the neoliberal political calculus governing AI infrastructures, and demand public interest solutions. This is at odds with contemporary AI governance approaches, which see the market as the main power-holder that should ensure environmental considerations in AI infrastructures. These findings provide insights into what is missing from contemporary AI governance approaches: a European state that wields its economic and technological statecraft to ensure sustainable futures.

Public Interest to Transcend Contemporary Infrastructural Politics

Participants propose different ways to design in scarcity, from small do-it-yourself solutions to structural reconfigurations of the technology industry. What binds these solutions is that they all prioritise social and environmental wellbeing in AI infrastructure governance over that of markets, accumulation of capital, and geopolitical influence—a shift which draws attention to contemporary governance deficits that have led to the concentration of power and wealth in the hands of a few technology companies, and in its wake a supply chain of injustice, exploitation, and pollution. We found that words like "public interest" and, to a lesser extent, "social justice" and "environmental justice" were used to refer to the values which are considered to align with emancipatory governance processes. Public interest was included in demands like "invest in public interest infrastructure" or "computing for the public interest". Participants did not define "the public interest", they assumed that there is a shared understanding of what is meant by it. Other research observed a similar trend, where public interest is used as a loosely defined concept to describe the role of the state in society vis-à-vis the market. Maxigas describes it as an approach that goes beyond economic logic, "the role of the state is to shape markets towards outcomes that serve the public interest rather than the narrow objectives of capital accumulation" (Maxigas, 2024). By centring public interest in AI infrastructure governance, participants express a desire for a state that prioritises societal wellbeing over capital accumulation. More specifically, while public interest concerns in the governance of technology have traditionally been understood in as privacy, access to knowledge, and freedom of expression (DeNardis, 2014), in the context of AI infrastructures should also include social and economic rights, such as public safety, health, or access to electricity. Departing from public interest helped participants formulate demands that transcend the status quo.

The limitation of the public interest concept is that it assumes that when state actors protect the common good, it will lead to equal access and rights in society. In contrast, the term social justice describes the desire to overcome historically determined inequalities, in terms of access and redistribution of computing power. Social justice concerns were surfaced by participants through questions such as, "How much compute is needed?" or "What is the bare minimum of compute needed for everyone to participate in the digital society?" or "Who gets harmed and who benefits?" This acknowledges that society is stratified and power and resources are distributed unequally, where equity, non-discrimination, and inclusion are achieved through the dismantling of oppressive structures. The concept of environmental justice was used when acknowledging pollution, oppression, and harm in the supply chains of AI hardware. The term emphasises that the climate and biodiversity crises are fundamentally unjust, communities and land that are most impacted by these crises have contributed the least to them, and their voices are not included in sustainability governance processes (Kazansky et al., 2022). The emphasis on public interest over social or climate justice underlines the participants' positioning of AI infrastructure governance within the framework of Western liberal democracies, where the "rational" state ensures the market also serves the public interest. The absence of abolitionist or more militant approaches to designing in scarcity suggests that participants do not imagine a future without AI infrastructures, emancipatory futures fit within the scope of the liberal rules-based order, and justice approaches relate more to questions of redistribution and access and are less about dismantling colonial, extractive, and exclusionary structures.

Limiting Unnecessary AI

Propositions for structurally reconfiguring the technology industry ranged from sufficient computing, public infrastructure, limiting claims on the electricity grid, and data waste. Two central threads that emerge from these solutions are: the desire to categorise AI—not on its computational techniques but on its uses or contribution to the public interest—and the need to understand AI infrastructure in relation to the broader ecosystem. We'll first discuss the desire for categorisation. Suchman (2023: 1) argued that the question "Just what are we talking about when we talk about 'AI'?" is needed to allow scholars to demystify AI and interrogate relevant genealogies, material practices, and politics. Similarly, when discussing sufficient computing, public infrastructure, and data waste, participants raised a comparable question, though their interest did not lie in differentiating between the computational techniques but in categorising their uses. Participants believed that designing in scarcity requires a governance practice that limits the expansion of AI infrastructures and prioritises public interest in existing computing capacity. To be able to differentiate between public and commercial interest, one "needs to know what compute is used for? Start classifying the purpose of AI; is it health care, education, military, finances, etc." (Workshop 3 2024). The idea is that if we can articulate what are desirable and undesirable uses of AI infrastructures, we can introduce computation taxes that incentivise public interest use and discourage unwanted or commercial uses. Or introduce a public use mandate on all AI infrastructures, meaning that a large percentage of the servers have to be allocated to the public interest (Workshop 1 2023; Workshop 2 2024). Important to recognise is that here desirable use relates to limiting and redistributing computing power and not to the social impacts, such as perpetuating stereotypes and reinforcing social inequality, that can emerge when AI models are introduced into public services like health care.

The discussions around energy use, the electricity grid, and Europe's sustainability objectives foregrounded the need to situate AI infrastructures in their broader ecosystem. Participants emphasise that currently AI infrastructures drive up the total volume of energy consumed by the tech industry (Jansen & Thorne, 2024) through actual and fictive claims on grid capacity (Velkova, 2024), which gets in the way of the decarbonisation of society. Their claim on renewable energy sources keeps other sectors dependent on fossil fuels and the practice of air-bookings reserves higher amounts of the electricity grid's capacity than needed (Velkova, 2024), pushing a narrative that there is a need for additional capacity. These dynamics make "AI infrastructure management an integral dilemma in our energy transition" (workshop 3). A low-hanging emancipatory future relates the real-time fossil fuel mix used for AI, where participants want the tech industry to move to matching renewable energy supply and demand locally rather than through green energy certificates. More fundamentally, participants believe that when designing in scarcity, an ecosystem approach allows us to prioritise energy allocation in accordance with social needs and Europe's sustainability objectives and not market demand. This shifts the discussion away from making AI infrastructures sustainable to ensuring a sustainable society that stays within planetary boundaries. AI infrastructures could potentially play a role in the energy transition, but not at all costs.

Re-Imagining the Role of the State in AI Infrastructure Governance

Many of the solutions formulated in the workshops speak to the role of the state in AI infrastructure governance. There are three ways in which participants conceptualised the role of the state: as a regulator, facilitator of different governance approaches, and an investor. At Privacy Camp, participants emphasised the regulatory role of the state, "we do not need to start from scratch, but we need to start enforcing existing regulation" (Workshop 2 2024). This emphasis on enforcement stems from civil society's frustration at the tsunami of regulations adopted by the von der Leyen Commission that lack effective implementation and enforcement. Looking towards the future, some participants suggested the creation of a "compute police", a state entity that could enforce prioritisation of public interest within a framework of sufficiency. This policing proposition was shot down almost immediately due to privacy and surveillance concerns. The second role assigned to the state was facilitator of different governance approaches. Bottom-up policymaking is needed to align European strategy with the reality of and respond to the challenges of communities and local governments, as municipalities are considered to be on the frontline navigating the tension between market interests, social needs, environmental harms, and public opinion. Top-down governance, through mechanisms like the OECD, is needed as participants believe that no single state can control the global technology industry nor develop and enforce a life cycle assessment (LCA) standard to promote transparency and accountability in the mining, production, and use of critical raw materials for AI hardware. The last role was that of the state as an investor. In the Montenegro workshop, participants demanded that "10% of Horizon Europe funding should go to post-silicon computing and community experimentation". This demand builds on Mazzucato's (2011) notion of the entrepreneurial state, where governments have and will continue to play a crucial role in funding research and innovation in new technologies. Participants felt that when the state invests in European AI, a significant part of this research and development funding should be allocated to new and more environmentally friendly types of computing. In addition, at the university workshop, participants argued that the state should invest in its own capacity to experiment with sufficient computing. The state is not merely a regulator, but also a consumer of AI infrastructures, and as such, it can be a testbed for sustainable innovation.

Conclusion: Demanding a Different State

The workshops highlighted a range of emancipatory futures that centre public interest in AI infrastructure governance over the narrow objective of capital accumulation and see the state as a primary power-holder to achieve this. State intervention is of course not the only solution or approach to designing in scarcity, small scale and community approaches were proposed in the workshop, but these did not get traction in the discussions. Confronted with contemporary global power constellations, in which the tech industry and countries are in a race to gain AI hegemony (Bareis & Katzenbach, 2022), people tend to attribute power and agency to those actors they believe can act on a certain scale. In the

Western European context, this is the state and not citizens, users, nor communities. In the process of demanding the state to take up responsibility in AI infrastructure governance, participants articulate the need for a completely different state. This imagined state echoes a certain nostalgia to the Western European welfare state, where the state provided for its citizens and in turn was trusted to be a competent entity that wields its power to ensure that social, economic, and human rights are protected. The attributes ascribed to this imagined state are that it can act at scale, operates from a rational and democratically established rule-based order, and prioritises societal wellbeing over capital accumulation. Societal wellbeing in relation to AI infrastructures is conceptualised as limits and redistribution of computing power, opposing the market-state entanglements that are central in contemporary statecraft. The role of the state in establishing and perpetuating colonial, extractive, and exclusionary structures, that are embedded and enacted through infrastructures, is left unaddressed.

The imagined states can be understood as a critique of the current market-state entanglements and interstate competition for AI hegemony. At present, the tech industry is capitalising on the new moment of geopolitical tension, a consequence of China as the rising hegemon and the United States and Europe as waning hegemons, where technologies such as AI and quantum computing are projected as the main battlegrounds of global competition and a new source for infinite growth (Bareis & Katzenbach, 2022). The techsolutionist imaginaries, where AI is hyped as the solution to societal and environmental problems, while ignoring its direct and immediate harms, masks the transition from neoliberal to predatory capitalism. In Europe, this transition is characterised by an understanding that infinite growth in the Global West is not possible anymore. From this vantage point, global competition becomes a zero-sum game where the development of one comes at the decline of another. The geopolitical anxiety, where states fear losing out to other states, manipulates the state to invest in technological development, promote strategic autonomy by on-shoring the exploitation of nature, to reduce the geopolitical dependency on China (Riofrancos, 2023), and further deregulate the rules and restrictions on the tech industry. Industry leaders are feeding on this global anxiety to push their AI growth agenda, which comes at the expense of society and nature, and suggest the government should bet on AI to solve these problems in the future (Solnit, 2024).

Instead of a wartime economy, where all economic production and natural extraction are coordinated in the interest of interstate economic competition, the emancipatory futures demanded the state to intervene to prevent further deterioration of our lives and environments. Here, the imagined state wields its might, through regulation, investment, and soft power, to prioritise the welfare of its citizens and the environment. In this future, economic and technological statecraft are directed at minimising global warming, ecological deterioration, and rising societal differences, and actively countering the geopolitical competition to the bottom and the accumulation of capital in the hands of the few through an ever-further militarised economy (Galeotti, 2022). Through the articulation of the imagined state, participants offer a fundamental critique of Europe's contemporary political rationalities and demand a radical shift in the state's ideology. Specifically, the European Union's quest for Europe to become a global leader in AI at all costs (European Commission, 2025) is at odds with the proposed public interest approach. In contrast, participants see the social and environmental crises as the real problem of our times, not the ability to cram more processor power on smaller wafers, more storage, or more computing. The current trend towards strategic autonomy could provide an opportunity more than a threat, as it allows Europe to take a step back from the neoliberal growth paradigm and centre on the welfare and wellbeing of people and the planet, as well as the role technologies and regulations play in realising them.

Acknowledgements We thank the participants of our workshops for brainstorming and thinking with us.

Competing Interests The Ford Foundation and the Internet Society Foundation supported research for this chapter.

References

Alcott, B. (2005). Jevons' paradox. *Ecological Economics, 54*(1), 9–21. https://doi.org/10.1016/j.ecolecon.2005.03.020

Balayn, A., & Gürses, S. (2024). *Misguided: AI regulation needs a shift in focus.* Internet Policy Review. https://policyreview.info/articles/news/misguided-ai-regulation-needs-shift/1796

Bareis, J., & Katzenbach, C. (2022). Talking AI into being: The narratives and imaginaries of national AI strategies and their performative politics. *Science,*

Technology, & Human Values, 47(5), 855–881. https://doi.org/10.1177/01622439211030007
Barlow, J. P. (1996). A declaration of the independence of cyberspace. *Electronic Frontier Foundation*. Retrieved January 5, 2025, from https://www.eff.org/cyberspace-independence
Bell, G., Blythe, M., & Sengers, P. (2005). Making by making strange: Defamiliarization and the design of domestic technologies. *ACM Transactions on Computer-Human Interaction, 12*(2), 149–173. https://doi.org/10.1145/1067860.1067862
Bender, E. M., Gebru, T., McMillan-Major, A., & Shmitchell, S. (2021). On the dangers of stochastic parrots: Can language models be too big? 🦜. *Proceedings of the 2021 ACM conference on fairness, accountability, and transparency*, 610–623. https://doi.org/10.1145/3442188.3445922
Bowker, G. C., & Star, S. L. (2008). *Sorting things out: Classification and its consequences* (1st paperback ed., 8th print). MIT Press.
Bridges, L. (2023). *Geographies of digital wasting*. Retrieved December 6, 2024, from https://www.geographiesofdigitalwasting.com/
Brodie, P., & Velkova, J. (2021). Cloud ruins: Ericsson's Vaudreuil-Dorion data centre and infrastructural abandonment. *Information, Communication & Society, 24*(6), 869–885. https://doi.org/10.1080/1369118X.2021.1909099
Chen, A., & Burrington, I. (2023). *Manufacturing: The semiconductor is an accretion of place*. Geographies of Wasting. https://www.geographiesofdigitalwasting.com/manufacturing-2
DeNardis, L. (2014). *The global war for internet governance*. Yale University Press.
Edwards, D., Cooper, Z. G. T., & Hogan, M. (2024). The making of critical data center studies. *Convergence*, 1–18. https://doi.org/10.1177/13548565231224157
Ensmenger, N. (2021). The cloud is a factory. In T. S. Mullaney, B. Peters, M. Hicks, & K. Philip (Eds.), *Your computer is on fire* (pp. 29–50). The MIT Press. https://doi.org/10.7551/mitpress/10993.003.0005
European Commission. (2025, April 9). *Commission sets course for Europe's AI leadership with an ambitious AI continent action plan*. European Commission. https://ec.europa.eu/commission/presscorner/detail/en/ip_25_1013
Falk, S., Van Wynsberghe, A., & Biber-Freudenberger, L. (2024). The attribution problem of a seemingly intangible industry. *Environmental Challenges, 16*, Article 101003. https://doi.org/10.1016/j.envc.2024.101003
Fay, B. (1987). *Critical social science: Liberation and its limits*. Polity Press.
Frenzel, J. (2023). Data rush: How 'green' computing is opening up a new frontier in Arctic Norway. In D. White, J. Peck, & C. Goldie (Eds.), *Disturbed*

ecologies: Photography, geopolitics, and the Northern landscape in the era of environmental crisis. transcript Verlag.

Galeotti, M. (2022). *The weaponisation of everything: A field guide to the new way of war.* Yale University Press.

Galloway, A. R. (2012). *The interface effect*. Polity Press.

Greenwood, D. J., & Levin, M. (2007). *Introduction to action research: Social research for social change.* Sage London

Grønhaug, K., & Olson, O. (1999). Action research and knowledge creation: Merits and challenges. *Qualitative Market Research: An International Journal, 2*(1), 6–14. https://doi.org/10.1108/13522759910251891

Gunderson, T. (2020). *Making the familiar strange: Sociology contra reification.* Routledge. https://www-taylorfrancis-com.proxy.uba.uva.nl/reader/download/2a963f06-3a59-4f8f-aed8-12e2320e8e3a/chapter/pdf?context=ubx

Hao, K. (2019, June 6). Training a single AI model can emit as much carbon as five cars in their lifetimes. *MIT Technology Review.* https://www.technologyreview.com/2019/06/06/239031/training-a-single-ai-model-can-emit-as-much-carbon-as-five-cars-in-their-lifetimes/

Hesmondhalgh, D. (2021). The infrastructural turn in media and internet research. In P. McDonald (Ed.), *The Routledge companion to media industries* (1st ed.). Routledge. https://doi.org/10.4324/9780429275340

Hogan, M. (2015). Data flows and water woes: The Utah data center. *Big Data & Society, 2*(2), Article 205395171559242. https://doi.org/10.1177/2053951715592429

Holt, J. (2024). *Cloud policy a history of regulating pipelines platforms and data.* The MIT Press.

Jansen, F. (2022, March 7). The politics of data centers. *Green Web Foundation.* https://www.thegreenwebfoundation.org/news/the-politics-of-data-centers/

Jansen, F. (2025). *A scalar mismatch: Sustainability approaches in an internet infrastructural ideology of infinite growth and abundance* [Unpublished manuscript].

Jansen, F., & Cath, C. (2024). *Down with data centres: Developing critical policy.* Critical infrastructure lab. https://doi.org/10.5281/ZENODO.11059837

Jansen, F., ten Oever, N., & Maxigas. (2023). *Exploring the public interest in media infrastructures through the lenses of geopolitics, standards, and the environment: Workshop report October 6th 2023.* Critical Infrastructure Lab. https://doi.org/10.5281/zenodo.10002322

Jansen, F., & Thorne, M. (2024). Predatory delay and other myths of "sustainable AI." In F. Kaltheuner, L. Saari, A. Kak, & S. Myers West (Eds.), *Redirecting Europe's AI industrial policy: From competitiveness to public interest.* https://ainowinstitute.org/publication/predatory-delay-and-other-myths-of-sustainable-ai

Kaomea, J. (2003). Reading erasures and making the familiar strange: Defamiliarizing methods for research in formerly colonized and historically oppressed communities. *Educational Researcher, 32*(2), 14–23. https://doi.org/10.3102/0013189X032002014

Kazansky, B., Karak, M., Perosa, T., Tsui, Q., & Baker, S. (2022). *At the confluence of digital rights and climate & environmental justice: A landscape review.* The Engine Room. https://engn.it/climatejusticedigitalrights

Lehuedé, S. (2021). *Governing data in modernity/coloniality: Astronomy data in the Atacama Desert and the struggle for collective autonomy. Dissertation, London School of Economics.* https://etheses.lse.ac.uk/4321/

Maphosa, V., Mangwana, J., Macherera, M., & Zezai, D. (2023). *Discard: Advocating for e-waste management in Zimbabwe.* Geographies of Wasting. https://www.geographiesofdigitalwasting.com/discard-2

Maxigas. (2024). *Network paradigms and infrastructural ideologies: Standards and protocols in a geopolitical context.* Critical Infrastructure Lab. https://doi.org/10.5281/zenodo.10912418

Maxigas, & ten Oever, N. (2023). Geopolitics in the infrastructural ideology of 5G. *Global Media and China, 8*(3), 271–288. https://doi.org/10.1177/20594364231193950

Mazzucato, M. (2011). The entrepreneurial state. *Soundings, Winter,* (49), 131–142. https://doi.org/10.3898/136266211798411183

Microsoft. (2024). *2024 Environmental sustainability report.* Microsoft. https://cdn-dynmedia-1.microsoft.com/is/content/microsoftcorp/microsoft/msc/documents/presentations/CSR/Microsoft-2024-Environmental-Sustainability-Report.pdf

Pasek, A., Vaughan, H., & Starosielski, N. (2023). The world wide web of carbon: Toward a relational footprinting of information and communications technology's climate impacts. *Big Data & Society, 10*(1). https://doi.org/10.1177/20539517231158994

Riofrancos, T. (2023). The security–Sustainability nexus: Lithium onshoring in the Global North. *Global Environmental Politics, 23*(1), 20–41. https://doi.org/10.1162/glep_a_00668

Rone, J. (2024). The shape of the cloud: Contesting date centre construction in North Holland. *New Media & Society, 26*(10), 5999–6018. https://doi.org/10.1177/14614448221145928

Solnit, R. (2024, October 16). Is it worse to have no climate solutions—or to have them but refuse to use them? *The Guardian.* https://www.theguardian.com/commentisfree/2024/oct/16/climate-crisis-technology-ai

Sridharan, H. (2025). "Sustainable" cloud computing: Fantasies and futures of Microsoft Azure's [Unpublished manuscript]. In A. Mollen, S. Kannengießer,

J. Velkova, & F. Jansen (Eds.), *AI infrastructures and sustainability—Expanding perspectives on automation, communication and media*. Springer Nature.

Starosielski, N. (2015). *The undersea network*. Duke University Press. https://books.google.com/books?hl=en&lr=&id=NtGqCAAAQBAJ&oi=fnd&pg=PT7&dq=starosielski+2015+undersea+network&ots=Ih7SFZCcU1&sig=fGsWo2o0RbnIYEYH4ksEBvI_FDY

Starosielski, N., & Walker, J. (Eds.). (2016). *Sustainable media: Critical approaches to media and environment* (1st ed.). Routledge.

Suchman, L. (2023). The uncontroversial 'thingness' of AI. *Big Data & Society, 10*(2). https://doi.org/10.1177/20539517231206794

Sutherland, B. (2022, June 21). Strategies for degrowth computing. *Eighth Workshop on Computing within Limits 2022*. https://doi.org/10.21428/bf6fb269.04676652

ten Oever, N. (2023). 5G and the notion of network ideology, or: The limitations of sociotechnical imaginaries. *Telecommunications Policy, 47*(5), Article 102442. https://doi.org/10.1016/j.telpol.2022.102442

Velkova, J. (2024, February 19). Dismantling public values, one data center at the time. *University of Helsinki*. https://www.helsinki.fi/en/researchgroups/reimagining-public-values-in-algorithmic-futures/whats-new/dismantling-public-values-one-data-center-at-the-time

CHAPTER 16

The Good Infrastructure: Digital Futures, Values and Friction

Johanna Sefyrin and Julia Velkova

Introduction

For more than a decade, scholars have been exploring the manifold harms and societal ruptures introduced by algorithmic systems. Exclusion through bureaucratic systems of identification and credit scoring (Singh, 2023), the dehumanization of online content moderation work (Roberts, 2019; Ruckenstein & Turunen, 2020), digital securitization, surveillance, care and control (Winter & Hermansson, 2025; Zakharova et al., 2024) and datafied racialization (Amaro, 2022; Benjamin, 2019; D'Ignazio & Klein, 2023; van Schie, 2023) are just some of the many issues that scholars have been raising. These issues have highlighted how algorithmic systems compromise public values of inclusivity, diversity, justice and fairness while they transform the social fabric of digitally mediated life.

J. Sefyrin (✉) · J. Velkova
Linköping University, Linköping, Sweden
e-mail: johanna.sefyrin@liu.se

J. Velkova
e-mail: julia.velkova@liu.se

A. Mollen et al. (eds.), *AI Infrastructures and Sustainability*, Palgrave Studies in European Communication Research and Education,
https://doi.org/10.1007/978-3-032-09748-4_16

Increasingly, the long list of harms has also come to include the digital infrastructure that enables the flow of data, audio-visual content and the calculations of AI systems, with data centres becoming a particularly salient concern.

Scholars in this book and elsewhere have documented the problematic relationship between data centres and their use of water and impact on nature, energy infrastructure and land (Bresnihan & Brodie, 2023; Brevini, 2020; Hogan, 2015; Lehuedé, 2022; Levenda & Mahmoudi, 2019), and the emergent community resistance to such developments (Lehuedé, 2024; Rone, 2024; Valdivia, 2024). The dynamic temporalities of data centre development that ebb and flow add further pressures, affecting communities unevenly as data industries produce simultaneously the infrastructural futures and the ruins of digitalization in many places around the world (Brodie & Velkova, 2021; Burrell, 2020; Velkova & Plantin, 2023). Collectively, these dynamic developments have more recently been gathered under the umbrella term of "sustainability" issues that engage the relationship of digital infrastructure to climate change, nature-culture relations and human and more-than-human collectives. In this context, we find it timely to pause and ask: What is a "good" and desirable digital infrastructure for algorithms and AI systems? What does it look like? How can it be imagined, and what is it made of? For whom and by whom?

Our interest in these questions was provoked by our encounter with the work of a Swedish company called EcoDataCenter (EDC) that specializes in co-location data centres for AI processing. The company advances an ecological and social profile. Founded in 2014, EDC owns data centres in Falun, Stockholm and Piteå in Sweden. It promotes "ethical business conduct, mitigating environmental and social risks in our supply chain, saying no to crypto, and ensuring transparency and compliance with laws and standards" (EcoDataCenter, 2023, p. 4). The company strives to have its data centres use fossil-free energy, share waste heat and become independent from groundwater for cooling. The company also works with diversity and equity based on the Swedish welfare values, respecting worker rights, parental leave, freedom of association and union-led collective salary negotiations (EcoDataCenter, 2023, p. 4). Furthermore, EDC works to foster a culture of transparency in an industry that has been overtly secretive about its workings, by publicly reporting data about the company's systems, performance metrics, sustainability work and how it follows legislative and industry standards. In other words, the company goes to lengths to respond to environmental criticisms, align to accepted welfare and inclusivity policies, and promote a model for operations that ticks many of the boxes for what today could be called a "sustainable" or, at the very least, non-harmful digital infrastructure. Nevertheless, despite its commitments, the company faces civic resistance and critique around its latest data centre development in the town of Östersund in Sweden. We were curious: why? What can this critique tell us about what a societally beneficial digital infrastructure looks like and how it comes into being?

In this chapter we explore the frictions that emerge when communities, industries and public institutions collectively try to imagine and materialize "good" digital infrastructure in Östersund, Sweden. We track how different propositions of the good were advanced and contested around plans to construct a sustainable data centre.[1] Mobilizing the notion of friction (Tsing, 2005) and ideas from valuation studies (Doganova et al., 2014; Dussauge et al., 2015), we argue that questions of justice, damage to land, community interests, and energy use emerge in negotiations between incommensurable versions of "the good." We show how there is no universally right thing to do to make a data centre sustainable or categorically good because the good is always plural and relational and made through situated relations, practices and valuations. In other words, good and bad are never properties of a technology per se but a result of sociotechnical relations, the values that they promote and the power structures that allow for certain versions of the good to flourish and to suppress others. We propose therefore to expand the current debate on the sustainability of digital infrastructure and to orient attention from questions of quantifiable and measurable harms, such as carbon emissions, to concerns with valuations through which the different qualities of "good" infrastructure come to fruition and contention, adding to calls to nuance scholarly debates about digital infrastructure and sustainability (see for instance Cellard et al., 2025; Pasek et al., 2023).

[1] These discussions were ongoing at the time of writing this chapter.

Friction and the Good

Digital infrastructure, including data centres, materializes through the movement of data, metals, materials and labour through distributed, globalized supply chains, as well as through relations with local, situated resources, infrastructure, institutions and communities (Johnson, 2023; Valdivia, 2024; Vonderau, 2018). The interlacing of the global and the local to produce data centres in specific places and make them infrastructural to a digital economy happens with friction. Friction, following anthropologist Anna Tsing (2005), is not synonymous with tension or conflict even if it certainly involves these in some ways, at some point in time.

Friction, in Tsing's meaning of the term, reflects the productive and compromising relations through which aspirations to fulfil universal schemes of global connection come to fruition. Following Gayatri Spivak, Tsing defines a universal as that which "we cannot not want, even if it so often excludes us" (Tsing, 2005, p. 1). Universals are the prerequisite for establishing a global connection, but they never come in the forms that their proponents have laid out for them, writes Tsing (2005). Instead, universals create friction and materialize through the heat of local encounters between different surfaces that meet across difference: "As a metaphorical image, friction reminds us that heterogeneous and unequal encounters can lead to new arrangements of culture and power" (Tsing, 2005, p. 5).

Sustainability is one such universal, a word and a discourse that everyone can claim to a different end and purpose.[2] It is an aspiration for an elusive "good" that becomes particular, and concrete, in situated, material and embodied encounters across difference. When digital infrastructure becomes localized, universal ideas of sustainability and "good" infrastructure rub against situated, local understandings of the good as practised by a diversity of actors. For example, in the context of large language model (LLM) AI systems such as chatbots, educational software, or applications to support decision-making in public authorities, friction arises from different organizational cultures, knowledge and value

[2] See Stacey Alaimo (2012) for a good discussion on the fraught epistemology of sustainability and its connection to techno-solutionism and to a long history of scientific objectivity.

practices in a particular context (Kaun & Männiste, 2025; Lehtiniemi, 2024).

Frictions also make evident that what good digital infrastructure comprises is a matter of valuation. Scholars working in the tradition of science and technology studies and drawing on a pragmatist tradition, define valuation as "any social practice where the value or values of something is established, assessed, negotiated, provoked, maintained, constructed and/or contested" (Doganova et al., 2014, p. 87) including "judging, improving, appreciating, and lots of other activities" (Hauge, 2016, p. 127). This approach assumes that values are not stable nor a property of people or cultures but something that is "grappled with, articulated, and made in concrete practices" and that can be studied by "looking at dissonances, discordances, and ruptures between values" and "situations of the explicit assembling, articulation, coordination, and negotiation" (Dussauge et al., 2015, p. 1) of what counts as valuable.[3] Therefore, the question "What is good technology?" and its corollary, "What is a good infrastructure?" are bound to always remain open and addressed through the friction between multiple global and local understandings of the good, and the different practices that define what is good in a given time, place and situation, be it a scientific laboratory or a site of a new technology implementation (Lee & Helgesson, 2020).

Valuation practices are exposed to analysis in moments of controversy (Bolin, 2013; Doganova et al., 2014). Controversies highlight the making of social, political and power relations in action. They open a black box of objects that seem fixed and contained, taken for granted, and show the politics of these objects coming into the world (Latour, 2003; Venturini & Munk, 2021). This chapter loosely follows a version of controversy analysis to map the frictions that arose in the making of "good" and "sustainable" digital infrastructure that supports AI systems, with a focus on the EDC establishment in Östersund.

Between 2023 and 2025, we tracked public debates on and contestations of the EDC establishment in Östersund in online materials, publicly available recordings of municipal hearings, sustainability reports written

[3] Such a practice-based approach to values is certainly not new. It can be dated at least to John Dewey and his work "Theory of Valuation" from 1939 in which he theorises values as an essence and as a practice, a noun and a verb. I am grateful to Göran Bolin for this comment, and for his chapter that elaborates more on Dewey's work and value as practice, see Bolin (2022).

by EDC, a Facebook group Save the Spikbodarna that was formed by citizens soon after the plans for the establishment of a data centre in Östersund were announced, and media coverage by the local newspaper, *Östersundsposten*. In addition, Johanna Sefyrin (the first author) held eight interviews with EDC, municipal employees, the regional power grid operator Jämtkraft, and the local Society for the Conservation of Nature.

Our aim in gathering these materials was to map the controversies, the actors involved (human as well as nonhuman), their different perspectives, understandings of the good, and their valuation practices. We analysed our collection of materials with a hermeneutical approach (Cole & Avison, 2007), moving back and forth between empirics and our questions and analytic perspective. The outcome discussed below shows how the good data centre emerges through friction between competing values of care for shared infrastructure such as energy grids and care for the global economy of AI systems development, as well as friction between competing understandings of what constitutes a good city and a liveable urban environment.

Friction Between Care for Local Energy and Care for the Global AI Economy

When a company establishes a data centre, it must cultivate relations with the community and with the infrastructural systems in a place. It is well known that data centres might claim very large capacities from local power grids that can lead to carbon emissions, as well as to social inequality that manifests through issues around access to energy (see Velkova in this volume, and Ortar et al., 2023). When EDC started planning for its new data centre for AI in Östersund, Sweden, in 2023, the company committed to minimize pressure on and disruption of energy provision in the region: "We do not want to cannibalize the existing electric grid," a company representative expressed EDC's vision of sustainability in an interview. Östersund is a medium-sized town in Sweden. Geographically, it is situated in the middle of the country, but it is still considered a northern town, and demographically, most of the population in Sweden lives south of this town. Most of the electricity in Sweden is produced in the northern half of the country, including around Östersund, but it is consumed in the south.

In this context, the EDC company wanted to see its data centre in Östersund as making a difference, by becoming "an enabler to bring in more capacity that will go to Östersund municipality and other industries around it" (interview) and emphasized the importance of contributing to energy developments (rather than consuming) as a key element of the corporate value palette. The representative stated that "A rightly placed data centre can add incredibly much in an electricity system. A wrongly placed one can cannibalize an electric system ... This is what we believe is the next step in our sustainability journey" (interview). In other words, data centres should be placed closer to where the electricity is produced rather than "in the large cities ... where this stresses the electric grids quite a lot" (interview).

Carefully selecting the locations of its data centres, EDC opted for operations in the northern part of Sweden. Östersund is sitting along the main backbone of the electricity grid transmission line in close proximity to more than a dozen major hydropower generation plants and many new wind power plants. Placing a data centre in Östersund would be beneficial for the grid, reasoned EDC. This vision resonated well with the vision of the local grid operator in the region, which foresaw many benefits from a data centre in the region. A large power consumer could justify the expansion of the area's power grid, which could in turn bring the capacity for new, electricity-intensive industries in the town, and with them more revenue and social development, such as jobs in this northern region that generally struggles with depopulation. Thus, the development of an electricity-intense data centre would help the grid grow locally and thereby enable the establishment of local companies and, by extension, further local growth.

EDC requested 150 MW from the grid, a substantial grid capacity which equalled the electricity consumption of the whole town of Östersund at the time. Capacities of this scale were not readily available for the data centre and had to be built through grid reinforcement and new powerlines. To that end, the local grid owner, the national energy backbone grid operator Svenska Kraftnät, and EDC teamed up to co-fund the development and scale up the grid until 2033. The grid operator tied these developments to a question of resource sovereignty. In an interview, an employee of Jämtkraft, the regional power grid operator, explained that the grid operator wanted to keep 500 MW in the region for local electrification and for electricity-intensive industries, rather than export it to other parts of Sweden as had been the common practice for decades. EDC became an element in a regional identity–building politics of making Jämtkraft more resource self-sufficient and autonomous from the south.

"Good" infrastructure here manifests through values of care for the power grid, care for the energy autonomy of the town, and care for enabling local self-determination over resources and industrial development, similar to other northern regions in Sweden (see Vonderau, 2018). These forms of care were in harmony and defined the good ultimately as infrastructure development that would enable multiple forms of local autonomy and sovereignty and convert the region from a zone of extraction to one of economic value production where the benefits of these developments would be exploited locally rather than by the economically stronger south of Sweden.

These visions of good data centre infrastructure were less resonant with the materiality and economy of AI development. EDC specializes in subletting space and infrastructure services to companies that run computation-intensive processes such as large language model training. The company knows that despite efforts to not "cannibalize" the grid, and do good, the servers would have to consume considerable resources of different kinds. EDC facilities are generally much more resource-intensive than ordinary data centres, due to the fact that they center on AI. The servers that would reside at Östersund EDC would be equipped with Nvidia graphic processing cards (see also Valdivia in this volume), and when used for AI calculations they "are more energy-demanding than ordinary servers," a company representative said, explaining to Sefyrin:

> One needs a specific kind of data centre that can operate these servers in a special way... it is much more cooling. You will need more power because you need more cooling. You need more people who are working... because it's much more intensive. You need more maintenance, because everything is run harder. The whole facility is run harder... it needs to be maintained more often in order to secure that absolutely nothing is broken.

This comment was exemplary of the friction between the resource intensity of the economy of AI computation that requires more of everything, and the attempts of EDC to make something positive from this intensity in order to produce economic value from AI as another kind of "good" that supports the company's core business. Mobilizing values of care for the grid, and local resource sovereignty, gave legitimacy to local infrastructure growth but did not reduce pressure on the grid—after all, the data centre did not focus on the existing grid as such; rather, care was directed towards a grid under pressure from electricity-intensive industries to expand. A lot more electricity would have to be produced and consumed in the region, and much of it would go to supply this data centre with electricity to spin the global economy for AI. The data centre created therefore both a demand and justification for grid expansion. While perhaps not "cannibalizing" the grid, EDC would be a major consumer of energy in the town, and that energy would go towards global computing. Furthermore, grid expansion and reinforcement might trigger land issues and conflict with the Sámi people who live on the territory of the municipality and practice reindeer herding.[4]

The friction between the value of care for the economy of AI and the care for local energy prompted EDC to search for other, creative solutions to do good for the town. For instance, EDC offered the heat from the data centre to a company centering on building large scale greenhouses heated with waste heat from industries, suggesting that it was an opportunity for the city to bring large-scale greenhouses for food production to the region and to create "a circular industrial symbiosis" (Via TT, 2023), thus transforming waste into use value[5]—a proposition that was welcomed by the municipality as a positive thing that could enable industrial growth and employment. EDC also joined the Climate Neutral Data Centre Pact, an association of data centre operators and trade associations committed to the European Green Deal, agreeing to make its data centres climate neutral by 2030. These solutions did not reduce the intensity of resource and energy use but instead shifted "the good" in another direction. In response, EDC also imagined its data centres as carers for keeping the grid in balance with the help of battery storage. The data centre would act as a mediator balancing supply and demand in the electric grid—a necessity since the grid must be kept within a specific frequency in order not to break down. Through this form of care, the company was to practise being "a good member of society"[6] and be able to balance the electric grid if need be, or other kinds of balancing services. "There is a lot that one can do there. Battery storage or how ... yes, that we look at," a company representative explained. But here comes again

[4] There is no space in this chapter to elaborate more on this relation, but for reference read for example Fjellheim (2023) or Lawrence (2014).

[5] See Velkova (2016).

[6] Swedish: samhällsmedborgare.

the friction with the economy of the data centre built on running servers for AI systems:

> Our customers are dependent on being able to run their stuff all the time, so we sit here with a problem about how to [do so]... and they are guaranteed a certain capacity, and then we can't put this capacity on something else either. So it's an ongoing discussion too... for our part, then, it's an endeavour to be flexible. (interview)

The latter comment exposes another friction between the idea of doing good through care for the grid and for the region, and the need to care for making a profitable data center that supports AI systems development. The friction is in the economy of retailing energy via the data centre, which promises AI companies that it will always have electricity available for their computers, and the fact that power grids do not work in this way. Electricity availability varies depending on dynamic consumption in the area, one shaped by many more practices than data centre operations, including people charging their electric cars or using electricity-intensive saunas (Velkova et al., 2022). The cultural expectations of a resource-intensive industry that operates on the premise of constant connection and computing 24 hours a day as a core business model are simply incongruent with fluctuations in electricity and shifting demand for energy in everyday practice. EDC's experiments with flexibility are symptomatic of this friction but do not resolve it. Instead, differing cultural expectations between energy and AI companies, and differing infrastructural sectors, remain in friction, giving a spin of the AI economy beyond the town of Östersund.

Friction Between the Good Data Centre and the Liveable City

Having arranged deals with the local energy provider, EDC continued with the planning and permitting process in Östersund to build the data centre. Towards the municipality, EDC developed another version of "the good" promoting values of democracy and trust. Following established and mandatory democratic processes was central in this local work: "We have a very rigorous, democratic consensus process in Sweden, overall. One must follow this," a company representative explained. In Östersund, the company did not yet engage the community, but in other towns in Sweden, it created metrics to assess its local contribution. EDC made impact analyses of its data centres with foci on tax revenue, data collection, transparency and educational initiatives while measuring these against negative impacts. Despite the promotion of values of democracy and trust, the data centre establishment in Östersund created a huge rift between the residents and the municipal administration over the identity of the town and conception of what was a good future for it – an industrial one or one with the existing infrastructure that promoted recreation and life in nature (see Fig. 16.1 and 16.2).

Simultaneously, the municipality is at pains to attract residents, aiming at increasing from 69,500 in 2023 to 75,000 residents in 2040. Town planners see jobs and new electricity-intensive industries as shortcuts for creating jobs to attract a new workforce and encourage population growth. In Östersund as in many northern towns in Sweden, the municipality faces demographic challenges and migration to the south. When they lose residents, they also lose tax money, and without it, budgets for public services shrink. In response to this tendency, the municipality in

Fig. 16.1 The beginning of the cross-country ski trail Spikbodarna in Östersund in winter 2024. The trail goes partly in forest, and partly under the pylons of the electricity grid to which EDC will eventually connect. *Photo* Julia Velkova

Fig. 16.2 People skiing on the Spikbodarna ski-track in December 2024. *Photo* Julia Velkova

Östersund had worked for many years to attract a large and electricity-intensive industry to the town in order to create local job opportunities. In 2011 there were far-reaching plans for the establishment of a Facebook data centre, but Facebook went for Luleå further north in Sweden (Vonderau, 2019).

The arrival of EDC to Östersund offered the municipality a possibility to develop a green industry (around which it imagined to be many jobs) and to attract people from afar. Industrial development resonated well with values of urban economic growth and local prosperity that historically have been more difficult for municipalities in the northern part of Sweden to fulfil. As discussed by Mager and Katzenbach (2021, p. 223), imaginaries of sociotechnological futures are increasingly dominated by technology companies that seem to "absorb public institutions' ability to govern these very futures." These "'prophetic corporations' seek to provide future visions of a better world to guide and legitimize their own digital technologies and business practices" (Mager & Katzenbach, 2021, p. 229) in ways that have significant and sometimes detrimental implications for local democratic practices. In the process citizens, civil organizations, activists, researchers and local governments might face a hard time asserting counter imaginaries against the dominant technology companies' visions and versions of the future.

Outdoor life, mountains, cross-country skiing and forest life are part of the core identity of the town. The municipality of Östersund maintains large forest recreational areas close to the town centre for cross-country skiing and hiking, as a source of well-being for residents and as "attractions" that contribute to local tourism and to making the town interesting for people to move to and live in (Östersund municipality, 2022). The vision of the good city made through industrial growth and AI infrastructure generated significant friction with the citizens who had a different idea of a liveable town. The EDC data centre would be sited in one of the forest areas used for recreation, called Spikbodarna, which is popular among residents for its hiking and cross-country skiing. Winter sports and especially cross-country skiing are central for many Östersund residents, and the town regularly arranges national and international ski competitions. The municipality has also highlighted parts of Spikbodarna as having substantial natural value, including wetland forest with older sallow and rowan and coniferous forest growing on limy soil. Sensitive or endangered species of bats, birds, orchids, butterflies and frogs inhabit the forest. Furthermore, the area features a number of old wooden buildings and hill farms that are considered part of Swedish cultural heritage. These elements contribute to define the identity of Östersund as a liveable and desirable city, dominated more by nature, and less by industry.

These two versions of the good city—the industrial Östersund developing AI and the Östersund of nature and cross-country skiing—collided when the municipality announced that it had granted a building permit to EDC in the Spikbodarna recreational area. Siting the data centre there was convenient from an energy perspective because the main high-voltage power lines pass straight through the area. However, it requires the demolition of large parts of the forest that citizens value as part of the liveable and attractive environment of the town.

The siting of the data centre became a source of public contention because of the municipal decision to change the purpose of the area. Even though some of the ski tracks would remain, the area was to be remade from a recreational area to an industrial lot that would be prepared for green industrial growth. In this conversion, the data centre would become the main source of sustainability for other industries that would be established as well, such as a massive, industrial-scale greenhouse, an extension of the power grid and new roads. In all, 140 hectares of forest would be cleared (Save the Spikbodarna webpage). In other words, the data centre came to stand for the good future of the town where the good was reduced to the growth of industries with an environmental profile. This growth would happen at the cost of the forest and the recreational infrastructure that existed in the town, something which became a source of contention with citizens.

The local chapter of the nationwide association Society for the Conservation of Nature engaged in a campaign to defend the recreational value of the forest. A group of citizens founded a Facebook group, Save the Spikbodarna, in order to influence and eventually sue the municipality and make it accountable for the public consultation and planning processes that were part of this transformation.

Backed by the local media, the two organizations emphasized how industrial developments, even when marketed as sustainable, compromised the public values of urban recreation and the cultural heritage of the area. In an interview with Sefyrin, a member of the local chapter of the Society for the Conservation of Nature expressed a critique and referred to natural values, the ski-tracks and the old hill farms in the designated area. He claimed that many residents lived in or had moved to Östersund because they wanted to live in a city with nature close by, and they did not want to live in industrial areas or in a larger city. As he argued, the closeness to nature was what made Östersund an attractive city to live in. This view was also expressed in several articles in the local newspaper.

To be sure, citizens were not against industrialization nor computing as such but rather against the destruction of the forest landscape as a public recreational infrastructure that they saw as already sustainable and part of their way of life. No industrial developments, from their perspective, would be able to craft a version of sustainability of higher quality than the sustainability and value offered by the forest. As the Facebook group Save the Spikbodarna mentions on their page, "Sometimes it is more sustainable to not do anything at all, as a participant in the dialogue with the citizens said it. In this case, it is without any doubt the best alternative" (Save the Spikbodarna, 2025).

This was a conflict between, on the one hand, public values of local economic development and the creation of local jobs and, on the other, public values of health and recreation and closeness to nature around which the identity of the town was built. The friction exposed differing understandings of the good sustainable urban life, one related to the creation of jobs, to industrialization and economic growth, and the other to living close to nature and caring for the forest through creative, small-scale farming and entrepreneurial practices. For example, the region is a member of the UNESCO Creative Cities network in the category of food (Golpayegani & Schmudde, 2024), and the whole province of Jämtland where Östersund is located has been promoting local, small-scale entrepreneurship in the fields of tourism, recreation and food by making the landscape of mountains, forests and rivers and small-scale farming a selling point.

This locally situated and creative way of producing economic value is oriented towards caring for rather than exploiting the forest, and it is incommensurable with the value of good industrial development advanced by EDC and the municipality of Östersund. Here we also see the incommensurability of multiple perspectives on the "good" and how each works with different materialities and qualities of the good, as well as different publics. A good energy grid and a good AI data centre are worth little to citizens who want to have a good forest to live with.

The question of whether to give priority to industrial or recreational values divided the municipal administration too. The division of urban planning argued that exploitation of the area would have an irreversible impact on the recreational qualities of the town and on the forest and public health. The division of culture and leisure at the municipality argued instead that Östersund's attractiveness as a town for outdoor activities would be damaged, and that the cultural heritage of old hill farms must be preserved. The division for environment and health held a third position and argued that the data centre location goes against the comprehensive plan for municipal development and would compromise public health and natural values.

The conflicting versions of good infrastructure and the good city as defined by different actors in the process raised questions about the democratic legitimacy of the planning process (see also Rone, 2024). A member of the local chapter of the Society for the Conservation of Nature feared that there would be uncontrolled industrial expansion, since the establishment of the data centre was already approved by the municipality. He questioned the democratic process and the power position of industries and parts of the municipal administration that would disregard civic opinion. His experience exposes how in the current regime of governance, in which politicians and EU-level institutions promote data centre developments, differing values and practices are not given the same weight.

Östersund municipality had many years ago decided that they wanted to attract large, electricity-intensive companies to increase market activity and local job opportunities. The conflict in Östersund and the negotiations on nature, sustainability, health and well-being occurred within this established frame.

Democracy was a public value held in high regard by all the parties involved, and the process followed established rules and legislation. Even so, the legitimacy of the process was repeatedly questioned by civic groups claiming that all arguments and actors were not being equally heard and valued.

Conclusion

The controversies surrounding the establishment of EDC in Östersund reflected the frictions of making the abstract notion of "sustainable" digital infrastructure for AI concrete and grounded in a place with its people, infrastructure and social relations. The "good" data centre for AI systems emerged in Östersund through a friction between the valuation practices of various actors who had differing understandings of what is a good future based on the distinct perspectives from which they saw the good – as residents of the city, as city planners, or as infrastructure providers. Common to these different actors is that they all express the "good" in terms of different forms of care: care for the economy of AI-centred computing, care for a destabilized power grid in need of expansion and management, care for the distribution of local resources and the recuperation of lost resource sovereignty, care for local industrial developments that promote the future of "green" industries, and as care for existing infrastructural landscapes and the values attached to them, such as cultural heritage, health, trust and democracy.

While equally important, these distinct forms of care as a particular valuation proved to be incommensurable in Östersund. The source of this incommensurability was two-fold. On the one hand, it exposed a fundamental incommensurability between measurable and unmeasurable valuations of the "good." When the data centre company, grid operator and municipality reasoned about the good future for the city with a "sustainable" data centre, they defined the good in measurable terms: through carbon emissions, megawatts of electricity growth and distribution, population size, number of jobs, or number and diversity of industries. Greater or lesser quantities of each of these measurable entities defined a good future for different industries and the city. Even though the data centre development was tied to values of sovereignty and economic prosperity, these values were premised on promoting quantifiable versions of the "good." On the other hand, the civic groups and environmental NGOs defined the "good" through qualities that are not easily measurable, such as a good life with a forest and its species, health and the ability to practise a culture of moving in the landscape on skis. Their understanding of the "good" was related to nurturing a relation of belonging to the town and the landscape and to the role of recreational infrastructure in nature in shaping this relation. It was these non-measurable qualities that the citizens felt were under threat and protested to protect.

In the friction between these incommensurable versions of the good, infrastructure providers and the municipality devalued the non-measurable positive qualities that make the town liveable for its citizens. In this process of devaluation, the "good" industrial future with a data centre for AI computing attains qualities of a destructive force for residents that pushes them to negotiate the loss of values and qualities that they cherish, such as everyday urban life in and with nature. Relatedly, the "sustainable" data centre, even if nominally ticking all the boxes of sustainability and promoting good industrial futures, also promotes losses that matter and to which people have to adapt: the loss of recreational infrastructure, of lifestyle, of forest inhabitants and of relationships with the landscape.

Losses bring to the fore larger question of governance and power. The urban future with a "sustainable" data centre is defined from differing vantage points and by actors who occupy different power positions. Planners and power grid operators have the institutional and infrastructural power to decide on future urban and regional developments, and decide who will lose and who will gain from them. Data centre industry developments, in turn, are strongly promoted by national policies in Sweden, as well as at the EU level, as vehicles enabling AI-based services and digitalization more broadly. Put simply, it is a prioritized industry that other actors have to accommodate to and make space for regardless of whether citizens like it or not. These institutions also promote liberal market values that assume that societal and environmental well-being can be created through governance mechanisms and economic benchmarks. Making sustainable futures is then about not only who has the power to make the decisions about an individual data centre but also who has the power to shift priorities and value non-measurable qualities that are vanishing: sense of place, belonging, trust and life with forests and nature. In the friction created by the encounter between global aspirations for sustainable, digitally mediated futures and their emergent legacies, a pressing question for further research calls for more engagement with the losses and endings that digital developments promote, and the things and qualities that are devalued and pushed aside.

Competing Interests

The chapter was written with the support of the "Megabytes vs Megawatts" research project funded by the Marianne and Marcus Wallenberg Foundation, grant no. MMW 2022.0070 and the REIMAGINE-ADM project supported by FORTE, under the CHANSE ERA-NET Co-fund programme, which has received funding from the European Union's Horizon 2020 Research and Innovation Programme under Grant Agreement no. 101004509. Julia Velkova's work is also supported by the Profutura Scientia programme of SCAS and the Riksbankens Jubileumsfond in Sweden.

Acknowledgements We would like to thank Anne Mollen, Fieke Jansen, Sigrid Kannengießer, Göran Bolin and Francis Lee for their attentive reading, comments, critique, patience and support in the development of this chapter.

References

Alaimo, S. (2012). Sustainable this, sustainable that: New materialisms, posthumanism, and unknown futures. *Pmla/publications of the Modern Language Association of America, 127*(3), 558–564. https://doi.org/10.1632/pmla.2012.127.3.558

Amaro, R. (2022). *The Black technical object: On machine learning and the aspiration of Black being*. Sternberg Press.

Benjamin, R. (2019). *Race after technology: Abolitionist tools for the new Jim code*. Polity Press.

Bolin, G. (2013). Questioning Entertainment Value: Moments of Disruption in the History of Swedish Television Entertainment. In *A History of Swedish broadcasting. Communicative ethos, genres and institutional change* (pp. 261–81). University of Gothenburg.

Bolin, G. (2022). The value dynamics of data capitalism: Cultural production and consumption in a datafied world. In A. Hepp, J. Jarke, & L. Kramp (Eds.),

New perspectives in critical data studies, transforming communications—Studies in cross-media research (pp. 167–86). Springer International Publishing.

Bresnihan, P., & Brodie, P. (2023). Data sinks, carbon services: Waste, storage, and energy cultures on Ireland's peat bogs. *New Media & Society, 2*(25), 361–383. https://doi.org/10.1177/14614448221149948

Brevini, B. (2020). Black boxes, not green: Mythologizing artificial intelligence and omitting the environment. *Big Data & Society, 7*(2), 1–5. https://doi.org/10.1177/2053951720935141

Brodie, P., & Velkova, J. (2021). Cloud ruins: Ericsson's Vaudreuil data center and infrastructural abandonment. *Information, Communication & Society, 24*(6), 869–885. https://doi.org/10.1080/1369118X.2021.1909099

Burrell, J. (2020). On half-built assemblages: Waiting for a data center in Prineville, Oregon. *Engaging Science, Technology, and Society, 6*, 283–305. https://doi.org/10.17351/ests2020.447

Cellard, L., Parker, C., & Haines, F. (2025). Beyond AI as an environmental pharmakon: Principles for reopening the problem-space of machine learning's carbon footprint. *Environment and Planning E: Nature and Space,* 1–26. https://doi.org/10.1177/25148486251332087

Cole, M., & Avison, D. (2007). The potential of hermeneutics in information systems research. *European Journal of Information Systems, 16*(6), 820–833. https://doi.org/10.1057/palgrave.ejis.3000725

D'Ignazio, C., & Klein, L. F. (2023). *Data feminism* (1st MIT Press paperback edition). MIT Press.

Doganova, L., Giraudeau, M., Helgesson, C.-F., Kjellberg, H., Lee, F., Mallard, A., Mennicken, A., Muniesa, F., Sjögren, E., & Zuiderent-Jerak, T. (2014). Valuation studies and the critique of valuation. *Valuation Studies, 2*(2), 87–96. https://doi.org/10.3384/vs.2001-5992.142287

Dussauge, I., Helgesson, C.-F., & Lee, F. (2015). *Value practices in the life sciences and medicine.* Oxford University Press.

EcoDataCenter. (2023). *2023 sustainability report.* https://ecodatacenter.tech/sustainability-data-center/sustainability-report-2023

Fjellheim, Eva Maria. (2023). Wind energy on trial in Saepmie: Epistemic controversies and strategic ignorance in Norway's green energy transition. *Arctic Review on Law and Politic*s, *14.*

Golpayegani, K., & Schmudde, U. (2024). Unleashing the power of social entrepreneurs for regional development: Insights from Jämtland Härjedalen. In A. Sörensson, M. Bogren, G. Grigore, A. Stancu, & A. Lundström (Eds.), *Creating new roles for a sustainable economy.* Palgrave Studies in Governance, Leadership and Responsibility. Palgrave Macmillan. https://doi.org/10.1007/978-3-031-61551-1_5

Hauge, A. M. (2016). The organizational valuation of valuation devices. Putting lean whiteboard management to work in a hospital department. *Valuation Studies, 4*(2), 125–151. https://doi.org/10.3384/VS.2001-5992.1642125

Hogan, M. (2015). Data flows and water woes: The Utah data center. *Big Data & Society, 2*(2), 1–12. https://doi.org/10.1177/2053951715592429

Johnson, A. (2023). *Where cloud is ground: Placing data and making place in Iceland*. University of California Press.

Kaun, A., & Männiste, M. (2025). Public sector chatbots: AI frictions and data infrastructures at the interface of the digital welfare state. *New Media & Society, 27*(4), 1962–1985. https://doi.org/10.1177/14614448251314394

Latour, B. (2003). *Science in action: How to follow scientists and engineers through society* (11th printed ed.). Harvard University Press.

Lee, F., & Helgesson, C.-F. (2020). Styles of valuation: Algorithms and agency in high-throughput bioscience. *Science, Technology, & Human Values, 45*(4), 659–685.

Lawrence, R. (2014). Internal colonisation and indigenous resource sovereignty: Wind power developments on traditional Saami lands. *Environment and Planning D: Society and Space, 32*(6), 1036–1053.

Lehtiniemi, T. (2024). Contextual social valences for artificial intelligence: Anticipation that matters in social work. *Information, Communication & Society, 27*(6), 1110–1125. https://doi.org/10.1080/1369118X.2023.2234987

Lehuedé, S. (2022). Territories of data: Ontological divergences in the growth of data infrastructure. *Tapuya: Latin American Science, Technology and Society, 5*(1), Article 2035936. https://doi.org/10.1080/25729861.2022.2035936

Lehuedé, S. (2024). An elemental ethics for artificial intelligence: Water as resistance within AI's value chain. *AI & Society, 40*, 1761–1774. https://doi.org/10.1007/s00146-024-01922-2

Levenda, A. M., & Mahmoudi, D. (2019). Silicon forest and server farms: The (urban) nature of digital capitalism in the Pacific Northwest.*Culture Machine, 18*, 1–14.

Mager, A., & Katzenbach, C. (2021). Future imaginaries in the making and governing of digital technology: Multiple, contested, commodified. *New Media & Society, 23*(2), 223–236.

Ortar, N., Taylor, A. R. E., Velkova, J., Brodie, P., Johnson, A., Marquet, C., Pollio, A., & Cirolia, L. (2023). Powering 'smart' futures: Data centres and the energy politics of digitalisation. In S. Abram, K. Waltorp, N. Ortar, & S. Pink (Eds.), *Energy futures: Anthropocene challenges, emerging technologies and everyday life* (pp. 125–167). De Gruyter.

Östersund municipality. (2022). *Översiktsplan Östersund 2040*. https://www.ostersund.se/bygga-bo-klimat-och-miljo/oversiktsplaner-och-detaljplaner/oversiktsplanering/oversiktsplan-ostersund-2040.html

Pasek, A., Vaughan, H., & Starosielski, N. (2023). The world wide web of carbon: Toward a relational footprinting of information and communications technology's climate impacts. *Big Data & Society, 10*(1), 1–14. https://doi.org/10.1177/20539517231158994

Roberts, S. T. (2019). *Behind the screen: Content moderation in the shadows of social media*. Yale University Press.

Rone, J. (2024). The shape of the cloud: Contesting date centre construction in North Holland. *New Media & Society, 26*(10), 5999–6018. https://doi.org/10.1177/14614448221145928

Ruckenstein, M., & Turunen, L. L. M. (2020). Re-humanizing the platform: Content moderators and the logic of care. *New Media & Society, 22*(6), 1026–1042. https://doi.org/10.1177/1461444819875990

Save the Spikbodarna. (n.d.). *Hjälp oss bevara Spikbodarna som naturområde*. https://raddaspikbodarna.nu/

Singh, R. (2023). The backend work of data subjects: Ordinary challenges of living with data in India and the US. In L. Parks, J. Velkova, & S. De Ridder (Eds.), *Media backends: Digital infrastructures and sociotechnical relations* (pp. 229–244). University of Illinois Press.

Tsing, A. L. (2005). *Friction: An ethnography of global connection*. Princeton University Press.

Valdivia, A. (2024). The *supply chain capitalism of AI*: A call to (re)think algorithmic harms and resistance through environmental lens. *Information, Communication & Society*, 1–17. https://doi.org/10.1080/1369118X.2024.2420021

van Schie, G. (2023). The datafication of racialization and the pursuit of equality: The case of the "Barometer Culturele Diversiteit." In K. Es & N. Verhoeff (Eds.), *Situating data: Inquiries in algorithmic culture* (pp. 141–158). Amsterdam University Press.

Velkova, J. (2016). Data that warms: Waste heat, infrastructural convergence and the computation traffic commodity. *Big Data & Society, 3*(2), 1–10.

Velkova, J., & Plantin, J. C. (2023). Data centers and the infrastructural temporalities of digital media: An introduction. *New Media & Society, 25*(2), 273–286.

Velkova, J., Rohracher, H., & Magnusson, D. (2022). Smart thermostats and the algorithmic control of thermal comfort. In S. Pink, M. Berg, D. Lupton, & M. Ruckenstein (Eds.), *Everyday automation: Experiencing and anticipating automated decision-making* (pp. 171–183). Routledge.

Venturini, T., & Munk, A. K. (2021). *Controversy mapping: A field guide*. Polity.

Via TT. (2023, April 20). Via TT. (2023, April 20). *Unik etablering i Östersund skapar 1 000 nya gröna job*. https://via.tt.se/pressmeddelande/3344944/unik-etablering-i-ostersund-skapar-1-000-nya-grona-jobb-?publisherId=3235911

Vonderau, A. (2019). Scaling the cloud: Making state and infrastructure in Sweden. *Ethnos, 84*(4), 698–718. https://doi.org/10.1080/00141844.2018.1471513

Winter, K., & Hermansson, K. (2025). (Dis)affordances and abandonment: Understanding everyday user engagement with security apps. *Sociologisk Tidskrift, 62*(1–2), 59–84.

Zakharova, I., Jarke, J., & Kaun, A. (2024). Tensions in digital welfare states: Three perspectives on care and control. *Journal of Sociology, 60*(3), 540–559. https://doi.org/10.1177/14407833241238312

Index

A
Abundant energy, 89, 90
Accelerationism, 123, 309
Access to electricity, 98, 104, 109, 330
Access to energy, 98, 106, 109, 110, 346
AGI, 305–307, 309, 310
AI adaptation, 202
AI chips, 15, 41
AI commodity chains, 15, 34–36, 42, 44
AI-driven efficiencies, 123
AI ecosystem, 85, 86, 216, 266
AI efficiency, 32
AI factories, 98, 191, 192
AI for all, 85, 86
AI for sustainability, 35
AI growth, 86, 91, 334
AI infrastructure, 3, 4, 6–9, 11–18, 21, 38, 43, 51–57, 59, 61–65, 85, 167, 168, 171, 173, 190–192, 194, 197, 199, 202–206, 216–218, 221, 223, 225, 227, 229, 230, 272, 284, 285, 304, 306, 308, 310, 314, 322–324, 327–334, 353
AI infrastructure governance, 20, 323, 326, 329–334
AI infrastructure in scarcity, 327
AI infrastructure value chains, 52
AI platforms, 118, 273
AI platform shift, 263
AI-powered acceleration, 173
AI's environmental costs, 33, 34
AI's environmental harms, 310
AI's environmental impact, 33
AI's extractiveness, 303
AI's infrastructural acceleration, 305
AI sovereignty, 224
AI supply chain, 3, 86
AI systems, 7, 10, 11, 19, 32, 35, 52–54, 62, 73, 90, 98, 99, 101, 104, 109, 117, 194, 199, 201, 203, 205, 247, 280, 281, 283, 303, 342, 344, 345, 350, 356

A. Mollen et al. (eds.), *AI Infrastructures and Sustainability*, Palgrave Studies in European Communication Research and Education,
https://doi.org/10.1007/978-3-032-09748-4

AI technologies, 3–8, 10, 11, 15, 16, 35, 62, 63, 171, 179, 194, 199, 216, 217, 237, 241, 248
AI tools, 19, 146, 148, 152, 155, 225, 287, 296
Algorithms, 4, 8, 33, 34, 36, 101, 102, 153, 202, 273, 281, 282, 287, 294, 303, 304, 342
Amazon rainforest, 56, 57, 61
Anthropic, 241
Apple, 167, 171, 173, 175, 176, 235, 244
Aquabyte, 119, 124, 129, 130, 133
Aquaculture, 117, 123, 124, 127, 129, 135
Aquatech, 118, 126, 130
Artificial Intelligence (AI), 1–21, 31–40, 43, 51–55, 59, 62–65, 73–76, 80, 81, 83–87, 89–91, 98, 99, 101–103, 105, 106, 109, 110, 117–121, 123, 125–127, 132, 133, 136, 143–147, 149, 151–158, 165–168, 171, 173, 174, 176–180, 182, 189–206, 215–230, 235–237, 240, 241, 243, 244, 247–250, 262–265, 267–269, 272, 273, 279–282, 285–287, 289, 295–297, 301–314, 322–335, 342, 346, 348–350, 353, 356, 357
Authoritarian regime, 229
Automation, 4, 9, 17, 179
AWS, 77, 98, 102, 119, 125, 130, 133, 173, 241

B
Big data ecologies, 149
Big Tech, 15, 17–19, 44, 77, 106–108, 118, 125, 134, 144, 148, 166, 200, 235, 237, 241, 249, 250, 266, 302, 303, 313, 326, 327
Blue revolution, 129
Botanical metaphors, 19, 264
Brazilian Amazon, 53, 55, 58, 59

C
Capacity deficit, 98, 103–105, 107
Capitalist growth, 17, 118, 135, 136, 157, 309
Capitalist sustainability, 135
Carbon emissions, 11, 33, 34, 37, 41, 98, 148, 151, 180, 302, 310, 322, 343, 346, 356
Carbon footprint, 33, 151, 224, 227, 325
Chip manufacturing, 38, 39
Circular economy, 64, 132
Climate change, 11, 33, 43, 64, 98, 143, 171, 177, 181, 196, 224, 263, 264, 279, 280, 282, 296, 305, 308, 310, 311, 342
Cloud computing, 14, 102, 103, 105–110, 135, 143, 152, 157, 177, 198, 219, 220
Cloud economy, 146, 149
Cloud for Sustainability, 17, 145, 150–152, 154, 156
Cloud infrastructure, 38, 84, 102, 135, 144–146, 149, 153–155, 157, 158, 166, 167, 171, 180
Colonial capitalism, 134
Colonial expansionism, 305
Colonial exploitation, 52
Commodification, 6, 35, 322
Commodity fetishism, 15, 35
Common good, 16, 17, 98, 283, 286, 330
Computing infrastructure, 102, 109, 110, 166, 177, 325
Control, 7, 130, 147, 148, 202, 205, 219, 223–225, 228–230, 238, 242, 267, 270, 273, 280,

288–291, 312, 314, 326, 333, 341
Controversies, 345, 346, 356
Convivial technologies, 313, 314
Convivial tools, 313
Corporate agreements, 243
Corporate ecosystems, 238
Corporate entanglements, 238
Corporate environmental communication, 18, 167, 169, 170, 181
Corporate sustainability, 144, 217
Cradle of AI infrastructures, 15, 52
Critical political economy, 239, 241, 242

D
Data analytics imaginary, 178
Data center, 32, 40, 73–75, 77–91, 104, 143, 145–149, 155, 156, 158, 166, 168, 173–175, 179, 204, 215, 227, 228, 328, 350
Data center hubs, 85, 87
Data centre, 2, 4, 7–10, 13, 16, 17, 21, 31, 32, 36, 38, 40–42, 44, 51, 55, 97–111, 123, 132, 133, 191–193, 198, 200, 215, 220, 222, 224, 227–230, 236, 249, 264, 267, 283, 301, 302, 305, 311, 314, 321–329, 342–344, 346–357
Data centre governance, 328
Data centres in scarcity, 328
Data colonialism, 120, 124
Data-driven capitalism, 121
Data-driven technologies, 125, 279, 280
Data infrastructures, 9, 33, 171, 177, 272, 282, 283, 286, 290–292, 296
Data systems, 281, 282, 286–288, 292, 295, 297
De-automatisation, 20, 312, 314
Decomputing, 311–314
Decoupling strategy, 147, 148, 156
Defetishisation of AI commodities, 36
Defetishise commodity chains, 35
Deforestation, 38, 58–61, 63, 155, 279, 280, 282, 286
Degrowth, 64, 311, 312, 314
Democratic practice, 239, 352
Democratic process, 295, 350, 355
Depoliticization, 219, 227
Designing in scarcity, 327, 329, 331–333
Desirable digital infrastructure, 342
Digital and energy convergence, 74
Digital capitalism, 131, 238
Digital efficiencies, 126
Digital energetics, 76
Digital governance, 289
Digital infrastructure, 4, 8, 19, 41, 73–77, 80, 81, 83, 85, 91, 98–100, 125, 167, 168, 175–178, 180, 194, 228, 229, 237, 280, 283, 287–289, 324, 325, 342–345, 356
Digital infrastructure hub, 16, 74, 75, 84, 89, 90
Digital innovations, 195, 279
Digital platforms, 124, 240, 266, 269
Digital sovereignty, 15, 18, 190, 216, 223–225, 227, 229
Digital transformation, 180, 195
Discourse analysis, 74, 145, 167, 173, 220, 221
Discursive infrastructuring, 220, 221
Discursive legitimation, 181
Discursive strategies, 168
Disinformation, 194, 200, 201
Distributional injustices, 14, 35
Distribution of profit, 239
Domestication, 118, 123, 133, 135, 136

E

Ecocritical metaphorology, 264, 273
EcoDataCenter, 132, 342
Ecological justice, 54, 285
Ecological metaphors, 262, 264, 265, 268, 269, 273
Ecological sustainability, 14, 15, 251, 252, 283
Economic concentration, 238, 239
Economic growth, 55, 64, 106, 120, 144, 146, 158, 324, 352, 355
Economic power, 239
Economy of AI, 346, 348, 349, 356
Eco-technological frames, 169
Effective altruism, 309
Efficiency, 6, 11, 32, 33, 39, 58, 118, 121–124, 126, 130, 131, 133, 145–147, 149–154, 156, 177–179, 194, 227, 228, 281, 283, 284, 286, 292, 305, 312, 325, 326, 329
Electricity grid, 41, 98, 101, 105, 106, 108, 310, 325, 331, 332, 347, 351
Electricity in Sweden, 346
Emancipatory futures, 324, 329, 331–333, 335
Emancipatory governance processes, 330
Embodied harms, 323
Empathetic perception, 281, 284–286, 290, 292, 295
Energy autonomy, 348
Energy consumption, 7, 32, 33, 39, 86, 89, 143, 165, 177, 227, 251, 301, 321, 326
Energy demand, 16, 80, 84, 86, 87, 105, 175, 249, 301, 302
Energy grid, 74, 90, 98, 103, 105, 279, 346
Energy sustainability, 228
Environmental datafication, 120
Environmental degradation, 33, 63, 84
Environmental destruction, 152, 264
Environmental footprint, 85
Environmental governance, 19, 20, 151, 279–287, 291, 295, 296
Environmental impact, 32, 34–37, 39, 41, 42, 144–146, 149–152, 154–157, 165, 167, 178, 179, 182, 224, 248, 249, 264, 269, 321, 326
Environmentalism, 17, 145, 153, 154, 157
Environmental justice, 3, 10, 16, 20, 39, 239, 252, 322, 330
Environmentally sustainable tech, 328
Environmental sustainability, 98, 149, 154, 166, 169, 171, 173, 175, 239, 242, 248, 249, 266
E.ON, 104, 105
Epistemic technology, 239, 242
ESG reporting, 156, 217
Evolutionary directionality, 271
E-waste, 15, 36, 42, 43
Expansionist strategies, 77
Extractive datafication, 121
Extractive epistemologies, 121, 126
Extractive practices, 57

F

Fish farming, 17, 117–119, 124–127, 129, 130, 132, 133
Follow the thing, 35, 41, 43
Forest governance, 288–290, 292
Forestry management, 287, 289, 291
Friction, 3, 7, 10, 13, 21, 120, 150, 151, 154, 343–346, 348–350, 353, 354, 356–358
Frugal computing, 313
Future visions, 176, 181, 352

G
GAFAM, 267, 268, 270
Gazeta Wyborcza, 197, 199
Generative AI, 6, 19, 31, 32, 41, 51, 53, 54, 62, 102, 143, 149, 150, 156, 166, 182, 235–252, 301, 302, 304, 321
Generative AI infrastructures, 236, 238, 240, 242, 251, 252
Generative AI providers, 235–239, 241–252
Generative AI value chain, 240, 241, 245, 246, 249, 251
Geology of media, 32
Geopolitical tensions, 13, 18, 38, 193, 201, 216, 334
Geopolitics, 4, 8, 16, 199, 200, 205
Global connectivity, 78
Global South, 41, 42, 52, 55, 78, 83, 89, 91, 246, 302, 310, 322, 325
Good AI data centre, 355
Good city, 346, 353, 355
Good digital infrastructure, 345
Good energy grid, 355
Google, 38, 77, 102, 107, 110, 119, 125, 126, 143, 156, 165–167, 171, 173, 175–179, 193, 199, 200, 219, 235, 244, 249, 267, 302, 305
GPUs, 9, 15, 16, 32, 34–40, 42–44, 57, 301, 304, 305, 307
GPU waste, 42
Green capitalism, 17, 119, 126, 144, 158
Green data capitalism, 145, 157
Green extractivism, 118
Green hydrogen production, 78, 81
Green industry, 352
Green revolution, 129
Grid capacity, 97, 104, 105, 302, 332, 347
Grid capacity shortages, 16
Growth ideology, 305, 311

H
Hyper-scalability, 101, 102, 107, 109
Hyper-scalable cloud infrastructure, 102
Hyper-scalable computing, 101, 102, 108, 110
Hyperscale data centres, 40, 311, 326, 329

I
Illegal mining, 16, 58–60
Imaginaries, 5, 15, 20, 21, 76, 79, 86, 123, 144, 148, 152, 153, 155–158, 170, 223, 229, 268, 273, 305, 309, 314, 353
Imaginaries of sociotechnological futures, 352
Imagined futures, 169
Implicit presuppositions, 263
Indigenous communities, 60, 61, 63, 147
Indigenous people, 108
Inequalities, 2, 4, 83–85, 90, 196, 246, 271, 283, 330
Infrastructural growth, 76, 91
Infrastructural (in)visibility, 144, 156
Infrastructural knowledge, 179
Infrastructural power, 18, 84, 145, 157, 166, 167, 178, 357
Infrastructural solutionism, 18, 173, 176, 177, 179
Infrastructural turn, 8, 144
Infrastructural violence, 303
Infrastructure misalignment, 16, 101, 103, 110
Infrastructure of sustainability, 17, 145, 150, 152, 156, 157
Infrastructure security, 228
Infrastructure sustainability, 227, 228

Infrastructuring, 53, 54, 62, 63, 220, 223, 230

J
Justice, 7, 10, 11, 17, 52–55, 63, 108, 196–198, 239, 252, 286, 311, 331, 341, 343

K
Knowledge infrastructures, 124, 246, 282, 288

L
Labour, 5, 31, 34–36, 52, 102, 122, 199, 204, 205, 269, 288, 293, 302–304, 311, 344
Labour exploitation, 43
Liveable town, 353
Longtermism, 309

M
Market concentration, 19, 236–238, 240–242, 252
Market power, 236, 238, 240, 243, 246, 248–251, 325
Master narratives, 221, 222, 228
Materiality of AI, 32, 36, 37
Materiality of generative AI, 240
Materiality of infrastructure, 323
Matters of care, 312
Media concentration, 238, 239, 241, 242, 251
Media diversity, 251, 252
Media ecologies, 19, 265
Media infrastructures, 9, 168, 181, 216, 218
Media studies, 4, 19, 129, 262, 265, 268, 325
Mercury poisoning, 60
Metabolic rift, 17, 118, 121, 122
Metaphor, 19, 123, 131, 143, 228, 261–264, 266–273
Metaphorical concepts, 263
Method of defamiliarisation, 322, 327
Microsoft, 77, 97, 102–104, 107, 110, 119, 125, 144–158, 166, 167, 171, 175, 177, 193, 198–200, 235, 237, 241, 243, 249, 250, 302, 321
Microsoft Azure, 17, 38, 102, 103, 143–146, 157, 193, 321
Military cybersecurity, 200
Mineral extraction, 34, 37, 38, 43, 52–55, 62, 63, 310
Minerals, 3, 9, 14–16, 33, 36–38, 42, 43, 51–59, 62–64, 204
Mining, 15, 16, 37, 53, 55–64, 117, 204, 323, 325, 333
Mining practices, 57, 58, 61
Misinformation, 201
Mobilisation, 285–287, 294, 306, 308, 310
More-than-human justice, 52, 53, 55, 63

N
National institutions, 202
National security, 189, 190, 200
News media, 15, 19, 75, 190, 194, 197, 236, 237, 239–252
News media partnerships, 236–239, 247
Non-harmful digital infrastructure, 343
Non-measurable qualities, 357
Nvidia, 32, 36–38, 57, 62, 241, 348

O
OpenAI, 6, 149, 182, 235–237, 241, 243–250, 307

Operational harms, 323
Optimization, 124, 126, 179, 279

P
Permacomputing, 313
Philosophy of technology, 265
Planetary boundaries, 11, 17, 20, 322, 327, 328, 332
Planetary Computer, 145, 153–156
Planetary limits, 118, 131, 305
Platform capitalism, 168
Platform companies, 262, 268, 270, 272
Platform ecology, 266
Platform infrastructure, 4, 19, 269, 273
Platformization, 238, 262
Platform society, 19, 262, 266, 267, 269
Platform studies, 19, 166, 262, 263, 266, 268
Poland, 13, 18, 20, 189–197, 199–206, 281, 287–290, 292
Polish digitalisation strategy, 194, 195, 206
Polish forestry, 287, 290, 292, 294, 295
Political ecology of data, 118–120, 282
Power grid, 98, 100, 101, 103–110, 346–348, 350, 354, 356, 357
Power relations, 75, 221, 271, 345
Practices, 2, 5–7, 9, 10, 12, 15, 16, 21, 52, 54, 57, 58, 61–65, 87, 89–91, 98, 100, 105, 109, 119, 121, 123, 124, 132, 134, 135, 147, 151, 154, 169, 176, 178, 190, 195, 217, 218, 221, 223, 228–230, 250, 251, 264, 273, 282, 283, 286–288, 290, 292, 313, 324, 331, 332, 343, 345–347, 349, 350, 352, 355, 356
Precarious labour, 39
Predatory capitalism, 327, 334
Promissory legitimacy, 181
Promissory stories, 166, 167, 169, 170, 173, 175, 176, 180, 181
Public digital infrastructures, 280, 281, 284, 287, 295–297
Public forestry infrastructure, 289
Public interest, 20, 237, 322, 323, 329–331, 333, 335
Public value, 9, 16, 17, 98, 99, 104, 109–111, 266, 267, 269, 273, 280, 283, 295, 341, 354, 356

R
Race for AI hegemony, 326
Reading infrastructure, 221
Recycling, 64, 148, 171, 175
Relationality of infrastructure, 218
Renewable electricity, 101, 103, 135
Renewable energy, 7, 39, 73–75, 78, 81–86, 89–91, 101–103, 132, 147, 149, 171, 173, 175, 200, 302, 326, 329, 332
Resilient infrastructure, 192, 195, 199, 201
Resolute engagement, 281, 284–286, 292, 294, 295
Resource extractivism, 38
Resource-making, 121
Resource sovereignty, 347, 348, 356
Resource usage, 149, 151
Responsible innovation, 281, 284
Responsiveness, 20, 281, 284–288, 295–297
Responsive state, 285, 286
Russia, 14, 18, 19, 189, 194, 195, 215–220, 223, 227, 328

S

Scalability efforts, 106
Scale, 9, 12, 17, 18, 20, 31, 40, 43, 55, 56, 58, 59, 61, 74, 83, 84, 87, 102, 103, 106–110, 119, 122–124, 126, 127, 129, 131, 132, 136, 146, 153–156, 166, 175, 177, 178, 191, 192, 194, 196, 205, 236, 247, 268, 280, 281, 284, 286–288, 292, 295–297, 302, 304, 305, 311–314, 322–324, 328, 333, 334, 347, 349, 353, 355
Scaled efficiencies, 118
Self-reliance, 18, 19, 190, 193, 199–201, 203, 205, 250
Social construction of AI, 218
Social inequality, 280, 286, 332, 346
Social justice, 8, 54, 56, 64, 239, 311, 330
Societally beneficial digital infrastructure, 343
Socio-environmental trade-offs, 83
Socionature, 121
Sociotechnical imaginaries, 144, 155
Sociotechnical systems, 7, 168, 218
Spillage effects, 61, 62
Stabilizing AI, 227
State-market entanglements, 325
State policies, 82
Strategic partnerships, 241–243, 246
Submarine cables, 77–81
Supply chain infrastructure, 73
Supremacism, 310
Sustainability, 3–8, 10–20, 32, 39, 43, 52–55, 58, 63–65, 74, 82–87, 89–91, 99, 102, 103, 109, 117, 118, 121, 123, 125, 126, 130–136, 144–146, 150–152, 154–158, 167, 169, 171, 175–181, 189–191, 194, 197–199, 205, 206, 216–218, 223, 228, 229, 236, 238, 239, 242, 243, 246, 249, 251, 252, 279–281, 288, 289, 294, 296, 314, 322, 323, 326, 329, 331, 332, 342–344, 346, 353, 354, 356, 357
Sustainability agenda, 325
Sustainability discourse, 18, 224, 230
Sustainability journeys, 145, 152, 347
Sustainability report, 130, 220–223, 226, 228, 345
Sustainability reporting, 18, 217, 218, 221, 223, 226
Sustainability transition, 176, 180
Sustainable acceleration, 178
Sustainable AI infrastructures, 8, 221, 327, 329
Sustainable cloud infrastructure, 146
Sustainable data centre, 21, 343
Sustainable development, 6, 55, 64, 76, 83, 91, 144, 189, 194, 195, 201, 217, 238, 247, 287
Sustainable digital tech, 134
Sustainable future, 145, 150, 152, 153, 157, 167, 173, 179, 181, 263, 297, 329, 357
Sustainable innovation, 333

T

Tailings, 58, 59, 64
Technocratic governance, 280
Techno-optimistic visions, 83, 181
Technopolitics, 312, 313
Technoscience, 121, 122, 125, 129, 135, 306
Technoscience-for-sustainability, 121
Technoscientific power, 306
Technosolutionism, 176, 308
Techsolutionist imaginaries, 334
Territorial tensions, 75
Tidal, 119, 125, 126
Total mobilisation, 306–314

Transformation, 3, 9, 16, 20, 31, 42, 74, 89, 118, 147, 180, 195, 284–286, 293, 297, 314, 354

U

Upscaling power grids, 17, 109

V

Valuation, 13, 120, 343, 345, 346, 356

Values of care, 346, 348

W

War in Ukraine, 18, 190, 197, 199, 200, 205

Water consumption, 34, 38, 39, 147, 149, 321

We Live in the Cloud, 145, 146

White supremacy, 309, 314

Wind generation, 78

Y

YaLM, 220

Yandex, 13, 18, 215, 217–230

Yandex Cloud, 222

YandexGPT, 220, 222

Kolibri 360 GmbH
Ferdinand-Jühlke-Straße 7
99095 Erfurt, Deutschland
produktsicherheit@kolibri360.de